INTERNATIONAL CONTRACTING

Contract Management in Complex Construction Projects

INTERNATIONAL CONTRACTING

Contract Management in Complex Construction Projects

John van der Puil
TiasNimbas Business School, Tilburg, the Netherlands

Arjan van Weele
Eindhoven University of Technology, the Netherlands

ICP
Imperial College Press

Published by

Imperial College Press
57 Shelton Street
Covent Garden
London WC2H 9HE

Distributed by

World Scientific Publishing Co. Pte. Ltd.
5 Toh Tuck Link, Singapore 596224
USA office: 27 Warren Street, Suite 401-402, Hackensack, NJ 07601
UK office: 57 Shelton Street, Covent Garden, London WC2H 9HE

British Library Cataloguing-in-Publication Data
A catalogue record for this book is available from the British Library.

INTERNATIONAL CONTRACTING
Contract Management in Complex Construction Projects

ISBN 978-1-908979-50-6

Typeset by Stallion Press
Email: enquiries@stallionpress.com

Printed and bound in Great Britain by
Marston Book Services Limited, Oxfordshire

Foreword

Nowadays, large contractors, like Ballast Nedam, act more frequently as a system integrator to deliver construction projects in the complex international environment. More and more clients request integrated solutions from a life-cycle perspective. Hence, contractors have to assume more responsibilities and risks to create added value for these clients. Requests for tender often include responsibility for design, maintenance, operation or even financing the project. As a result, our clients' contracts have become very complex to manage and execute.

Creating maximum value and mitigation of risks can only be realized if all parties in the supply chain work together effectively. Aligning the objectives and agreements among all parties involved is essential to create a seamless team in projects. It is also essential to avoid conflicts and, when conflicts occur, to solve these effectively. Every manager in the contracting business, that is, area managers, tender managers, project managers, and procurement managers, should have sufficient knowledge of the principles of contract management and the most important contract models that are used. In Ballast Nedam's vision, contractual awareness is an essential competence for such specialists in order to be able to improve the added value for our clients, for ourselves, and for our supply chain partners.

Because of this vision, Ballast Nedam was one of the founding partners of the International Contracting Program at TiasNimbas Business School, at Tilburg, the Netherlands. This international program is specially designed to satisfy our company needs for an executive training on contractual awareness, based upon a mix of academic knowledge and practitioner experience. The true value of the program is that it has been organized around real-life case studies taken from the international contracting business. It has been a great success since it began in 2008. This success is the result of the effort of all participants: trainees, trainers, founding companies, and TiasNimbas Business

School. I am delighted that all the knowledge that has been built up during these years is brought together in this book. I would like to thank John van der Puil and Arjan van Weele for their enthusiasm and effort during the development of the program and the writing of this book.

International Contracting: Contract Management in Complex Construction Projects is easy to read and very practical, due to its unique mix of practitioner insight and academic theory. It is a must for project managers, tender managers, area managers, and project engineers working in a complex international context. Enjoy reading this book and good luck with your next international challenge!

Romeo Malizia
Chief Operational Officer
Ballast Nedam N.V.
The Netherlands

Preface

Local contractors need to make great efforts to win a contract from a client in a very competitive arena. When the contract is signed, subcontractors and materials suppliers need to be mobilized. Different requirements, with different business partners, will result in different relationships within different contractual arrangements. Most construction firms today are orchestrators of fairly complex supply chains. They need to orchestrate the activities of a wide range of different business partners and to do so meticulously, in order to meet the client specifications and requirements. They also need to orchestrate the commercial arrangements underlying these relationships.

International contracting is even more complex. Large contractors today operate in different cultural environments to deliver multimillion or even multibillion road and rail works, airports, harbors and adjacent industrial areas, oil platforms, power plants, wind-energy farms, energy-distribution infrastructures, and a wide range of buildings.

For many years, the scope of Dutch contractors has been truly international. The Dutch have a good reputation for designing and realizing complex infrastructural works across the world. Over the years, engineering and project management have become more sophisticated. As well as contract management, large employers and clients today use complex contracts to create maximum value for money and mitigate risks related to their investments. Rather than just constructing what an architect or client may have envisaged, contractors are now faced with assuming design and engineering responsibilities. In some cases, they also may be requested to finance, operate, and maintain the infrastructure that they built! As a result of this, the risk exposure has changed dramatically in the contracting industry. Large clients and employers increasingly want to shift their risk to their contractors. International contracting has become a risk game; hence, international contracting has become a contracting game.

Where traditionally contractors have invested heavily in design and engineering, project planning and management, contract management still needs important improvements. Most project engineers and managers have a technical background. Increasingly, apart from technical challenges, they are faced with interface problems that need to be solved in the relationship between the contractor and the employer on one hand, and the contractor and its suppliers and subcontractors on the other hand. In doing so, effective arrangements need to be made between all parties involved and, when agreed, these arrangements need to be followed up. In complex projects, it is understandable that conflicts will emerge. This explains the need for project managers to be acquainted with the principles of contract management, and the most important contract models that are used. Project managers need to understand what they can do to avoid conflicts with business partners, and when they occur, how to solve them.

Surprisingly, the opportunities to get acquainted with modern contracting in an international context are limited. Most training courses and executive education are aimed at accountants, lawyers, and legal counsels. Here, business law, tax law, and contract management are taught from a specialist, legal perspective. Little training and education on contract management and international contracting is provided from a business perspective. Such a perspective would allow project managers to understand the principles underlying business law and contract management. Next, it would allow them to get an insight into the main legal arrangements laid down in rules and regulations, in order to judge at what time they need to solicit specialist legal advice. In essence, they need knowledge and insight, which does not need to be as detailed as legal counsels would require. Therefore, general training for legal counsels and specialists would not be attractive to them.

In 2007, the authors were requested by TiasNimbas Business School, the Netherlands, to design a program on international contracting for its three consortium partners, Ballast Nedam, Royal Boskalis, and Heerema Fabrication Group. The program was to be aimed at project managers, tender managers, regional managers, and project engineers. To meet their specific training needs, we decided to organize a workshop with representatives of these companies. This resulted in a program that we have conducted many times since then. As most people primarily learn by doing, we opted for an interactive course design built around real-life case studies, which were obtained from the practices of these companies. This format proved to be very successful. On top of that, it proved to be very enjoyable. The settings, which were designed in close collaboration with the steering committee, consisting of representatives of the three companies and TiasNimbas Business School, allowed for learning, both by participants and teachers. During our discussions, many new insights and ideas were developed, and many gaps in knowledge were identified. As a result, we decided to write this book, in order to honor our participants and their leaders; also, to contribute to the international contracting domain.

This book offers a blend of theory and practice. Chapters are built around introductory cases, practical illustrations and core text. Each chapter ends with an overview of the most important conclusions and findings. We include a large number of subjects and describe them in different chapters. In relations with an employer, a subcontractor, a surveyor, an agent, a supplier, a vendor or a banker, discussions are never restricted to one chapter only, because in one meeting multiple aspects come together. Therefore, the index will help the reader to find their way.

We are thankful to all project managers, tender managers, procurement managers, financial directors, technical directors, design engineers, account managers, company lawyers and company secretaries, technical assistants, draftsmen, foremen, logistic managers, captains and marine officers for their openness; they gave us an insight into their interesting, urgent or important problems. We made cases out of their experiences, changing the reality where necessary in order to retain confidentiality.

It was a challenge and a pleasure to write this book. We hope it will be a challenge to read it. And yet, not all subjects are included. We did not write about the "as-built" principle, and a chapter about insurance is absent. If any reader is missing other topics, please do not hesitate to contact us. We hope to come back to supplementary subjects in a second edition.

John van der Puil
Arjan van Weele
Rotterdam/Maarssen, September 2013

Acknowledgments

First and foremost, we appreciate the confidence and trust which the steering committee showed when they put a small fund together to allow us to write this book. Without their motivational support, this book would not have been feasible. We therefore want to thank Rik Lammes, Director of Projects at Heerema Fabrication Group; Erik Kruizinga, Head of Legal Affairs at Ballast Nedam; Marjolein Zeebregts, HR consultant; and Jan de Hartog, Director of Human Relations at Boskalis; and also, through them, their companies.

In order to make sure that the book would truly meet the needs of business practitioners, a review committee was formed. Its members went over the text meticulously. We would like to thank again Erik Kruizinga, as well as Jeroen Hein, Project Manager, Ballast Nedam; Jan Willem Prakke, Head of Legal Affairs, Schiphol Airport; Tino Vinkenstein, Vice President at Heerema Fabrication Group; and Bernd de Looff, Legal Counsel of Boskalis, for having read the text so carefully and for having provided us with so many constructive comments and suggestions. As a result of their interventions, the structure of the book was changed and the text has become more readable, focused and, more importantly, more relevant.

Over the past years we have worked intensely with the staff of TiasNimbas Business School. Being an outstanding business school in the Netherlands, we thank its Dean, Professor Doctor Philip Joos, and his management team — first of all, its Director, Miranda Bol, for allowing us to explore international contracting as a business domain. We also want to thank TiasNimbas Program Managers Mark Vincken, Wim Gent and, especially, Sanne Bruinstroop, who took care of all contractual arrangements and who proved to be a very professional contract and relationship manager by nature! A special word of appreciation goes to Marieke Boudewijns, who acted without exception, and relentlessly, as a professional and efficient support manager. It has been a true pleasure to have worked with you all.

Finally, we also want to thank our publisher, Imperial College Press, for the constructive collaboration. We are thankful for the positive comments of the reviewers who were summoned by ICP to judge the quality and commercial opportunities for this book. We are very grateful to have worked with Commissioning Editors Kellye Curtis and Lance Sucharov. Editorial Manager Jacqueline Downs was our editor; her support was more than expected.

We have tried to be very careful when making appropriate references to external resources, to make sure that we have not used quotes or any material without proper reference or permission. In those cases where we have been neglectful, we would appreciate it if you would let us know. We will then do everything possible to correct errors that have been made. We are responsible for them.

Being able to teach to practitioners and seasoned managers is both a challenge and a privilege. This is how we see it. It is a challenge to keep their minds and brains focused during classroom sessions, since we know how precious time can be for busy people these days. It is also a privilege to be able to engage in discussions and real-life problems, which participants do share, in and outside our classrooms. These discussions have opened our eyes and hearts to the interesting contracting world. As the saying goes: "Nothing is more practical than good theory." However, we would add: "...provided that the theory is derived from the best practices". It is of extreme importance that practitioners open up to academics and researchers. This is what they did. We are grateful for that.

Of course, many of the discussions have been done in our spare time. Writing takes a lot of time; it cannot be done during working hours. Thinking about how to structure the book, what concepts and examples to include or to leave out, requires time for contemplation and reflection, which the working environment does not allow for. We are very fortunate to live our lives with partners who understand our personalities and our zeal and zest for new knowledge. Some people like to go abroad when they travel; we like to travel with our minds. This explains why we were not always present, even when at home. We are aware that we have sacrificed precious time that we could have spent with the persons who are most dear to us in life. We thank you, Florine and Ineke, for having given us the time and freedom to work on what we felt was something that we needed to do. We will make up for it!

Contents

Introduction

Where it all started

This book is the result of an executive program on international contracting, which has been taught by the authors since 2008 to project directors and managers of large contracting companies in the Netherlands. In 2007, three of these companies, Ballast Nedam, Boskalis, and Heerema Fabrication Group, requested that TiasNimbas Business School of Tilburg University design and arrange such a program for their international project and engineering managers.

In order to arrive at a unique blend of academic knowledge and practitioner insight, we, during a workshop, invited a selection of project managers and legal experts to design an initial program structure. This resulted in one of the best — and one of the most attractive — programs that we have ever taught.

We decided to build the program around a few key principles.

First, the program should reflect every aspect of the contract cycle, beginning with the invitation to tender, up to the delivery of the project and handling of guarantee claims. Our objective was to show how interrelated each part of the contract cycle is and how that interrelationship affects business and personal relationships. Obviously, the contract cycle needed to be discussed in relation to business strategies and project management practices.

Second, it was decided to build the program around real-life case studies, taken from the actual practices of the companies involved. Project managers are pragmatic people. They have a busy agenda. They don't like theory, as they don't see the practical value of it. They have a lot of experience. They do not want to sit and listen. They want to act and engage. Therefore, we decided to develop case studies, which could serve as vehicles for discussion and the exchange of knowledge and experience among future participants.

Hence, we devoted ourselves to the time-consuming activity of writing cases based on their rich and fascinating stories. You will not find all of them in this book.

Third, we opted for a mix of academic knowledge and practitioner experience. Each case study would be discussed, and, at the end, put into some theoretical perspective or framework. Theory helps practitioners to structure their ideas and practices. As authors, we feel that nothing is more practical than good theory. However, in management, these theories should be derived from actual practices.

After having designed the program, we submitted our ideas to a steering committee with representatives of the founding companies, and TiasNimbas Business School. Some of these members were present during the first pilot of the actual program. Today, this steering committee is still around. Twice a year we review the program based on participant evaluations, and discuss what needs to be improved. Discussions are always constructive and insightful, and provide a vehicle for learning to all who are present.

Teaching the program is always a pleasure to us. We learn so much from it. Due to the interactive design, practitioners present their ideas and suggestions, as well as new business problems that they are confronted with in the exciting world in which they live. For every course, we have summarized the results of small group and plenary discussions into case reports, which later may serve as references for the participants. The contents of these case reports, as well as the many ideas, problems, and case studies that were shared during the program, inspired us to write this book. As the international contracting world is becoming more professional and complex, and our world becomes more dependent on the success of large infrastructural projects (and, in some cases, is becoming increasingly exposed to societal damage when projects go wrong), we felt that practitioners and project managers operating in this world could benefit a lot from our experiences and insights.

What this book is about

This book is about international contracting and contract management. These subjects are discussed from an international perspective, as large engineering, construction, and contracting firms operate all over the world. However, since the founding companies of the program are Dutch, we have also given our attention to the specific European context. Most of the book, however, deals with international contexts. Large infrastructural, engineering, and construction projects create the background for the book. In international contracting, projects range from oil platforms that need to be built by contract engineers for large oil companies, to the design and construction of harbor facilities in an emerging country, which are financed by the World Bank. Projects like these form the background of our book. The international contracting world is a fascinating one.

In conceiving and creating these large international projects, a lot of stakeholders are involved. We had to choose what perspective to use when dealing with the different topics. We decided to write the book from the perspective of the contractor. This may be considered a weakness, since successful projects are always co-created, i.e. realized in close collaboration between employer, contractor, subcontractors, and other stakeholders (e.g. local governments, investors, consultants). We chose the perspective of the contractor since he is, for the completion of the specific project, the central actor. The contractor needs to translate the requirements from the employer into a design and project plan. Next, he needs to negotiate a contract. After signing the contract, he needs to align subcontractors and materials suppliers. Finally, it is the contractor who has to deliver the realized permanent works to the employer. He also needs to secure and arrange all necessary permits. An increasing complexity is represented by stakeholder management, i.e. managing the interests and interrelationships with parties that are or may be affected by the project (neighbors, environmental associations, trade unions, local pressure groups, etc.). Contractors are confronted with most of the complexity in the value chain and therefore may serve as an excellent subject for our study.

In our book, we will use the term employer for a client, customer or principal, i.e. a person, company or public institution that has a specific need and wants to have a specific project completed. We will use the term contractor to designate the engineering firm, construction firm, the consortium or alliance that is selected by the employer for accomplishing the work. We will differentiate between the subcontractor and suppliers. Suppliers are those providers that deliver primarily components and materials to the work. Subcontractors are those companies that provide a combination of knowledge, services and materials to the work of the contractor.

Other terms that will be used are project manager, tender manager, procurement manager, contract manager and legal counsel. The project director, or the project manager, is the person responsible for managing the project within the targets and boundaries provided by the corporation. The tender manager is the person responsible for analyzing an invitation to tender from a potential employer and preparing the bid, which is going to be presented. The procurement manager is the person responsible for selecting and contracting subcontractors and materials suppliers. Next, the contract manager is responsible for managing all contractual aspects in a relationship with employer, project partners, and key suppliers and subcontractors. The legal counsel is the legal specialist, who is called on for specific legal advice for putting contracts together and to solve specific legal issues, which may emerge during the project.

The book is structured around the contracting cycle. Some of the book deals with the role of the contractor in international contracting, the tender process, landing and negotiating the contract, the types of contract that are used, problems that may occur during project execution, project delivery, and handling guarantee claims. Some chapters will deal with very specific issues that may occur during project execution. Other chapters deal with issues such as how to manage variations, how to handle damage to contract parties and third parties, differences between responsibility and liability, *force majeure*, dispute resolution, and how to deal with lawyers.

Target audience

This book is primarily written for business practitioners operating in the international contracting industry. It is assumed that the reader has a clear picture of his industry and/or experience in it. Furthermore, the book assumes a basic understanding and knowledge of theories related to project management, construction engineering, business law, and economics.

This is not an academic book. However, due to its unique blend of practitioner insight and academic theory, it can be taught in courses at universities at the master level. As most engineers will, beyond a doubt, deal with contracts in their work, this book is specifically recommended for engineering programs both at the Bachelor (BA) and Masters (MSc) levels. Lawyers will find the book useful for understanding the business context in which their customers and/or colleagues work. A legal framework is not a purpose in itself. It needs to enable companies and public institutions to conduct better business and develop better business relationships. Since, in most legal literature, this perspective is missing, we feel that this book fills that gap.

Given the scope of this book, the prime audience for it consists of:

- Project directors and managers of large, international engineering and construction contractors, who are responsible for managing complex technical projects within targets imposed by the corporation.
- Area managers, who are responsible for supervising different large projects in different cultural and legal environments.

- Tender managers, who need to analyze invitations to bid from employers, and who need to orchestrate the process of bid preparation.
- Field engineers, who frequently interact with employers and subcontractors to get things done in their projects.
- Procurement managers and professionals, who need to select the right subcontractors and materials suppliers for the projects and who need to align these to the project objectives.
- Legal counsels, who need to support tender managers and project managers in preparing and finalizing contract documents in a relationship with both employers, subcontractors, materials suppliers and, in some cases, investors.

The various chapters may explain why contract management is a key activity for project directors and managers. The book should help them understand that clear contracts are perfect instruments for delivering top quality in business. Also, it should help them to understand what specific legal issues may come into play. As a consequence, as soon as the scope of the work has been designed, the project manager will be able, based upon this book, to involve his legal counsel or contract manager more effectively in his daily work.

How this book is structured

This book has 25 chapters, which are divided into three parts. Each chapter is structured around a consistent format:

- Introduction. Each chapter begins with an introductory case, which highlights the practical relevance and provides an introduction to the topic.
- Core text. Next, the chapter will provide core text to acquaint the reader with the topic.
- Boxes. Boxes in the chapter will provide small case studies and/or best practices.
- Figures. Figures are used to illustrate the text.
- Conclusions. Each chapter concludes with a summary presenting the most important teachings and recommendations.

In this way, we hope to contribute to a better readability and understanding of the topics that are described.

Part I: International contracting: Defining the playing field

This part sets the scene. It explains the context of the book and provides definitions and concepts that will be used in later chapters. It also describes the relevance of the subject to international contractors and society.

Chapter 1 presents one of the most disastrous projects that the modern world has been confronted with: the BP oil spill. Based upon public documents, an analysis is made of the sequence of events that led to this disaster. As in most cases, various causes lie at the heart of the BP oil spill. Apart from an analysis of the damage done to various stakeholders, the effects on future rules and regulations for the contracting sector are discussed. This chapter sets the scene for the rest of the book.

Chapter 2 discusses the role of contracting in international business. International competition forces large contractors to deliver integrated solutions to their employers. Contractors need to choose to specialize in specific activities or to provide integrated solutions. Most Western contractors choose the latter. This implies that increasingly they are moving up the supply chain and are operating as supply-chain integrators. In this role, they should be able to orchestrate the activities of a network of subcontractors and materials suppliers in order to meet customer requirements. This orchestration requires a careful contracting strategy.

Chapter 3 discusses different clients. In international contracting, assignments may be obtained from private customers, as well as public clients. Tender procedures among these two types of clients are vastly different and become more systematized and bureaucratic. Next, different structures are used to realize complex projects. In this chapter we will discuss the specifics of public–private partnerships.

Chapter 4 provides an overview of important contract management concepts and definitions. Common problems, which may occur in customer relationships and project completion, are discussed. Different perspectives are presented in how to structure relationships in the project industry. These perspectives include the dyadic perspective, supply-chain perspective, and the value-chain perspective. The chapter will make clear that, depending on the perspective, different alternatives for solving problems may arise.

Part II: The contracting cycle

Chapter 5 discusses the various elements of the contracting cycle. Subjects discussed are the invitation to tender, how to land the contract, contract negotiations and closure, subcontracting and project execution, testing delivery and payment, as well as claims handling and dispute resolution. As such, this chapter serves as an important reference for the following chapters.

Chapter 6 discusses the process of European tendering. Public institutions are not free in how they award business to contractors. In Europe, they are bound to the European Directives on Public Procurement. The principles underlying these directives are discussed. Next, the most important procurement procedures that are used by public institutions are presented.

Chapter 7 presents an overview of downstream contracting, i.e. the way contractors could select and collaborate with materials suppliers and subcontractors. Definitions on procurement and supply management are provided. Important purchasing procedures are discussed and a portfolio-management method is provided to decide how to differentiate among subcontractor and supplier relationships. Next, specific operational and legal problems related to subcontracting are discussed.

Chapter 8 discusses the role and importance of standard contracts in international contracting. First, different basic contract types are presented. Here we will discuss the lump-sum contract, cost-reimbursable contract, and the unit rate or charter contract. Many contracts use a mix of these basic contract types. In preparing a contract, employers, as well as contractors, fortunately, can use different international templates that are utilized to arrange for contractual relationships. Here, FIDIC, LOGIC, and BIMCO contracts will be highlighted.

Part III: Project and risk management

Chapter 9 is about project and risk management. Managing complex engineering and/or infrastructural projects is all about managing risks. Risks need to be identified at the tender stage. Such an analysis should result in a risk classification: high, medium, and low risks that may affect the project outcome. It may also appear that some risks cannot be accepted, due to the companies' risk policy.

Chapter 10 deals with the important subject of managing variations. Variations are natural to any project. However, they can have severe financial consequences for project lead time, project results, and employer and supplier relationships. In this chapter we will provide clear guidelines on how to act on variations and how to arrange for variations in a contract. It will become clear that a good project-management administration is key to this activity.

Part IV: Legal issues in international contracting

This part deals with various legal issues that may occur at several stages of the contracting cycle. Each chapter results in some clear and practical guidelines on how to handle and act on specific legal issues.

Chapter 11 discusses the Letter of Intent and Memorandum of Understanding. It will become clear that both documents differ in nature. However, both have an important role to play in getting parties closer to a deal.

Signing a contract requires particular attention, as Chapter 12 explains. A loophole lies in the circumstance that most standard contracts contain clauses, which exclude all foregoing proposals and deviations discussed during negotiations. The final negotiated scope of work is added to the contract and that's it. What is not in the signed documents is of no value to the parties. There are more points for attention, which are highlighted in the chapter.

Next, liability versus responsibility will be discussed in Chapter 13. A project manager is responsible for performing a certain task; in case of non-succeeding, the company as a legal body is liable under the contract. Here, referred issues are discussed, as well as indemnities that may be asked for among the contract parties.

Chapter 14 deals with the difference between guarantee clauses and warranty clauses. This seems a rather theoretical issue for specialized lawyers, but it is better to understand the difference.

There is not a single project that has been accomplished without damage. Damages may relate to contract parties or to third parties. Here, a difference between contract law and tort law is made. Chapter 15 deals with this difference, and with contractual mechanisms for arranging for damage control in contracts. Such arrangements may relate to preventing damage upfront or settling for damage when it unfortunately occurs.

Chapter 16 is about consequential losses. Different legal systems deal differently with this subject. In common law, the definition is strict. In continental legal systems, it is the attributable cause that decides whether a party is liable and up to what amount as a consequence of their non-fulfillment of contractual obligations, their actions or omissions.

Chapter 17 is about intellectual property. Knowing how to deal with intellectual property is important, to prevent project managers from being confronted with unexpected claims from third parties.

Chapter 18 describes how to assess damage. We will analyze different causes of damage and how to deal with them. Three causality theories will be explained. We will look at solutions for preventing future damage and find out how this is done by engineers and by lawyers. It appears that there is a fundamental difference between the two.

Chapter 19 describes an important instrument for risk allocation in the maritime industry, i.e. the knock-for-knock arrangement. English courts have dealt with a number of cases; the principle is not often brought before courts in other jurisdictions. However, in a number of legal systems, gross negligence and willful misconduct will not be honored as arguments to escape liability.

Chapter 20 deals with disasters and parties' responsibilities towards the general public. In this chapter several examples will be presented, where, as a result of natural or other disasters, projects incurred great losses. Suggestions are made to prevent disasters in future. In dealing with the damage of these events, the theory of causality is important.

Chapter 21 is about *force majeure*. *Force majeure* is often used as an argument to avoid damages. However, this chapter will describe what *force majeure* is. It will become clear that only in a very few cases may it be used as an argument before court. Some practical ideas are suggested on how to deal with and minimize the consequences.

Chapter 22 describes the problems around bribery. It informs the reader that bribery is not a firmly defined subject, which in all different cultures covers the same idea. In the UK and the USA, very strict legislation is in force. A warning to all project directors and project managers is in place.

Chapter 23 presents dispute-resolution mechanisms. The major message of this chapter is: beware before you go to court. Firstly, because so many other vehicles for dispute resolution exist; secondly, because going to court takes a lot of time, money and energy; and thirdly, because it is extremely difficult to align the lawyers' interests with your business interests. The chapter also discusses the impact of different law systems on contracts.

Chapter 24 delves more specifically into the similarities and differences between continental law, English law and USA law. There are families of legal systems, which are based on different human values. This chapter will make clear how to deal with the different systems.

Chapter 25 explains that, as contracts are closed between companies and, more specifically, between people, cultural differences greatly impact the relationship and the way in which people deal with contracts. This chapter presents a framework that project managers can use to assess cultural differences. In doing so they can predict what problems might occur during the initial contracting stage, and later at project execution. Contract law is not an exact science. Judgment will always play a role, not only at the business level but also certainly when going to court. This is why the cultural dimension of international contracting deserves a place in this book.

How to read this book?

Most readers probably will find the first chapters interesting and easy to read. The objective of Part I is to provide an overview of the trends and developments in international contracting and contract management. The BP oil spill represents a warning for the offshore industry and society. As such, it sets the scene for the remainder of the book. Different types of employers (private versus public sector) are explained and different perspectives towards contract management are provided. Therefore, Part I is recommended to all readers.

Part II describes the contracting cycle. In order to become familiar with the contracting cycle, Chapter 5 must be read. As Chapters 6 and 7 are related to European tendering and downstream contracting, these may be skipped by those readers who have only a general interest in the topic.

Part III is about project and risk management. Experts who are already familiar with these topics may skip this part.

Part IV deals with specific legal issues in international contracting. As the variety in standard contracts is very large, reading these chapters is recommended. Readers may choose only the topics that they are most interested in. However, for a proper understanding of the many issues that may emerge prior to or during project execution, we recommend taking notice of all chapters, so that later on, when specific issues in the project may emerge, the reader knows the specific section to consult.

Part I

International Contracting: Defining The Playing Field

Chapter 1

International Contracting: How a Project Can Turn into a Nightmare

1.1. Case — An uneasy event

On April 20, 2010, a range of explosions crippled the Deepwater Horizon. Flames spread rapidly, power went down. Eleven men lost their lives, seventeen were seriously injured. The economic loss amounted to tens of billions of dollars. BP had to set aside $40 billion to compensate for damage to third parties. The BP Oil Spill probably has grown into the biggest disaster in offshore contracting. The story is as incredible as are its lessons. Figures 1.1 and 1.2 show the giant module in perfect condition before the disaster and when it burned before going down to the bottom of the Gulf of Mexico.

The literature about project management and risk management is abundant. Most project managers are familiar with the basics of project and risk management — they practice them every day. Rather than discussing what it takes to implement professional project and risk management, we have decided to present these topics via an actual case study to show the gap between theory and practice that often exists. We use the BP oil spill as an example. The next sections discuss what actually happened and what went wrong when testing the production pit. We also describe how the contract partners and stakeholders reacted when things went wrong and when they were brought to investigation committees for initial interviews. We conclude the chapter with the important lessons that can be learnt from this dramatic case study. In doing so, this chapter sets the stage for the remainder of the book.

1.2. The BP oil spill: what happened?

BP contracted a number of parties to prepare a well for exploration. The two most important partners were Transocean and Halliburton. Transocean delivered the platform and technical installations under a long-term

Figure 1.1. The Deepwater Horizon before the disaster. (Photo: Transocean Inc., 2013, www.deepwater.com/fw/main/lDeeptwater- ..... - 419C151.html.)

Figure 1.2. The Deepwater Horizon burning on April 22, 2010, before it sank to the sea bottom in the Gulf of Mexico. (Photo: www.crisispictures.blogspot.com, courtesy Bojar Baretic, February 2013.)

contract. Halliburton was responsible for providing and installing the cement, as described in Box 1.1 and under Figure 1.4. BP was the legal operator, whilst all oilfield service activities were subcontracted to specialist companies.

With the help of the Deepwater Horizon, BP arranged for drilling a well, enabling access to the oil reserves of the Macondo area at a depth of 5,500–6,000 meters below sea level. Locally, the sea floor is at about 1,500 meters below sea level. A special multitubular casing was drilled through three different layers in the soil in order to arrive at the oil and gas layers (see Figure 1.3). Care was taken so that the oil and gas would not come to the surface. This was arranged by injecting a heavy drill fluid ("mud") in the drilling pipe. During the production phase, which was planned to take place later on by a different production platform, the oil and gas would come upwards through the central metal riser. The outside casing and the inside metal tubing were, at the time of completion of the drilling, blocked by cement to prevent oil and gas coming up. Injecting the cement was contracted to Halliburton. Right on the sea floor a blowout preventer (BOP) was mounted. This important piece of apparatus was part of Transocean's equipment. It was designed and manufactured by Cameron.

Box 1.1. Casing and tubing below sea level.

Figure 1.4 shows the casing and the inner pipe under the sea bottom. The casing together with the central production tubing penetrates three different layers under sea level before arriving into the oil- and gas-bearing layers. The central tubing was intended, in the future, to transport the hydrocarbons up to a production platform and, therefore, is called the production tubing. The casing, when coming to depth, has smaller diameters. When mounting the casing and the inner piping, heavy drilling liquid is put into it in order to prevent oil and gas blowing out. Later on cement is poured between the casing and the central transport tubing. Cement is also put on the well annulus at the lowest possible point of the production pipe and outer casing. The tightness of the cement is verified by means of a pressure test. If the pressure test shows negative results (which indicates that the casing and production tubing have been effectively closed), the heavy drilling liquid can be changed for sea water, which is much lighter than the drilling liquid.

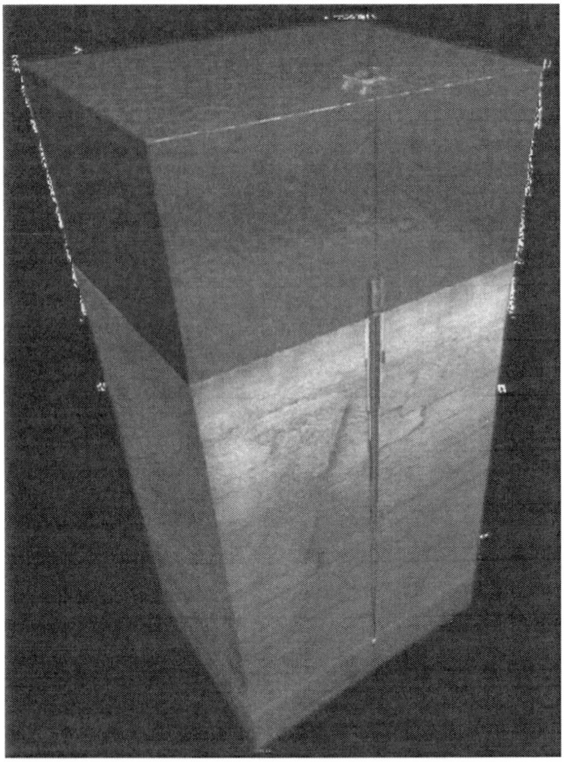

Figure 1.3. The BP well design and the drilling platform above; the object on the sea floor is the blowout preventer. (Source: Artist rendering of the Macondo well from rig to 'rathole', National Commission on the BP Deepwater Horizon Oil Spill and Off Shore Drilling, Chief Counsel's Report, February 17, 2011, p. 53.)

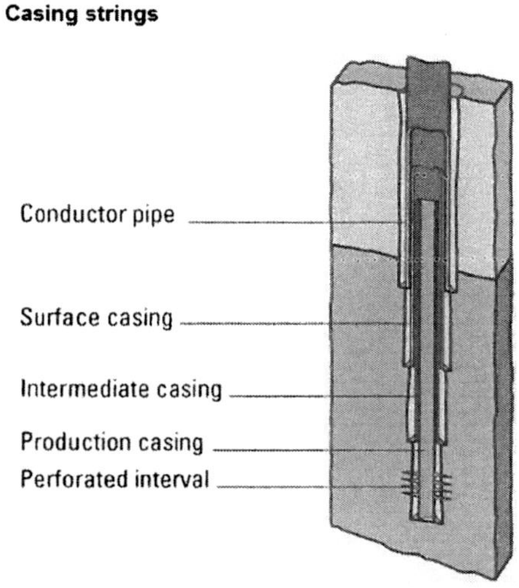

Figure 1.4. Schematic view of drilling pipe design. (Source: Oil and Gas Dictionary, January 2013.)

BP's engineering team designed the well and specified in detail how it had to be drilled (see Box 1.1). BP contracted out the work. On April 20, 2010, only 7 out of 127 persons on board the platform were BP employees.

1.3. The test

It is common practice to test the closure of the well through a pressure test. Engineers call such a test a negative pressure test. If nothing happens the result is positive. The cement down the casing and the production tubing should be sufficiently tight to resist all pressure from the oil and gas below. Cement is the barrier. In the event hydrocarbons could have penetrated between the outer casing and the production tubing a second barrier was in place. A strong seal underneath the BOP should prevent oil and gas passing through the tubing — this BOP is the third barrier and could be closed in the event hydrocarbons would, unexpectedly, come to the surface through the production tubing or through the outer casing.

After the "successful" pressure test, the crew started to replace the heavy drilling fluid with sea water. This is much lighter than the heavy drilling fluid. In the event oil and gas penetrated the cement, this would be recorded by an increase of the pressure, which would mean that the cement was still insufficiently tight. If a rise in the pressure was registered, measures could be taken to interfere on time.

After testing, everything seemed to be under control. Obviously, the well passed the test in good order. Things appeared to be okay and the well site leader concluded that the operation was successful...

The reality was quite different. There were leaks. However, these remained unobserved due to the fact that procedures were not followed, and also to an unclear line of command among the parties involved. As the crew replaced the drilling fluid with sea water, the pressure on the well was reduced. At 20:50 hours, the well became unbalanced. The weight of the lighter sea water could not resist the pressure of the gas deep down. Suddenly, the oil stream pushed the cement upwards, taking parts of it with it on its way to the surface. The BOP refused to operate. First, enormous quantities of mud, cement and sea water spread out on the drilling deck. Shortly afterwards, the dangerous methane gas escaped and found an ignition source. Methane is heavier than air and probably could have entered through ventilation openings to arrive in the engine room, where several hot objects of machinery, such as diesel engines, were operating. This set the methane gas on fire. Now the oil came up, burning the giant platform to total destruction within a mere 36 hours. When the $365 million rig slowly sank to the sea floor on April 22, oil and gas continued to flow from the open well underneath into the open waters of the Gulf. It took 87 days to get that stopped. As noted above, BP had to put aside $40 billion as compensation for claims for damages.

What can we conclude from this story so far? Firstly, all parties involved, i.e. BP, Transocean, Halliburton and others, including the subcontractors, are experienced contractors who are familiar with drilling and offshore operations. All parties have extensive procedures on health, safety and environmental issues. All parties are professionals in risk management. This is particularly true for a company like BP, which does not make any major investment decision without a thorough risk analysis. Obviously, safety procedures were set aside or were not followed with sufficient diligence.

Many parties needed to work closely together. However, they obviously failed to do so since the line of command was not entirely clear to them. Obviously, subcontractors were (or felt) overruled by the BP engineers who actually decided what needed to happen. It is a fact that, for reasons that were unclear, parties decided to deviate from standard routines.

1.4. The first investigations

Two weeks after the disaster, public hearings before the US Senate were held. A public investigation before a joint Coast Guard and Interior Department Commission started. The US Departments of the Interior and Homeland Security started an investigation to assess the damage on land. The US Department of Justice put a team of lawyers on the case to investigate criminal liability of companies and individuals. President Barack Obama installed a special committee to investigate the disaster.[1] This was "an independent non-partisan entity, directed to provide a thorough analysis and impartial judgment".[2]

Immediately after the first hearings of the US Senate and the Joint Coast Guard and Interior Department Commission, and after the *Wall Street Journal* interviewed dozens of witnesses to the disaster, this newspaper reported on how risks were estimated by BP's responsible chiefs-in-command and how opinions from specialized service providers were misjudged.[3] What

[1] Deep Water, The Gulf Oil Disaster and the Future of Offshore Drilling, Report to the President, National Commission on the BP Deepwater Horizon Oil Spill and Offshore Drilling, January 2011.

[2] National Commission, Foreword, p. 1.

[3] Deep Trouble; PB Decisions Set Stage for Disaster; There Was Nobody in Charge, *Wall Street Journal*, May 27, 2010, www.wsj.com.

emerged was a startling picture of the last operating day of the Deepwater Horizon. Later on, the preliminary conclusion was confirmed by the National Commission in its report in January 2011. The commission found that BP, contractors and subcontractors working for them had conducted a number of hazardous and time-saving activities, without adequate considerations of the risks involved. Their report concludes:

> ...There are recurring themes of missed warning signals, failure to share information, and a general lack of appreciation for the risks involved. In the view of the Commission, these findings highlight the importance of organizational culture and a consistent commitment to safety by industry, from the highest levels on down.[4]

The Chief Counsel's report, when describing his technical findings, is in line with these observations, when it states: "Behind this simple story is a complex web of human errors, engineers in misjudgment, missed opportunities, and outright mistakes."[5]

The BP drilling operation appeared to be way over budget and far behind schedule. The budget was exceeded by $20 million on the original sum of $155 million, while the planning schedule was 43 days behind. BP's contract required it to pay approximately $533,000 per day for the charter of the platform. In addition to that amount was fuel, expenses, salaries, service providers and suppliers. It was estimated that the total cost for BP amounted to about $1 million per day. Members of the Congress, industry experts and workers on board accused BP's engineers of having cut corners to save time and money.

Drilling was finished 11 days before April 20, and the well was lined with cement and steel, in this way preventing gas and oil from leaking and causing an explosion or fire. The well could then temporarily be abandoned. Thereafter, a production platform could re-open the well for production of oil and gas.

Normally, rig workers would remove about 100 meters of mud below the BOP and replace it with sea water. But BP engineers decided to remove 10 times as much mud as was deemed normal before running the test. It was unusual, but the engineers stated before the Joint Commission that they had their (technical) reasons.

During the test, at 17:00 hours, pressure increased unexpectedly. Nobody could explain why. The personnel of the control room struggled to interpret the

---

[4] National Commission, Foreword, p. 4.

[5] Chief Counsel's Report, BP Deepwater Horizon Oil Spill and Offshore Drilling, February 17, 2011, p. 35.

data. Senior management did not think the problem was serious. It was decided to tighten the valve on top of the BOP. This seemed to resolve the problem, although not everyone involved was completely satisfied. Some uncertainty remained. After discussions among managers, it was decided to do another test.

The second test resulted in an unexpected reading. One smaller tube that led up from the well showed no pressure, while this tube was connected to the main pipe where readings actually showed pressure. Conflicting information is always confusing. It may be interpreted in different ways. Finally, the well site leader for the evening decided to inform BP engineers in Houston that he was satisfied with the test.

Analyzing the available electronic data after the disaster provided clear indications that leaks actually occurred. It is amazing that none of the experienced personnel observed these signs from their control systems. Executives and workers were busy with "other things".

We may conclude that the fact that the project was running behind schedule and over budget caused significant stress among all key managers involved. During the weeks before the blow out, work plans were changed frequently, causing a lot of frustration and uncertainty among the staff involved. The platform was needed elsewhere and the crew was already demobilizing before the pressure tests were finished. BP wanted to finish the job as soon as possible. All staff members were engaged in different activities. This may explain why, during two hours, the instruments that reported clear leakages were not monitored. When, finally, the leakages were observed, it was too late. Obviously, the leadership was lacking and failing, not only during the time of the blow out, but certainly also in the weeks before. Bad leadership was responsible for frequent schedule changes, with neglect of procedures resulting in stressful situations and frustration among personnel. Formal contracts and risk management procedures are of no value in such a situation. Risk management can never replace bad leadership.

1.5. The blame game

Three main parties were involved in the disaster. First, BP plc, which held the concession for drilling and exploration of oil and gas below sea level in the Gulf of Mexico. The next party is Transocean, i.e. the owner of the platform. The third party is Halliburton, i.e. the specialized service provider, who performed a variety of services on the rig and who was responsible for the cement operations.

As far as the concession is concerned, US laws and regulations apply, issued by institutions such as the competent ministries, the supervising bodies, the environmental inspection bodies and, last but not least, the US Coast Guard.

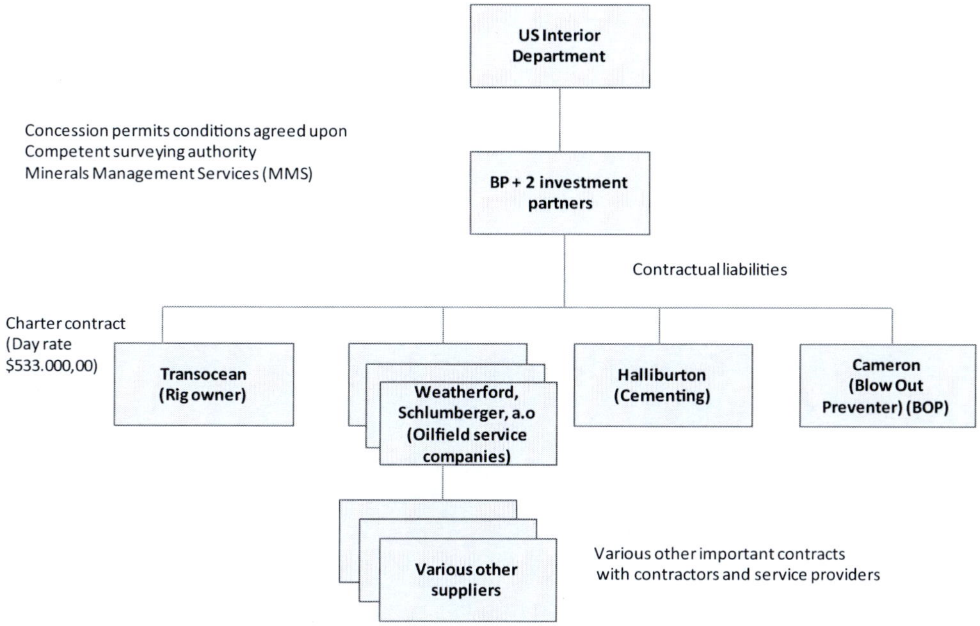

Figure 1.5. Contract structure BP Macondo Project (major contract parties).

These rules and regulations apply to all companies searching for oil and gas. There were also some special local issues for the well. These legal rules are applicable to all partners who were on board at the platform and in the offices on shore. The parties were linked by contracts as showed in Figure 1.5.

In May 2010, during the official hearings before the national Congress, the responsible parties started what later on became known as "The Blame Game". The cooperation among the parties involved was far from perfect — they were divided beyond words.

BP stated that the BOP did not work. All equipment was managed and maintained by Transocean. Consequently, Transocean, being the owner of the rig, was to be blamed. Transocean, in turn, mentioned that the cement system was not in order, so Halliburton's negligence in operating the cement system was to blame. Halliburton, in turn, said that on board the platform nothing was done without BP's consent. Therefore, BP was to blame. All persons who were interrogated declared that all safety procedures were exactly and prudently respected, so that "they were not to be blamed". "It was not my fault" — that was what all of them seemed to express.

When preparing Congress's investigation, it appeared that the Minerals Management Services Department, being the competent surveying authority, issued regulations "in general" and left the details, including whether these complied with the regulations, to the oil sector. In Congress the question arose: why? Was that body not capable of issuing detailed regulations? Did it not have to inspect and monitor compliance to these rules and guidelines? It was noticed that one and the same body cashed the concession fees. This resulted in further questions: why the same body? Was this not to be considered a conflict of interest?

In order to cut corners and to prevent even more critical questions, one day before the first hearing, i.e. on May 11, the Ministry announced that these practices were to be changed as soon as possible.

1.6. Kinds of damages caused by the disaster and claims

It was expected that BP would have to pay billions of US dollars to small enterprises and individuals to cover 200,000 of claims that were deemed eligible. It was clear to everyone that the local economy would suffer from the effects of the oil spill, which came on top of the financial crisis, together with its reduced house prices and bad balance sheets of local banks. A major difficulty, both for private citizens and companies, was to prove before the court the causal relationship between the oil spill and the damage that occurred. Another problem was to quantify the financial damage done to external stakeholders.

Table 1.1 provides a schematic overview of damages that were incurred as a result of the disaster. Table 1.2 provides an overview of the major claimants.

1.7. Court proceedings

BP and various other BP entities are among the companies named as defendants in approximately 600 private civil law suits resulting from the disaster, and further actions are likely to be brought.[6] The pending lawsuits have been brought in US federal and state courts. Plaintiffs include individual, corporations, insurers and governmental entities, and many purport to be class actions. Claims come from claimants from different US states. The US filed a civil complaint in a multidistrict litigation under the Oil Pollution Act 1990 and civil penalties under the Clean Water Act. A summary is shown in Table 1.2.

Experts foresee that settlement of litigations will take about 20 years before everything will be completed. BP faces tens of billions of dollars more in governmental fines and legal costs. BP claimed Transocean, Weatherford, Halliburton and Cameron International Corporation, the manufacturer of

---

[6]BP Annual Report 2011, p. 160, www.bp.com/annual report 2011.

Table 1.1. Categories of damages.

Kind	Direct suffering	Consequences
Material damages	Platform Oil well BP partners in the exploration enterprise MOEX Offshore and Anadarko Petroleum Company	Financial losses by BP plc, its partners in the venture and Transocean — changing relations between personnel, reorganization, check on and improvement of internal health and safety procedures
Personal injuries	11 persons killed 17 injured persons	Families, companies USA — citizens
Physical damages	Environmental damage	Birds, fish, alligators, vegetation, etc
Immaterial damages	Families, companies, colleagues Psychical damages	Sadness, anger, loss of confidence in oil and gas industry and in government
Financial damages	450,000 individuals, companies and institutions; companies involved in commercial fishing, oyster or shrimp industries, sea food processing/packaging industry. Waterfront property owners and restaurants Dock and marine owners and operators and business owners Commercial and private boat owners, cruise lines, travel agencies City, County or State Institutions Local transfers of housings Local Gulf Coast banks Loss of shareholders' value for BP shares Civil prosecution costs	Insurance companies lose money; US economy: Fishermen and families cannot spend money, companies have less business or not at all, restaurants, bars, shops suffer financially, unemployment due to the disaster, local supply chains earn less, housing agents no activity Shareholders, banks, investment companies, Pension funds
Reputation damages	BP plc, Transocean, Halliburton, oil and gas industry in general CEOs and staff of companies concerned Tony Hayward, president BP Numerous BP managers before criminal courts	BP Shareholders Transocean shareholders Halliburton shareholders Hayward and family Shareholders and banks Managers losing their jobs

Table 1.2. Stakeholders of the claim war.

Claiming institution	Activity	Accountable party
State of Alabama and 11 other states of America: Increased public service costs, loss of government revenue	Prosecutor of Alabama Criminal prosecution	BP, Transocean and Halliburton, their executing officers, directors and project managers
USA President Obama	Cleaning of sea surface 4400 vessels — 33.000 persons involved Civil prosecution	BP and its contract partners
US Department of Justice	Installation of 23 claim centers for the registration of claims	BP and its contract partners
Installation of Central Claim Court in New Orleans	Common judgment of all claims before courts related to the oil disaster	Ministry of Justice, who will claim against BP and contract partners for compensation
US Department of Justice	Criminal Prosecution	BP, Halliburton and Transocean board members, directors, key and project managers
A few hundred solicitors on behalf of offenders	Supporting claiming parties	BP, partners, service providers and sub-subcontractors
BP, Transocean, Halliburton, subcontractors	Private civil law suits against each other	BP, Transocean, Halliburton, subcontractors
200,000 private claimants under civil private laws of the states around the Gulf of Mexico	Deposing private civil law suits	BP, partners, service providers and sub-subcontractors
BP shareholders under civil British law	Deposing private civil claims at the London court	BP
Security Exchange Commission of the New York Exchange	Deposing law suits based on manipulation of exchange notification	BP and Financial directors

the BOP. BP sued Transocean for $40 billion for the oil spill.[7] The August 2010 hearings, when parties attempted to understand the causes of the Deepwater Horizon explosion, were dominated by disagreements among lawyers of the companies involved. Later on, all contractual parties claimed

[7]http://www.tonwhall.com/news/us/2011etc, January 21, 2013.

against BP or filed cross claims or counter-claims based on several issues, such as state law, maritime law, the Oil Pollution Act 1990, the Clean Water Act, as well as on the basis of comparative fault. Shareholders of BP started a class action against BP plc and are suing BP for lost revenues and reduced shareholders value.[8]

Without awaiting any court decisions, President Obama presented the US's first invoice of damages, amounting to $69 million. It was May 3. Specification: cleaning costs in general. Motive: reimbursement under the Oil Pollution Act 1990 and other laws. In July 2010, additional bills were dispatched to BP and other parties, such as MOEX and Anadarko (BP's partners in the concession) and Transocean. The first 11 bills were reimbursed by BP; a 12th bill was pending at that time. The total cleaning amount was reaching $715 million. The Administration will continue to bill the responsible parties.[9]

BP took responsibility for the cleanup, reserving billions for losses.[10] BP opened a $20 billion trust fund that is available to satisfy the foreseeable claims and litigations; as per 31 December, 2011, BP's total contributions to this fund amounted $15.1 billion.[11] BP remains of the opinion that the amounts it put aside for paying damages will not be sufficient to finalize the claims. "The total amounts ... are subject to significant uncertainty and the ultimate exposure and cost to BP will be dependent on many factors (including ... determination of BP's culpability based on any findings of negligence, gross negligence or willful misconduct)."[12]

In the meantime BP was able to arrange some settlements with contract parties for some of the claims. MOEX and Anadarko, who were partners in the joint venture Deepwater Horizon, paid $1 billion and $4 billion respectively to BP. Cameron, the producer of the BOP, paid $250 million to BP. A deal was realized between BP and Weatherford, a subcontractor that supplied and installed pressure control valves to the Deepwater Horizon. The company agreed to pay a sum of $75 million to BP.[13] These amounts were transferred to the $20 billion trust fund mentioned above.[14]

In March 2012, a settlement was reached between the Plaintiffs' Steering Committee, representing the economic and medical interest of approximately

---

[8] www.prnewswire.com/news-releases/etc, June 30, 2010.
[9] www.restorethegulf.gov/release/2011/etc, July 12, 2011.
[10] www.bp.com/sectiongenericarticle800.do, January 21, 2013.
[11] BP Annual Report 2011, p. 77.
[12] BP Annual Report 2011, p. 193.
[13] www.bloomberg.net, June 22, 2011.
[14] BP Annual Report 2011, p. 77; under Legal Proceedings, p. 161.

100,000 persons and businesses around the Gulf. BP will help to restore the economic losses and property damage related to the Gulf Seafood Industry, and other economic interests such as tourism and boating; the total amount referred is $7.8 billion.[15] The deal needed approval from the US District Court in New Orleans, which was granted on 22 December, 2012.[16]

In turn, Transocean reached a $1.4 billion settlement with the US over the spill. Transocean decided to plead guilty to violation of the Clean Water Act 1990 ($400 million in criminal fines and $1 billion in civil penalties).[17]

BP also agreed to pay $4 billion to the US Justice Department, pleading guilty to several counts, including 11 for the manslaughter of seamen. BP will pay an additional $525 million to resolve claims by the Security and Exchange Commission that the company misled investors about the rate of oil flowing into the Gulf in April and May 2010.[18]

There are some personal charges as well. The well site managers, who supervised testing, were charged with involuntary manslaughter, seamen's manslaughter and Clean Water Act violations. The US states that they ignored multiple indications that the well was not secure before the explosion. A former BP vice president was charged with obstruction of Congress and false statements related to the size of the spill. A former BP engineer is charged with destroying evidence and obstruction of justice for allegedly deleting text messages from his mobile phone.[19] These are not the only personal cases related to the disaster. More persons will be invited before the court.

1.8. Further investigations and reports

BP is subject to a number of further investigations related to the oil spill by numerous agencies of the US government. The related published reports are available on the websites of the referred agencies and commissions.[20]

- On January 11, 2011, the National Commission on the BP Deepwater Horizon Oil Spill and Offshore Drilling, established by President Obama, published its report on the causes of the incident and its recommendations

[15] APNews, Townhall.com/news/us/2012/, 2012/05/02; BP Annual Report 2011, pp. 77 and 163.

[16] www.Bloomberg.net, December 22, 2012.

[17] The New York Times, January 3, 2013; www.bloomberg.net, January 9, 2013.

[18] www.bloomberg.net, December 12, 2012.

[19] www.bloomberg.net, November 29, 2012 and January 14, 2013.

[20] BP Annual Report 2011, p. 164.

for policy and regulatory changes for offshore drilling. On February 17, 2011, a separate report regarding the causes of the disaster followed. (See also Section 1.4 of this chapter.)

- In a report dated March 20, 2011, with an Addendum dated April 30, 2011, the Joint Investigation Team (JIT) for the Marine Board of Investigation established by the US Coast Guard and Bureau of Ocean Energy Management (BOEMRE) issued the Final Report of the Forensic Examination of the Deepwater Horizon Blowout Preventer (BOP) prepared by Det Norske Veritas. To that purpose, the blowout preventer was carried up from the bottom of the Gulf of Mexico by the US Coast Guard and transported to test facilities as shown in Figure 1.6.
- On April 22, 2011, the US Coast Guard issued its Maritime Report focused on the maritime aspects of the incident. The US Chemical Safety and Hazard Investigation Board (CSB) also conducted an investigation that is focused on the explosions and fire.
- Also, at the request of the Department of the Interior, the National Academy of Engineering/National Research Council established a Committee to examine the performance of the technologies and practices

Figure 1.6. The blowout preventer of the Deepwater Horizon dismantled into two parts during transport on the Mississippi River into Jeux de Fille at New Orleans, September 2010. The blowout preventer was used to help the Joint BOEMRE/US Coast Guard investigation determine the circumstances surrounding the explosion, fire, pollution and sinking of the Mobile Offshore Drilling Unit Deepwater Horizon. (Photo: US Coast Guard Petty Officer 3rd class Stephen Lehmann. http://www.deepwaterinvestigation.com/index_fichiers/360339.JPG.)

involved in the probable causes of the disaster and to identify and recommend technologies, practices, standards and other measures to avoid similar future events. On November 17, 2010, the Committee publicly released its interim report.
- The Flow Rate Technical Group (FRTG), Department of the Interior, issued its final report, titled Assessment of Flow Rate Estimates for the Deepwater Horizon/Macondo Well Oil Spill, on March 10, 2011. The report provides a summary of the strengths and limitations of the different methods used by the US government to estimate the flow rate and a range of estimates from 13,000 b/d to over 100,000 b/d.
- On March 18, 2011, the US Coast Guard ISPR team released its final report noting lessons learned from the incident as well as making recommendations on how to improve future oil spill response and recovery efforts.
- There are hundreds of investigations on the consequences of the disaster. These relate to the local economies of the areas around the Gulf, the disturbed wildlife, the mental health of individuals concerned, and many disturbed human relations.

All reports are extensive and time-consuming to read. Most reports require detailed understanding of various applied sciences. In short, these reports seek to identify the alleged root causes of the disaster, the failures of the safety systems and safety equipment, such as the BOP that did not work when it was needed. Also the maintenance operations and safety culture of companies are reported. The contractual relations between companies are examined. Communications between human beings, such as directors, staff members, design and construction engineers, project managers, representatives and operating personnel are investigated. As such, the reports will be part of the numerous court proceedings that will be going on for years to come. The official reports also will serve for the improvement of design and construction standards of the authorities and the classification societies.

This extensive reporting will lead to improvements to industry practices, and to regulatory programs to prevent recurrence and mitigate potential consequences. Inspection authorities are now equipped with additional personnel and executive authority. Stricter procedures on health, safety and environment will follow worldwide. All countries where oil and gas are explored learned their lessons: dramatic oil spills could happen anywhere in the world.

Many reports had critics, though. Transocean and BP issued their own reports, expressing different viewpoints, which were not mentioned in the reports of the competent authorities. BP investigated the accident with the help of a dedicated special team of experts.[21] Their report denies a number of causes that were indicated as root causes by the National Commission and the JIT committee. BP is clear in analyzing that Transocean's equipment was not up to standard and Halliburton's cement and mud treatments were inadequate, while the well monitoring failed. Also, the malfunctioning of the failing BOP is mentioned.

Obviously, BP went to great lengths to obtain financial compensation from its business partners. However, BP admitted making major mistakes and misjudgments. BP's investigation unveiled a complex, interlinked series of implementation and team interface failures, involving several companies, including BP, which contributed to the accident. The BP team made 26 recommendations specifically for its drilling operations, which now are implemented worldwide. Two of the recommendations relate to the strengthening of contractor management and personnel competence. There is an integrated action plan which will apply for BP, its partners and its service providers.

Halliburton disagreed with the cement testing, performed on behalf of the Commission, and disagreed with the findings of the National Commission in its January 2011 report. "The National Commission selectively omitted information provided to it by Halliburton in response to its numerous inquires", the company said.[22]

Also Transocean investigated the disaster and published its findings. Transocean's report says BP failed to properly assess the risks around the troubled well and did not communicate these to Transocean. BP used a poor well design which led to the failure of the cement around the well casing, allowing gas to escape, the report states. Transocean also said its BOP was properly maintained, but the extreme pressure from the well forced drill pipes to bend, preventing it from functioning.[23] "Transocean blamed BP for the Deepwater Horizon Platform Disaster .... the disaster resulted from BP's

---

[21] BP, Deepwater Horizon — Accident Investigation Report, September 8, 2010, http://www.bp.com/liveassets/bpinternet/globalbp/. Deepwater_Horizon_Accident_Investigation_Report.pdf

[22] Halliburton Press Release: Halliburton comments on National Commission Cement Testing, October 28, 2010; Press Release: Halliburton comments on Final Report from the National Commission on the BP Deepwater Horizon Oil Spill and Offshore Drilling, January 11, 2011.

[23] Transocean Ltd, Internal Investigation Report on Causes of Macondo Well Incident, June 22, 2011, www.deepwater.com and http://phx.corporate-ir/net/phoenix/etc, August 29, 2011.

faulty decision-making and inadequate attention to risk management. Transocean blamed BP for changing its plans for Macondo five times in the two weeks preceding the blow out."[24] Transocean rejected its responsibility for the oil spill and believed it was indemnified from liability in the contract with BP.[25]

Notwithstanding the fact that BP and Transocean were successful in settling their private civil litigation where they claimed damages, cross claims and counter-claims under their contract, as well as damages in tort, Transocean's defending opinions will remain valuable in the remaining criminal proceedings which were started by the US Department of Justice. Sharing the guilt for the offences may result in sharing the upcoming penalties and fines. As well as that, top executives of both corporations are still individual suspects in the proceedings.

1.9. What went wrong? — The causes and proposed reforms

Looking at the many reports which were analyzed, we conclude the following:

- When designing the production tubing and the casing, BP had the option to choose from different designs. The Chief Counsel's Report remarked about this issue: "BP's decision to use a 'long string production casing' increased the difficulty of achieving zonal isolation during the cement job. While the decision did not directly cause the blow out, it increased the risk of cementing failure."[26]
- Halliburton advised BP to install numerous devices to make sure the riser was centered in the drilled shaft before injecting cement between riser and casing. Otherwise, small channels in the cement might give way for the gas to squeeze through. However, BP decided to have only 6 center-devices installed instead of the 21 recommended by Halliburton. In doing so, BP obviously overruled the expertise of a specialist subcontractor (probably for cost reasons).
- More mud than usual was replaced by lighter sea water; up to 10 times more, it was reported. In this way the risk that the oil pressure from below

[24] www.bloomberg.com/news/2011-06-22/transocean

[25] http://www.nypost.com/p/news/national/transocean_rejects_responsibility, December 15, 2010.

[26] Chief Counsel's Report, Chapter 4.2.

could match and even override the pressure from the weight of the sea water was increased. In discussing this item, Transocean disagreed with BP about how much drilling mud should be removed and replaced by water. BP clearly won the argument. Here, again BP did not listen to, and overruled, its expert subcontractor.

- In general, comparable tests to check the cement would last 10 hours. BP ordered that the negative test should last only 30 minutes, during which time any risk that the pressure would rise would not be identified. The test needed to be longer so that the risk would become apparent. Here, BP clearly did not respect standard procedures on cement testing.
- It was clear that the well was not tight — the gauges gave different indications after the second test, while the responsible well site leader concluded the test to be successful and he apparently was wrong. Transocean personnel also agreed that the test was okay.[27] Due to the time pressure imposed on them, and the urge to speed up the work, staff had become careless in their analysis of measurements and interpreting data.
- In the two hours between the decision, "test successful", and the start of the fire, the digital measurements in the control room showed gas and oil leakages. During these two hours, engineers could have given orders to intervene; mud and cement could have been added. "If rig personnel had identified the problem earlier they could have prevented the Macondo blow out."[28] Due to other duties, staff did not keep track of instruments and measurements. Both crew and their supervisors fell short of executing their tasks.
- The BOP did not work at the moment it should have closed the well. The Chief Counsel's Report mentions that it could have prevented the killing of 11 persons. However, it could not have reduced the oil spill.[29]
- Transocean did not maintain its BOP according to the manufacturer's instructions. There were also "other maintenance problems on the Deepwater Horizon".[30]
- A chapter of the Chief Counsel's Report is dedicated to underlying management causes. "Management failures lay at the root of all technical failures."[31]

---

[27] Chief Counsel's Report, Chapter 4.6.
[28] Chief Counsel's Report, Chapter 4.7.
[29] Chief Counsel's Report, Chapter 4.9.
[30] Chief Counsel's Report, Chapter 4.10.
[31] Chief Counsel's Report, Chapter 5.

Proposed reforms of regulations

In September 2011 the United States Coast Guard (USCG) and BOEMRE completed their joint investigation.[32] The Joint Report of Investigation contains the findings, analyses, conclusions and recommendations of the JIT. It contains the issues within the jurisdiction of the Coast Guard, specifically the vessel and its systems and the subsequent evacuation, firefighting and search-and-rescue efforts; it addresses the causes of the blow out, including factors related to the Macondo well drilling, well abundant procedures and well control that are within the jurisdiction of BOEMRE. Both institutions are already undertaking significant reforms of the domestic regulatory and oversight regime for Mobile Offshore Drilling Units (MODUs). They will keep pace with changing industry practices and drilling procedures "... to effectively manage risks to ensure safe, secure, and environmentally responsible operations".[33] That message is loud and clear. When the industry does not manage its risky operations, we — in our role of public institution — will.

The Coast Guard made 52 recommendations for changing regulations. These refer to: a) coastal state requirements; b) flag state requirements; and c) international requirements, established through the International Marine Organization (IMO). To mention some recommendations, they refer to design of MODUs, fire and exposure strategies, layout of machinery, ventilation systems, persons in charge, regulatory inspections, fire-fighting systems and components, engineering evaluation, performance standards of systems and components, life-saving issues, introduction of compulsory shore-based operation centers, more comprehensive inspection standards for foreign-flagged MODUs[34] and risk assessment models.

The USCG received 282 comments that took issue with numerous findings and conclusions in its joint report. They came from five entities — i.e. the main contract partners — and only a very few of them were acceptable to the Coast Guard: the Coast Guard disagreed with most comments and believed that the JIT's recommendations were supported by the evidence of the investigation. The comments were considered but did not impact the decisions reflected in the Commandant's Final Action.[35]

[32] Joint Cover Memo, September 9, 2011, Volume I and Volume II, plus Appendixes, September 16, 2011, http://www.deepwaterhorizoninvestigation.com/go/doc/3043/1193483, 25th, September 2011.

[33] Joint Cover Memo Introduction letter to Joint Report, September 9, 2011.

[34] Bear in mind the Deepwater Horizon was registered in the Republic of the Marshall Islands.

[35] Joint Report, Response to Comments on the Coast Guard Deepwater Horizon Report of Investigation, Enclosure to Volume I of the report.

1.10. Violation of laws, regulations, procedures and policies

The BOEMRE report of September 2011[36] covers the same subjects as the earlier Report to the President of January 2011.[37] Its objective was to analyze the causes of the disaster, to mention the violations of US regulations and make recommendations to improve the safety of offshore drilling. BOEMRE found that seven compulsory US-regulations were violated. The report also analyzes company practices and written procedures which had to be followed by all employees. The report states that eight company practices with regard to safety and risk management were violated, mainly by BP itself.[38] Six out of eight were contributing causes of the Macondo blow out, while two were classified as possible contributing causes. "As a prudent operator, BP should have complete control of operations and issues surrounding operations on its lease."[39]

Earlier, BP stated that Halliburton and Transocean were to blame, being responsible and liable for their own activities, as — according to BP — they are the specialists in their area of knowledge. The lesson to be learned from this case by all technicians operating at dangerous projects: you may contract out your responsibilities and liabilities to contractors, subcontractors, service providers and suppliers, but contracting out is a risk in itself. Transferring risks is common practice in the construction and oil and gas industry. In reality, risks never disappear. In all events, the party who contracted out the risk remains responsible and accountable with regard to the competent local authorities having jurisdiction over local activities.

1.11. Sharpening regulations

Drilling activities in the Gulf of Mexico were interrupted for two months. All drilling rigs and further installations were inspected. Safety policies were checked. When this moratorium was lifted, new rules were imposed.[40] The US administration temporarily barred more than 3,800 contractors from winning new federal work in 2012. Not all of these bans were related to the oil

[36] Volume II of the Joint Report.

[37] Deep Water, The Gulf Oil Disaster and the Future of Offshore Drilling, Report to the President, National Commission on the BP Deepwater Horizon Oil Spill and Offshore Drilling, January 2011.

[38] Pp. 191–193, Volume II.

[39] Joint Report, p. 191, Volume II.

[40] *New York Times*, October 13, 2010.

spill disaster. In BP's case, the ban was imposed because the company's conduct during the 2010 Deepwater Horizon disaster showed "a lack of business integrity". The action does not affect existing contracts.[41] One of the reasons for barring some oil and gas contractors was that they appeared to be not up-to-standard as far as HS&E regulations were concerned.

Competent authorities in Denmark, the Netherlands, Norway, the United Kingdom, Ireland, Sweden, Germany and other countries checked their existing regulations. All of them scrutinized the supervision of all existing oil and gas concessions. The number of inspections has been intensified everywhere. All offshore operating companies had to forward their procedures for ongoing drilling activities, to inform authorities which equipment was used, what competences were attributed to the regular workers and their emergency and rescue plans in the event of a disaster. Companies had to report which safety measures were taken during recent years.

Awarding licenses and concessions has become much stricter. As a consequence, operations costs for all oil and gas companies have increased dramatically in a very short period of time. International public authorities sharpened their regulations with regard to design, maintenance and inspections, notwithstanding the fact that there is no proof that systems or components (for instance the electrical equipment and installations) were in bad condition or failed, neither that they contributed to the disaster. In the future, building and operating the assets will require increased investments and costs. Contractors of drilling platforms will be faced with inspection authorities who keep stricter regulations in stricter hands. The bad risk management of a few private parties has increased future investments and costs for the entire oil and gas industry all over the world. Laws that arrange for damages after oil disasters have been changed and the maximum fine has increased from $75 million to $10 billion damage compensation in the USA.

Four oil exploration companies announced the foundation of an alliance and provided funding of $250 million each to develop a system, capable of catching up to 100,000 barrels a day, in case a comparable disaster to that of the Macondo well should occur. They hope that new licenses and concessions will be granted. The companies involved are ExxonMobile, Chevron, ConocoPhilips and the Dutch-British Shell.[42]

---

[41] Bloomberg, December 20, 2012.

[42] New Oil Spill Containment System to Protect Gulf planned by Major Oil Companies, Chevron press release, July 20, 2010.

1.12. Causality and risks

The management of BP, responsible for the operation of the well, had an appetite for risk, or it disregarded the risks involved. The job was over schedule and over budget. Simon (2000) analyzed the circumstances and the conditions in assessing internal risk pressure.[43] The job was over time and far over budget. Working under pressure results in stress, and stress in its turn may jeopardize clear thinking, clear reading of gauges and test result values and coming to balanced conclusions to implement the correct actions.

In the offshore and construction industries, damage is very seldom caused by one element; in most cases, two or more causes come together. Here, in the BP disaster, at least six risk-accumulating causes occurred at the same time. Most probably all of those were *sine qua non* causes. That means that if one such cause had not happened, the disaster would not have taken place. Management's inappropriate disregard for risk assessment created the climate where all causes were overlooked; the signals were ignored by the staff responsible for safety and risk assessment.

There is another phenomenon that requires attention. Before the disaster, the US surveying authority was the Minerals Management Services Department, which monitored oil exploration and drilling activities. During the hearings, it appeared that the rules and regulations were formulated in general terms only, leaving the details up to oil companies (in this case, BP). BP was able to change testing procedures five times without being questioned by the surveying authority. Apparently, BP had much more knowledge concerning the operations and the risks involved than the surveying institute. This may be true for most international, high-tech contracting activities.

When you, as a project manager, are responsible for a job — in, for example, the Great Republic of Swania — it may happen that you are in a position to convince the surveying authorities that a certain way of operation is "absolutely safe", without the inspectors of the official institute being able to criticize you. In such a situation, you obtain a permit, while you know that the institution that issued the document is not in a position to judge all risks involved. This gives you an ethical dilemma. Is your proposed action a full 100% safe, and does it sufficiently meet the risk management policy and guidelines of your company? Or are you cutting corners to speed up your time schedule and to limit your financial losses, through accepting more risk than you normally would do?

---

[43] R. Simon (2000), *Performance Measurement & Control Systems for Implanting Strategy.* Upper Saddle River, NJ: Prentice Hall, pp. 264–269.

What happened in the BP oil spill could happen in any project. Engineers, project managers, project directors, engineering staff and operators should realize that, from time to time, working under pressure is not dramatic, as long as you keep a cool head. Any project can be placed under pressure. That was the case here: over time and over budget. The rig was committed to the next job and was squeezed between two deadlines. In those circumstances, BP, as well as Transocean, had good reasons to speed things up. However, by neglecting normal safety procedures, tremendous risks were accepted. The pressure to finish the job came from senior management, both at BP and at Transocean. The project failed due to failure of management and leadership.

1.13. Conclusions

BP was rather autonomous in setting the rules for the negative test. In this self-governing position BP could summon a changed test procedure in the morning meeting on April 20. BP overruled the advice of its specialized service providers Transocean and Halliburton. In any project design technical choices have to be made. They are always connected to project costs and project risks.

From our analysis we may conclude the following:

- *Risk management starts even before tendering for projects.* When tendering, one has to investigate and list all possible risks. The design of the drilling pipe was made by BP. The rig was hired by BP. Oilfield service activities were subcontracted to a number of specialist subcontractors. Subcontractors accepted BP's instructions. Subcontractors should remain cautious and critical about risks which are related to the design and engineering of a project. Why does the employer decide on a certain design? How many redundancies were built into the design? Analyze your own company's technical, project and safety procedures. Provide timely feedback to your employer. Don't accept everything that is submitted to you.
- *Project management and international contracting are all about risk management and risk allocation.* All contract parties involved had excessive technical and safety procedures. All staff probably were well trained. But what about the basic risk mentality that was conveyed? Why were these technical and safety procedures not followed?
- *Assess risks carefully.* Do so in a joint discussion among all contract parties involved. Write down which potential causes for damage may be hidden in the intended operations. Distinguish between *sine qua non* causes ("show-stoppers") and consequential causes. Ask yourself if the total risk of an operation is increased if two or more causes occur at the same time.

- *Value the expertise of your subcontractors.* Discuss what will happen in the event that damage occurs. Listen to specialized service providers and their subcontractors. They know more about specialized activities than you do. Use their experience; your company is paying for it. You have the right to be informed about the best advice that you can get. Analyzing project risks is done in concert with your business partners. Your risk is their risk, and the other way round. It is better to cooperate with your contracting parties than blame your business partners afterwards when things go wrong. Leave your ego at home.
- *Take good care of your equipment.* Do not neglect maintenance. Be respectful of maintenance procedures, and of the maintenance schedules of your equipment. If maintenance appears to have been neglected, you put your company in a risky position before any court.
- *Keep your nerves under control.* When top management puts increasing pressure on you to stay within budgets, and when you are squeezed to meet deadlines, realize for yourself that your personal responsibility will never disappear. At any time, and under any law system, you will remain responsible for your actions or non-actions. This is even true when your boss, your contractor or your employer orders you to put aside safety procedures. Don't forget that tens of high-ranked persons of the companies, as well as the individuals involved in the Gulf disaster, will be brought before court, this time not as witnesses, but as suspects. The responsible site managers of the Macondo project were amongst the first to be sued.
- *When private companies fail to manage their risks adequately, compulsory and stricter legislation will follow.* The best ways to cope with risk management are excellent leadership, managing by example, personal wisdom and integrity. Failing risk management leads to increasing costs and investments for the entire offshore and contracting industry.
- *Risk management occasionally may suffer from the egos of arrogant senior management.* Such management operate from a large distance and who issue orders without really understanding and knowing what is going on at the work site. No risk management system can replace or cover for a bad relationship between senior executives of companies that are supposed to cooperate.

In modern society, project managers and project engineers hold very responsible positions. Being a project manager and project engineer is wonderful, that's for sure. The work offers challenges and adventure. However, it also brings responsibilities towards society and the environment. No contractor can escape from risk and responsibilities. When managing risks, project managers and engineers are recommended to think and plan before they leap.

Chapter 2

The Role of Contracting in International Contracting

2.1. Case — What is reasonable?

Some years ago, a major Dutch contractor got the challenging assignment to do specialist dredging work to deepen the fairways to Rio de Janeiro. The agreement between the Port Authority of Rio de Janeiro and the contractor was a FIDIC Dredging and Reclamation Contract, which stipulated the works to be delivered "fit for purpose".

Based upon the soil investigation, which was conducted by a specialist consultant on behalf of the Port Authority, the Dutch contractor prepared his work plan and time schedule. As the soil investigation showed, no specific problems were to be expected in the dredging area. However, a few weeks after the work commenced, the dredger stumbled on some unexpected hard rock formations. As a result of this, the cutter teeth and adapters of the dredger needed to be replaced more frequently, leading to higher operational costs and a delay in the time schedule. When the job was finished, there was no profit and the contractor was cited by the Port Authority for late delivery. The contractor was appalled, since he had worked exactly according to the Port Authority's instructions and the technical data that was provided. In reaction, the contractor claimed against the Port Authority for its defective and incorrect soil investigation, and the negative consequences that resulted.

When both parties went to court for settlement, the Judge sentenced the contractor. He argued that since the work was to be delivered fit for purpose, it would have been the contractor's responsibility to check the validity of the results of the soil investigation. By not doing so, the contractor assumed the risk that data would not be complete or correct, so damages should come from the contractor's account. Furthermore, he decided that the Port Authority's claim for late delivery should be awarded against the contractor, since this was arranged in the contract.

Another large Dutch contractor conducted a major work in Berlin, Germany. After the fall of the Berlin wall in 1989, a major reconstruction of the city was decided upon. In the next decade, billions of euros were invested to improve Berlin's infrastructure. As a result, it happened that two contractors would conduct construction works next to each other, i.e. at adjacent sites. The German contractor had assembled a large construction pit, which was secured by major sheet piling. However, one Saturday morning, after heavy rainfall, the sheet piling started to crack, causing a flood of water to flow into the construction pit. As the Dutch contractor's crew were aware of what was happening, and since only security personnel were around at the German contractor's site, they immediately mobilized equipment, sand and concrete, to stop the sheet piling from further breaking down. In doing so, they were able to limit the damage for the German contractor. In the week following this incident, the sheet piling was repaired and the Dutch contractor's equipment could be moved to its own site.

Since the Dutch contractor incurred considerable costs for this operation, the project manager deemed it reasonable that these costs would be reimbursed by the German contractor. However, the German project manager referred to his contract manager. The contract manager acted rather formally: since there was no contract between the German contractor and the Dutch contractor, the latter was not entitled to any compensation. The German contractor felt it was only obliged to payment to any third parties, and only if it had engaged formerly in a contract with those parties...

The Dutch project manager was appalled; he was of the opinion that it would be absolutely reasonable to have the cost of his rescue operation fully covered by his German colleague. However, no payments were ever made in this respect by the German contractor.

These cases lead to a few observations. One is that Dutch contractors, for many years, have operated in a truly international environment. Most Dutch contractors obtain more revenue and profits from employers abroad than from employers in the Netherlands. As a result, project managers and contract managers have to deal with different cultural settings and environments.

As the Rio case shows, the type of contract between contractor parties defines roles, responsibilities and liabilities between parties. When a work needs to be delivered fit for purpose, the contractor is held responsible and liable for the design of the work. As such, the contractor needs to validate the technical information that is provided by the employer or the employer's engineer. Having a good understanding of the different contract types that can be encountered in the international offshore industry is crucial for a successful completion of the work — and to prevent unpleasant surprises!

The Berlin case shows that different cultures may have different interpretations of what is reasonable. The German contractor operated from the principle that if you have no agreement, you would not be liable or responsible for any payment. The Dutch contractor operated from a different principle: in a case where you see a disaster strike, you need to act immediately. In the German view, there was nothing wrong with that, provided that the Dutch contractor made an immediate phone call to the German project manager for his permission to act.

2.2. Changing relationships in international contracting

Globalization is, already for many years, a characteristic of the international contracting and construction industry.[1] Projects, by definition, are large, complex and, as a result, carry a lot of risk. Managing these projects requires superior project management as well as a careful orchestration of all disciplines and stakeholders involved.

In general, the future of the international contracting and construction industry seems bright. This is due to a number of factors:

- *Increasing world population.* It is expected that the world population will grow from its current 7 billion people to 9 billion people by 2050.[2] This will result in an increasing demand for infrastructure, not only in terms of houses to be built, but particularly also in terms of trade infrastructure that will be needed to support transportation and logistics flows within and among nations. As most of the population growth is to be expected in coastal areas, this will call for a greater demand for land reclamation projects, deep-water harbors and ports.
- *Newly constructed infrastructure* to be developed in the next decades will be needed in areas outside Europe and North America. Economic development and new land reclamation will be concentrated in Africa, Asia, Oceania and Latin America. More and more economic power will move from the developed Western countries to upcoming economies.[3] This

[1] Throughout this book we will use "contracting industry" to refer to the international offshore and construction industry, i.e. industries which are characterized by large construction projects offshore as well as onshore.

[2] United Nations, Department of Economic and Social Affairs, Revision of World Population Prospects, 2010; UN Press Release, May 3, 2011.

[3] J. A. Goldstone (2010), The New Population Bomb, The Four Mega Trends That Will Change The World, *Foreign Affairs*, January/February, http://www.foreignaffairs.com/articles/65735/jack-a-goldstone/the-new-population-bomb, January 21, 2013.

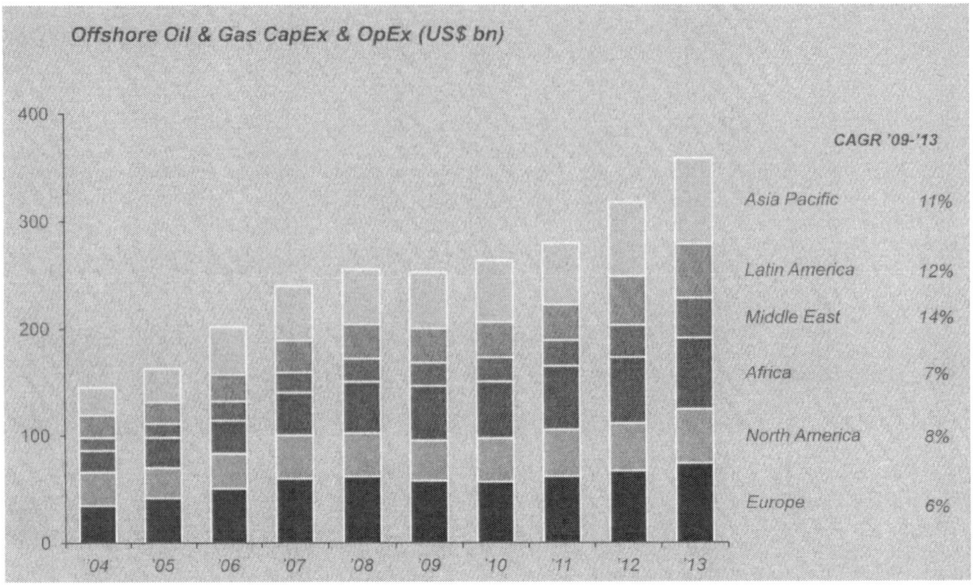

Figure 2.1. Offshore oil and gas capital expenditure (US $ bn). (Source: Douglas-Westwood and Energy Files: "World Offshore Drilling Spend Forecast 2009–2013".)

means that Western European contractors will largely book their orders in foreign cultures and foreign legal systems.

- *Increasing energy consumption.* The increasing world population will require more energy in terms of oil and gas. Due to the exhaustion of traditional oil wells and gas fields, new and more difficult energy reservoirs will be exploited. Next, investments will be made in renewable energy infrastructure (e.g. offshore wind parks, submarine cables). This will require massive investments in new technology (see Figure 2.1). To cite an example: as Brazil has now found one of the largest oil reserves in the world, located three and a half miles off the coast at a depth of three to five kilometers, Petrobras[4] has announced investment plans of over $225 million for the period 2012–2017.[5] Similarly, other oil companies have significant investment portfolios.
- *Growing needs for terminal and transport capacity.* Given the growth of the world population and the increasing energy consumption, countries will need to expand their terminal and transportation capacity. To accommodate new terminal capacity, existing ports need to be expanded

[4] Petrobras: the Brazilian state oil company.

[5] S. Pearso and J. Leahy (2011), Perrobras in $225 bn investment plan, *Financial Times*, July 23.

and new ports need to be built. The current investment plans of China and other Southeast Asian countries are good news for international dredging, engineering and construction companies.

During the past decades, some markets have changed dramatically. The oil and gas industry has witnessed an ongoing concentration. Today, a handful of large, powerful, professional oil companies dominate the competitive arena. As a result, the relationships between these companies and contractors also have changed dramatically:

- *Complex value chains.* Large companies in general have focused on their core competencies, whilst outsourcing their non-core activities to specialist providers. This has resulted in complex, international value-chain structures where contractors may need to work together in different constellations (e.g. joint ventures, alliances) in combination with a myriad of subcontractors and materials suppliers. Managing these supply networks has become extremely complex. Adding to this complexity is the fact that clients in different parts of the world operate with different degrees of bureaucracy and ethics.
- *Risk management.* Given the increasing size and complexity of projects, financial and technical risks have increased. As a result, large companies now try to move these risks to their business partners, using advanced risk allocation and contracting methods and techniques.
- *Contract management.* Many large companies today have segregated project management and contract management, which are considered to be closely related but separate disciplines. As a result, contract management has become a specialist discipline and has made interorganizational relationships more complex and detailed. In general, this has resulted in even more formal relationships between contract parties.
- *Claim culture.* As contracts have become more complex and formal, relationships between parties have become more tense. Any change in the scope of work by the employer during project execution may immediately result in claims for extra time and budget and resources from the contractor. Vice versa: any failure by the contractor to meet the employers' requirements may immediately lead to claims. As a result, the culture between parties has changed during the past decade. Traditionally, the claim culture has prevailed in Anglo-American countries. However, this is now making inroads in other Western countries.

The way in which large employers deal with their contractors clearly has affected the contractors' business strategies, business models and ways of working. It has also affected relationships with suppliers and subcontractors, who, in general, have been confronted with more formal behavior from the contractors they work for. In general, the following observations can be made:

- *Focus on core competencies.* Given the excessive pressure that employers impose on their contractors, contractors started to specialize. The basic idea was: focus on what you can do best, and outsource or subcontract non-core activities to specialist subcontractors and materials providers. This has become apparent, for instance at Dockwise, a specialist provider of heavy transportation in the maritime industry. Dockwise decided in 2004 to outsource its entire ship management in order to concentrate on customer-relations management and engineering. Oil companies like BP decided to outsource their drilling and maintenance activities to specialized service providers.
- *Differentiated value propositions.* Large employers nowadays expect integrated solutions from their contractors. When constructing a port, this needs to come with terminals, storage and transportation infrastructure, which should be arranged for by the contractor. As a result, the contractor has moved into the role of supply-chain integrator and orchestrator, sometimes being responsible for getting all the permits from the government and managing all the agreements with subcontractors and materials suppliers. Landing and executing these integrated contracts has dramatically changed the risk profiles of contractors.

  However, since competition for large infrastructural projects is intense, contractors also need to be able to do routine, less complex works at competitive prices to maintain a high level of equipment utilization. As such, contractors need to provide different value propositions to different markets and market segments.
- *Validated ways of working.* As employers move more risks to contractors, this calls for a full tracking and tracing of their activities. This is not only true for activities that are conducted by the contractors' personnel; it also holds for activities conducted by subcontractors and suppliers. Given the complexity of the networks that project managers need to manage today, this is quite a challenge.

Apart from these changes in strategies, business models and ways of working, project managers need to be able to deal with different clients. Executing a major project for an international oil company is quite different from working for a governmental institution in a third-world country. Project managers need to work in different environments, for different types of customers and to be able to work with different types of contracts.

2.3. Contract management and contracts

Parties that operate in the international construction value chain are linked to each other through contracts. As we have discussed, contracts have become more complex. They also have become more varied. Today, different contracts are used for different situations and different objectives.

In this book we define contract management as: "The process that ensures that all parties to a contract fully meet their obligations, in order to satisfy the operational objectives of the contract and the strategic business goals of the customer."[6]

This definition warrants some more discussion. The definition refers to contract management as a process, which is aimed at successful and profitable project delivery. Usually, different stages can be identified in the process of contract management, i.e. the pre-contractual stage, the contract-negotiation stage and the post-contractual stage.[7] These three stages are interrelated: problems that have occurred in the pre-contractual stage between contract partners may surface during project execution. Therefore, it is important to be aware of the full contracting cycle when engaging in a contract.

The definition also refers to the obligations from both parties, which should be fully met. Obviously, it is difficult to put all obligations in writing. As projects differ in terms of complexity, their outcome may be more or less predictable. Therefore, a good contract will allow for specific arrangements[8] or contract parties, when, during the course of project execution, circumstances may change.

The third aspect is that a contract does not focus only on activities that are necessary to realize the project objectives. A good contract also takes into account the strategic business goals of the final customer. The final customer may, in many cases, not be the contractor's contract party, i.e. employer. In the case of dredging for a new port, the employer may be the port authority. However, the final customer may be the city (or the country) which has an economic interest in having the harbor completed. In such a situation, both

[6] Obtained from various sources on the Internet (see www.cips.org, https://sonsultations.rics.org, www.business.govt.nz).

[7] Post-contractual stage refers to those activities that are commenced after contract closure.

[8] I.e. contract clauses.

the employer and the contractor may have one common interest: to jointly serve the interests of the city's council. Later in this book we will discuss different perspectives from which contracts may be considered.[9]

A major problem that underlies contract management is how to transform a conflict system into a cooperative one.[10] Traditionally, the major problem between contract parties is how to overcome conflicting interests. Usually, the employer's main interest is to pay as little as possible for the job to be done. However, the contractor's main interest will be to get as much money as possible from the assignment. This conflict of interest is, in most cases, dealt with by negotiation. Prior to the negotiation, each party will consider its interests, what it wants to get out of the negotiation (maximum versus minimum position) and what tactics it will use to attain its goals. Negotiation usually leads to solutions where one party gives in to the benefit of the other party. It may lead to situations where a party feels outsmarted and where concessions were made that were later regretted.

Negotiation may be an effective coordinating mechanism for less complex, one-shot deals. However, for more complex and risky projects, where parties will be engaged for a long period of time, other mechanisms may be needed. Parties should avoid the situation where objectives are not jointly consistent (conflict system). The challenge is how to transform a conflict system into a cooperative one, in which individuals act rationally in the name of a common objective. In practice, this is a challenge that can barely be overcome.

A conflict system is one in which parties have objectives that do not concur. It is organized through exchanges and other interactions between parties. A cooperative system is one in which parties act rationally in the name of a common objective. Conflict systems can arise through bounded rationality (participants would like to act rationally but fail to do this) and/or opportunism (participants try to optimize their position at the expense of others). Later in this book we will discuss how to overcome the disadvantages of conflict systems.

This book will cover different types of contracts to a fair degree of detail. A difference will be made between three basic contract types: lump-sum contracts, cost-reimbursable contracts — i.e. time and materials — contracts and unit-rate contracts.[11] Most contracts are a combination of these three

[9] See Chapter 3.

[10] This discussion was taken from J. R. Turner (2001), *Project contract management as a theory of organization*, ERIM Report Series, ERS-2001-43-ORG, Erasmus University, Rotterdam, the Netherlands.

[11] See also Section 8.2 for a discussion of these and other contract types.

archetypes. Next, we will discuss different contract forms, which are covered by international standard contracts. Our discussion of contract forms will include: Construction contracts, Design and Construct contracts, EPC contracts, DBFM contracts, engineering contracts and subcontracts. Most international standard contracts cover these contract types. Standard contracts that will be discussed include FIDIC, LOGIC and CMM. Next, some specialist contracts for the offshore industry (BIMCO, TOWCON, TOWHIRE) will be discussed.

2.4. The role of project managers and contract managers

The role of project managers in international contracting projects is crucial. Working at places that are often very remote from their headquarters, project managers need to manage their projects within the corporate guidelines, the contract, the project budget and timeline. As projects become more integrated, this calls for new tasks: arranging permits from the local government, communicating with local stakeholders on the progress of work, communicating with the employers and the employers' engineer, negotiating and contracting the subcontractors and the materials suppliers, staffing the project and managing the workers, keeping control of progress and quality of work, keeping control of budgets and cash flow, to name a few.

Today, project management means stakeholder management rather than only managing a project in a technical way. This is why project managers are recruited increasingly from non-technical disciplines. On the road to project success, the project manager needs to align all stakeholders' activities with the client's business interests. As, in most projects, a large part of the work is contracted out to subcontractors, this calls for effective contract management.

This book describes the role of project managers in the full contracting cycle. It describes how project managers can create alignment among contract partners. It also describes what problems may be expected in relation to the different contract types that can be encountered, and how to solve these problems.

2.5. Conclusions

The world of international contracting is a dynamic world. As the global economy and world population grow, the need for energy and infrastructure grows. This is not only true for civil infrastructure such as ports, airports, railways, and roads, it is also true for industrial infrastructure such as power plants, renewable energy farms, petrochemical and chemical installations. As such, the future outlook for international contracting firms seems bright. However, as investment in such infrastructure becomes larger and projects more complex, risk management has become a key issue in managing projects successfully. Many large clients, private as well as public employers, try to cover part of these risks through detailed contracts, which stipulate the rights and liabilities of the parties involved. In dealing with contractors, employers have introduced contract management increasingly as a separate discipline to manage their projects. Over time, projects have become more integrated and multidisciplinary. As a result, risks and responsibilities have been shifted to the contractors.

Contract management has developed into a separate discipline. The client's contract managers are involved at an early stage of project development to define what contract types and templates to use, given the background and technical complexity of the project. During project execution, they support their internal project leaders by following up the contractors' activities against what has been contractually agreed.

The increased sophistication, which at client-side is apparent in many industries, poses interesting challenges to contractors. In managing projects successfully, the contractor's project managers need to understand the different contract forms or contract types that they might encounter. More particularly, they need to understand in what circumstances these contracts are used and what responsibilities and liabilities result from these contracts. Moreover, they need to have a thorough understanding of the different pricing mechanisms (such as lump-sum/fixed-price, reimbursable and unit-rate mechanisms), which may be used in these contracts. These subjects are the core of this book and will be dealt with in detail in subsequent chapters.

Chapter 3

The Client[1]

3.1. Case — No discrimination

During the early 1980s, the government of Denmark issued a tender for the construction of a bridge, spanning six kilometers over the Great Belt. The bridge was part of a 17-kilometer highway connecting the islands of Funen and Seeland. Following the European Directives on Public Procurement, the tender was announced in the EC Tender Electronic Daily (TED). Based on the unique nature of the project, the Danish government had opted for the negotiation procedure with prior publication. Having received the bids, five consortia were shortlisted. Finally, the European Storebaelt Group (ESG) was selected.

However, before the assignment was awarded, one of the other consortia submitted a claim to the European Commission because of a violation of the EC Treaty. The tender documents stipulated that the work needed to be performed, as much as possible, with Danish employees and Danish subcontractors. Such conditions were deemed to be a violation of the non-discrimination principle of the EC Treaty.

Next, objections were made against the fact that the quotation by ESG was used as a benchmark to compare the other bids. This was considered not to be fair to all bidders. Finally, the competition claimed that ESG's quotation did not meet the requirements of scope of work, the technical specifications, as well as the award criteria that had been announced in the publication prior to tender.

Even before the contract was awarded, the European Commission informed the Danish government about the claim that it had received. Notwithstanding, the Danish government awarded the contract to ESG. In response, the

[1] In the remainder of this book we will use the following synonyms for client: "customer", "employer".

European Commission summoned the Danish government to cancel the award. When the Danish government refused, the European Commission started a legal case before the European Court. As part of the claim, the European Commission demanded that the Danish government suspend all construction activities until the European Court came to a judgment.

During the preparation for the trial, the Danish government admitted to the European Court that the non-discrimination principle of the EC Treaty had been violated. Therefore, the Danish government proposed to come to a settlement with the opposing consortium. Once such a settlement had been concluded, the case was closed by the European Court. Although the exact amount was never made public, rumors are that the Danish government settled for 10% of the total contract price.

The case of the bridge over the Great Belt in Denmark is a classic one. It was one of the first cases where a local member state was sued by the European Commission for violation of its European Directives on Public Procurement, with regard to a large infrastructural project. These directives are mandatory. Member states cannot put them aside. This is also true for those contractors that act on behalf of European governments on their projects. These European directives also need to be taken into account by, for instance, Shell, in respect of its exploration or drilling operations in the North Sea. As Shell operates under a concession from the government, it automatically follows that all subcontracting undertaken by Shell needs to be in accordance with the European Directives on Public Procurement. The fact that Shell is a private company does not exonerate it from acting in accordance with these directives.

The world of international contracting is a complex and diverse world. Construction firms and offshore companies deal with a variety of clients, operating in diverse environments in different cultures and legal systems. This makes every project unique — not only in the technical sense, but also in the sense that project managers need to deal with different companies and organizations, personalities and legal rules and guidelines.

This chapter deals with that variety. It briefly describes the trends and developments going on in large private companies that deal with international contractors. Next, developments in the public sector will be described. In doing so, we provide a short description of the role and value of public–private partnerships (PPPs). Differences in the value systems of clients lead to different practices in projects and contracting. We will briefly discuss the implications for obtaining permits, financing projects, the role of advisors and the impact of different law systems and cultures. This chapter provides the project manager with insights that will be key for project success: the values and interests of the clients whom he may work for.

3.2. Private sector

The private sector for international contractors consists of different market segments. Usually these market segments include the oil and petrochemical industry, energy producers and public utility companies, shipping and trading companies and real estate companies.

In general, these large customers are increasingly searching for an all-inclusive service offering, as well as early contractor involvement, in their dealings with international contractors.

The following trends can be observed in the contracting behavior of, in particular, large clients:

- *Cost, schedule and flexibility.* Due to heavy international competition, projects need to be accomplished against very competitive budgets and tight schedules. The sooner a platform is in production, the sooner the oil company can earn back its investment. Given the strong price competition in these markets, international contractors are played off around the world. Hence, European contractors need to compete head-on with their American and Asian counterparts.
- *Risk management.* As supply chains have become much more visible due to Internet technology and social media, large companies impose increasing demands in terms of health, safety, labor conditions and environment (HS&E requirements). Problems — like with Brent Spar[2] and oil spills in Nigeria — have put companies like Shell in the spotlight. This has resulted in a strong focus on risk assessment and management. Where possible, clients try to shift their risks to the contractor without additional compensation.
- *Strict and formal tender procedures.* In order to reduce risks, large companies impose increasing demands on contractors in terms of quality, operational performance, craftsmanship and HS&E. As a consequence, the tender process becomes more laborious and it has become more difficult and laborious to qualify as a contractor.

[2] Brent Spar was a North Sea oil storage loading buoy in the Brent oilfield, operated by Shell UK. Brent Spar became an issue of public concern in 1995, when Greenpeace organized a worldwide, high profile media campaign against Shell's plan to dump the Brent Spar in the Atlantic.

- *Role of advisors and engineering firms.* Many companies operating in the oil and petrochemical sector have focused on their core activities. Non-core activities are subcontracted increasingly to specialized firms. Detailed engineering work, which used to be done in-house, nowadays is outsourced to specialized architects and engineering firms, who provide the liaison between client and contractor. As a result, large firms have lost significant technical knowledge, for which they now rely on engineering firms and contractors.
- *Lifecycle costing and management.* As the investment cost of many projects is just a small part of the total lifecycle cost, large companies sometimes award projects based on Total Cost of Ownership (TCO)[3] rather than price alone. Moreover, they want their contractors to take part in financing the project and maintaining it after completion. This requires totally different capabilities and resources from contractors to win contracts. It also demands different requirements of project managers, who increasingly need to be familiar with the financial engineering of projects.
- *Early Contractor Involvement (ECI).* As contractors are often specialists in their business, large customers want to involve them early in the design process. Contractors are invited to participate in design contests or beauty contests or, sometimes, they are pre-selected on the basis of their input, i.e. ideas on basic designs. Often, these activities need to be conducted without full payment. Although this system offers participating contractors no guarantee of being awarded part of the project, it could be advantageous for the client to have a contractor implement its "own" design.
- *Changing demands.* The contractor is often confronted with continuously changing customer requirements during the tender process. However, this may also happen during project execution, with clear (or, more often, unclear) consequences for the project budget and schedule. A good example of this is the High Speed Line project in the Netherlands where, after approval of budgets and project plans, political leaders decided on an extra underground tunnel under the green heart of Holland. Not surprisingly, this had dramatic consequences for both the project budget and the project schedule.
- *Integrated solutions.* Where large companies traditionally focused on contracting for a single activity, today they increasingly seek integrated solutions. This is true for a company like Boskalis, for instance, which made its reputation in international dredging work. Today, the company has to

[3] Also referred to as "Life Cycle Cost".

deliver a Turnkey coastal-protection infrastructure, the accomplishment of which includes many more disciplines than only dredging.

These examples show that international contractors today face a varied world of private customers with different demands and requirements. Demands and requirements differ between market segments, but may even differ within a market segment. These multifaceted requirements should be met by the contractors with multistaged value propositions, which need to be delivered through integrated supply chains. This is not always easy for the more traditional contractors, who do not have the required expertise in the fields of engineering, financing and multidisciplinary scopes of work.

This idea is depicted in Figure 3.1. Different customers with different needs require different value propositions and different contracts. A major challenge in doing so effectively is how to align the interests of all stakeholders involved.

In conclusion: a project manager should keep a keen eye on the interests of his clients, which underlie the project that they commissioned. It is not so much the completion of the project that the private client is interested in; he is more interested in what commercial interests and benefits he may accrue from the project. As a result, the project manager should have a good understanding of these commercial interests, which are not always clearly

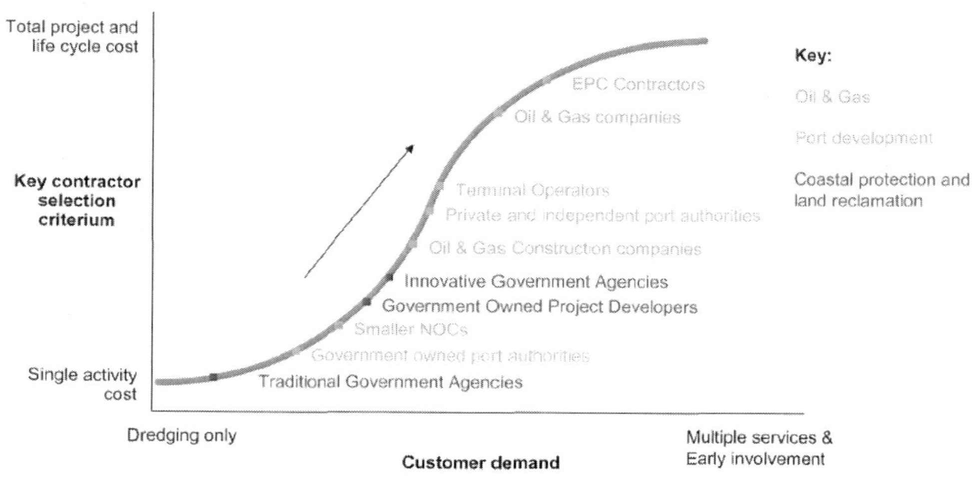

Figure 3.1. Changing market requirements in the offshore industry lead to more integrated value propositions in projects. (Source: Boskalis[4] internal document, published with permission.)

[4] Boskalis, officially Royal Boskalis Westminster NV, www.boskalis.com.

communicated to him. Small engineering changes or schedule improvements (early delivery) may be of great value to the client. On the other hand, small delays and quality flaws may have severe financial consequences for the client. The project manager should be aware of the client's key interests, so that he can make an adequate assessment of his options whenever he needs to decide on a course of action.

3.3. Public sector

Some of the trends and developments that have been described in the previous section also apply to the public sector. However, in essence, clients from the public sector operate quite differently from those in the private sector. The key difference is that public-sector officials and politicians need to justify their decisions to their taxpayers and are subject to complex political regimes. Decision-making on large infrastructural projects in this sector is, therefore, often bureaucratic and surrounded with uncertainties. It is highly political in nature. Since the political climate in the country can change overnight, long-term collaboration with governmental institutions, which is often needed in large infrastructural projects, is quite a challenge. Moreover, in many countries, specific laws and directives may apply on how to engage in contracts for large civil works.

Below, we describe the most important trends and developments in dealing with governmental institutions as clients:

- *High political visibility.* Large governmental investments in infrastructure projects usually have high political visibility. Given their complexity, the investments involved and the opposing views among politicians, these projects are closely monitored by the press. Decision-making and planning is complex due to the large number of stakeholders involved. This makes the timing and planning of these projects highly insecure. To cite an example: it took the city council of Amsterdam about 15 years to decide on the construction of the extension of its metro system. It took the city about another 15 years to execute the project. Another example in the Netherlands is the 7-kilometer section of the A4-motorway between Delft and Schiedam. The estimated investment will amount to approximately €650 million in total, over €90 million per kilometer. This work will therefore result in the most expensive road project ever. The first design and proposals date from 1953. Since the investment and plans were finally approved in 2011, we conclude that the public decision-making process took a stunning 58 years.

- *Consultants and engineering firms.* Large infrastructural projects require specific knowledge and expertise. Usually, contractors have an advantage in this respect. For them, designing and executing civil works is a matter of routine. However, for the local government or city council, the project is often unique and a one-off event. In many cases, the leadership, expertise and knowledge required to serve as a partner to the future contractor are not present. Frequently, the apparent lack of knowledge and expertise is solved by recruiting and hiring specialist consultants. However, involving these specialists is usually costly and time-consuming and slows down project activities, as they first need to be selected and contracted. Sometimes, these external parties pursue their own commercial interests, rather than serving those of their employer. In such situations, the contractor is caught between two parties, who in some cases are difficult to align.
- *European Directives on Public Procurement.* Most European countries have now committed to European Directives on Public Procurement, which regulate the procurement process for large infrastructural projects and large-scale service contracts (e.g. contracting for large IT and software contracts). These directives prescribe to a high level of detail regarding how to deal with bids from contractors and services providers, how to evaluate these bids, and how to engage in a contractual relationship with contractors. Any mistake in the procedure may lead to either an extension or even cancelation of the tender procedure, or claims from contractors who didn't win the bid. Public procurement law has developed into a fast growing and highly profitable domain for specialized law firms. Chapter 6 deals in more detail with the importance of the European Directives on Public Procurement for Works, i.e. construction projects.
- *Finance and payment.* Since the financial situation in many European countries and emerging countries is tight, local governments have become very creative with ways to get public initiatives financed. One is to initiate DBFM contracts for large infrastructural projects, where future contractors are obliged to participate in financing the project, its operational execution and future maintenance. Having a detailed insight into the financial engineering that underlies the future project is key to accepting or not accepting any invitation for tender. This is certainly true for projects that are executed in emerging and developing countries, and that are financed by the World Bank and other international financial institutions. When these institutions are involved, increasing demands with regards to risk management and liabilities emerge. In any project, it is important to contractually arrange for how actual payments will be made. Usually, the

government will rely on engineering firms or external advisors to validate the work that the contractor claims to be completed. Any debate on this will immediately lead to the extension of planned payments. This may, as a result, jeopardize the project's cash flow.

These characteristics make successful project management in the relationship with public-sector institutions quite a challenge. The public context requires the project manager to keep a keen eye on the political interests that are served through his project, and the personal interests that key officials may have in the realization of the project. This dimension may be of greater importance than the technical aspects.

3.4. Public–private partnerships

A public–private partnership (PPP) can be described as a government service or private business venture, which is funded and operated through cooperative institutional arrangements between public and private sectors.[5] PPPs may have different forms: the PPP may perform all activities itself, or the PPP may act as a principal, i.e. taking care of all project coordination activities, whilst subcontracting most of the work to subcontractors and service providers. Public–private partnerships are sometimes referred to as PPP, P3 or P.[6] PPP involves a contract between a public-sector authority and a private party, in which the private party provides a public service or executes a project and assumes substantial financial, technical and operational risk in doing so. In some types of PPP the cost of using the service is borne exclusively by the users of the service and not by the taxpayer. In other types (for instance, Private Financed Initiative projects), the private sector provides a capital investment on the strength of a contract with a local government to provide agreed services while the cost of providing that service is borne wholly or in part by the government. Government contributions to a PPP may be in kind rather than in money (notably the transfer of existing assets). In projects that are aimed at creating public facilities, like in the infrastructure sector, the government may provide a capital subsidy, so as to make it more attractive to the private investors. In some other cases, the government may support the project by providing revenue subsidies, including tax exemptions.

---

[5] See C. Greve and G. Hodge (2005), *The Challenge of Public–Private Partnerships*. Northampton: Edward Elgar Publishing, p. 359.

[6] Sometimes also referred to as Build–Operate–Transfer (BOT) or Private Financed Initiative (PFI) projects.

A PPP could be structured as a special purpose company (also "special purpose vehicle", or SPV). In that case, each partner will be a shareholder in the SPV, with voting rights in accordance with the "weight" of his shares. The SPV offers the opportunity to organize the partners' cooperation in a legally sound manner and also to limit their individual liability for the financial wellbeing of the SPV. In a worse case scenario, the SPV could go bankrupt, leaving the shareholders with nothing of value, but at least they would not be liable for any debts of the company.

In the context of a PPP, the shareholders in the SPV would typically consist of a building contractor, a maintenance company and bank lender(s). It is the SPV that signs the contract with the government and with subcontractors to build the facility and then maintain it. A typical PPP example would be a hospital building financed and constructed by a private developer and then leased to the authority. The private developer then acts as landlord, providing housekeeping and other non-medical services while the hospital itself provides medical services.

An additional example would be a plan by the Ministry of Infrastructure to have a road constructed, based on functional requirements, that needs to be maintained and financed by the contractor for a period of 20 years. In return, the contractor is entitled, for example, to levy a toll on the road users, with the idea that, in this way, he will recover his costs and earn a profit, sometimes backed by government guarantees as to a minimum traffic volume or revenue. Winning such an assignment requires the active involvement of investors, construction firms, installation firms and maintenance firms, whose activities need to be carefully orchestrated by the main contractor. In doing so, the main contractor will need to be able to handle different types of contracts in the relationships with its key stakeholders.

Although the perspective of a long-term contract may be attractive, in practice some major risks can be found related to public–private partnerships. One is that strong leadership from the side of the government can be lacking. Usually, different governmental institutions need to cooperate in such projects, whereas their professional and political interests are difficult to align. Where this happens, the effectiveness and the quality of decision-making will suffer. As a result, the contractor may wait a long time before decisions are made on scope changes, schedule changes and/or claims. As has been mentioned before, advisors and consultants that are hired by the government to run such a project may add to the problem, due to lack of communication, lack of expertise and, sometimes, different agendas. An example is the north–south metro line in Amsterdam, where the project schedule was significantly delayed due to the lack of cooperation between the different departments that were involved in providing the required permits to the different contractors. Political problems as well as differing personal agendas were at the heart of these issues.

To cite another example of a project that suffered from significant delays and financial problems: in the HSL[7]–South project (a major infrastructural railway project in the Netherlands in 2000–2006) decision-making on the new railway safety system (ERTMS) took a long time, leading to a situation where the system was not available when the trains needed to be purchased. This was one reason why trains and carriages were ordered late. Next, the supplier was not able to deliver the trains within the required timeframe. Needless to say that the anticipated benefits from this prestigious PPP project will probably never be realized.

In conclusion, PPP appears to be a concept that can work only in a perfect world, where all parties have the same objectives, share the same views on how to realize those objectives and commit sufficient resources (time, money, equipment, personnel and expertise) to the project. Also, clear lines of responsibility must be defined, including the appointment of a leader.

3.5. Working with clients: specific issues

Working with private and public clients in the international contracting sector poses a challenge in itself. Some specific issues need to be taken care of. We mention here:

- *Obtaining permits.* Due to their impact on the local environment, infrastructural projects require specific permits from the government. For large infrastructural works, the government requires an Environmental Impact Assessment to be conducted before permits are provided. In many cases, these assessments require specific investigations on soil conditions, effects on air pollution, effects on wildlife, etc. Permits need to be obtained by the client; however, in many cases, the client is happy to shift this task to the contractor. Conducting the necessary investigations and obtaining the permits needed will require significant time and effort. It is important that these activities are sufficiently recognized in the overall project schedule. In practice, this is seldom the case. Many tender processes are started before environmental assessments are finished and permits obtained.
- *Financing and payment.* Before putting his signature on any contract, the contractor should make sure that sufficient financial arrangements have

[7] High-speed line.

been made by the client. First, the project manager should assess whether the financial resources available are sufficient to conduct a job. Secondly, he should be secure that the investors involved will be able to last during the project (and will not go bankrupt or withdraw). Next, the project manager should see to a previously defined payment schedule related to clear milestones in his project planning. He should assess the risk of overdue payments and may even consider export credit insurance.

- *Consultants and engineering firms.* Since these parties play a dominant role in almost every project, developing good personal relationships with these firms and their representatives is paramount. Too often we have experienced in practice that a project is delayed or affected by miscommunication or a relationship gone sour.
- *Legal system.* As we will see later in this book, legal systems may vary to a great extent. The continental European legal system, which is based on Roman law, is a far cry from the Anglo-Saxon and Commonwealth system based on common law. In general, the legal systems of Western countries are much more developed than in developing countries. Sometimes legal systems hinder the effective economical development of countries. In Mexico, the state-owned PEMEX (Petroleos Mexicanos) holds the monopoly for exploration and production of oil and gas. For a long period PEMEX lacked both the capital and the know-how to manage the exploration of its energy reserves. In that case, alliances may be formed to make such exploration possible. This is what happened. Foreign companies set up alliances with PEMEX for the investment in new drilling platforms or refineries. However, compulsory legislation prescribes that the title of any assets is transferred to the State of Mexico automatically. Obviously, if a contractor is invited to tender for work in Mexico, he should ensure that the State of Mexico will make or guarantee all payments, which in practice is quite a challenge.
- *Stakeholder management.* Whatever the project, stakeholder management is of paramount importance for project managers in international contracting, considering the interests of both the client, co-contractors, subcontractors and, of course, their own employer. We have observed that in many projects the social complexity of the project clearly outweighs its technical complexity. This may come as a surprise for project managers, who predominantly have a technical background. Aligning the internal and external stakeholders in the project may be more crucial for the success of the project than the way in which it is technically executed.

Evidently, many aspects need to be considered in delivering international projects successfully. Both the private and public sectors are subject to different legal systems and contracts. Next, there are cultural differences when dealing with private clients and public clients. This all poses significant challenges to those project managers who want to succeed.

When contracting for projects, parties may use different legal frameworks. Rather than using company-specific contracts, standard international contract frameworks can be used (such as FIDIC, LOGIC, BIMCO). These contract frameworks relate to different contract forms (such as Construct, Design and Construct, Engineer/Procure/Construct, DBFM, Dredging and Reclamation contracts). Such subjects are discussed in the next chapters. Reading these chapters will not make project managers legal specialists. However, it will assist them in understanding why a certain legal framework and contract type were chosen for the project for which they are responsible.

3.6. Conclusions

The competitive landscape for construction contractors and engineers is complex and diverse. As a result of the growing world population, the outlook for the sector is bright.[8] Contracts are awarded from a wide range of clients. In general, a distinction is made between clients who operate in the private sector and those who operate in the public sector. Within the private sector a distinction can be made between the oil and gas industry, petrochemical industry, mining industry, energy producers and public utilities, terminal operators and the transportation and shipping industry. Clients in these sectors have changed their contracting behavior dramatically during the past decade. In general, projects and contracts have become more complex, involving many stakeholders whose interests need to be satisfied simultaneously. Another trend that can be observed is that large clients try to shift their business risks to the contractor through the use of more integrated contracts. As a result of these changes, international contractors need to be able to offer a diversity of value propositions, ranging from low-cost single project work to integrated, turnkey projects.

As discussed before, international clients have changed their buying and contracting behavior for investment projects. During the past decade, many companies have focused on their core activities, outsourcing non-core activities to specialist providers. In the past, most clients' contractors were much more vertically integrated, subcontracting only specifically defined activities, i.e. jobs to contractors. In many cases, the coordination of the different activities was conducted by the client himself. Today, large clients often contract large

[8] See Chapter 1.

projects to consortia and alliances that have been formed specifically for these projects. As a result, these consortia and alliances have become responsible for managing complex multidisciplinary, multistakeholder, integrated projects.

The implications for the project manager's job are considerable. Traditionally, the project manager was focused primarily on performing a single job to his client's detailed specifications. The relationship was predominantly dyadic, i.e. involving only two parties. Today, the project manager is manager of an integrated supply chain or supply network, consisting of specialist subcontractors, many of whom have been engaged already during the tender phase, and who need to collaborate intensively side-by-side with the contractor's own technical staff and workers. As a result, the qualifications needed by today's project managers are not so much those of a technical specialist but those of an executive manager, managing a wide range of external and internal stakeholders. Each of those stakeholders is engaged through specific contractual agreements, which need to be carefully managed in order to secure the project interests.

Successful project management in international contracting requires a good understanding of the client's objectives. Here, interests are different among private clients and the public sector clients. The first category normally utilizes the project (for instance: the construction of the oil platform or the construction of a jetty for a refinery) to serve other business objectives. The project manager needs to understand the overriding commercial objectives and interests of his client, since this may be crucial for managing and solving operational problems.

Successful tendering for projects in the public sector requires a good understanding of local laws in order to be able to submit competitive bids for tender, especially those laws that relate to procurement directives (such as the European Directives on Public Procurement). If the project is obtained, the project manager needs to have a good understanding of the political interests that may underlie the project, and the personal interests and sensitivities of key public sector officials and leaders. This makes stakeholder management almost a full-time job and the key issue for successful project completion.

Some specific issues may hamper or complicate discussions with future clients. In this chapter we mentioned obtaining permits, financing and payment, consultants and engineering firms, legal systems, and stakeholder management.

When contracting for projects, parties can use a wide variety of standard contracts, templates and contract forms. The remainder of the book will cover these subjects in a fair degree of detail.

Chapter 4

Contract Management: Definitions, Concepts and Perspectives

4.1. Case — The Amsterdam underground metro line

In April 2003, work started on one of the most challenging projects ever undertaken in the Netherlands: the construction of the metro in Amsterdam. This new subway should connect the northern part of the city with the southern part and will cover a distance of 9.7 kilometers. A complication was that the construction work needed to be conducted 40 meters under the old city center. As the soil below Amsterdam is very weak, many disasters were forecast before the work commenced. And many of those disasters actually happened. One of the major incidents was the damage done to six historical houses in Amsterdam's hot spot, the Vijzelgracht. As a result of the construction work, the owners of another seven historical buildings needed to leave their properties for considerable time. Of course, the damage to their properties was claimed from the contractor and the city of Amsterdam, resulting in complex court cases. At the time of writing these cases are still not settled.

These and other problems caused significant delays, resulting in a predicted total construction time of 14 years. In the meantime, the original budget that was anticipated in 1996 (€678 million), increased to an astounding €3.1 billion. Altogether, these problems have put an end to the career of many promising local politicians and city officials.

As in many of these cases, the reasons underlying the problems of this prestigious construction project are manifold. Firstly, the city of Amsterdam's project office decided to apply many civil-engineering techniques that were unknown to them. Part of the tunnel would be drilled using specialized equipment, with which the city of Amsterdam had no experience (see Figure 4.1). Secondly, in order to save costs, the project office decided to

Figure 4.1. Drilling head of equipment used by Bouygues for the Amsterdam metro. (Source: AD, December 8, 2009.)

work with different contractors for different parts of the project, instead of selecting one main contractor. As a result, many conflicts and discussions arose around the interfaces between the different contractors (the project office had to manage relationships with over 45 contractors). Thirdly, the fact that many of the contracts were open-ended was a prime reason for the extreme budget overruns. Fourthly, the project office decided not to insure the project for cost reasons. As a result, all risks for this complex project were to be carried by the city of Amsterdam. Finally, it appeared that a sound risk analysis for some critical parts of the project was totally absent. This was the reason why the project office was taken by surprise in some technical cases.

Although many of the difficulties were attributed to technical issues, the major cause of most problems was assigned to significant failures in project and contract management. The project office was operating without a clear mandate from the Amsterdam city council, which obstructed clear and efficient decision-making. In the relationship with most contractors, there was not a clear line of command. Since the authority of the project office was debated within the city, different departments, who are responsible for submitting permits and licenses, went their own way.

The important lesson from this case study is that complex construction projects require professional project management as well as contract management. Without these activities these projects are certain to fail — often at the cost of the taxpayer!

4.2. Contract management: concepts and definitions

Earlier, we defined contract management as: "the process which ensures that all parties to a contract fully meet their obligations, in order to satisfy the operational objectives of the contract and the strategic business goals of the customers."[1] When discussing this definition we observed that the major challenge underlying professional contract management is to overcome the conflicts of interest which may arise between the client (employer) and the contractor (supplier). These conflicts of interest arise from different objectives, which contract parties may pursue. The employer wants to pay as little as possible for the project that needs to be accomplished; the contractor wants to generate as much money as possible from the contract. This problem is referred to in literature as the problem of opportunism: when closing a deal with another party, each party primarily wants to serve its own interests.

The question is: how to overcome this classic conflict of interest in commercial contracts between parties? Different solutions and coordination mechanisms will be suggested here.

One approach is to increase and improve the communications flow on the project, to ensure all participants have sufficient information to behave rationally and to reduce the possibility of deceit, on which opportunism depends. The idea here is that if every partner in the project is informed regularly about its progress, its planning, its budget, and the parties are clear about their interests, rational decision-making will be facilitated. Improved communication will also create a much better mutual understanding. Clearly, this idea calls for a sound multilevel communications structure between parties, in which senior management, project management and workers are engaged on a regular basis.

Another suggestion is to incentivize the project participants in such a way that all participants indeed share a common objective. Health, safety and environmental issues may serve as an example here. Employers of large projects set clear targets in terms of the number of accidents without injury, the number of accidents with injury and/or absence, etc. Actual performance by the contractor and his subcontractors results in penalties to be paid or for bonuses to be received. Similar agreements may cover quality aspects, lead time and cost performance issues. Incentivizing contract partners in this way seems to be an effective means for achieving goal-alignment among all parties involved.

---

[1] See Section 2.3 of this book.

In the construction industry, most contracts are fixed-price, lump-sum agreements. The advantage for the employer in the case of such contracts is that the price to be paid is established in advance, as well as the work schedule. A disadvantage is that he will not get any insight into the contractor's cost price and profits. Most risks for project execution and delivery are with the contractor. For the employer, the benefit of such a contract is that he knows exactly what to expect when commencing the work. In case the employer wants to change his scope of work or other requirements, a revised budget and time schedule need to be made and negotiated. This will make the employer reluctant to suggest any changes along the way. An advantage for the contractor is that he can abstain from detailed weekly reporting on cost, progress, man-hours, etc., to the employer. This example illustrates that an important aspect of contract management is to manage and provoke certain behavior from contract partners. Different contract types will evoke different (and sometimes undesired) types of behavior among partners in the value chain.

In the remainder of this chapter we will discuss several important aspects of contract management. Different perspectives on contract management are presented. Thereafter, we will discuss different attitudes towards contracting. And finally, we will discuss the contract cycle, i.e. the phases that parties may go through from tendering to completion of the project and its delivery. However, first we will describe what problems may occur in the practice of contract management.

4.3. Problems in contract management

Realizing a successful project in international contracting is a far from simple task. Project managers often report the following issues in the relationships with their clients:

- *Misalignment of objectives between client and contractor.* When signing the agreement, parties may communicate enthusiasm and drive for accomplishing the work. However, when the work progresses, the client comes forward with extra requirements that he doesn't want to pay for. Often the contractor is confronted with the employer's managers and staff, who are unfamiliar to him, and who do not seem to be properly briefed about the work and its contractual agreements.
- *The employer lacks knowledge and expertise.* Many international companies and large governmental institutions have focused on their core activities. Non-core activities have been outsourced to specialist providers. As a

result, the knowledge and expertise with regard to specific design, engineering and construction solutions and techniques have suffered. In such situations, technical requirements are often unclear, whilst the employer has engaged a range of consultants and/or interim managers who interfere, and the contractor is overwhelmed with extra work resulting from an overload of detailed questions.

- *Active involvement of engineering and other consultants.* Often, employers require approval for (parts of) the work from specialist engineers and consultants. In many cases, these engineers and consultants operate at a high level of detail in the relationship with the contractor, since every problem that they might find will lead to extra work and, next, a higher fee for them. Depending on the arrangements made between the engineer and the employer, and more specifically on their risk allocation model, engineers may represent an important inhibiting factor for successful project completion.
- *Contract management.* Many large organizations (e.g. oil companies and the chemical industry) have initiated special contract managers to deal with the contractual side of the relationship with their contractors. In most cases, these contract managers appear to act rather straightforwardly (as the second case at the beginning of Chapter 2 shows); what has not been agreed contractually will not be discussed and compensated for. Many project managers in the construction industry, who used to solve issues on a personal basis with their employer, are often surprised by this new, direct and straightforward approach, which they need to get used to.
- *Inefficient decision-making.* In large organizations and governmental institutions, mandates and the authority to make decisions are not clear (see Box 4.1). The contractor is confronted with staff that are underqualified and have no mandate to act. As a result, decisions with regard to suggested scope changes, planning changes and cost changes are often postponed and delayed; however, the project completion date remains unchanged. This is why project managers increasingly are suffering from a squeeze on time.
- *Frequent scope and planning changes.* Certainly in complex projects, the employer becomes aware of flaws in his design during the course of the work, and wants to change his specifications. This may not only happen in Construct contracts[2] (where the employer is responsible for the detailed design), but also in Design and Construct (D&C) contracts (where the contractor is responsible for the design). In the latter case, this may lead

[2] In this book we will use "construct" and "construction-only" contracts interchangeably.

to a discussion about the responsibilities and liabilities of contract partners, which may hamper the technical completion of the project.

- *Misunderstanding of what has been agreed.* At the time of completion, the employer has a different interpretation of what should have been accomplished than the contractor. This problem may arise in D&C and EPC (Engineer, Procure and Construct)[3] contracts where the work to be delivered needs to be described in functional terms and where the contractor is responsible and liable for the design. The contractor's design may meet the functional specification of the employer but not his aesthetic preferences. In practice, defining the right functional specifications is quite a challenge. Another one is to manage the contract in a proper way. Operating under a D&C or EPC contract requires the contractor to provide a work that is fit for purpose or functionality. Contrary to Construction-only contracts, under these contracts, variations for extra work are often not justified and cannot be claimed. Working with D&C and EPC contracts therefore requires a different approach from both the employer as well as the contractor to the work to be delivered.
- *Payment problems.* Some project managers report that they spend about 20% of their time trying to make the employer pay for work that has been delivered. Often, this requires a careful orchestration of all stakeholders involved, who may influence the employer's decision-making. Most employers require extensive evidence that the actual work has been delivered to the correct standard. However, providing such evidence in unequivocal terms is often troublesome.
- *Local political pressure.* Pressure may emerge from stakeholders with whom the contractor has no contractual relationship at all. They may influence the running of the project and the permanent works to be created. Examples of these institutions are trade unions, local deciding authorities, local public opinion leaders of political parties and local competition between sub-subcontractors for participating in the project.

Another problem that was often reported was one related to the transfer of the responsibility for the project to the project manager, after the contract has been signed. Until that moment, sales managers and tender managers work intensively together to prepare the bid. After winning the contract, the project is handed over to the project manager. However, he is not always properly briefed about the history of the project, the detailed discussions with the client and the problems and issues that were discussed.

---

[3]To be discussed in detail in Chapter 5 of this book.

Box 4.1. Decision-making in Saudi Arabia.

Many large Dutch contractors have accomplished a lot of work in Saudi Arabia and the Middle East, where they experience different decision-making structures than at home. The ample financial resources and wealth of some Arabian families and sheiks has resulted in massive investment programs in housing, commercial real estate and infrastructure. In many cases, local engineers and consultants are hired to contract construction firms and subcontractors. Also, these engineering firms and consultants are responsible for following up on the work. In all their dealings with American and European contractors, contact with their employers are carefully secured. However, contractors are highly dependent on the consent and approval of the final customer, i.e. the investors themselves. In these countries, payments may be deferred many times for unknown reasons and for uncertain periods of time, while differences in the legal systems may exacerbate this problem.

These examples illustrate that successful project completion is far from simple. In practice, employers may deal with D&C as an EPC contract, and forget that not all risks can be attributed to the contractor. Contractors, on the other hand, may act in the case of a D&C contract as if it were a Construction-only contract, trying to charge the employer with all costs related to variations. Project management and contract management require a thorough understanding of the risks and liabilities of the different contracts that are used. As employers increasingly want formal evidence that work has been delivered and quality requirements have been met before making any payment, excellent project administration is required.

Next, project and contract management are equal to stakeholder management. As projects have become more multidisciplinary and integrated, the emphasis in project management has shifted from a technical orientation to a stakeholder orientation. Rather than engaging in technical discussions, most of a project manager's time goes into aligning communications with stakeholders. If relationships in the construction value chain are not properly managed, these may give rise to all kinds of disputes and conflicts, and even legal claims, which could have been prevented. A good contract can never replace a bad employer–contractor relationship.

Given the many problems that may affect successful project completion, we recommend that for larger projects companies differentiate between project management and contract management. The project manager at all times assumes responsibility for every aspect of the project. Project managers should ensure excellent communications on a day-to-day basis with the employer and major subcontractors. Contract managers act on their behalf, and in close coordination, in dealing with specific contractual matters, either in the relationship with the employer or in the relationship with the subcontractors and materials suppliers. It is important that contract managers follow up on what has been agreed contractually with all parties involved. In fact, the contractor's contract-management approach ideally should be mirrored by that of the employer. It is useful to separate discussions on business matters and contractual issues. Only if a contract manager is not able to solve specific contractual issues, should he seek support from his project manager.

4.4. Perspectives on contract management

Usually, contracts in construction are agreed between two parties, i.e. the employer (customer) and the contractor (supplier). However, in complex projects other parties can be involved in the main contract negotiations. Such is the case in many infrastructural projects where the employer negotiates a contract with a consortium of specialist contractors. The specialist contractors may organize themselves through different coordination mechanisms. They may use different legal entities to engage in the relationship with their prospective employer. Legal entities may range from the creation of special purpose companies (where parties legally act as shareholders) to joint ventures and alliances, sometimes with the help of venture capital from third parties. A joint venture (JV) is defined as a contractual agreement joining together two or more parties for the purpose of executing a particular project or business undertaking. A key characteristic is that all parties agree to share the risks, profits and losses of the project or business undertaking. Joint ventures may take the form of a consortium or an alliance. A consortium is usually considered to be a group of companies that undertake an enterprise or an activity that would be beyond the capabilities of the individual members. An alliance differs with a consortium in the sense that the client is a partner in the entity. Also, it may occur that a client acts as subcontractor, due of its specialized know-how in a niche market. In both a consortium and an alliance, all parties share risks and rewards (the "pains and gains") of the project.[4]

---

[4] For an overview of widely used business terms and definitions, see www.investorwords.com.

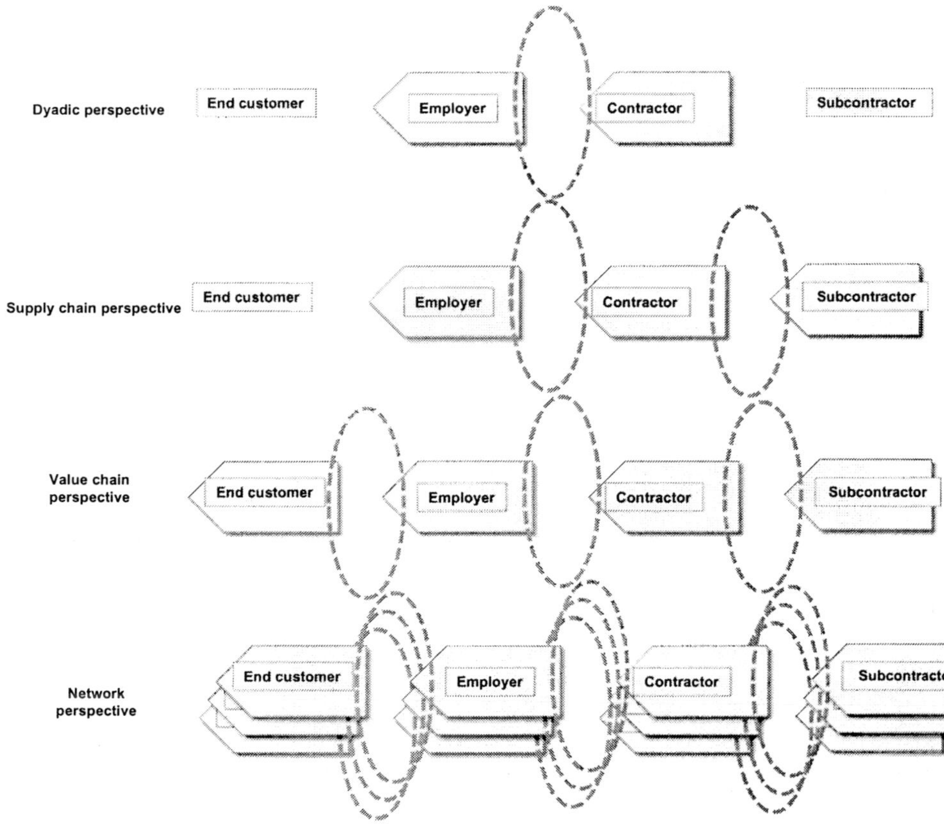

Figure 4.2. Different perspectives on contractual relationships.

Whatever contract is made among the parties involved, contracts may be perceived from different perspectives. Here, we introduce the following four perspectives (see also Figure 4.2):

- *Dyadic perspective.* Contract parties are limited to the employer and the contractor. When negotiating the agreement, both parties assume that they can act independently from other parties in the sector in which they operate, and/or the value chain that they belong to. This perspective applies when parties allocate all risks among themselves and when parties think that all problems related to their agreement need to be solved by themselves.
- *Supply-chain perspective.* Here, contract parties are aware, when negotiating the agreement, that the completion of the work will depend to a fair extent on the contribution of subcontractors and suppliers downstream on

their supply chain. As a result, key subcontractors and suppliers may be consulted when preparing the contract, or even may be involved in the contract negotiation itself. This happens in the case of so-called back-to-back agreements, where the major conditions of the contract between the client and the contractor are translated one-to-one in the contracts with downstream subcontractors and suppliers. The supply-chain perspective usually emerges in projects where major supplies (such as steel piles, pile sheets, prefabricated concrete elements) or specific supplier capacity and expertise (design, special molds for concrete elements, telemetry) represent bottlenecks in the project planning.

- *Value-chain perspective.* When adopting this perspective, the contractor, subcontractors and suppliers are aware that they have one common interest: to jointly serve the current and future interests of the employer. All contract parties are aware that they may influence the project results and that they are mutually interdependent. As a result, parties will engage in close collaboration and information exchange (see Box 4.1 for an illustration). The value-chain perspective usually results in gain and risk sharing agreements, based upon the actual project outcome.
- *Network perspective.* This perspective builds on the previous ones and recognizes that no company can act in splendid isolation. All parties are aware of the interdependencies that may exist in the relationships of other companies that belong to the same industry. This becomes clear in tenders, where a contractor wants to involve a specific subcontractor early and therefore wants exclusivity from him. However, the subcontractor is reluctant to provide such exclusivity, since he is not sure which contractor will win the tender. Therefore, he also engages in relationships with other potential contractors, which he assumes may win the tender. Obviously, such behavior impedes longer-term and close collaborative relationships among partners in the construction industry. Adopting a network perspective recognizes the interdependencies that may exist in different stages in the construction industry's value chain.

Knowledge of these four perspectives on contract management is important when designing a contract or when discussing a conflict between parties. Some examples will illustrate this. In the case that a subcontractor makes up a significant part of the total project, this would call for early involvement of that subcontractor in the tender stage. When constructing a harbor in a developing country, a large part of the project sum may go to the dredger, who needs to provide for sufficient depth in the bay and its seaway. We have seen many situations where the contractor sent out an invitation to tender to the employer and, in his final negotiations, had to reduce the bid price, leaving almost no profit for the work. In most of these cases, the contractor will push its subcontractors for further cost reductions. However, in the international dredging market, news travels fast. Most of the time, the dredging contractors will be informed about the deal that has been closed between the main contractor and the employer. As a result, the dredging company will not move an inch with regards to their initial offering to the main contractor.[5] In such situations, it seems preferable to involve the dredging contractor at the tender stage and to create a partnership with them for the project involved. When concessions need to be made in order to win the contract, the main contractor and the dredging contractor can jointly decide what to do and what to give in to. This is one illustration of how to apply the supply chain perspective to contracting management.

Most disputes that we have been involved with are confined to discussions between employer and contractor. After ample discussions, in the case of severe disputes, parties may decide to go to court. However, by expanding their dyadic view to a value-chain perspective, new possibilities to solve the conflict may open up. For instance, an employer may stick to the completion schedule that has been agreed in the contract with the contractor, and since the work has been delayed, he calls for a penalty. This is because the final customer has also negotiated for a penalty in the contract with the employer. In such a situation, both the employer and contractor could jointly discuss with the final customer what leeway he has in his planning. This may lead to a situation where all parties agree not to exert any penalties (although these were contractually agreed).

4.5. Attitudes towards contracting

When we discussed contract management with colleagues and legal counsels, we heard the view that contract management is similar to war games. As contract parties have different objectives, they will pursue their own self-interest, often at a cost to, and to the detriment of, the other party. When such disputes arise, there is no other way to solve them than to either outsmart the other party (providing new data and information that he was not aware of) or to exert power ("if you do not agree with me in this case, this is the last contract that I will award to you"). The prevailing coordination mechanism for settling disputes and conflicts is negotiation. In these negotiations, contract parties will probably not be 100% clear about their intentions, their commitments, plans and resources.

---

[5] For a more extensive description of this case, see Chapter 5, Section 5.1.

This view, contract management as war, is quite common among lawyers and legal counsels. Often, these parties benefit from enlarging disputes and conflicts and making these more complex. This is comprehensible, if one is aware of the business model that underlies most legal practices. The more complicated the case, the more hours need to be spent on it and the greater the resulting fee will be.

However, another view on contract management is possible. Based upon our definition (see Section 4.2.) we propose a collaborative view towards contract management. Essentially, a contract is a vehicle to serve and facilitate the collaboration between parties involved. As we saw earlier, the contract can be aimed at meeting the project objectives and meeting the business objectives and strategic goals of the final customer. A collaborative attitude towards contract management requires a careful orchestration of four dimensions in the interaction between employer and contractor (see Figure 4.3), i.e.:

- *Information flow.* In organizing for the work to be done, parties need to agree on what information will be provided by whom, in what form, when and to whom, with regard to the functionality of the work, its technical requirements, the planning that will apply, etc. Moreover, it should be agreed what information will be exchanged between parties during the course of the project.
- *Goods flow.* Arrangements need to be made on how materials will be delivered to the work and when the work will become the property of the

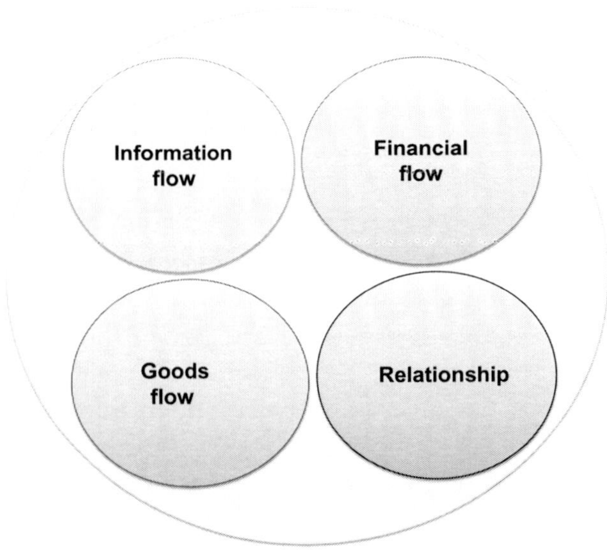

Figure 4.3. Contract management: four dimensions need to be managed in parallel.

employer. Arranging for the goods flow implies agreement on how tracing and tracking of the project deliverables between parties will take place.

- *Cash flow*. As large projects will require sufficient and timely funding, parties need to arrange for specific agreements for when payments will be made against what warranties. Also, they need to discuss what will happen if payments are postponed or deferred for whatever reason.
- *Relationships*. Most construction works are conducted in highly complex networks consisting of different parties, companies, managers and employees, who may come from different cultures. As experience has shown, the human factor is key to project success. Therefore, specific arrangements are needed for how to improve and maintain the relationship quality among all key stakeholders involved.

Experience shows that better outcomes can be achieved through collaboration.[6] Experience also shows that the nature of the relationship can change from one phase of the contract to another — contract management is a dynamic phenomenon.

4.6. The lifecycle of a contract

Contracts may go through different stages and may have different lead times. The comparison may be made with the different seasons of the year. In spring, parties may get acquainted and orientate themselves about a future relationship. At this stage, the employer sounds out the market for a potential contractor to get a specific job done. He may do this through his network, through intermediaries or through the Internet. Usually, he will differentiate between pre-selecting the potential contractors based upon their capabilities, experience and references from other customers, and the actual tendering when, based upon the bids received, the contract is awarded to the best bidder. Summer is marked by globalization and the kick off. Now, both parties are full of hope and confident about their collaboration. Both parties need to get used to each other. They will provide each other with the benefit of the doubt. At this time, there are few clouds in the sky. In autumn, parties have gotten to know each other. By this time, the work has progressed. However, a number of issues have appeared. Some of these issues were caused by the

---

[6]See for example: M. Nicholas and J. Nicholas (2011), *Lean Production for Competitive Advantage*. New York: Productivity Press; J. P. Womack and D. T. Jones (2003), *Lean Thinking: Banishing Waste and Creating Wealth in Your Corporation*. New York: Free Press; J.L. Liker (2004), *The Toyota Way: 14 Principles from the World's Greatest Manufacturer*. New York: McGraw Hill.

employer, who wanted to change the scope of the project. Other issues were caused by the contractor, who was not able to deliver part of the work at the required quality levels and within the agreed time frame. The sky is gradually becoming overcast with clouds. In winter, the parties involved have a realistic picture of what the result of their collaboration is going to be. Some conflicts have caused irritations in the relationship between the managers and staff involved. Some of these irritations have been communicated; however, some important ones have remained under the table and are now going to surface at the time of the full project delivery.

Most project managers and contract managers will recognize these stages in the contract lifecycle. The fact that projects have a clear beginning and a clear end makes work in the construction industry bearable — at the end of a project, there is always a new project on the horizon.

In reality, the following stages may be identified in the contract lifecycle:

Pre-contractual stage

- *Sales and marketing.* Through its sales and marketing activities, the contractor makes itself known to the outside world. It is important to communicate to future employers the firm's capabilities, specialties, experience and reputation in order to qualify for future work. Here, different publication channels, ranging from personal sales to publication through the Internet, are used to influence all members of the employer's decision-making unit.
- *Invitation to tender.* At this stage, the employer communicates the future project to the market. Private companies have more degrees of freedom in doing this than governmental institutions. The latter need to satisfy all kinds of public interests and national or local policy, including opposition from the leading politicians. In Europe, public institutions are bound by the European Directives on Public Procurement, which prescribe how to engage in the delivery of works and goods to external parties. In this case, they are bound to specific lead times, which allow for construction firms to react to requests for information and bids. Construction firms should be allowed sufficient time in order to prepare their proposals, calculations and risk plans, including contracting their suppliers, service providers, sub-suppliers and vendors.

Contractual stage

- *Landing the contract.* Most bidders will not make it to this phase. Based upon a number of competitive bids, the employer will pre-select one or two contractors, with whom he will negotiate. Contract negotiations will follow after having made agreements on the base price. Such contract discussions can be lengthy, detailed and tedious. This stage results in the contract, which will serve as a basis for the future collaboration.

Post-contractual stage

- *Engineering and design.* After landing the contract, the engineering begins in order to prepare for detailed technical specifications and drawings. Based upon the detailed engineering, budgets are prepared for the man hours that will be spent, the materials and materials volumes that will be needed and the subcontractors that need to be hired. This stage is a crucial project phase. In many cases, unexpected technical challenges need to be solved, for which client approval is needed. Next, government permits need to be acquired, which may also take more time than planned for. As a result, preparing the technical specifications and project planning will require much more time than anticipated, whilst the delivery date of the work contractually can not be changed. This explains why project managers and their downstream supply partners are often faced with a significant time squeeze from the beginning of their project.
- *Subcontracting and procurement.* As soon as the agreement has been reached on the main contract, the agreements with the subcontractors and materials suppliers should be finalized. Here, the contractor has different options: he could choose for a back-to-back agreement, to make sure that all major performance clauses are mirrored in the subcontractors' contracts; he may choose to go for the best competitive bid, selecting the subcontractors and suppliers on the lowest price possible; or he could use a mix of these options.
- *Realization of the scope of work.* Usually, project work commences before all contracts have been finished. Since the construction industry does not operate in an ideal world, variations are a fact of life. These need to be discussed, agreed, documented and archived. Smaller disputes and conflicts need to be dealt with on a day-to-day basis.
- *Testing and delivery.* As the project moves beyond its major milestones, work needs to be approved by the employer or its representative/engineer. This may take time depending on availability of staff, reports, etc. Payment schedules need to be managed in line with the project milestones, which in reality is quite a challenge.
- *Maintenance and guarantee period.* After delivery of the work the contractor remains liable for potential defects and failures that may be found.

- *Claims.* Long after the project has been finished, legal counsels and lawyers may be busy for years settling claims from the employer and/or subcontractors. Depending on the outcome of the legal conflicts, a project profit may turn into an unsuspected deficit.

The concept of the contracting lifecycle is key to understanding contract management. Chapter 5 will deal with it in detail. Here, we argue that the different stages of the contract lifecycle cannot be considered in isolation. Every step of the cycle is put into the next step. Problems that may occur in one step of the process can only be understood if what happened in the previous stages is understood. For practical reasons, some contractors make a differentiation between the pre-contractual stage, the contractual stage and the post-contractual stage. The pre-contractual stage is dealt with by sales and marketing managers, tender departments, tender managers and cost analysts. Contract negotiations are conducted by directors and lawyers. When the contract is launched, it is handed over to the project organization, i.e. the project manager, often without a proper and detailed briefing. Frequently, project managers are confronted with projects that technically can barely be executed and whose profitability is highly uncertain. Depending on their complexity, operational problems can occur during the execution of the work, resulting in disputes and conflicts with employers and subcontractors. Having finished the project, these problems are handed over to the legal counsels and lawyers, who can be busy for years to come.

In order to solve the interface problems, which by definition are related to the different contract stages, some companies have adopted the practice of involving the intended project manager in the tender stage. Very few companies have adopted the practice, for complex strategic projects, of working with tender teams, consisting of senior project staff and competing tender teams, who need to prepare a bid based on identical tender documentation. As experience has shown, these practices will lead to more careful, complete and realistic bidding practices. Good preparation means half the work is already done!

4.7. Conclusions

In this chapter we defined contract management as: "the process which ensures that all parties to a contract fully meet their obligations, in order to satisfy the operational objectives of the contracts and the strategic business goals of the customer." A major challenge underlying professional contract management is to overcome the conflicts of interest that may arise between the client and the contractor. In short: the client wants to pay as little as possible for his project, whereas the contractor wants to get maximum payment for the works delivered. Overcoming this business dilemma calls for excellent communication and information exchange among parties. This will facilitate rational decision-making, and it will also create a better mutual understanding. Another suggestion is to incentivize project participants in such a way that they all indeed share and work towards a common objective. Preparing a thorough risk assessment and jointly discussing the outcome of this exercise is a third idea to create alignment among contract parties.

In practice, such business alignment is hard to realize. Since most projects are unique, problems are likely to occur. Operational problems may result from misalignment of objectives between client and contractor; parties involved lacking knowledge and expertise; interference of engineers, consultants and experts; playing the project too much by the book; misunderstandings of what has been agreed; and frequent scope and planning changes. Executing projects successfully is far from simple. In order to deal with these problems, project managers should be aware of the contractual context of their projects. Contracts differ in scope and nature and hence imply different rights and liabilities for contractors. Large clients today use integrated contracts in their dealings with contractors to shift business risks to them. As a result, contract management and stakeholder management have become key for successful project management. For large projects, project managers should seek assistance from professional contract managers.

In order to solve operational problems, project managers can adopt different perspectives, such as those discussed in this chapter. Knowledge of these four perspectives is important when designing a contract or when discussing a conflict between parties. The more participants who are included in the project manager's perspective, the broader the range of options for solving problems. Integrating key subcontractors early in the tender stage may help to arrive at more suitable and competitive bids to customers.

In this chapter, we have proposed a collaborative view towards contracting, which requires a careful orchestration of the four dimensions discussed. Each of these dimensions should receive sufficient attention from contract parties during the lifecycle of the contract.

The lifecycle of a contract has, in fact, three main stages, as noted above. All these stages are interrelated in the sense that problems that have occurred during a previous stage are likely to impact subsequent stages of the contract lifecycle.

Contract management is a dynamic game. This means that managing the transitions in the contracting lifecycle is of utmost importance, both for the client and the contractor. The next chapters of this book discuss how these transitions can be successfully managed.

Part II

The Contracting Cycle

Chapter 5

From Tender to Final Payment

5.1. Case — The offer and the main subcontractor

A major Dutch contractor tendered for a large construction job in a developing country. The construction work included the building of a harbor, including facilities, within one of the country's beautiful bays. The work was a multimillion-dollar project and contained a lot of uncertainties and risks. The work was to be executed under a FIDIC Design and Construct contract. The project was financed by the World Bank. The tender was coordinated by a local engineering firm on behalf of the State Port Authority. The volume of the dredging work to be conducted was unknown. Reports covering a sound soil investigation (for the dredging work) were not available. As the Dutch contractor did not have in-house dredging capabilities, a French dredger was contacted to estimate an initial sum for the dredging work, based on the general information that was available.

The Dutch contractor requested a bid clarification meeting, which was approved, and the contractor presented many questions to the prospective client. It was decided at that meeting that the State Port Authority would summon the soil investigation immediately, at its own cost. More detailed information was provided about the client's needs and requirements, which allowed the contractor to prepare a first bid. In preparing the tender, a lot of discussion took place between the members of the contractor's board. Some senior executives were of the opinion that, since the company needed new work badly, the bid should be based on the lowest cost possible. Some members were in favor of presenting a competitive price, combined with a large number of reservations. In doing so, the company ran the risk that the bid would be rejected by the client, since the tender documentation explicitly requested an all-inclusive price, i.e. covering all risks and uncertainties. Other senior executives were in favor of providing this all-in price, as requested by the client. In this situation, the other members of the board feared that the company could be confronted with some unpleasant surprises during project execution, which would prevent the company from making a profit on the project. Next, it was feared that the contractor's price might come out too high compared to competitive bids.

Finally, after many discussions, it was decided to go for an offer that was a compromise between both views.

The contractor was pre-selected, together with another major competitor. The State Port Authority continued their discussions with these two contractors. Obviously, the client was "cherry picking" during the conversations. Good ideas that had been obtained in the interviews with contractor number one were brought into the discussions with contractor number two and vice versa. Clearly, the client was playing off both competitors. Cost information, which was obtained in discussions with contractor number one, was used in discussions with contractor number two to drive down his price. A complicating factor here was that both contractors had the intent to subcontract the dredging work to the same French contractor. To the Dutch contractor's relief, the client chose its final offer as the best one. An important consideration was that in the final discussions the board had approved a reduction of the already very competitive offer by another 5%. Shortly after this concession was made, the State Port Authority decided in favor of the contractor's proposal. Since the dredging work would make up about 25% of the total contract sum, the contractor's procurement manager was instructed to negotiate a discount of 10% with the French contractor. However, the French contractor would not move an inch in that direction and was not willing to give in on his initial estimate, which he considered fair. The procurement manager had the impression that there were strong personal bonds between the general manager of the French dredger and some high-level people at the State Port Authority.

As this introductory case shows, the initial stage of a project can be complex and time-consuming. In theory, it is easy to differentiate among the stages in the contracting cycle. In practice, these stages seem to be very much intertwined and it is not easy to distinguish between them.

This chapter deals with the contracting cycle, covering the initial stage of projects, i.e. the tender stage, the stage of contract negotiations, as well as the stage of project execution and delivery. More specifically, we will discuss how to tender for new contracts. We will explain how the arrangements made in the tender stage will affect project execution and contracting subcontractors and material suppliers. An important stage in the tender process is the bid clarification meeting, after which contract parties engage in more detailed discussions. Here, we will discuss the value and importance of the Letter of Intent (LOI). Next, we will discuss how to land the contract. A crucial decision in international contracting is how to decide which contract type to use. We will mention some important contracts as well as the value and importance of standard contracts in international contracting. Furthermore, an important issue is how to contract effectively for subcontractors and materials suppliers. Some specific issues and problems with regard to subcontracting (sometimes referred to as downstream contracting) will be discussed. All these activities set the scene for project execution. Since project business is a one-off business, operational problems will definitely occur. Variations are a fact of life! The chapter concludes with a discussion on testing and delivery, guarantees and how to handle claims and disputes. However, the chapter commences with an overview of the contracting cycle.

5.2. The contracting lifecycle

Earlier in this book, we stated that projects and contracts in international contracting may go through different stages throughout their lifecycle.[1] Here, a parallel with the seasons of the year is made.

During springtime, contract parties first contact each other for work to be conducted. The client expresses his requirements and wishes, and the contractor expresses the intent to comply with these and conduct the project. During summertime, contract parties engage in more intimate discussions and explore each other's values and intents. Summertime usually ends with a contract (or not). During autumn, contract parties need to work closely together to execute the project successfully. A multitude of technical and operational problems will occur and parties will be put to the test of solving these problems effectively. At this stage of the relationship, the strength of the bonds between parties will show.

Depending on the complexity of the problems and the expertise of the parties and staff involved, problem-solving may be blurred by the egos and personalities of the persons involved. Although how disputes and conflicts will be solved between parties has been agreed contractually, political, social and personal controversies may prevent effective decision-making. Depending on how parties solve these controversies, winter will have different conditions. During wintertime, parties may go their own way, each satisfied about the outcome of the project. In that case, winter will be a mild season to them. However, parties may also go their own way even though some major conflicts still have not been solved. In that case, projects cannot be closed and results cannot be assessed, due to the fact that lawyers of both parties will be busy on claims for many years to come. In that case parties will face a long, cold winter.

[1] See Chapter 4, Section 4.5.

As this description shows, parties will experience different stages and situations as they go through the contracting cycle. Issues that happened in the past will affect their relationships today. Clearly, the different stages of the contracting cycle are connected.

In Chapter 4 we described the nine stages of the contracting cycle. Given the scope of this book, we will concentrate our discussion on the following stages:

- *Invitation to tender.* This stage is characterized by exploring the needs and requirements of the client, analyzing the client's upstream network, clarifying tender documents, initial negotiations with regard to risks and variations and checking the credentials of the parties involved. These subjects are part of Chapter 11.
- *Landing the contract.* This stage is characterized by complex negotiations among different specialists from the parties involved. Legal specialists are heavily involved, which results in very detailed agreements, which are hard to understand for non-legal professionals. Many specific legal issues are discussed in Part IV of this book.
- *Subcontracting and procurement.* This stage is characterized by hard-pressed negotiations with subcontractors and materials suppliers, who need to give in dramatically on their initially quoted prices and rates. This results in initial disappointment and frustration for all parties involved. As time pressure usually is high, contracts with downstream partners are less carefully prepared and less detailed. More details on subcontracting and procurement can be found in Chapter 7.
- *Contract execution.* This stage is characterized by many discussions on the variations caused by changes in the client's requirements. Any change in requirements leads to extra costs, charged by the contractor who wants to make up for the bad project margin. Discussions on these issues lead to disputes, which cascade up-and-down the organization of the parties involved. Chapter 10 discusses the complexities that may arise out of variations and how to manage these.
- *Testing and delivery.* Here, the client and the client's engineer are overly meticulous and ruthless in assessing the contractor's actual performance. Variations from the initial scope of work will always be found, as well as variations in performance (in case of delivery of complex installations). These variations will be used to uphold or extend payment to the contractor. Part IV, again, will discuss many of the problems that may occur at this stage and how to prevent or overcome these.
- *Guarantee period.* As these disputes will continue during the guarantee period, the client will withhold final payment of the retention fee. Details

about liabilities, indemnities, warranties and guarantees are to be found in Chapters 13 and 14.

- *Claims.* Based upon problems that occurred during the previous stages, lawyers will be busy for years. Given the importance of the subject, Chapter 24 deals exclusively with dispute resolution mechanisms.

Figure 5.1 provides a schematic overview of these contract stages.[2] In the following paragraphs, we will look into each of these stages in more detail.

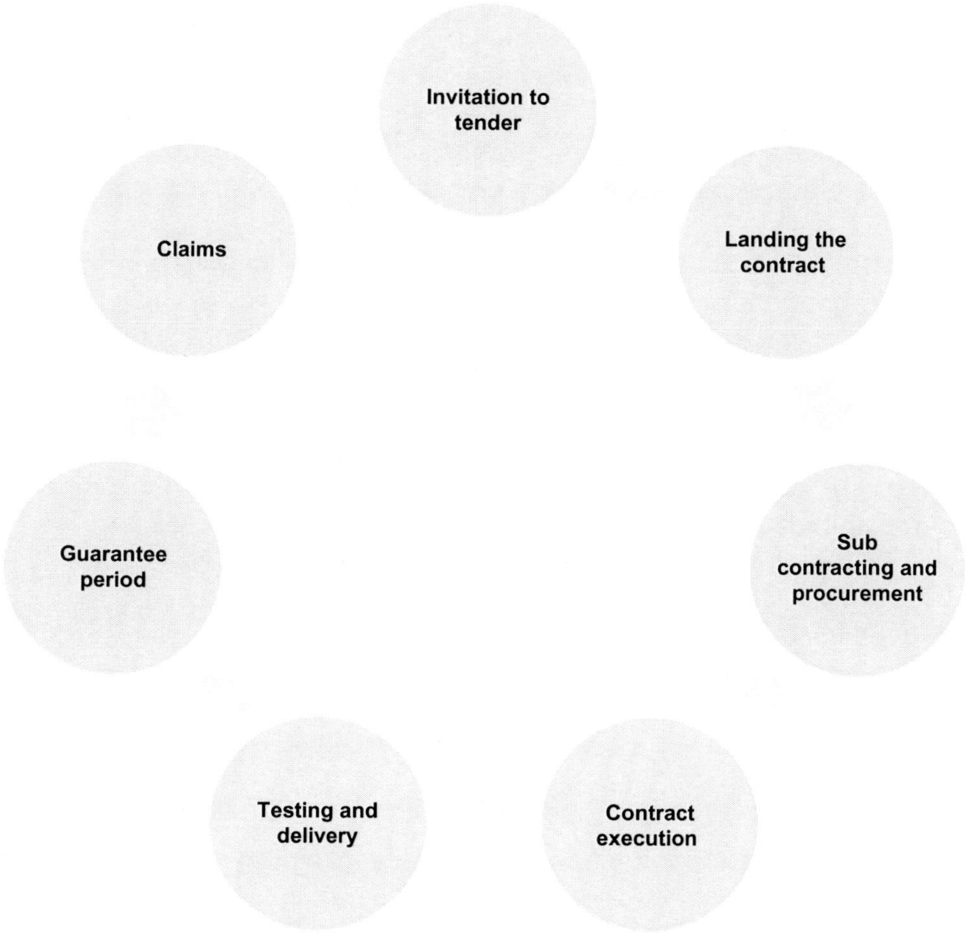

Figure 5.1. The contracting cycle: key elements.

[2]This figure reflects a cycle, since experiences gained during one project are used to prepare for an invitation to tender for the next project. Contractors learn from previous experiences and integrate their expertise and knowledge into future project proposals.

5.3. Invitation to tender: the tender process

The first step in the contracting process is when the contractor receives the tender documents from the client. The receipt of these documents needs to be confirmed. These documents need to be checked against specific requirements with regard to the client's tender procedure. Usually, explicit milestones and deadlines are mentioned that already may create problems for the contractor; for example, the time allowed for preparation of the bid might be too short. It is important that a tender manager or tender team is nominated and assigned with the job of preparing a detailed bid and to submit this bid for approval to the board of management.

At this stage we would recommend the following activities to be conducted by the tender manager or tender team:

- Check the completeness of the clients' tender documentation.
- Check the specific milestones and deadlines, as communicated by the client.
- Prepare a time-based work plan for effectively preparing the tender, including a list of the key persons that will be solicited for advice and actions.
- Prepare a concise tender document summary, to be sent to all those concerned in the internal organization.
- Prepare a detailed risk assessment plan, covering the major risks and flaws in the proposed project, documents and conditions.
- Develop initial ideas about the tender strategy, respecting the company's overall business values and strategic principles.

See Box 5.1 for how to handle the risk assessment at this stage.

In practice, the tender process is conducted under severe time pressure. The reasons for this are manifold. One reason is that the client needs a long time for its decision-making about the project and getting all financial resources arranged. As a result, less time remains for project completion, which means that the contractor needs to make up for the lost time. Another reason is that tender managers (if available) have a heavy workload and are not able to give their attention to the incoming invitations to tender when required. A third reason is that, where tender managers need to rely upon the capabilities and expertise of other specialists in the organization, these specialists are not readily available. The same is true for specific information from subcontractors and suppliers, who respond late to the procurement organization (which is already late in its request for initial quotes on subcontracted work and materials). A final reason is that senior executives, who need to decide about final proposals, appear to have

Box 5.1. Risk identification and risk assessment.

Preferably, the tender manager will use a pre-defined list or questionnaire to methodologically assess the risks that are related to the proposed project. It is recommended, for strategic projects, to set up a multidisciplinary tender team, consisting of specialists from different departments. The risk assessment, in that case, should be conducted together with the tender team, which is requested to: identify the most important risks, using the questionnaire; assess the risks identified in terms of their gravity (small, average, great, non-acceptable); and assess how these risks will be managed. With regard to the last point, risks can be classified as: risks that should be accounted for by the firm; risks to be accounted for by the client; risks that should be carried jointly; and risks that should be transferred to other parties.

To support the discussion between the disciplines involved, a risk assessment grid would be useful (see Box 5.2). Risks may be categorized as follows:

- Risks associated with employer's design.
- Risks associated with contractor's design.
- Technical risks associated with execution.
- Risks from subcontractors and suppliers.
- Risks regarding logistics and equipment.
- Contractual risks.
- Country specific risks.
- Financial risks.
- Political risks.
- Risks in hiring local labor.
- Risks concerning HS&E.

The financial risks may be sub-divided into a number of categories, such as financial and credit risk, market risks (for instance, currency risk, changing prices of materials and interest risk) and liquidity risk. These risks will be discussed elsewhere in this book.

different ideas at the time the proposed bids hit their desks. All of these circumstances may lead to a situation in which bids for tender are not getting the attention that they deserve. As a result, the company may be subjected to unnecessary risks when decisions about these proposals need to be made (see Box 5.3).

Box 5.2. Risk assessment grid.

Before coming to an agreement with a client, a careful risk analysis needs to be made. After the objectives and the deliverables of the services to be provided have been defined, it is useful to analyze all factors that may impede the realization of the agreement and deliverables.

These risk factors should be assessed based on two criteria: 1) the negative impact on the project's financial performance and/or operations and 2) the likelihood with which the risk factor probably will occur. Based on these two criteria, a risk assessment grid can be developed (see Figure 5.2) that allows for developing specific risk mitigation strategies and activities per risk factor. Of course, most efforts should be concentrated on those risk factors that would represent both a high negative impact on the project's performance and that could occur with high probability.[3]

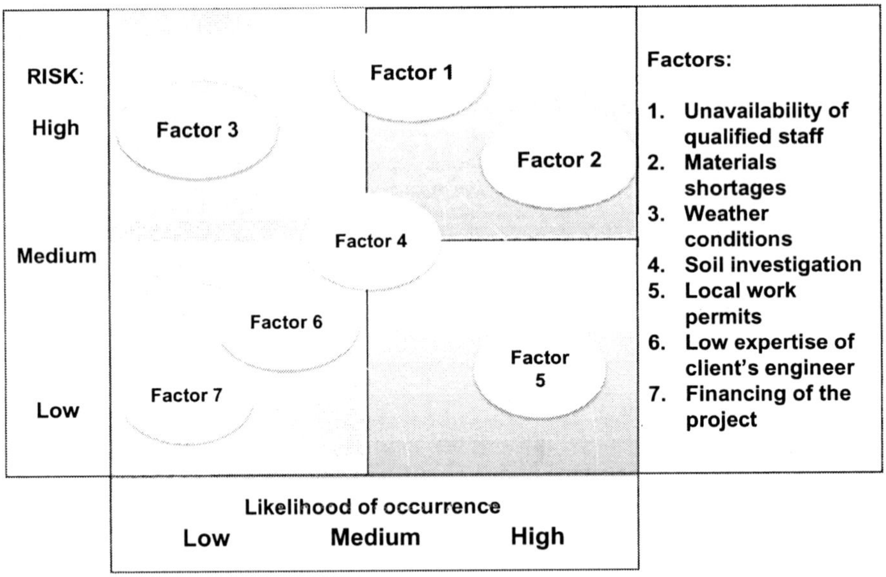

Figure 5.2. Risk assessment grid: systematic analysis of risk factors.

Based upon our experience with tender managers and project managers, we recommend for important tenders to work with competing tender teams. The contractor will benefit beyond doubt from the insight given by the different specialists involved. Another recommendation is to take sufficient time and spend sufficient effort in preparing a bid.

[3]For further details see Chapter 9, Section 9.7.

Box 5.3. Different tender teams arrive at different proposals.

During our program on International Contracting at TiasNimbas Business School at Tilburg University, the Netherlands, project managers are assigned to tender teams, who need to prepare a bid for tender. All teams are provided with the same tender documentation, which concerns the construction of a new port in an emerging country. Tender documents contain technical specifications and requirements. Next, a draft contract, which is submitted by the client, is provided to these teams.

Before arriving at the program, all participants have to study the tender documentation carefully. They have to identify risks and prepare remarks or reservations and have to calculate a bid price. They have to list all risks that are to be found in the tender documents. On the first day of the course, the individual findings are discussed in small sub-groups of, in general, four or five persons.

Our observation with regard to the outcome of this pragmatic exercise is that tender teams arrive at totally different solutions and proposals. To begin with, the risks discovered in the tender documents varied: the lowest score was 18%, while the highest amounted to 72%.

We have seen that proposed bid prices differed as well: the highest offer was approximately 24% above the lowest offer proposed.[4]

We did see a relationship between the number of risks identified and the proposed bid price. Time and time again, we observed that the team which actually won the tender was the one that observed the least risks in the client's tender documents. Our conclusion is that international contracting in construction is essentially a risk game.

A few companies have made it their standard practice to include the future project manager in the tender team. Usually, this is avoided, since senior project-management expertise is needed elsewhere in the organization and project managers cannot free themselves up for the time-pressed tender work. In such a situation, the tender team, as well as its board of management, is faced at a later stage with the so-called transfer problem. When the client assigns the project to the contractor, a project manager needs to step in — one who was not acquainted with the project, and who was not able to bring in his ideas. Given the positive experiences of some companies, we recommend involving senior project-management capacity early in the tender process, especially in strategic projects.

[4] Details of our experience are listed in Chapter 9, Section 9.6.

A major question to be asked is: are we going to tender or not? This is why the tender documents and the client information need to be checked for their compliance with the contractor's business values. What factors will be real problems for this project and will prevent us from submitting an offer? These need to be clear from the beginning. At that very early stage, the tender manager also needs to decide what type of contract needs to be pursued in the relationship with the prospective client.

Normally it is the customer who chooses the contract type and the form of contract, which as a rule are part of the tender documents. It is the customer who invites the contractor to enter into a Construction contract, a D&C contract or an EPC contract. But sometimes it is of interest to suggest a different contract type than originally required by the customer. This depends upon the contractor's experience and his core business. We once witnessed an invitation for an office building near a town, with parking lots, adjoining roads and flood lights, which originally was put forward by the client as a D&C contract, being offered by an experienced contractor as a Turnkey offer. The price was "a little bit" higher than expected by the customer, but if the functional specifications to be agreed upon are clear, the customer may arrive at interesting savings on its building and the supervising team during execution. The proposed Turnkey contract was attractive for the customer due to its shorter project lead time.

The same can be true for an invitation to tender for a Construction contract, which may be upgraded to a D&C contract by the contractor. The contractor will have to scrutinize the customer's design, but the advantage of a D&C contract is that the contractor shows the potential customer that it is not afraid of taking over the full responsibility for the design.[5]

Later in this book[6] we will see that the tender manager has different options here. Deciding about the right type of contract is crucial for the remainder of the contracting cycle in the discussions with the client. If they opt to go for tender, the tender strategy needs to be decided on. Here, two options are available: to go for a rock-bottom offer in combination with a large number of provisions, i.e. reservations or to go for an all-inclusive offer on a lump-sum basis, while accepting all project risks.

The preferred tender strategy is always the result of a number of considerations, including the hunger for work by the contractor, the specific project characteristics, the contractor's risks policy, the relationship with the client,

---

[5] For a detailed discussion of different contract types and forms, see Chapter 8.

[6] See Chapter 8. See also later in this chapter.

the personalities and seniority involved in the tender team, etc. When interviewing senior executives of large contractors, we overheard the following interesting statements:

- "Success in international contracting is decided by the way in which you are able to manage risk in the relationship with your key stakeholders. Risk management should be at the core of the activity of any tender team."
- "Tender teams that continuously get second or third place will automatically adjust their risk attitude. Nobody likes to lose constantly. Negative experiences will affect the risk attitude of tender teams. Eventually, this will come out okay."
- "Additional work, i.e. variations, should be identified at the tender stage. Identifying flaws in the client's specifications and requirements is key to tender teams."
- "At the tender stage it is extremely important to know how the client, i.e. the project, is financed. It is not so much project profitability that tender teams should be concerned about, but also future payments made by the client. Will we get the cash in?"
- "We should be careful not to involve lawyers, i.e. legal counsels, too early in the process as they usually lack a business perspective. On the other hand, some lawyers are good with small print. They may be helpful in identifying hidden risks in tender documents; but they shall not prevent us from tendering where risks are acceptable."

Finally, this stage should result in a professional bid to the client. However, before this stage can be arrived at, discussions and negotiations with the client may influence this task.

5.4. Landing the contract: the Letter of Intent (LOI)

The tender process is part of the pre-contractual stage. At this stage, contract parties need to get acquainted and accustomed to each other. One way to explore the other party is to ask questions and request clarification on issues that are observed in documentation and communication. This allows parties to engage in dialogue and discussion. From the client's point of view it's important that a level playing field is developed in the relationship with all bidders.

The client's procurement managers generally will ensure that no single contractor comes into a favored position. This is difficult, since what is allowed and not allowed at this stage is different per culture, per sector and per type of company. In general, oil and petrochemical companies are very strict in their dealings with contractors. No fringe benefits will be accepted whatsoever, be it in the tender stage or later in the project execution stage. However, when dealing with emerging countries, personal favors may be highly appreciated and may lead to a favored position. Here, the company's ethical policies and local laws may decide what is allowed or not allowed.[7]

In most cases, clients will organize face-to-face meetings with all the contractors concerned to answer questions that may have emerged or been put forward by contractors. Usually, the questions will be cited and documented, as well as the client's reactions. In some cases a bid clarification will be provided on a bilateral and personal basis. In other cases, this may be done in a bid clarification meeting with all the contractors present. Through its interactions with contractors, a preference may emerge at the client for one of them. Gradually, the long list of contractors will be brought down to a shortlist containing the two best contractors. These two contractors will be requested to submit a detailed bid, on the basis of which a final selection will be made.

Prior to making a final selection, parties may draft a letter of intent. Usually, this is seen by both parties as a pre-stage to the final contract negotiations. In practice, misunderstandings may occur about the legal value of a Letter of Intent. This is because in most standard contracts (such as FIDIC, LOGIC and the Dutch CMM contract), the LOI is not described.

In general, a LOI commits parties to what has been agreed in it and nothing more. If parties have agreed to explore opportunities to engage in a final contract, they should make their best effort to do so. However, although every party went at it with the maximum effort, a final contract may not be closed. This is all in the game. If parties have agreed in the LOI to deal with each other on an exclusive basis, they cannot engage with other parties at the same time. If the client has committed in the LOI to a soil investigation by an outside research agency, he should do so and pay for it.

The LOI can be considered as a preliminary contract, which helps parties to gain experience in working together more closely and to get a feel for the chance of success in the future collaboration for the entire project. This is the purpose of a LOI.

As we will see in Chapter 6, it is much more difficult for public institutions to engage in a similar way of working, due to the rigid procurement

---

[7] See also Chapter 25 of this book.

directives that they are subject to. This is one reason why working for public institutions as a contractor is much more difficult.

5.5. Contract negotiations and closure

At this stage of the contract cycle, it has become clear what type of contract will be closed with the client. Alternatives here are:

- *Construction-only contract.* This is recommended for building or engineering works designed by the employer or by his representative, the engineer. Under the usual arrangements for this type of contract, the contractor constructs the works in accordance with the design provided by the employer.
- *Contract for plant and design build (Design and Construct contract).* This is recommended for the provision of electrical and/or chemical plants, and for the design and execution of building and engineering works. Under the usual arrangements for this type of contract, the contractor designs and provides, in accordance with the employer's requirements, plant and/or other works. This may include any combination of civil, mechanical, electrical and/or construction works.
- *Contract for Engineer, Procure, Construct (EPC) projects/Turnkey projects.* This may be suitable for the provision on a Turnkey basis of a process or power plant, a factory or similar facility, or often an infrastructure project or other type of development, where a higher degree of certainty of final price and time is required and the contractor takes total responsibility for the design and execution of the project, with little involvement of the employer.
- *Design, Build, Finance, Maintain (DBFM) contract.* This is used in situations where the employer does not have the technical knowledge to design the project, nor has the financial resources to pay for the total investment up front, and nor wants to engage in the maintenance of the project. All of these activities are to be transferred to the contractor, who in many cases will need to team up with other specialist subcontractors in order to apply for the contract. Usually, this leads to very complex contracts, which extend to a long period of time (20 years or more).
- *Design, Build, Finance, Maintain, Operate (DBFMO).* Here, the contractor accepts the obligation to operate the permanent works for a certain period of time. When doing so, the employer's personnel may become familiar with the operating secrets of the referred works, in this way obtaining the necessary experience. Delivery of a toll road may serve as an example.

These and other contract forms and types are discussed in more detail in Chapter 8. A basic understanding of contracts is important, since every contract defines the responsibilities and liabilities among contract partners.

In Construct contracts, the risk and liability for design and engineering lies with the client or the client's engineer. The contractor is liable to the degree to which his work meets the client's specifications. When a Construct contract applies, the client should be aware that every change in its technical requirements could result in an extra cost to be charged by the contractor. Engineering changes should be documented carefully, their consequences on cost should be followed up and they should be approved by the contractor prior to execution. Experienced contractors may act very rigidly on this and probably will not commence any work on changes if the client has not agreed the financial consequences.

This situation is totally different when an EPC contract applies. Here, the project manager is responsible for ensuring that the work delivered meets the customer's design, which beforehand was checked and accepted by the contractor and as such became part of the contractor's responsibility. Stated otherwise, his work should be fit for the functional requirements of the design, whereas the design should be fit for purpose. Both types of contracts have different implications for the roles of the parties involved.

When an EPC contract applies, the contractor is responsible, when taking over, for ensuring that the works meet the definitions of the intended purposes as provided by the employer when concluding the contract. Above that, the contractor should ensure that the works meet the criteria for testing and performance. The client and the client's engineer should refrain from detailed instructions with regard to the construction and execution of work with an EPC contract. Preferably, the client should adopt a hands-off approach.

In industry, several standard templates are available for these different contract types. Examples of standard contracts are FIDIC and LOGIC for construction and offshore installations, and BIMCO for shipping and towing activities. These standard contracts are derived from the best practices in the sectors and have been agreed among major players in these sectors (both clients and contractors). FIDIC, for instance, was developed by the international federations of engineers, who were supported by the United Nations, World Bank, the International Development Association and the IMF, just to mention a few. LOGIC was developed by a large number of experts in the oil and gas industry. In general, the decision on which form of agreement will apply for the future project is up to the client. In the meantime, standard contracts cover Construct contracts, Design and Construct contracts, specialized dredging agreements, contracts for ship management and towing, contracts for Turnkey projects, contracts for Design, Build, Finance and Maintenance, etc. The use of these international contract standards is widespread.

Using these contract templates improves communication between parties in international business, saves a lot of time and cost, since agreement exists about the terminology and conditions of use, and contract parties can benefit from the vast experience from which these standard contracts have been derived. In these standard contracts, all subjects are covered in a methodological and systematic way. As Chapter 8 is devoted to this subject, we refer the interested reader to this part of our book.

With regard to contract negotiation strategies and tactics, we have observed a rich range of practices, which unfortunately are beyond the scope of this book. The reader is referred to the specialist literature on this topic.[8]

5.6. Subcontracting and project execution

In international contracting, it is quite common that projects are won at a price level that is barely profitable. As our introductory case shows, during the final negotiations the contractor gives an additional discount on its already competitive contract price. When the contract is captured in this way, the project manager is faced with a problem: how to make this project a profitable one? Of course, in many cases, efficiency gains can be made by meticulous work preparation and a reduction of operational costs. However, since subcontractors and materials suppliers easily make up 50–70% of the contract price, the procurement organization is summoned to squeeze these external partners. This approach is called: "Procurement needs to secure the margin for the project." The procurement organization may or may not succeed in chopping off a few percentages of the total procurement expense. However, in all cases, the procurement organization will face a tense relationship with its supply partners, who will use every opportunity to cut costs, charge heavily for extra work, and give in on quality and delivery. What's even worse: the supply partners will have no interest at all in making the project a success for the project manager, the contractor and/or the client.

---

[8] Harvard Business School (2003), *Harvard Business Essentials Guide to Negotiation*. Boston, MA: Harvard Business Press; R. Fisher (2006), *Getting to Yes: Negotiating Agreement Without Giving In*. London: Random House Business Books; G. Richard (2006), *Negotiation Strategies for Reasonable People, 2nd edition*; R. Dawson (2010), *Secrets of Power Negotiating*. Pompton Plains, NJ: Career Press.

This case is an illustration of what we have referred to earlier in the book as a "dyadic perspective" on contracting, which is characterized by a "win-lose" attitude by contract partners.[9] Although this approach has its merits (it is easy to practice), its major disadvantage is that parties will pursue only their self-interest at the detriment of the client's interest. This traditional approach towards subcontracting and procurement should therefore only apply for non-strategic, low-volume subcontractors and suppliers. Engaging strategic subcontractors and suppliers would, preferably, call for a more careful approach: these supply partners should be contracted using back-to-back agreements, which cover the risks and liabilities of the main contract as much as possible, as the case may allow. Otherwise, the risks for non-performance are fully carried by the contractor. Back-to-back agreements in general create a stronger interest from supply partners to meet the contractor's and client's needs. For strategic supply partners, full business alignment should be realized, i.e. alignment between the supply partners' interests and the contractor's and client's interests. Back-to-back agreements are helpful in creating a supply chain, i.e. value-chain orientation.[10] Parts of these back-to-back agreements are penalty and incentive schemes, which may motivate the supply partners to constructive behavior and contributions. For more details on how to deal with subcontractors and materials suppliers, see Chapter 7 of this book.

Subcontracting and procurement precede the stage of project execution. In theory, this may be true. In practice, subcontractors may have commenced their job and materials suppliers may have delivered their materials before a proper contract has been put into place.

In dealing effectively with supply partners, the project manager could do the following:

- Have a proper supplier selection procedure in place, documenting which supply partners are pre-selected, i.e. pre-qualified, how bids are evaluated and decided upon, what contracts need to be used and what general purchase conditions will apply. This would require a dedicated project buyer to be assigned to the project, who can act as a liaison between the project engineers and the procurement organization.
- Have a proper contract administration in place covering all contract documents and related documents. Obviously, this is a key requisite for successful contract management.

---

[9] See Chapter 2.

[10] See Chapter 2.

- Have a proper order-to-pay system in place, allowing the project support staff to order materials and services using the company's corporate purchase agreements and allowing for a full tracing and tracking of materials.
- Send a copy of general purchase conditions when necessary.
- Provide for effective expediting, following up on project strategic materials, subcontractors and suppliers.
- Have a quantity surveyor or contract manager on site who follows up per subcontractor and supplier on the number of man hours actually spent, the quantity of materials actually consumed and the equipment availability and usage.
- Have a clear incoming and quality inspection procedure in place for all incoming materials. Shipments should be checked with purchase orders in terms of quality, quantity and timeliness of delivery.
- All materials should be kept in secured inventory locations.
- Have a clear procedure for handling invoices coming from supply partners. All invoices should be subject to a three-way matching principle (order matches delivery document; delivery document matches with invoice, to be checked by an independent person; invoice matches with the order). All exceptional invoices should be checked by the project manager. Invoices without a purchase order number should be returned to the supplier/subcontractor.
- Have a proper subcontractor and supplier evaluation procedure in place, allowing for a ranking of supply partners in terms of partners, preferred suppliers and suppliers, and those suppliers with whom the relationship would need to be terminated due to bad performance.

If these procedures (which would call for adequate staffing and resources) are put in place, the project manager easily would save 3–4 % of the materials cost on his project. These savings are the result of less waste, less theft and actual payment for performance or goods delivered.[11]

It is our observation that expediting, materials control, quantity surveying and contract management are, in most projects, undervalued, underrated and understaffed activities. Our suggestion is not to see these activities as a cost to the project, but rather as an investment (which will be recouped within a couple of months).

When making payments ahead of time, as some suppliers may require or need, the project manager should make sure that the supplier issues a bank guarantee or concern guarantee. Through a statement called the Transfer of

---

[11] In some industries suppliers may invoice higher volumes than have actually been delivered.

Title of Ownership he should assure that materials (e.g. piping, steel plates) that are produced by the supplier are kept separate from other materials and are labeled with the name of the contractor, i.e. project. This will prevent serious problems in case the supplier gets into financial difficulties or faces bankruptcy.

5.7. Testing, delivery and payment

Having arrived at the project's milestones, the client or the client's engineer shall want to inspect the progress of work. Approval of both the quality of the work and its quantity by the engineer or client is needed to be able to send the invoice, which is linked to the respective milestone in the planning schedule, and get this approved for payment. Therefore, the project manager needs to manage the relationship with both the client and its engineer in order to prevent delays that might occur.

What to do if the work has been approved, the invoice has been sent, but the actual payment, for some obscure reason, is suspended? Most project managers will continue with their work, taking the risk that the company will finance most of the project eventually. Some financial directors have issued strict guidelines to their project managers and will summon their project managers to cease all project work. Of course, this can only be done if the client has been summoned through a first and second reminder to pay, and finally, has been officially put in default.

The jurisprudence provides many examples of situations where a contractor fell short of delivering a work according to what had been agreed in the contract. More often than not, parties settle their positions themselves without going to court or to arbitration, although one of the parties involved is in default. A contractor, who is a specialist in offshore pipe laying and sub-sea construction, may serve as an example here. For this work, the contractor uses specialist vessels. Recently, the decision was made to modify one of its special purpose vessels, i.e. a vessel that was used to cover sub-sea pipelines with stones and sand. The reason was a major project that was won from an international client for such work, totaling £60 million. The two existing electrical deck cranes were deemed to be outdated. Their movements were slow, and spare parts were no longer available. It was decided that both deck cranes would be replaced by a Hitachi 870 excavator. The Hitachi 870 would be used to move stones from the holds 4 and 5 of the ship into a vertical piping structure, which would manage the positions of the stones onto the seabed. However, in order to increase its productivity, it was necessary to increase the capacity of the original Hitachi bucket. A larger bucket was needed in order to be able to deliver a large project within the client's tight deadlines.

For the modification, an experienced subcontractor was selected, and he produced detailed technical specifications and drawings. These included the deck's frame construction, which should be supported in order to carry the heavy excavator and its loads. Next, many issues were discussed, such as lifting certifications, ship stability in various loading conditions and wind directions, maintenance, maximum residual charge remaining after unloading, cycle times of the bucket, anchoring system and safety while operating and during sailing. It was contractually agreed that the subcontractor would need to deliver the project Turnkey, including the reinforcement of the deck's frame. Next, the subcontractor was responsible for carrying out all maintenance work. It was also agreed that the Hitachi 870 would be operated by a certified driver, who needed to carry out daily maintenance and inspections. Of course, the performance of the bucket was specified. The bucket should be able to discharge full loads of 1–8" sand stones with a standard operating bucket of 4 m^3, from holds 4 and 5, whereas the cycle time for the bucket was specified to be one minute.

However, after completion of the work, the first tests with the Hitachi showed that the construction that was conceived was too light. The bucket deformed when gripping the stones in the cargo holds. Additional stiffeners needed to be attached. However, these would make the bucket too heavy to handle. Then, the subcontractor proposed using a smaller bucket of 2.5 m^3. When tested by the contractor, this seemed to work. However, using this smaller bucket had some major disadvantages: the residue that remained in the holds appeared to be three times higher than with the larger bucket. Next, 1,500 movements were now needed instead of the 1,000 movements for the larger bucket, reducing the excavator's productivity and implying that the anticipated project could not be achieved within the agreed timeline. See Figure 5.3 for a picture of the situation.

Obviously, the contractor faced severe problems. If the project could not be executed within the agreed timeframe, considerable penalties for delay would be executed. Of course, the claim could be passed on to the subcontractor. However, since this was only a small firm, executing the penalty would result in its bankruptcy; another party would have to be found to do the future maintenance.

The question rising from this case study is: what is the legal position of both parties and what claims can be executed by the contractor? A few observations may help to understand the situation:

- Since the contract between the contractor and subcontractor is a construction contract, the subcontractor can only be held liable for meeting that client's technical requirements. The technical solution was provided by the subcontractor and probably approved by the contractor. Next, the

Figure 5.3. The modified Hitachi 870 in action.

contractor varied the contract according to his approved specifications and drawings to the subcontractor to conduct the job.

- In the case that an EPC contract had been used, the subcontractor would have been liable for assuring that its technical solution would meet the contractor's business objectives and purpose: to be able to conduct the pipe-covering project within the agreed timeframe. In such a situation the subcontractor clearly would have been held liable for all direct damages. These could relate to the contractor's project if that was clearly communicated to the subcontractor from the beginning.
- Furthermore, the legal system of the referred contract plays a role. Under common law, in contrast to Dutch law, penalties in contracts are not allowed. This is why, in common law, parties normally arrange for liquidated damages to recoup the costs accrued by rectifying problems arising from malfunctioning equipment.
- Under LOGIC contracts (UK law) a contractor cannot successfully sue a subcontractor for consequential damages. Claims should be limited to liquidated damages that were caused by malfunctioning equipment.
- As a rule, indirect, i.e. consequential, damages are limited or excluded in contracts through specific clauses on the issue.[12] In this case, liquidated damages for the contractor were limited to 0.5% of the contract sum per

[12]See Chapter 13, Section 13.7 for a detailed discussion of consequential damage.

week overdue, i.e. £300,000 per week. Obviously, this far outweighs the subcontractor's total contract sum (which amounted to £200,000).

When brought to court, the outcome might be different based upon the legal system that applies. If English law applied, the judge would discard any claims for consequential damages in the event the subcontractor was not informed about the contractor's heavy liquidated damages under the main contract between employer and contractor. The judge probably would agree on claims related to damages incurred by the malfunctioning of the excavator's bucket and the deck's reinforced steel structure, if it could be verified that the subcontractor's work had deviated from the client's technical specifications. Under Dutch law, the outcome might be similar. However, a key issue would be the judge's consideration regarding whether the subcontractor was responsible for the proposed design of the bucket and the variation in the scope of the work, where a contractor's consent was given before installing a smaller bucket. Would a judge hold the subcontractor liable for the contractor's financial losses in such a case? Was there sufficient causality between cause (smaller bucket) and effect (contractor's liquidated damages)? Who will finally bear the losses?

What should the contractor do to solve this case? Two options are open to him. The first is to go to court and sue the subcontractor for all damage that was directly incurred from the malfunctioning bucket. This would not solve his current issue of an underperforming excavator. Moreover, such a court case would take considerable time and effort. Another option would be to discuss the matter again with the subcontractor to see what alternatives could be found to improve the excavator's productivity and reliability, and to solve the negative side effects of using a smaller bucket. Next, the contractor should engage in a discussion with his client to create more leeway in his delivery schedule for the pipeline-covering project.

5.8. Claims and dispute resolution

Given the complexity of most construction works, there is almost no job that does not end without a dispute or conflict among parties. Of course, preventing problems in the work and relationships is better than curing them afterwards. As we have seen in our practice, disputes and conflicts escalate due to bad personal relationships and egos, which get in the way (see Chapter 1 on the BP oil spill). Good contracts will never be able to replace damage from bad interpersonal relationships. It is preferable to solve issues that may arise through a concerted effort among parties, with the personal involvement of the key participants, than going to court or arbitration. As a rule, the contractor's project manager should interface personally, formally and informally with the client's key stakeholders and engineer on a very regular basis. We recommend project managers do everything possible before handing over the case to legal counsels within the firm. Legal counsels will mostly go for the letter of the contract, rather than the intent of the contract among parties. As a result, disputes and conflicts will increase in complexity. It is a delicate matter to decide to hand things over to the legal specialists. Obviously, this is decided best through a well-informed discussion between the project manager, contract manager and legal counsel.

Finally, when cases have been submitted to the legal department, and/or external legal counsels, the project manager still needs to have a role in solving the dispute. He should make sure that he is informed in such a way that he can take the lead in the relationship with his client. Leaving this to specialized legal counsels may complicate things, and may postpone a satisfactory outcome of the dispute. A prime reason for this is that the business model underlying successful legal practices[13] differs dramatically from the business model that underlies contracting firms. In many court cases, the business model of legal counsels may take priority over the interests of the parties involved. In practice, the relationship between project managers representing the client and the contractor may be tense. In such cases, the intervention by professional, rational contract managers may help to solve the issues at hand and prevent problems from unnecessarily escalating.

The chapters in Part IV deal extensively with specific problems and disputes which may arise in international contracting. How to resolve conflicts and disputes is dealt with in Chapter 24. The interested reader is kindly referred to these chapters.

5.9. Summary

Initially, this chapter discussed the parallel if the contracting cycle with the changing seasons of the year. Contractual relationships may move through the different stages of spring, summer, autumn and winter. In contrast to the seasons, the stages within the contracting cycle are interrelated. Previous stages may impact the relationships during later stages in the contracting cycle. In this chapter we identified seven specific stages which a contractual relationship may go through.

The first stage is the invitation for tender. Here, the client issues a request to the contractor to engage in a project. This invitation may have different

[13] I.e. making as many billable hours as possible.

forms, such as the aforementioned RFI, RFP or RFQ. International offshore projects are usually very complex; apart from the technical requirements that should be met, the interests of a wide variety of stakeholders also need to be met. In practice, clients put their prospective contractors under significant time pressure to produce their proposals. For this reason, this stage of the contracting cycle should be thoroughly prepared and organized. Sufficient time must be taken for a careful analysis of the tender documents and identifying the risks that are related to the project, the project environment, the client and its stakeholders. This is why we have spent significant time in addressing risk analysis and management. Every major project offering should be accompanied by a concise risk-management plan. Based upon these activities, the contractor should decide about his tender strategy. Options here are to go for a rock-bottom price with a long list of reservations, or a higher all-in price with all risks borne by the contractor. Of course, there is also a mixed solution: to discuss with the client what risks will be incurred by him, by the contractor and by both parties jointly. As practice shows, investing in sound preparation leads to a much better understanding and weighing of the risks involved. This is why we have stressed the value of working with focused tender managers and tender teams and involving the designated project manager at this stage.

Next, the second stage of the contracting cycle emerges, i.e. landing the contract. A thorough analysis of the project and its related risks may lead to questions being posed in the client's bid clarification meeting. Rather than entering into a contract right away, parties may sign a Letter of Intent. As we have argued, the LOI serves as a preliminary agreement. Parties are only committed to the issues agreed in this document and nothing more. The LOI allows parties to get acquainted with each other and to test each other's culture and commitment. After things have been sorted out under the LOI, parties may engage in more serious discussions and negotiations and land the contract. This is the third step of the contracting cycle.

At the contract negotiations and closure stage, parties need to agree and substantiate what contract model will be used. In this chapter, we discussed four major contract models, i.e. Construction, D&C, EPC, and DBFMO contracts. Each of these contract models is used in different situations and represents different roles and responsibilities for both client and contractor. Next, these contract models can be found in different international standard contracts (such as FIDIC, LOGIC, BIMCO). In fact, these standard contracts, which are widely used in international contracting, represent templates that can be used for the different contract models. Finally, parties need to agree on what legal system (UK law, Dutch law, Norwegian law) to use for their contracts.

The fourth and fifth stages in the contracting cycle are subcontracting and project execution. Both are mentioned together since it is common practice (however, this is not without risk) for subcontractors to start their work for the project without proper commissioning. Crucial elements in subcontracting are: deciding when to involve which subcontractors in the project (some of them might need to be engaged at the tender stage), how to pre-qualify or pre-select them, how to structure the bidding process and how to select the best offer. We also discussed the need for their activities to be meticulously planned, and to follow up on their activities, technically, in terms of quality and financially.

It is common for operational problems to emerge during project execution because every situation is unique. Therefore, not all problems can be anticipated. When these occur, parties need to react and act. We provided a real-life case on what might happen during project execution. Although contracts may be of help in making outcomes, roles and responsibilities explicit, they are of little help in actually solving stressful situations. Here, the quality of the relationship between parties is much more important in finding successful solutions.

The last two stages of the contracting process are the settling of guarantees and claims handling. As in most situations the client will negotiate for a retention fee, it is important to keep in contact with the client during the guarantee period to sound out upcoming problems with the work or installation delivered. A professional project administration that enables a good tracing and tracking of the project may be of great value in addressing disputes and conflicts that may emerge at this stage.

Chapter 6

European Tendering[1]

6.1. Case — Objectives[2]

Many infrastructural and construction projects are awarded by governmental institutions. As this chapter describes, the government is not free in deciding how it buys. It needs to follow strict procedures on public procurement. In Europe, European Directives on Public Procurement apply, that need to be translated into national legislation. For the UK government, general principles were issued by HM Treasury.

Good procurement means getting value for money — that is, buying a product that is fit for purpose, taking account of the whole-life cost. A good procurement process should also be delivered efficiently to limit the time and expense for the parties involved. Successful procurement is good for the public, good for the taxpayer and good for businesses supplying government.

While there is no single method that will guarantee the delivery of those objectives for all procurements, the following general principles set out the key steps to successful procurement in most cases. A procuring authority should:

- Be clear on the objectives of the procurement from the outset.
- Be aware of external factors that will impact on the procurement, such as the policy environment or planning issues.
- Communicate those objectives to potential contractors at an early stage, to gauge the market's ability to deliver and explore a range of possible solutions.

[1] Parts of this chapter are derived from A.J. Van Weele (2010), *Purchasing and Supply Chain Management*. London: Cengage, Chapter 6. This chapter discusses public procurement predominantly from a European perspective. However, the principles underlying European procurement practices are common in other parts of the world.

[2] HM Treasury, Transforming government procurement, UK, January 2007.

- Consider using an output or outcome-based specification, to give contractors — who naturally know more about their business than potential buyers — more scope to provide innovative solutions to solve the underlying problem the procurement is designed to deal with, rather than deciding what the precise solution should be at the outset.
- Follow a competitive, efficient, fair and transparent procurement process, and communicate to potential contractors at the outset what that process will be. This will give contractors greater certainty about the costs and benefits to them of submitting a bid, which should encourage effective competition. As all contractors have the same knowledge going into the process, and will be assessed in the same way, the successful bidder can be chosen purely on its ability to provide the best solution.
- Be clear about affordability — the resources available to spend on particular goods or services. The procurer has to select on the basis of whole-life value for money, but in setting budgets for individual projects, departments also need to make decisions about relative policy priorities and needs. If more is spent on one project than originally allocated, that will mean less is available for other priorities. Conversely, if savings are achieved, then these can be redeployed into frontline services.
- Establish effective contract management processes and resources in good time to drive excellent contractor performance throughout the contract.

Introduction

Notwithstanding the good intentions, which are described in the introductory case, the actual experiences with governmental institutions in regard to public procurement are disappointing. In many countries, the government represents the most important customer for construction and offshore contractors. In general, public procurement and tender processes and practices are highly bureaucratic, tedious and time-consuming, price driven and allow for little innovation and creativity from the construction industry. For this reason they are subject to considerable public debate.

In some sectors, public institutions and public utilities may have the position as a monopolist.[3] Demand for weapon systems and tanks are limited to the Ministry of Defense. Demand for water purification installations is limited to water supply companies, which are usually owned by the government. Tendering for civil infrastructure, such as roads, bridges, canals, harbors,

[3]See Chapter 7.

tunnels, etc., is for a large part limited to ministries, regions and municipalities in many countries.

The total volume of the market for governmental contracts in all EC countries is considerable. In 2002, the European Commission estimated this volume at 16.3% of the Gross Domestic Product (GDP), representing a contract value of about €1,500 billion.[4] This figure excludes the value of the GDP of the 12 member states that have entered the European Union since 1995.

Representing 16.3% of GDP, governmental institutions play a crucial role in developing the internal market within the EU. The idea behind the European Treaty is to create one European market without trade barriers, based upon a liberal market mechanism, so that free exchange of supplies, persons, services and capital can be accomplished. We will see in this chapter how these ideas, which underlie the EC, have a profound impact on how European government deals with its contractors and service providers.

This chapter discusses the public procurement practices in Europe. More particularly, it discusses to whom public procurement laws and directives apply and how they work. A good understanding of the subject is important in order to land contracts with governmental institutions successfully.

6.2. Principles and scope of the European procurement laws and directives

The European Union consists of the following member countries (the number is related to the year of entry to the EU): Austria 1995, Belgium 1951, Bulgaria 2007, Cyprus 2004, Czech Republic 2004, Denmark 1973, England 1973, Estonia 2004, Finland 1995, France 1951, Germany 1951, Greece 1981, Hungary 2004, Ireland 1973, Italy 1951, Latvia 2004, Lithuania 2004, Luxembourg 1951, Malta 2004, the Netherlands 1951, Poland 2004, Portugal 1986, Romania 2007, Slovakia 2004, Slovenia 2004, Spain 1986 and Sweden 1995. The total number of inhabitants is 480 million.

A compartmentalized market of government contracts, where national governments favor their national and local contractors, is in conflict with the realization of one common European market. For this reason the EU introduced strict procurement directives, which prescribe to a high level of detail regarding how governmental institutions and municipalities should buy. The basic idea behind these directives is that the massive EU market should be accessible for all contractors and contractors within the EU.

[4] European Commission, A report on the functioning of public procurement markets in the EU benefits from the application of EU directives and challenges for the future, February 3, 2004.

Principles

Four major principles underlie each of these procurement directives: the principles of non-discrimination, equality, transparency and proportionality. When applying the procurement directives, governmental institutions should comply with these four principles.

- *Non-discrimination.* The principle of non-discrimination should safeguard the market for government contracts so it is accessible to every contractor, whatever his nationality and country. For this reason, it is not permissible to prescribe that a company should be located, for instance, in the Netherlands, or should have done business previously with the Dutch government. Neither is it permissible to require a specific fabricate or brand. The only discriminating requirement that is allowed is that contractors should be able to speak and write in the language where the contracting authority is established, if this is considered to be necessary for a successful completion of the contract.
- *Equality.* The principle of equality stipulates that all competitors that compete for the same government contracts should be dealt with in a similar way and that they should be provided with the same information at the same time. In this manner the procurement directives try to create "a level playing field" for every contractor.
- *Transparency.* The principle of transparency forces governmental institutions and public utilities to publish those contracts, the value of which exceeds certain financial thresholds,[5] in the Tender Electronic Daily (TED), the EU database that keeps a record of all European tenders. This principle also demands, in case there is a clear interest from contractors in the other member states, that even the smaller contracts, which do not meet the financial thresholds, are communicated to the European business community. In these cases, public institutions may in addition use their websites or may place specific advertisements in European newspapers. The principle of transparency also demands that the public institution communicates in advance what procurement procedure will be used, what requirements will be imposed on the contractor and how the contract will be awarded among competing contractors. In general, these procedures also prescribe that contractors are informed about the reasons for not being selected.

[5] See later in this chapter.

- *Proportionality.* The principle of proportionality holds that the requirements and conditions that are imposed on the future contractor are reasonable. This means that they should be in balance with the scope and volume of the contract.

These four principles underlying public procurement are the backbone of what will follow in this chapter. An important concept that will be used in this chapter is the concept of the contracting authority. The contracting authority is in general a public institution or public utility that is subject to the European Directives on Public Procurement.

Public tendering: legal framework

The purchasing policy of the classical government (the state, regional or local authorities, bodies governed by public law, associations formed by one or more of such authorities or bodies governed by public law) has some specific characteristics. These characteristics do not specifically apply to the public utilities sector (public transport, water control, energy supply and ports authorities). Therefore, for this sector, an enlightened regime exists.

Tendering is a crucial part of the public procurement function. It may be surrounded by all kinds of specific legal rules and complexities. This is less true for public utilities, which increasingly are subjected to the laws of supply and demand. For this sector, there are many more similarities with how the private sector makes its purchases.

Public tendering includes supply-market research; developing a sourcing strategy based on a detailed specification for the delivery of supplies and services and/or construction; selecting the right procurement procedure; preparing the tendering documents, which will include the technical requirements, contractor selection and award criteria and contractual conditions; evaluating contractor data and contractor bids; contracting; writing up the final version of the contract and the follow-up of the tender procedure. In general, the public tender process is split into two different stages: (1) pre-qualification of contractors; (2) bid evaluation and the award of the contract to the best contractor.

Public procurement law is based upon the body of international and European law, national laws and directives and jurisprudence. Public procurement law prescribes in a formal way how to go about government contracts, i.e. how to deal with contractors and how to award public contracts. Over the years, it has become clear that national governments violated European procurement laws and directives when awarding contracts to contractors. In most cases, they kept protecting national interests by placing contracts with local and national contractors. For this reason, during the early 1970s, the first European Directives on Public Procurement were introduced. Initially, specific directives were made for "Works" and "Supplies".[6] In the early 1990s, the directives related to "Services" and "Public Utilities" followed.

European procurement directives and national legislation provide the legal framework upon which national contracting authorities should act. However, apart from these laws and directives, contracting authorities in the EU member states also have to comply with the regulations resulting from the Agreement on Government Procurement (GPA), that has been agreed upon within GATT (General Agreement on Tariffs and Trade), now the WTO (World Trade Organization). The following countries participate in the GPA: the European Union, Aruba (the Netherlands), Canada, Hong Kong, Japan, Iceland, Israel, Liechtenstein, New Zealand, Norway, Singapore, South Korea, Switzerland and the United States of America. Contractors from these countries have free access to the large market of central governmental contracts in the areas of construction, products and services. A consequence of GPA is that countries need to acknowledge lower financial threshold levels for the central government (the state).

In summary, the government needs to acknowledge complex legislation when making purchasing decisions. A thorough understanding of international and European procurement law is necessary in order to prevent problems in the relationship with contractors. Contractors should be dealt with in a fair way, respecting the four principles of non-discrimination, equality, transparency and proportionality. Procedural mistakes may easily cause delays to happen in project execution, and may unnecessarily result in contractor claims that are brought before court.

With regards to the scope of the European Directives on Public Procurement, we need to differentiate between what contracts need to be tendered according to these directives and to whom the directives apply.

Scope

In general, the European directives apply to all governmental institutions, including the state, regional or local authorities and bodies governed by

[6]The European Directive on Public Procurement on "Works" originates from July 26, 1971 and the European Directive on Public Procurement on "Supplies" originates from December 21, 1976.

public law. The latter may include specific research organizations, universities, academic hospitals, educational institutions, police authorities, new town development corporations and water supply companies. These examples already illustrate the wide range of institutions to which the European directives may apply. In the remainder of this chapter these institutions will be referred to as "contracting authorities".

The procurement directives define "supply, works and service contracts" as "contracts for pecuniary interest concluded in writing between one or more of the contracting entities and one or more contractors or service providers". This definition has two important elements. First, the agreement must be in writing. Second, the agreement must stipulate an exchange of value between parties. To be more precise: one party needs to provide supplies and services, for which the other party is willing to pay. A formal agreement does not need to imply a large, complex contract. It can also relate to a purchase order, which has been sent by e-mail. Or, it may simply relate to an invoice that has been accepted by the customer for payment.

The exchange of value between parties assumes that both parties have rights and obligations. One party needs to deliver, whereas the other party needs to pay. Payment does not necessarily have to happen in terms of money. Payment can also be made through exchange of a special permit or could simply relate to exchange of supplies (barter). As an example, a real estate company might acquire the property rights to a piece of land from a city against the promise that it will develop the area and that it will build a new City Hall for the city council free of charge. Hence, the European procurement directives apply to any contract for which a customer wants to pay with a return that can be put in monetary terms. As discussed before, the contract may relate to works, supplies and services.

"Works contracts" are contracts that have as their objective either the execution, or both the design and execution, of a project. A work means the outcome of building or civil engineering work taken as a whole, which is sufficient in itself to fulfill an economic or technical function. Purchase of immovable properties is excluded, but when a contracting authority hires a contractor to build real estate according to his specifications (terms of reference), it is considered as a Works contract. In practice, contracts for the delivery of a ship, acoustic installations for a theater or pumps for a water purification installation have been mistakenly defined as a work. These are examples of supplies deliveries. This is why the appendices of the European Directives on Public Procurement have been included. These appendices describe exactly what needs to be considered as a work. In case of doubt, the contracting authorities can use them to find the exact answer.

Supplies relate to physical products like computers, office furniture, helicopters, trucks, etc. However, supplies also relate to leasing and rental contracts of these physical products. If a public institution decides to lease its car fleet, this is considered to be a supplies delivery and not a service. This is also true when a vessel is being rented. Additional services, like installation services when acquiring a new telephone center, may be part of the supplies delivery. This is important when it comes to assessing the total value of the contract involved.

Services are in fact a rest category. Services relate to assignments, which can be considered neither a work nor goods. In reality, the differentiation between goods and services is very hard to make. The European Directives on Public Procurement differentiate between A- and B-services. A-services are fully subject to the European legislation. For B-services an enlightened regime exists — enlightened because the public procurement procedures do not fully apply. However, in all cases, these services need to be acquired recognizing the aforementioned general public procurement principles. And in case there is a clear interest from contractors from the other member states, there should be a certain degree of publicity of the contract. Examples of B-services are, amongst others, catering services, rail transport, transport by vessel, temporary labor, legal support services, healthcare and education.

6.3. European procurement procedures

From all the arrangements, the European procurement procedures have raised the most discussion. A European procurement procedure is defined here as "the total set of rules and regulations that are aimed at selecting the best contractor for the best product against the best conditions, recognizing European laws and regulations". The European Directives on Public Procurement include the following six procedures: (1) Open procedure, (2) Restricted procedure, (3) Competitive dialogue, (4) Negotiated procedure with prior publication of a contract notice, (5) Negotiated procedure without prior publication of a contract notice and (6) Design contest. All of these procedures will be briefly described. However, first we will discuss the threshold levels that need to be taken into account.

Threshold levels

The European procurement regime only applies to contracts that meet certain threshold values. Table 6.1 provides an overview of the threshold values

Table 6.1. Threshold values, European Directives on Public Procurement.

Classical government	Threshold values in euros
Works	5,000,000
Supplies: Central government	180,000
Supplies: Local contracting authorities	200,000
Services: Central government	130,000
Services: Local contracting authorities	200,000
Public utilities	**Threshold values**
Works	5,000,000
Supplies	400,000
Services	400,000

involved. The structural values, which are listed here excluding VAT, are updated every two years.

The reason for the lower threshold values for the central government is the fact that contracts also need to comply with the regulations as stipulated by the GPA, as shown earlier in Section 6.2. When estimating the value of a contract, all costs need to be recognized that will be incurred during the execution of the construction assignment, the delivery contract and/or the service contract, including all supportive activities. For example, when contracting for a new telephone installation, the contracting authority needs to recognize all costs related to the acquisition of the handsets and other accessories, as well as the acquisition cost of the installation itself. It is not permissible to cut the total assignment in pieces to work around the European procurement procedures. It is forbidden to split a larger assignment into a few smaller ones, just for this purpose. There is, however, one exception to this rule. A larger assignment may be split into smaller, coherent lots. For example, when buying office and computer supplies, the contracting authority may split the contract into one for office supplies and one for computer supplies, allowing prospective contractors to bid on the total contract, or to bid on each individual lot. This arrangement is also relevant for construction contracts. It is permissible, for instance, to take the contract for installation work out of the total contract and to solicit bids from competing installation firms, just for this part of the work. However, when doing so, the contract value of the lot should be less than €1,000,000. Next, the total value of the lots, which are separated from the total contract, should not exceed 20% of the total contract value. When tendering for a contract for railroad maintenance by a European railroad authority, with an estimated value of €50 million, the value of all lots together may not exceed €10 million, whereas each separate subcontract should not exceed the value of €1 million. These examples illustrate how complex and detailed procurement directives may be.

In general, governmental institutions can choose among the different public procurement procedures. Public utilities have the largest degrees of freedom. The next section discusses the public procurement procedures in more detail.

Public procurement procedures

- *Open procedure.* The idea underlying the open procedure is that every market party within the EU should be able to subscribe to a governmental tender. The maximum term for submitting bids is 52 days, starting with the day that the notice has been made public. These 52 days are calendar days. Where an information notice was published previously, this term may be reduced to 22–36 days. When sending all tender forms electronically to interested market parties, the contracting authority may further reduce the maximum term by seven days. If all tender documents (including technical information and drawings) are sent electronically, the maximum term may be reduced by another five days. When communicating electronically, the contracting authority may reduce the maximum term for contractors to react by 12 days, leaving them with a minimum term to react of just 15 days. Of course, contracting authorities should be reluctant to reduce the reaction time for contractors by too much. The risk will be that too few bids are obtained and that bids will be badly prepared. This will serve the interests of no one.
- *Restricted procedure.* Although the name of this procedure suggests otherwise, every EU contractor may compete for contracts that are tendered through this procedure. This procedure is different from the previous one due to the fact that the tender process is split into two distinct stages: the stage of selecting interested contractors, and the stage in which the pre-selected contractors are invited for tender. Therefore, a better name for this procedure would be the procedure with pre-selection. However, in this chapter we stick to the original name. When discussing this subject, we will differentiate between the traditional government and public utilities.

For governmental institutions the minimum term for the notice amounts to 37 days, to be calculated from the day that the notice has been sent to

TED. The contracting authority invites the selected companies to express their interest for tender. The minimum number of market parties to be selected needs to be at least five, matching the pre-qualification criteria that has been published by the contracting authority.

The contracting authority needs to provide 40 days at least to the pre-selected contractors to submit their bids, again to be calculated from the day that the invitation to bid has been published. When a prior information notice has been made, this term can be reduced to just 36 days.

As in the case of the public procedure, the contracting authority can reduce the term for submitting the actual bids by five days, when submitting all tender documents electronically to interested market parties. However, the minimum term should not be shorter than 22 days.

In case of urgency (not to be confused with extreme urgency), the contracting authority may go for a shorter reaction time. The time for pre-qualification of contractors then may be only 15 days, whereas the time needed to solicit bids from the pre-selected contractors may be reduced to a mere 10 days. The urgency may, however, not be related to circumstances with the contracting authority itself. The urgency may be that, after awarding a contract to a specific contractor, the contractor cannot deliver. In such cases, the contracting authority may go for a second, speedier, tender process. Whatever the reason, the contracting authority should mention the background for reducing the reaction times in its notice. Urgency only is acknowledged in the case of the non-public procedure. The public procedure does not have any specific arrangements for this.

The terms for public utilities are as follows: for the stage of pre-selecting contractors, the term of 37 days may be reduced to 22 days minimum; for the tender stage, the minimum term is 37 days. However, in consultation with market parties, this term may be reduced. In the case that the contracting authority and market parties do not come to an arrangement, the legal minimum term will amount to at least 24 days.

- *Competitive dialogue.* The competitive dialogue is a special procedure, which may be applied by governmental institutions in specific circumstances and for very complex projects. It is not relevant for the public utilities sector. A project is considered to be very complex when a contracting authority is not able to come up with a detailed specification and when the legal and financial terms and conditions of the project cannot be defined. In such cases, the competitive dialogue may be used. The procedure is as follows. First, just like the restricted procedure, a pre-selection of qualified market parties is made. This should result in at least three parties being interested in and qualified for the assignment. Next, these parties are consulted on the solutions that best fit the functional specifications that have been submitted by the contracting authority. The dialogue ends when the contracting authority has selected the best possible solution that was presented by one of the market parties. Next, the contracting authority will put a detailed specification together and invite comprehensive bids from the market parties that were solicited earlier. Bids are evaluated by the contracting authority based on the most economic offer (rather than price only). Just like the open and the restricted procedures, it is strictly forbidden to negotiate on the final arrangements.

The minimum term for pre-qualification of market parties amounts to 37 days. This term may be reduced to 30 days if the notice is made electronically. For obtaining the bids and final offers, no minimum terms are mentioned in the European regulations.

- *Negotiation procedure.* The negotiation procedure can only be followed in special circumstances. Here, the contracting authority can negotiate face-to-face with market parties about the contents, execution and costs related to the contract. The negotiation procedure can be used with or without (pre) announcement. The negotiation procedure with prior publication of a contract notice starts with a pre-selection of interested and qualified market parties. The term for this is 37 days minimum. Again this term may be reduced by seven days if all documentation is sent electronically. In situations of urgency, the selection may be reduced to 15 days or 10 days when the notice is made electronically. For obtaining bids from contractors, no minimum terms are stipulated in the directives. These only state that the term should be reasonable for contractors to prepare their bids.

For the public utility sector, only minimum terms apply for the selection stage. This term needs to be 20 days minimum. If the notice is made electronically, this period may be reduced to 15 days. Also here, no minimum term is stated for soliciting the bids from the contractors involved.

The negotiation procedure with a contract notice can be applied by contracting authorities only in very specific cases. The four most important cases are:

- When, in the case of a public or non-public procedure or competitive dialogue, irregular bids by suppliers have been obtained. This may apply to situations in which contractors obtrusively have made price agreements with each other.

- When the bids that have been solicited are in fact unacceptable. This may be the case when the prices that have been offered are way off the available budget or when the offers that have been made simply do not meet the minimal requirements.
- When the cost related to executing the assignment cannot be estimated in whatever way due to unforeseen circumstances. This may be the case when restoration of historical buildings or old paintings is needed. In such cases, the contracting authority may engage in face-to-face discussions with the limited number of experts that are available.
- When it is impossible to specify the work to be conducted and the product to be delivered in a fair level of detail. This may apply to specific research assignments or when consulting support is needed for major personnel restructuring.

These limitations do not apply to the public utilities sector.

As the name already suggests, the negotiation procedure without a contract notice does not need to be published. The contracting authority may approach contractors independently to obtain their ideas and bids. Some of the situations where this very special procedure may be used are:

- When the contracting authority did not receive any bids, or bids that were totally unsuitable.
- In situations where only one specific contractor is available, due to technical or artistic reasons, or due to exclusive rights that may relate to the product or service to be acquired. In such cases the contracting authority needs to demonstrate and prove that only one contractor was available and that only one way of working was possible.
- Extreme urgency due to unforeseen circumstances that cannot be ascribed to the contracting authority. Examples here are the acquisition of supplies needed in case of war or natural disasters (such as a wildfire or a flood).
- In the case of additional delivery of supplies and services, that could not have been foreseen in the original contract, but which due to unforeseen circumstances are necessary.

For both negotiation procedures, the general principles, discussed in Section 6.1, also apply. In all cases, the contracting authority should publish which party the contract was awarded to through TED.

In the case that the contracting authority decides to go for the competitive dialogue or the negotiation procedure, it should explain its decision in the procurement dossier.

- *Design contest.* The design contest is a procedure that is used to obtain a plan or a design based on competition among expert parties. The design is judged by a professional jury. Market parties may be rewarded in terms of a monetary price or otherwise. The design contest is used for architectural work, but also for the design of complex ICT architectures. It may also be used for procurement projects that require a high degree of innovation. Contracting authorities are free to orchestrate a design contest however they wish. It is not necessary to explain their motivations. There are no specific terms, i.e. lead times, that one needs to consider.

6.4. Implications for contractors

The previous paragraphs show that public tendering is a highly complex issue, due to its detailed and complex legislation. Although the sanctions for not following up on European public procurement law and directives are weak, public institutions cannot escape from them. Chances for success in obtaining jobs from the government increase when contractors acknowledge the following:

Pre-contractual stage

- Active lobbying may pay off when the contractor is able to influence the specifications, the procurement procedure that will be used, the contractor selection criteria and more particularly, the contract model that will be applied by a public institution. The contract model should be in line with the allocation of risks and responsibilities of the parties involved. This kind of lobbying may be against the European Directives on Public Procurement. Contractors, therefore, have to operate carefully.
- Contractors should have a thorough knowledge of the public procurement procedures that are used most, i.e. the open procedure and the restricted procedure. It is important to acknowledge the minimum response times that are allowed according to these procedures. This is a specific task for the contractor's tender manager.
- Contractors should be keen on the principles that need to be followed by public institutions. Once the tender process has started no changes in scope and requirements can be made unless approved by all market partners. Contractors should keep an eye on the level playing field, which needs to be created by public institutions. All contractors should receive the same information at the same time. No single contractor may be put in an advantageous position by the public institution.

- Specifications and requirements should be checked regarding specific brand or supplier-specific characteristics, as these will limit competition. Vice versa, it is unrealistic to expect that a public institution will integrate a contractor-specific solution in its technical package.
- Contractors need to be informed about the criteria and rating schedules, which will be used by the public institution to pre-select contractors and evaluate the bids. During the tender process, criteria and weighting factors may not be changed anymore.
- Contractors should be prepared to deal with an army of consultants and legal counsels, which are hired by the client to do the job and to minimize risk. As these consultants and counselors usually work on hourly rates, they will extend the discussions where they can.
- Keep on asking questions. As employers will need to respect fair play and a level playing field in their dealing with contractors, individual contractors can create an advantage through asking more questions than others, in order to be better informed about requirements and stakeholder interests.

Contractual stage

- In order to be pre-selected, contractors need to meet the information needs of the public institution as communicated in its tender documents. The contractor needs to abide by the specified response times. Being five minutes overdue in delivery will mean that all your work will be put aside.
- Bids should reflect all technical, quality, maintenance and commercial requirements as communicated in the tender documents. Not meeting these requirements will mean that your offer will be put aside. In case of options or alternative solutions, these can be included next to the original offer, without the expectation that the contracting authority will look at them.
- Most public procurement procedures do not allow for negotiation after the tender. As this happens all the time, the contractor could enforce its negotiation position by keeping a detailed diary of their discussions with the prospective client. This information may be used to put the client under pressure, when necessary.
- If the contractor did not get the job, he should review the process. Based upon his detailed dairies and reports, he should assess the weaknesses of the client's procedure and assess whether a case could be brought to court for compensation. Here, the so-called Alcatel response time applies, which holds that contractors who did not win the tender have 15 days to

formally react against the employer's decision to award the contract to the most favored party.
- The contractor should not mobilize for the work, unless it has obtained a contract signed by the customer.

Post-contractual stage

- When the contract is signed, the contractor can mobilize for the start-up of the work. This should be done only after all permits have been gained.[7]
- Any scope change or change of technical requirements and specifications should be checked and the cost consequences identified and agreed before implementing them.
- Contractors should have frequent face-to-face meetings with the client and/or its engineering representative, given the often fast-changing political landscape and client environment.
- Contractors need to take care of a flawless tracing and tracking of all their activities and those of their subcontractors and suppliers in order to be able to mitigate and/or share the burden of claims, when issued by the client.
- Contractors should keep an eye on the roles and responsibilities of the client, given the scope of the contract that was signed. In the case of an EPC contract, the client should demonstrate a hands-off attitude and not interfere in the contractor's design and project execution. If this happens, the contractor should stipulate its role, and point out consequences for the client.

6.5. Summary and conclusions

This chapter has provided an inside picture of the procurement policies and practices of governmental institutions. Due to the European treaty, member countries and European institutions are not free in the way they do business with contractors. European procurement law and directives prescribe how to act in specifying contractors' work, how to pre-select contractors, how to award business and how to engage in a contractual relationship. In doing so, public authorities should acknowledge the four basic principles, which underlie European procurement law, as noted above (non-discrimination, equality, transparency and proportionality).

---

[7]This is only true for those works for which permits need to be obtained. Many works can be started without permits.

The legal framework for public procurement is partly European, and partly international. The European framework consists of specific public procurement laws and directives for supplies, works and services. The international legal framework consists of the GPA, which opens up the public procurement market within the European community for suppliers and contractors of countries that are covered by it. Both frameworks are relevant for all governmental institutions, and for companies that conduct work on behalf of those institutions. Apart from the procedures to be followed, they also prescribe what threshold levels to take into account when engaging in a contract with an external party.

In this chapter, we described five European procurement procedures. These procedures differ in the way supply markets are informed about future jobs and orders, the way in which suppliers are selected and the bids evaluated and awarded. Different response times relate to these procedures. Detailed knowledge of these procedures and response times may put contractors in an advantageous position. As these procedures are very formal, the contractor needs to keep detailed records both during the pre-contractual stage and the post-contractual stage. Given the many changes in the political landscape during the course of the project, frequent face-to-face contact with the client and its engineering representative is recommended.

Chapter 7

Downstream Contracting: Managing Suppliers and Subcontractors

7.1. Case — The subcontracted steel piles

Some years ago, a leading international contractor acquired a major offshore project to build 80 windmills in the North Sea. The objective of the project was to enable the country to meet its goals in reducing its carbon footprint. The wind-energy park that was conceived should enable the country to do so. A main contractor was selected for the design and construction of the project. After completion of the park, it would be operated by a national energy company.

A consortium was formed with some major contractors, who would provide for the cable to the mainland, the rotor blades and the turbines. The main contractor would provide all foundations, the necessary infrastructure and the steel piles for the windmills. As the steel made up a significant part of the main contractor's total project budget, steel requirements were contracted as soon as the contract with the employer was signed. The procurement manager was able to negotiate a fair price for the total steel volume and was able to secure sufficient production capacity for bending and welding activities. However, the contract stipulated that the main contractor would pay its subcontractor three months in advance through pre-payments.

After delivery of the first piles, the supply from the subcontractor came to a sudden stop. The reason was its financial situation. Soon it appeared that the subcontractor was not able to pay for salaries and outstanding invoices. As a result, it declared bankruptcy. The local court nominated a trustee, who took over the management of the subcontractor. The main contractor immediately contacted the trustee and urged the handover of the steel piles that were already paid for. However, the trustee did not comply with this request. He simply argued that in order to get the piles delivered, the main contractor first would have to make new payments for them.

Figure 7.1. Offshore wind park.

This case illustrates what may happen if agreements with subcontractors have not been made carefully. As in any other business, the construction industry is subject to the business cycle. In the case of economic growth, companies need to be able to speed up quickly; in an economic downturn, companies need to scale back their activities in a flexible manner. Bankruptcies are a frequent phenomenon in the construction industry, and some companies cannot escape from this. Therefore, procurement professionals in the construction industry should be always on guard. The careful supplier-selection process would have two stages: one is to pre-qualify and pre-select suppliers. At this stage, the financial situation of the supplier should be checked. Only after a careful pre-qualification procedure should the next step in the selection process be made: selecting the best offer from the pre-selected suppliers and/or subcontractors.

In this case example, no payments should have been made without having received either a bank guarantee or a formal statement, signed by the subcontractor, that the property — the specific set of piles — was transferred to the main contractor. Next, the statement should secure that the piles concerned were put aside from the company's main stock and labeled with the name of the subcontractor. In this way, the main contractor could have prevented the major supply problems that it was now suffering from.

This chapter describes the essentials of procurement and subcontracting for the offshore and construction industry. This is often referred to as downstream contracting. As some materials' suppliers and subcontractors will be on the critical path in the project planning, these contacts should be managed with great care. Suppliers and subcontractors are not equally important to contractors. Therefore we will propose a differentiated way of dealing with these important business partners. Before doing so, we provide some important definitions and concepts. Next, we will discuss the essentials of the procurement process and how to contract for materials and subcontracts.

7.2. Downstream contracting: definitions[1]

Today, large construction projects in the offshore industry cannot be dealt with by one company only. The expertise that is needed, the complexity of the project activities and the uncertainty and risk that are related to these kinds of projects warrant close cooperation among all partners of the value chain. This becomes visible in the cost structure of projects (see Figure 7.2). The majority of project cost is related to materials and subcontracts, usually ranging in a ratio of 1 : 2 to 1 : 3. To put this in other words, for every employee on the main contractor's payroll, two or three people are paid for at the suppliers' and subcontractors' end. The suppliers and subcontractors do not only determine the project cost, but also the project's profitability.

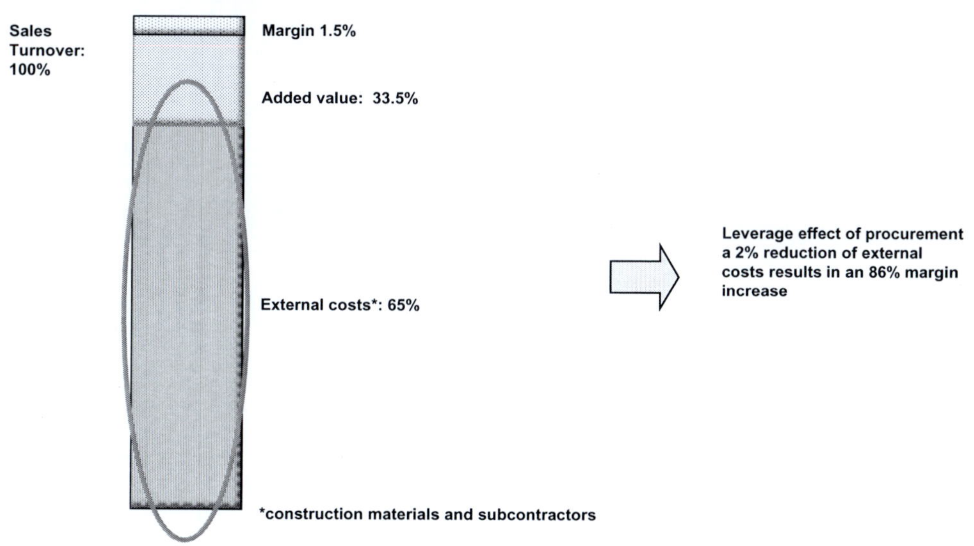

Figure 7.2. Typical cost structure of a main contractor.

[1] Part of this section is derived from A.J. Van Weele (2010), *Purchasing and Supply Chain Management*. London: Cengage, pp. 8–10.

From the example in Figure 7.2 it can be concluded that a 2% reduction of all external costs would result in an 86% increase of the company's profitability. This explains why, in the construction industry, strong price orientation exists in the dealings and negotiations with external partners. However, this price orientation may work to the detriment of the quality of the project, project schedule and targeted total cost of ownership. As we explained in Chapter 1, a strong price orientation may foster a culture of opportunism and deceit. This is not only true in the relationship between the employer and main contractor; it also holds for the relationship between the main contractor and his many materials suppliers and subcontractors.

The impact of suppliers and subcontractors on the project profitability is only one part of the story. The other part of the story is that, based upon Figure 7.3, these suppliers and subcontractors are also responsible for 65% of the employer's satisfaction with the work, project delivery and the project's carbon footprint. Next, suppliers and subcontractors will be responsible for about 65% of the innovation capability that could be mobilized to improve the project value to the employer. It goes without saying that if suppliers are squeezed by their main contractors, their willingness to participate in actions to improve project solutions or project processes will be minimal.

This explains why procurement professionals will be careful in their dealings with their suppliers and subcontractors, and why a differentiated approach towards managing relationships with external partners is warranted.

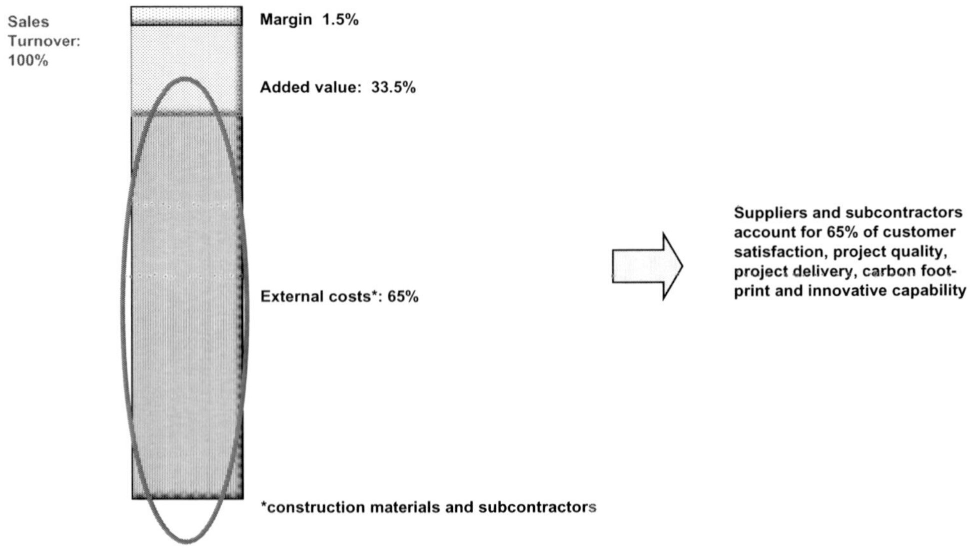

Figure 7.3. Supply chain partner effects on project performance.

The purchasing function traditionally encompasses the process of buying. It involves determining the need, selecting the supplier, arriving at a proper price, specifying terms and conditions, issuing the contract or order and following up to ensure proper delivery. In the old days it was argued that the purchasing function should also include obtaining the proper equipment, materials, supplies and services of the right quality, in the right quantity, at the right price and from the right source. In this description, the purchasing function is regarded predominantly as an operational activity.

In practice, as well as in the literature, many terms and concepts are now used in the area of purchasing. However, no agreement exists about the definition of these terms. Terms like procurement, purchasing, supply and supply-chain management are used interchangeably.

Here we define purchasing as:

> The management of the company's external resources in such a way that the supply of all goods, services, capabilities and knowledge which are necessary for running, maintaining and managing the company's primary and support activities is secured at the most favorable conditions.

The purchasing function in this definition specifically covers activities aimed at:

- Determining the specification (in terms of required quality and quantities) of the goods and services that need to be bought.
- Selecting the most suitable supplier and developing procedures and routines to select the best supplier.
- Preparing and conducting negotiations with the supplier in order to establish an agreement and to write up the contract.
- Placing the order with the selected supplier and/or to develop efficient purchase order and handling systems.
- Monitoring and control of the order in order to secure supply (expediting).
- Follow up and evaluation (settling claims, keeping product and supplier files up-to-date, supplier rating and supplier ranking).

Figure 7.4 schematically illustrates the main activities of the purchasing function. It shows that all these activities are closely interrelated. This picture is referred to as the purchasing process model.

The purchasing function does not include the responsibility for materials requirements planning, materials scheduling, inventory management, incoming inspection and quality control. However, in order to be effective,

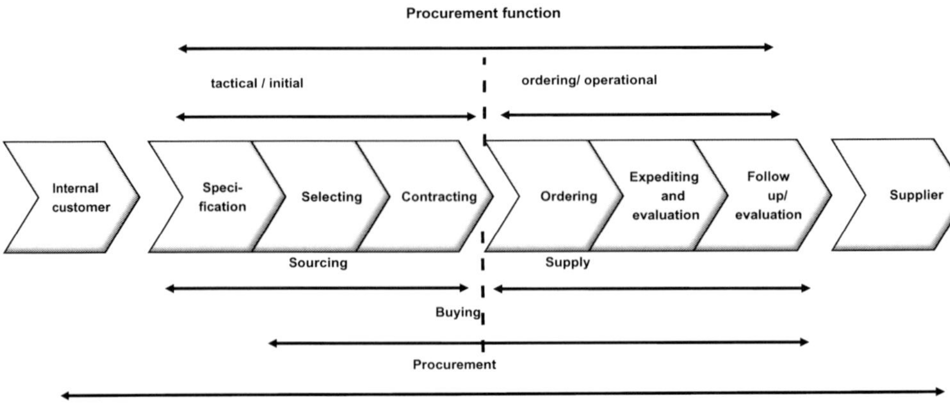

Figure 7.4. Purchasing process model and terms.

purchasing operations should be closely linked and interrelated to these materials activities. A purchasing manager should support each of the six activities mentioned above. However, this does not necessarily imply that all these activities should be conducted by the purchasing department.

The scope of purchasing covers all activities for which the company receives an invoice from outside parties. Hence, the scope of purchasing includes inter-company business, counter-trade arrangements, hiring of temporary personnel from outside agencies and contracting for advertising. Usually, many of the activities for which the company might receive invoices from suppliers may be arranged for without interference from the purchasing department. Therefore the scope of the purchasing function is usually much broader than that of the purchasing department.

The term "ordering" refers to the placing of purchase orders at a supplier against previously arranged conditions. Furthermore, this term will be used when purchase orders are placed directly, without questioning the supplier's conditions and without sufficient supplier market testing. Call-off orders fall into this category, as telephone orders for products bought from a supplier catalog. Ordering is considered to be a part of the purchasing process. In fact, it relates to the last three steps of the purchasing process. The use of the term "tactical purchasing" refers to the first three steps.

Purchasing differs from buying and ordering in two ways. While specifications may be a given when ordering and buying, these specifications are challenged when it comes to purchasing. In that case, discussion may start about the degree to which the specifications are really fit for purpose. Features that are not necessary for meeting the function that the product needs to fulfill are skipped. This often leads to a situation where an (expensive) supplier-branded product is replaced by an identical product from a lesser-known supplier. Another difference is that purchasing relates to finding the best possible supplier, based upon a broad supplier market definition.

In the construction industry, usually the term procurement is preferred over purchasing.[2] As seen from Figure 7.4, procurement is a somewhat broader term. It includes all activities required in order to get the product from the supplier to its final destination. It encompasses the purchasing function, stores, traffic and transportation, incoming inspection, quality control and assurance. Some firms also consider salvage and recycling (as they are related to materials) as a part of procurement.

To summarize: procurement is concerned with the management of the external resources of a company, based upon its articulated business requirements. It covers all activities for which companies receive an invoice. Hence, a differentiation must be made between the procurement department and the procurement function.

7.3. Purchasing process and procedures

The procurement process model shows the interconnectedness of all procurement-related activities. Each of the different steps in the model should be treated with great care in order to get the best possible performance from suppliers. Many quality and delivery problems related to supplied materials and services can be traced back to either insufficient specifications and requirements, the wrong supplier selection or a wrong contract model that has been applied in the relationship with the supplier. Especially in a project environment, where the repetitiveness of supply activities is low, a professional approach on how to apply the procurement process model is crucial.

Here, we describe what activities to take into account for each step of the procurement process model:

- *Specifications.* In projects, specifications can be defined at different levels of abstraction. Here we differentiate between:
    - *Functional specifications.* These are often provided by the employer and relate to the functionality of the work to be delivered. An example is an assignment to design and construct a road that should accommodate 5,000 vehicles per hour, 24 hours per day, and 365 days per year, without any maintenance, during a period of five years. Functional

[2] In the remainder of this book we will use the term "procurement".

specifications are common in Design and Construct and EPC contracts.

- ○ *Design specifications.* Here, the contractor is provided with the global design outlining the general features (length, breadth, number of layers, foundation) of the road to be constructed. However, based upon this information, a detailed design, including a detailed budget estimate, needs to be prepared by the contractor.
- ○ *Technical specifications.* Here, the employer or the employer's engineer provides detailed technical instructions on how the road should look and how the road should be constructed. Technical specifications are common in Construct contracts. Normally, the employer already has a detailed cost estimate against which the contractor's budget will be compared.

- *Supplier selection.* The specifications will largely define the qualifications and capabilities of future suppliers. When a Design and Construct contract is to be used, future contractors clearly should have advanced engineering capabilities and references. This is less true for a Construct contract. Supply selection usually encompasses two important steps, i.e. pre-qualification and bid award.
  - ○ *Supplier pre-qualification.* In the pre-qualification stage, suppliers are invited to register based upon a general description of the work. Detailed checklists covering the capabilities and the references of the suppliers need to be filled in. It is not uncommon at this stage to request general information about rates and tariffs for particular activities. Having obtained this information, the procurement specialist will bring down the long list of suppliers to a shortlist. The shortlisted suppliers will be invited for a bid to tender.
  - ○ *Invitation to bid.*[3] Bidding procedures can be complex and demanding. Criteria that will be used to do bid evaluation can be submitted or not to suppliers prior to the award. Procurement professionals may decide to use electronic auctions or not. Having obtained the bids, these are compared and the best offer is chosen (in the construction industry, this is usually the offer with the lowest price).
- *Contract negotiation and closure.* Usually, contract negotiation starts with the preferred supplier, keeping the next best in reserve. Contract negotiations are again complex and time-consuming, since many internal stakeholders will be involved. The contract manager will support the project

[3] Also referred to as Request for Proposal (RFP) or Request for Quotation (RFQ).

manager and will act as liaison between him and the specialist legal counsels of the firm. There may be different versions of the contract documents before a final arrangement is made. Contract documents may be based on standard, international contracts such as LOGIC, FIDIC, UAVGC (NL) or others. The type of work to be accomplished and the type of relationship with the supplier usually determine what type of contract to use.

- *Ordering.* When the contract is agreed, materials and services then need to be ordered from the supplier or subcontractor. As project schedules can change many times, this activity usually is done at the project level. It is important to refer to the contract number in every order that is submitted. Every purchase order has a unique purchase-order number, to which all other delivery documents and invoices need to refer. In this way, one obtains a closed loop which enables "three way matching": when the invoice matches the delivery document — which specifies the number of products to be delivered, the time for delivery and the quality, all of which needs to be in line with the original purchase order — the payment to the supplier can be made. Keeping record of all documents is quite a challenge, given the variety of products and services that are delivered and the number of parties involved. This calls for a professional procurement and supply administration at the project level. In case actual performance delivery deviates with the contract, the project manager immediately needs to mobilize the contract manager or procurement professional.
- *Expediting.* Expediting is a typical procurement job, which is related to following up on actual deliveries made by suppliers and subcontractors. The prime task is to prevent late deliveries and quality problems from suppliers. Therefore, critical parts and suppliers are followed up in advance by follow-up reports, audits or even supplier visits. Part of expediting is quantity surveying, where deliveries of suppliers are closely monitored in terms of quantity and quality. Next, the quantities that are actually consumed in the project are compared with the quantities that are invoiced by the supplier. Given the large amounts of money that are spent on materials and subcontractors, a professional expediter or quantity surveyor is worth his weight in gold.
- *Evaluation and follow up.* Even when the project is finished, the work is not yet done. It is important to reflect on the actual supplier performance during the entire project. Which suppliers performed well, which suppliers performed badly? Actual supplier performance should be monitored and registered in order to feed the company's supplier-performance management system. This information will help the company qualify and select even better suppliers for future projects. Based upon their

actual performance, suppliers are ranked as A, B and C suppliers. This ranking may help the company in future projects to identify quickly the best performing suppliers.

7.4. Portfolio management and supplier segmentation[4]

Not all suppliers are equally important for a project or firm. Some are more important and critical than others. This is why strategic suppliers need to be dealt with differently than routine suppliers. When designing differentiated supplier strategies, the portfolio approach originally suggested by Kraljic (1983)[5] is recommended. Crucial in developing procurement and supply strategies is the issue of influencing the balance of power between the company and its key suppliers. The balance of power should preferably be in favour of the main contractor. Obviously, when a company is too dependent on a supplier, something should be done to change this situation. In developing effective supplier strategies, the following questions may be helpful:

- Does the present procurement strategy support your business and project objectives and does it meet your company's long-term interests? Are opportunities for benefiting from synergies between divisions/business units fully exploited, for example, by joint contracting for common project materials and services?
- What is the balance of power between your company and your major suppliers? For which products/materials does the company have a dominant position in the supply market and for which products/materials is the company dependent on one single supplier?
- Are the strategic products and services sourced from the best-in-class suppliers? To what extent have the procurement requirements and volumes been evenly spread over several suppliers and geographic regions?
- What difficulties or interruptions in supply can be expected in the near future and how can these problems influence the profit and growth objectives of your company?

---

[4] This paragraph has been based upon A.J. Van Weele (2010), *Purchasing and Supply Chain Management.* London: Cengage, pp. 194–202.

[5] P. Kraljic (1983), Purchasing must become supply management, *Harvard Business Review*, September/October, pp. 109–117.

- What opportunities exist for collaboration with suppliers with regard to product development, quality improvement, lead-time reduction and cost reduction? Are these opportunities sufficiently being used?

An analysis of the company's procurement spend per category and its supplier base in general will show that the 20—80 rule applies: 20% of the products and suppliers will represent about 80% of procurement turnover. This analysis is a first step in identifying the company's strategic commodities and suppliers. It also reveals the often huge number of small expense items and small suppliers, who in general are responsible for 80% of the company's internal handling costs. After this step the analysis can be refined using Kraljic's procurement product portfolio approach. In this approach, the procurement turnover and the supplier base are analyzed based on two variables:

- *Procurement's impact on the company's bottom line* — the profit impact of a given supply item measured against criteria such as cost of materials, total costs, volume purchased, percentage of total purchase cost or impact on product quality or business growth. The higher the volume or amount of money involved, the higher the financial impact of procurement on the bottom line.
- *Supply risk* — this is measured against criteria such as short-term and long-term availability, number of potential suppliers, cost of changing a supplier, competitive structure in supply markets, make-or-buy opportunities, storage risks and substitution possibilities. Sourcing a product from just one supplier without an alternative source of supply represents a high supply risk. Supply risk is low when a (standard) product can be sourced from many suppliers, while so-called switching costs are low.

The combination of these variables yields a two-dimensional matrix with four quadrants; these represent the product groups or suppliers, each offering different interests to the company (see Figure 7.5).

- *Strategic products.* These are high-tech, high-volume products, which are often supplied to customer specification. Only one source of supply is available, which cannot be changed in the short term without incurring considerable costs. Usually this type of product represents a high share in the cost price of the end product. Examples are engines and gearboxes for automobile manufacturers, turbines for the chemical industry and bottling equipment for breweries. Communication and interaction between subcontractor and supplier are usually intensive, and, as they relate to different aspects of the relationship, complex.

- *Leverage products.* In general, these are the products that can be obtained from various suppliers at standard quality grades. They represent a relatively large share of the end product's cost price. A small change in price has a relatively strong effect on the cost price of the end product. This is the reason why the buyer exerts aggressive sourcing and tendering among a small sample of pre-qualified suppliers. Using e-auctions may be useful here to arrive at competitive prices in an efficient way. Examples are bulk chemicals, steel and aluminium profiles, packaging, steel plate, raw materials and standard semi-manufactured commodities.

Characteristic for this situation is that the contractor has freedom of choice regarding his selection of suppliers. There are various suppliers and the "switching costs" are low. Abuse of this power, however, can lead to

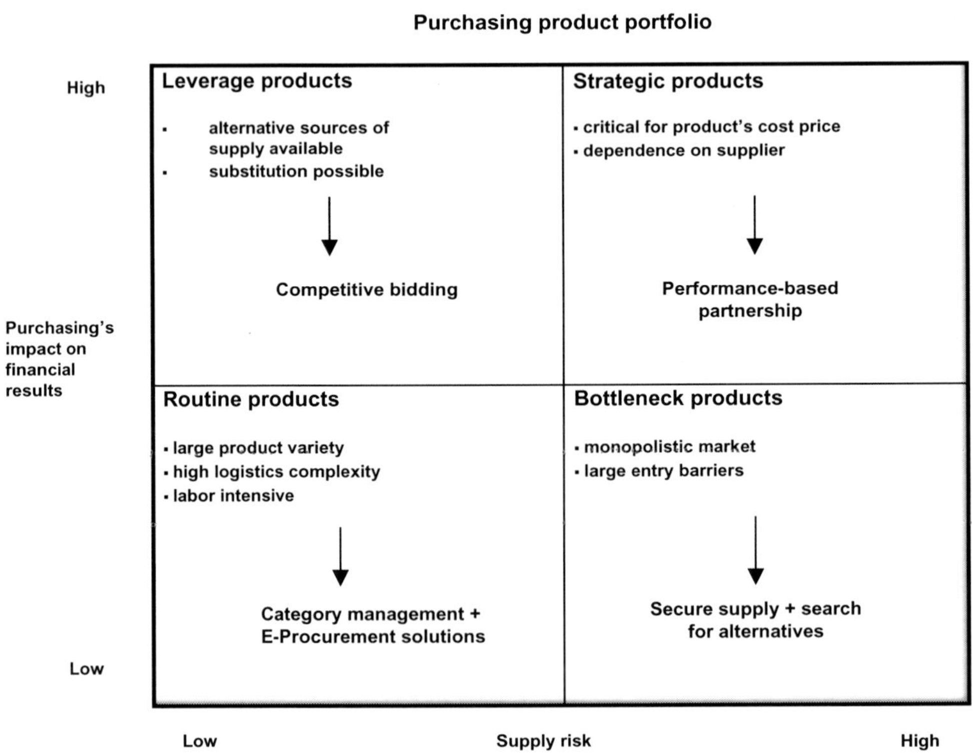

Figure 7.5. Purchasing product portfolio.

cooperation among the suppliers. Cartels and price agreements, though forbidden under EC law, may develop in these situations, shifting the commodity to the right side of the matrix.

- *Bottleneck products.* These items represent relatively limited value in terms of money, but they are vulnerable in regard to their supply. They can only be obtained from one supplier. Examples are specialist moldings, specialist technical services, engineering software programs and spare parts for earth moving equipment and machines (e.g. cutter teeth and adapters for dredgers). In general, the supplier is dominant in the relationship with the contractor, which may result in high prices, long delivery times and average technical service.
- *Routine products.* These products produce few technical or commercial problems from a procurement point of view. They usually have a small value per item and there are many alternative suppliers. In practice, most items fall into this category; examples are cleaning materials, office supplies, maintenance supplies, fasteners, hand tooling, safety products, etc.

The problem with this group of products is that the handling often costs more money than the value of the products itself. Usually, 80% of the time and energy of procurement is used for these products; this is a reason why procurement is often seen as an administrative job. The procurement of these normal products should be organized efficiently, in order to spare time for the other, more interesting products.

Depending on the product segment of the portfolio, the procurement strategy will differ. The emphasis should lie with the strategic and leverage products. The work related to normal products has to be limited as much as possible.

The procurement product portfolio provides the opportunity to identify and analyze the company's risks in its procurement markets. This is illustrated below in Figure 7.5.

For every segment of the portfolio a different strategy is possible. The strategies are:

- *Performance-based partnership.* Strategic products together with the leverage products make up 80% of total turnover. Depending on the relative power position of the different parties involved, the procurement policy for strategic products will be aimed at partnership or collaboration. The goal is to create mutual participation based on pre-planned and mutually agreed cost and operational improvement targets. A relationship based on "open costing" is preferred. With these partner suppliers, efficiency programs are developed to achieve cost reduction, quality improvement, process improvement and improved product development. Such cooperation can, in the end, lead to the fading of borders between the different companies. An essential aspect of this partnership strategy is the thorough selection of the supplier-partner. Early in the development, the market is scanned for the "best-in-class" suppliers. These suppliers are screened on their references, financial stability, production capacities, the quality of their logistics and quality systems, and, of course, their research and development and engineering capabilities.

- *Competitive bidding.* For leverage products a procurement policy based on the principle of competitive bidding or tendering will be pursued. Since the suppliers and products are basically interchangeable, there will be, as a rule, no long-term supply contracts. Long-term contracts and annual agreements will be combined with "spot" procurement. In most cases, buyers will adopt a multiple sourcing strategy. Buying at a minimum price while maintaining the required quality level and continuity of supply will take priority. Small savings (small in terms of percentages) represent a large sum of money. This justifies an active market scanning through continuous market and supply research. Regularly, outsiders will be introduced so as to avoid price arrangements between the present suppliers.
- *Securing continuity of supply.* The procurement policy concerning bottleneck products has focused on securing continuity of supply, if necessary at additional cost. At the same time, activities are conducted aimed at reducing the dependence on these suppliers. This is done by developing alternative products and finding alternative suppliers. However, the costs involved in these actions (for example, tests in laboratories) often exceed the cost savings obtained, which is why management often has difficulty in approving this type of action. A risk analysis to determine the most important bottleneck items in the short-, middle- and long-term supply is necessary. Based on this analysis, contingency plans are made. With contingency planning, measures are prepared in case one of the established risks actually occurs. Examples of measures are consigned stock agreements aimed at keeping the stock of the materials concerned at the supplier's or the company's own premises, preparing alternative modes of transportation and actively investigating product alternatives.

- *Category management and e-procurement solutions.* For reasons mentioned earlier, routine, MRO products require a procurement strategy that is aimed at reducing administrative and logistic complexity. Buyers will have to work out simple but efficient ordering and administrative routines with the pre-selected suppliers in the form of electronic catalogs from which employees can order directly. A few aspects relevant to the policy for these products are: standardizing the product assortment (article catalog), reducing the number of suppliers, pursuing systems contracts for categories of MRO items (office supplies, technical maintenance products, cleaning products, catering, etc.), working with electronic catalogs, ordering through Internet technology, electronic payment or using the Procurement Card. A final example is to contract out the procurement of these articles to specialized procurement offices and/or trading houses.

The use of the procurement portfolio leads to a differentiated procurement strategy. It points out that suppliers represent a different interest for a company.

To conclude this section, we should discuss the limitations of using the purchasing portfolio. From practice, we have observed that this approach may have an important shortcoming. If a product is positioned for the buyer in the strategic segment of his purchasing portfolio, this does not necessarily imply that this product is also of strategic relevance to the supplier involved. In order to develop effective collaboration, a good fit between the position of the product in the buyer's purchasing portfolio and the position of the product in the supplier's customer portfolio is necessary. Detailed knowledge and a good understanding of the dependence of both parties on each other may prevent disappointment. This is the reason why some companies have introduced the "Dutch Windmill" as an extension to their purchasing portfolio analysis (see Figure 7.6). This portfolio approach allows the buyer to mirror his view to the one used by the supplier. In general, combining both the buyer's portfolio approach and the supplier's customer portfolio approach leads to more realistic expectations and plans with regard to future buyer — seller collaboration. Based upon the Dutch Windmill, 16 buyer — seller relationships are possible, out of which probably one is suitable for long-term collaboration. In most cases the position of the buyer versus the seller will be different. In most business-to-business relationships, either the buyer or the seller will be dominant.

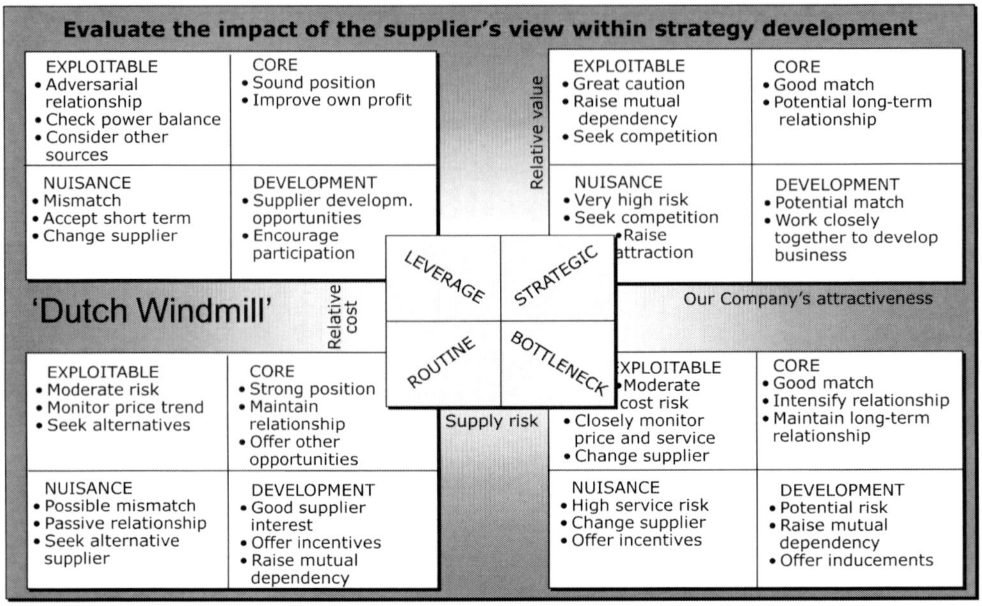

Figure 7.6. Dutch Windmill: analyzing buyer–seller interdependence. (Source: Purspective, 2002.)

7.5. Specific operational and legal problems related to procurement and subcontracting

This section describes some operational and legal problems that may occur in the relationship with materials suppliers and subcontractors.

Securing materials supply

A frequent problem that may jeopardize the project schedule is late delivery of materials and subcontractor services. The reasons for this may be many. In order to reduce the risk related to late deliveries, the following actions may be considered:

- Classify products and suppliers depending on how critical they are for the project. List the most critical products, services, suppliers and contractors.
- Assign a junior engineer to follow up on these critical products and external parties. Follow up should consist off up-front phone calls, e-mails, inspection reports, planning documents, etc., which would

secure timely supply. In special cases, site visits to the critical suppliers should be made.

- Provide incentives for those suppliers with 100% on-time delivery. Exert penalties for those suppliers that fail to do so. Using penalties in contracts would make sure that tight supplier capacity will be made available for your project. However, it should be realized that penalty-based contracts usually do not foster innovative thinking from suppliers and subcontractors.

Given the dependency of projects on suppliers and subcontractors, engaging a project-supply planner specifically for this job is recommended.

Back-to-back agreements

The widespread practice of playing off suppliers against each other should be avoided for critical supplies and suppliers. Especially in EPC and Design and Construct contracts, part of the responsibilities and liabilities that the main contractor has accepted should be transferred through back-to-back contracts to suppliers and subcontractors. This is especially recommended for suppliers that are on the critical path of the project. Incentives engaged in the main contract should be transferred to contracts with critical materials suppliers and subcontractors.

This is easier said than done, given the fact that after the main contract has been awarded, procurement professionals are assigned with the job of squeezing suppliers to the maximum to compensate for the price concessions that have been made to the employer in the final round of contract negotiations. However, project managers that fail to transfer incentives may suffer from a lack of goal alignment among the company's interests and the interests of the supplier and subcontractor.

Supplier bankruptcy

Certainly in projects with a long lead time, the financial status of key suppliers should be followed up regularly. If this is not done by the procurement organization at the company's headquarters, this should be done at the project level. Early warning indicators for financial problems are the supplier's willingness to provide large discounts in exchange for large pre-payments, its hesitation to provide for corporate guarantees or bank guarantees in case of pre-payment and hassles about all kinds of small cost items.

Pre-payments of any kind should be made against bank guarantees and/ or against statements that arrange the transfer of the legal title of materials from the supplier to the contractor. Next, as the case at the beginning of this chapter shows, the materials concerned should be stored separately from other materials and be labeled with the contractor's name. In this way, the project manager can avoid severe problems when lightning strikes.

Testing and delivery

Certainly in the construction industry, where negotiations are fierce, material deliveries and service deliveries should be followed up by detailed inspections. Materials that are delivered should be accompanied with technical and quality documentation, outlining the batch in which materials were produced, while identifying the major process parameters. When materials need to be shipped from faraway countries, quality reports can be sent for approval prior to shipment. However, the project manager should make sure that these quality reports relate to the batch in which the products to be delivered have actually have been produced (in some regions in China it is common to send a product sample or a quality report from batch A, while the products shipped come from batch B). Thus, the project manager should ensure that quality reports are made by independent auditors. These specialists of course cost money; however, their revenues clearly outweigh the investment.

Follow-up reports, quality reports, audit reports, site visits, etc., should be documented carefully as part of a professional project administration.

Payments and guarantees

Project managers should pay their suppliers and subcontractors on time, i.e. according to what has been agreed in the contract. They should avoid situations in which the financial administration pays according to its own insight. Nothing motivates a supplier or subcontractor more than timely payment! However, the type of work to be delivered might require scheduled payments. It is important to arrange these payments in line with the milestone payments that have been agreed in the main contract with the employer. Here, managing the cash flow of the project is of extreme importance. The project managers should see to a situation in which the money from the employer is received before the payments are made to suppliers and subcontractors. In doing so, he will contribute to reducing the company's working capital and, hence, reduce the loans needed from banks to finance the project.

A similar reasoning applies to guarantees. Supplier and subcontractor guarantees should not cover a period that is shorter than the guarantee period provided to the employer.

Dealing with claim situations by the employer (which are part of life and cannot be avoided) require a sound project administration, where the performance of suppliers and subcontractors can be tracked and traced. In many practical situations, part of the liability for claims could have been transferred by the main contractor to external partners; however, flaws in the project administration prevented the companies from doing so.

General procurement terms and conditions: the "battle of forms"

A common phenomenon in international trade is the battle of forms. Many project managers will recognize the following situation: company A sends out a purchase order for the delivery of materials, referring to its procurement terms and conditions, to supplier B. Supplier B responds by sending an order confirmation, referring to its sales terms and conditions. Company A confirms the message of supplier B, referring to its procurement terms and conditions. At delivery, company A needs to sign for delivery on the delivery document of supplier B, which refers to its sales terms and conditions. Supplier B sends an invoice referring to its sales terms and conditions. Question: what terms and conditions apply? Answer: it depends. On what? On the legal system of the parties involved. Under Dutch law, in general, the terms and conditions of the party that first sent a document to the other party will apply. Under UK law, the terms and conditions of the party that sent the last document will apply, while the other party (sometimes implicitly) accepted such terms and conditions. In some legal systems, none of the referred terms and conditions are applicable. This, by jurisprudence, is the case in Belgian and Italian law.

Under Dutch law, terms and conditions of the other party can only be deferred if, and only if, these have been clearly and formally discarded. Just referring to your own procurement terms and conditions will not be sufficient.

How to solve this issue? How to prevent lawyers from being the only ones who benefit from this argument? Our suggestion is to leave the matter for routine deliveries from routine suppliers that do not have a critical role in a project. However, for critical supplies and subcontractors, we recommend a tailored contract that is agreed among all parties involved. For such a specific, customized agreement, standard contracts can be used as a template.

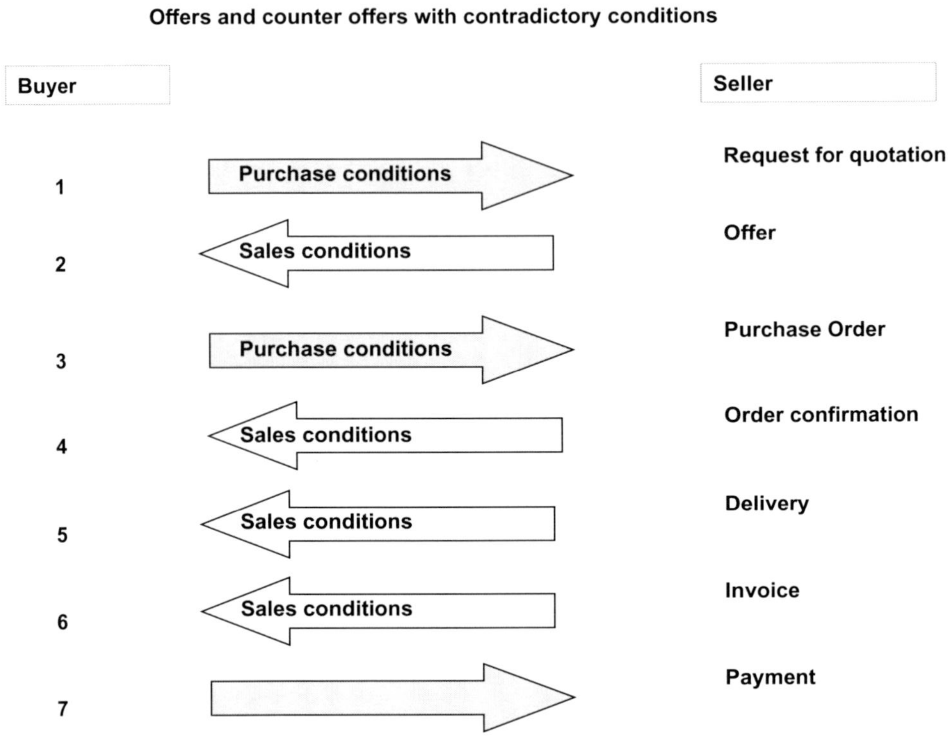

Figure 7.7. Seven steps between buyer and seller disputing terms and conditions. (Source: John van der Puil, 1986.[6])

7.6. Summary

As materials and subcontractors make up the majority of the project cost, procurement and subcontracting is a critical activity. Not only are materials suppliers and subcontractors crucial for the project's profitability, they also determine a large part of the company's social capital and its performance in the relationship with its customers. Since not all suppliers are of the same importance to the project, the differentiated approach in dealing with them is necessary.

In this chapter we have discussed different definitions. Important concepts are purchasing, procurement, supply-chain management, ordering and expediting. In the construction and engineering industries, procurement is the term most commonly used. It covers the range of activities from specifying the requirements that are needed from external parties, selecting reliable

[6] J. van der Puil (1986), *Inkoopvoorwaarden in de praktijk, 2nd edition.* Deventer: Kluwer, p. 183.

project partners and suppliers, negotiating and closing contracts with them, actual ordering of materials and services, expediting and quantity surveying, i.e. follow up on supplier activities, and performance measurement and evaluation. The scope of procurement covers the activities from the supplier up to the point of consumption of his products and services.

The procurement process model, which we have introduced in this chapter, shows the interrelatedness and interconnectedness of each of these activities. All of these activities should be executed with great care in order to secure superior supplier and subcontractor performance. A supplier and contractor can just be as good as the project manager for whom he works!

The purchasing product portfolio approach enables a differentiated supplier approach resulting in four basic supplier strategies. For strategic products and services, a performance-based partnership with external parties is suggested. For leverage products and services, a business-driven competitive approach is recommended. Routine items should be supplied using efficient supply mechanisms such as electronic ordering, electronic catalogs and electronic payment. Bottleneck items usually represent the largest risk to the project, since these can only be obtained from single, monopolistic sources of supply. With these items, the project manager should seek alternatives, both in terms of products and in terms of suppliers. Whatever sourcing strategy is going to be developed, it can only be effective if considered from both the buyer's and the seller's perspective. Here, the Dutch Windmill can be a useful concept.

Finally, we discussed a couple of frequently occurring problem areas in the relationship with suppliers and subcontractors. In order to prevent these problems, project managers need to be able to get the support from dedicated materials planners and project administrators. A sound project administration, allowing for an excellent tracing and tracking of the work of subcontractors and suppliers, can prevent a lot of problems, and can also provide a basis for handling claims. Given the amount of money and the complexity related to suppliers and subcontractors, the benefits of a professional procurement organization will clearly outweigh its cost.

Chapter 8

Contract Models in International Contracting

8.1. Case — The missing rescue boat

A European engineering contractor obtained an Engineering, Procurement and Construct (EPC) contract from an energy company for a sea-based compressor station to be located in the East Sea. At the contract negotiations stage, the contractor observed that a rescue boat facility was missing in the client's specifications. As the compressor station would operate primarily without staff, the energy company stated that such a facility would not be needed. The engineering contractor provided the detailed engineering, which was approved by the client, and constructed the compressor station within schedule and budget. In order to ship the station to its final destination, certificates were needed from the maritime authorities. Then, it appeared that a rescue boat facility was a prerequisite. The authorities involved referred to the detailed safety, environmental and technical requirements, which needed to be adhered to in this part of the maritime world. Since the engineering firm was a specialist in this business, it should have been aware of this requirement. Hence, a major problem emerged: without the approval of the maritime authorities, there was no handover of the project to the client. And without a rescue-boat facility, there was no approval from the authorities.

Therefore, the engineering firm had to negotiate with the energy company about the extra cost of the rescue boat facility (about €200,000). However, the energy company was of the opinion that, since an EPC contract was in place, the engineering firm was solely responsible for the compressor station's functionality and therefore had to pay for this facility.

Cases like this show the importance of understanding the scope, responsibilities and liabilities of different types of contracts that can be negotiated between partners in the contracting industry. In the case of an EPC contract, the engineering contractor commits to delivery of an installation which is fit for purpose and which is delivered Turnkey. Hence, the engineering contractor was liable for the rescue boat facility.

In this chapter we will discuss different contract models. In international contracting, a wide variety of contracts are used. Important contract models are Construct, Design and Construct (D&C), EPC/Turnkey, DFBM, and DBFMO contracts. We will discuss three important elements of contracts: (1) pricing mechanisms, (2) payment mechanisms and (3) risk allocation mechanisms. Finally, we will discuss the value and importance of standard contracts, which contract parties may use to facilitate their contract negotiations.

8.2. Pricing in contracts[1]

Before entering into the contract negotiations stage, the decision needs to be made by the client on how to pay the contractor for his work. Here, the employer has a choice, whether the work will be paid for based on a fixed-price basis, cost-reimbursable basis[2] or unit rate.

Fixed-price

When work is executed based on a fixed-price contract, the client orders the contractor to perform the required activities at a fixed price, and to have the work completed by a pre-determined date. The advantages of this pricing method are that the client knows exactly where he stands financially. Moreover, after completion of the work, there is no need for settlements because all risks are carried by the contractor. A final advantage is that the employer has certainty about the completion date.

As the price is fixed, it is in the contractor's interest to execute the work as efficiently as possible. The fixed price is an incentive to complete the work, or deliver the goods, as quickly as possible within the agreed terms.

---

[1] This section is partly derived from A.J. Van Weele (2010), *Purchasing and Supply Chain Management*. London: Cengage, pp. 34–42.

[2] Also referred to in literature as "Time and Materials" contracts.

A major disadvantage of this method is that it is difficult for the client to get insight into the contractor's cost breakdown if the client lacks expertise. Another disadvantage is in judging the price quoted by the contractor. This problem can be avoided by requesting quotations from more than one contractor. A third disadvantage of this manner of contracting is that it requires thorough preparation, and hence, a lot of time is needed to prepare the detailed specifications. The question is whether there is enough time to prepare a detailed specification and have a formal bidding procedure. Finally, one does not know in advance which contractor will turn out to be the best.

Cost-reimbursable

When the contractor is going to be paid according to a cost-reimbursable basis, the exact activities to be performed do not have to be known. The client orders the contractor to perform the required activities and/or to provide equipment at a pre-determined hourly rate, in combination with a pre-arranged percentage to cover the overhead costs. Next, a profit percentage is agreed. Settlement follows after completion of the activities based on the contractor's day reports, stating the man hours worked and the materials that have been consumed.

An advantage of this method is that the client can start the work immediately. Next, he obtains an exact picture of the cost structure of the work. Naturally, there are also some disadvantages related to this type of contracting. First, there is no pre-determined fixed price, so the buyer is not sure about the financial outcomes. Next, there is no incentive to work faster, as the contractor is reimbursed for every hour he works; every setback is charged to the client. This is why, in many reimbursable contracts, incentives for safe, accurate and speedy work are included. Furthermore, the client needs to follow up on the quantity and quality reports of the contractor. He needs to make sure that no more quantities are invoiced than actually consumed. This is why in some countries (e.g. the United Kingdom) quantity surveying has developed into a specialism. Quantity surveyors keep track of all materials delivered and consumed and the actual hours spent on the job. Their reports can be used to check the invoices submitted by the contractor.

An additional disadvantage of this method is that the client is not forced to specify exactly what it is he wants. Frequently, this specification is left to the contractor for the sake of convenience. Due to the uncertainty of the final cost, many employers avoid working with cost-reimbursable contracts. Some only use them in the case of specific, minor maintenance/ repair activities, for which the financial risks are relatively clear. Another problem is that the client is uncertain about the exact project delivery date. Cost-reimbursable contracts are not without problems, and need to be managed with great care. A common misunderstanding is that the contractor is not liable for mistakes and errors, i.e. that extra work to cover such mistakes and errors can always be charged to the client. This is not the case!

Cost-reimbursable contracts, if combined with proper incentives for all contractors involved, and if well managed, may represent a useful vehicle to allow for effective collaboration between employer and contractor. In fact, it represents a situation where all parties involved work based upon an open-book calculation, i.e. full transparency, which would in principle allow for better decision-making and mutual understanding. Well-chosen incentives should prevent opportunism among parties.

The decision in favor of either fixed-price or cost-reimbursable contracts is determined by a number of factors, such as:

- *Scope and comprehensiveness of the specification.* The scope of a project determines what contract type can be used most effectively. In case complex engineering is required, this may be offered on a reimbursable basis, whereas the actual construction (later on) can be offered at a fixed price. The availability of detailed specifications is a crucial prerequisite of fixed-price contracts. The absence of specifications makes a fair comparison of the various quotations impossible.
- *Available time.* Does the client have enough time for a tender procedure and price negotiations, or should the work be started immediately?
- *Technical expertise.* If the work requires specialized knowledge and skills, which are not present at the client organization, a cost-reimbursable contract is often preferred.
- *Knowledge of the industry.* The degree to which the client knows the methods and price arrangements that apply in that particular industry.

Unit rate/charters

A third type of contract, which is often used in the international contracting world, is the unit-rate contract or the charter contract. These contracts determine the cost per activity for repetitive or standardized and routine work.

Petrochemical companies, for example, annually negotiate unit rates for repetitive installation and maintenance activities which are subcontracted to contractors (for instance, unit rate per metre of piping that is installed, or unit rate per square metre of space that is painted). Unit-rate contracts are used for activities which are common, repetitive and/or standardized, but which are difficult to estimate in terms of volume and time. In the offshore industry this is often the case. Therefore unit-rate contracts, in this industry referred to as "charters", are used in terms of day rates per dredger, barge or tow boat.

In general, the client should, for smaller and less complex jobs, insist on a fixed price, arrived at through competitive bidding or negotiation. The agreed price should be acceptable to both client and contractor. Financial obligations between parties should be defined unequivocally. In fixed-price jobs, the client will try to impose as many risks on the contractor as possible. A fixed price is definitely preferable from the perspective of cost control or budget management. However, in complex jobs that allow for a lot of interaction between employer and contractor, a reimbursable contract, in combination with unit rates, may be a better solution. A fixed-price contract, in most cases, will cause opportunism to develop between parties. A reimbursable contract, if properly incentivized, would allow for much better and more constructive interaction among the parties involved.

Additional arrangements on pricing

In practice, additional pricing mechanisms and arrangements are used in contracts.

- *Fixed price with economic price adjustment.* This contract is used when some cost elements are subject to significant change during the contract period (e.g. fuel, steel and labor). Adjustments can be based upon actual costs incurred by the contractor, target costs or a price index. Parameters should be chosen, such that they cannot be influenced by one of the contract parties.
- *Fixed price plus incentive fee.* This type of contract is designed to motivate contractors by means of rewards to execute the work above the agreed standard. The incentives do not have to relate to immediately visible cost reductions, which are realized by the contractor. They can also relate to

earlier delivery and/or a better quality performance than agreed. In the offshore industry, incentives related to safety performance (HS&E) are common.

- *Reimbursable contracts.* This type of contract may have different forms: cost-plus with a percentage fee, cost-reimbursable plus a fixed fee, and cost-plus with a guaranteed maximum. In practice, this type of contract often turns out to be more expensive for the client than other types of contracts. Cost-plus contracts are used in situations where the work cannot be specified adequately, or when a fixed price constitutes too big a risk for both the contractor and the buyer.
- *Target-sum contracts.*[3] These are a variant of cost-reimbursable contracts. At the outset of the contract, targets are agreed in respect of cost, time and, when applicable, planned performance. Next, formulae are devised for the distribution between parties of the gains or losses arising from actual variations to the targets. Usually, a target cost for the project is proposed by the contractor, then checked and agreed by the employer. This target, which does not include any profit for the contractor, becomes the principal instrument in budgetary control of the works. It is updated at regular intervals until the end of the work, when a final target cost is established. Key steps are the following:

    - A schedule and target time for completion are agreed, and these are regularly updated to recognize any new circumstances arising during the execution of the project.
    - Similarly a performance target is agreed.
    - Payment of the actual cost of the work as it is incurred is made from a fund established under the financial provisions of the contract.
    - The contractor receives a fee for his work, the amount of which is related to his performance against the agreed targets. Usually, the contractor is paid a stated minimum fee per project milestone. Specific bonuses can be paid for early completion.

- *Unit-rate contracts.* This type of contract is usually based on fixed hourly rates for labor and equipment. However, without a bonus or penalty clause, these contracts provide little incentive to minimize

[3] This section is adapted from http://www.misronet.com/targetcost.htm, January 23, 2013.

labor hours or costs. The employer should therefore always make sure that:

- The contractor keeps a detailed cost administration, so that inspection is possible.
- A maximum contract price is recorded in the contract.
- This maximum is only to be exceeded after formal agreement has been obtained from the employer.
- The costs that are to be reimbursed are made payable to the contractor based upon on a well-specified invoice.

When contracting for equipment, it is recommended to record optional prices for future deliveries of spare parts, and, when appropriate, service rates. Finally, when buying from foreign contractors, currency risks need to be dealt with. This is quite a challenge for international contractors that operate in the offshore business. The time that elapses between the date of winning the order and the date of completion of the project can easily be a few years. During that period, currency exchange rates may alter significantly. There are several ways to deal with this. One way is to contract for the materials and services in the same currency that the customer will use to pay the company. Another way is to work with currency exchange clauses in the contract, which define how the company will be compensated by its customer in case a currency exchange rate fluctuates. Hedging of currency risk is another option, but this is usually an option for contracts with a shorter completion time.

8.3. Payment terms

When capital goods, installations, infrastructural and other construction projects are contracted for, it is common practice that payment takes place in several installments, partly because the contractor will have to make large investments to be able to produce the desired work. If this method of payment is used, account should be taken of the influence of the payment terms on the final price, as well as the cash flow of the project. Attention should also be paid to covering the currency risk related to paying for goods that have not yet been delivered.

In general, the preferred method of payment is based on the contract's milestones. For instance: payment of 20% of the total sum when 25% of the work is completed, 45% when 50% of the work is completed, etc. The last 5 or 10% of the payment is held back until the client is absolutely sure that the equipment operates exactly as it should or, in the case of a service, that the contractor's work has been completed to the customer's satisfaction. Of course, payments can also be made as a lump sum, a single payment covering the entire price for the project.

Advance payments are typically covered by a bank guarantee in which the contractor agrees to fulfill his obligations. Such a bank guarantee completely covers the prepaid sum and is valid for the period of delivery of the part that the bank guarantee relates to. If appropriate, a concern guarantee from the holding company (which is often less expensive) will suffice.[4] Similarly, when large payments are made to suppliers or subcontractors, these also should be covered by a bank guarantee in order to prevent unpleasant surprises.

In many cases, payments are covered by a performance bond. A performance bond includes a written guarantee from a third party guarantor (usually a bank or an insurance company) submitted to a client by a contractor on winning the bid.[5] A performance bond ensures payment of a sum of money (not exceeding a stated maximum) in case the contractor fails in the full performance of the contract.

8.4. Activities and risk allocation

Today, project managers are confronted with a myriad of contracts in their daily practice. Box 8.1 is based on a selection of discussions with project managers about what contracts they encounter in their daily life.

The most important contract models used in international contracting are: Construct contract, Design and Construct contract, the EPC contract and the DBFM contract. The latter contracts are referred to as integrated contracts. When contracts become more integrated, the duties, responsibilities and liabilities that are incurred by the contractor increase.

In defining these contracts, we follow the definitions that are provided by the Federation Internationale des Ingenieurs-Conseils (FIDIC)[6], the UK Leading Oil & Gas Industry Competitiveness (LOGIC)[7] and the Baltic and International Maritime Counsel (BIMCO)[8] in Copenhagen.

---

[4] For details on guarantees, see Chapter 14.

[5] This definition is taken from www.businessdictionary.com/definition, January 23, 2013.

[6] See FIDIC (1999), Conditions of contract for Plant and Design Build, Foreword.

[7] http://www.logic-oil.com/contracts2.cmf.

[8] www.bimco.org.

Box 8.1. Contracts in the "daily life" of project managers.[9]

Contract models

Standard contracts

- FIDIC 1999 — red book — Construction
- FIDIC 2006 — blue book — Dredging and Land Reclamation
- FIDIC 1999 — yellow book — Design and Construct
- FIDIC 1999 — silver book — EPC/ Turnkey Projects
- FIDIC 2006 — white book Client — consultant agreement
- FIDIC 2008 — gold book Design Build Operate Projects
- FIDIC Short Form of Contract
- FIDIC Form of Contract
- FIDIC 2011 — Subcontract
- FIDIC 2005 — Services Agreement
- FIDIC 1992 — Joint venture (consortium agreement)
- LOGIC 2003 — Construction
- LOGIC 2004 — Marine Construction — Design and Construct
- LOGIC 2003 Design[10]
- LOGIC 1997 — Mobile Drilling Rigs
- LOGIC 2005 — Purchase Order Terms & Condition
- LOGIC 2003 — Services
- LOGIC 2005 — Supply of Major Items of Plant and Equipment
- LOGIC 2002 — Well Services
- LOGIC 2001 — SME Services
- LOGIC 2001 — Subcontract for SME Services
- BIMCO Charter Party
- BIMCO Supplytime 89
- BIMCO Supplytime 2005
- BIMCO TOWCON 2008
- BIMCO Time Charter parties

NF 07 Norwegian Fabrication Contract
NTK 07 Norwegian Total Contract EPC/ EPIC
NTK 07 MOD Norwegian Total Contract Modification

Engineering and construction contracts

- Construct contract (C)
- Design and Construct (D&C)
- Design, Build and Maintain (DBM)
- Design, Build, Finance and Maintain (DBFM)
- Design, Build, Finance, Maintain and Operate (DBFMO)
- Engineering, Procurement and Construct (EPC)
- Engineering, Procurement, Installation and Construct (EPIC)
- Public Financed Initiatives (PFI)
- Public–Private Partnerships (PPP)

[9] This list is a result of discussions with participants of TiasNimbas International Contracting program. The list is far from complete.

[10] Earlier standard models (before 2000) in England were developed by CRINE.

Apart from this list, a large collection of standard contracts is available; they have been drafted and issued by a variety of institutions. To name a few of these institutions: ZipForm, Business Integrity, ACA, NEC, ICE, Finer Edge, SEC Info, Onecle, TechAgreements and the former English NEDC.[11] The scientific institute CORI shows a collection of approximately 116,000 real building contracts that were drafted after standard contracts.

A Construct contract is recommended for building or engineering works designed by the employer or by his representative, the engineer. Under the usual arrangements for this type of contract, the contractor constructs the works in accordance with the design provided by the employer. However, the works may include some elements of contractor designed, additional civil, mechanical, electrical and/or construction works.[12]

A contract for plant Design and Build[13] is recommended for the provision of electrical and/or chemical plants, and for the design and execution of building and engineering works, infrastructural works, harbors, jetties, quays, etc. Under the usual arrangements of this type of contract, the contractor designs and provides, in accordance with the employer's requirements, plants and/or other works. These may include any combination of civil, mechanical, electrical and/or construction works.

A contract for EPC/Turnkey projects may be suitable for the provision on a Turnkey basis of a process or power plant, a factory or similar facility, or often an infrastructure project or other type of development, where: 1) a higher degree of certainty of final price and time is required; 2) the contractor takes total responsibility for the design and execution of the project, with little involvement from the employer. Under the usual arrangements for Turnkey projects, the contractor carries out all the engineering, procurement, and construction, providing a fully equipped facility, ready for operation (at "the turn of a key").

A DFBM contract is used in situations where the employer does not have the technical knowledge to design the project, nor the financial resources to pay for the total investment upfront, nor wants to engage in the maintenance of the project. All of these activities are to be transferred to the contractor, who, in many cases, will need to team up with other specialist subcontractors

[11]The standard contracts are available via the Internet. Type the name of the institute and find the site.

[12]I.e. in addition to the main works to be delivered.

[13]Design and Construct (D&C) contracts are also referred to as Design and Build (D&B) contracts.

in order to apply for the contract. Usually, this leads to very complex contracts, which extend to a long period of time (20 years or more).

A DFBMO contract is used under conditions that are identical to a DFBM contract; additionally, the contractor is obliged to operate the works for a certain period time.

The "F"-element in the above-mentioned standard contracts may be left out in case the employer does not require financial support from the contractor. In such an event, the standards become DBM and DBMO respectively.

8.5. Standard contracts

Standard contracts are templates that can be used by employers and contractors to support their contract discussions and negotiations. Usually, standard contracts have been developed through professional associations of engineers. Examples are FIDIC, LOGIC and BIMCO, among the many standard contracts that are available and which parties can choose from. Standard contracts cover most contract models that were discussed earlier. However, some standard contracts, such as BIMCO, cover additional, specialized (maritime) activities, such as hiring tugboats or barges. In practice, there is not a single contracting activity that is not covered by some kind of standard contract. Table 8.1 provides an illustration of the general structure of standard contracts.

In conceiving these standard contracts, the expertise and knowledge were mobilized from industry experts and technical experts, as well as legal experts. As such, these standards contain templates that reflect actual contracting practices in the industries for which they have been developed. In general, standard contracts are structured following the project, i.e. contract, cycle. Following the framework, contract documentation for projects is substantial and requires careful handling.

Apart from these international standard contracts, most countries have developed their own local standard contracts. In the Netherlands, the UAV contracts are popular and widely used.[14] The UAV 1989 is a construction-only contract. UAV GC 2005 relates to integrated contracts (D&C).[15] UAV TI 1992 is used for technical installation works. Other countries have similar national contract standards. It is important to note that these local standard contracts usually deviate in important details from the international standard

[14] UAV stands for Uniforme Administratieve Voorwaarden (Uniform Administrative Conditions).

[15] UAV GC relates to Geintegreerd Contract (Integrated Contract).

Table 8.1. Standard contracts framework.

Standard contracts framework			
1. Definitions 2. General obligations of parties 3. Design 4. Personnel 5. Plant, materials and equipment 6. Planning — start-up — delay — suspension 7. Variations 8. Tests 9. Taking over	10. Defects liability period 11. Price and price structure 12. Payment structure 13. Taxes and tax exemption, custom procedures 14. Patents and other proprietary rights 15. Termination 16. Risks and liabilities 17. Insurances 18. Confidentiality 19. *Force majeure* 20. Laws and legal regulations 21. Assignment 22. Audits	23. Appendices lists of: • Employer-provided items • Employer-provided services • Contractor-provided items • Special equipment • Employer-provided technical information • Employer-approved subcontractors • Employer's representatives and key personnel • Contractor's representatives and key personnel Insurance policies Safety manuals QA/QC manuals Bank guarantees Parent-company guarantees Models of reports and records Model of variations order Transport of personnel, equipment, employer-provided items, contractor-provided items Penalty or liquidated damages	24. Sections • Drawings, etc. • Specifications • HS&E regulations • Scope of work • Time schedule • Technical specifications • Permits and licenses • Administration procedures

Table 8.2. Some national standard contract models in different countries.

Country	National model
Australia	Standards Australia
Austria	Oenormen
Canada	Canadian Construction Documents Committee
China	GF-99–0201
Finland	YSE 1998
France	AFNOR
Germany	VOB/B
Japan	MLIT
Netherlands	UAV 1989 / UAV 2012 UAVTI, UAVGC
Norway	NS
Qatar	Qatar Petroleum
Singapore	Real Estate Developers' Association
Sweden	AB
Switzerland	SIA
Turkey	General Specification of Public Works
Ukraine	Model Construction Contract
United Kingdom	JCT/NEC
United States of America	AIA/AGC

contracts. This is due to the fact that local rules and working habits have been integrated in these contracts. Table 8.2 provides an overview of some standard contracts that are used by different countries.

8.6. Contract models overview

Listed below, we provide a summary of the most popular contracts in offshore and international contracting. In each case, a definition is provided along with a description for when to use these contracts, and what information should be obtained from the client. Table 8.3 provides a schematic overview of the roles and responsibilities of the employer and contractor, depending on the different contract models.

Table 8.3 illustrates that, as contracts become more integrated, the responsibility shifts more to the contractor, where the employer needs to monitor the contract and project execution at a distance ("hands off").

Table 8.3. Roles and responsibilities of employer and contractor per contract model.

Contract model	Construct	Design and Construct	EPC/ Turnkey	DBFM	DBFMO
Project stages					
Initiate					
Research					
Definition					
Basic design					
Detailed design					
Final design					
Technical design					
Project start-up	Note[16]				
Project execution					
Maintenance					
Operation					
Financing					

Orange	Responsibility Employer
Green	Joint responsibility
Blue	Responsibility Contractor

Contract model: fixed-price

When to apply?

- In the case of projects of low/medium complexity.
- In the case of a clear project description and requirements.
- In case a client wants to have certainty about contract price.
- In case a client has a detailed cost breakdown available.
- When the risks are limited, controllable and measurable.
- When a client has sufficient time to prepare a detailed scope of work, i.e. technical requirements.

[16] Start-up at Construct or employer or contractor.

- When it is clear what performance needs to be delivered.
- In the case of sufficient available parties in the market to choose from.

What information is to be obtained from the client?

- Clear, unequivocal scope of work, i.e. technical requirements.
- No changes in scope and specifications.

Major risk factor for the client:

- Scope changes.
- Work variations.

Contract model: reimbursable/time and materials

When to apply?

- Scope of work is not clear.
- Only initial design available.
- Client has confidence and trust in contract.
- Project lead time is not critical but work needs to be started quickly.
- If tendering would lead to unacceptable price levels (sellers' market).
- For variations and extra/less work.

What information is to be obtained from the client?

- Agreement on uplift (for profit, risk, general cost and overhead).
- Approval procedures.
- Supporting evidence for invoices and payments.
- Global picture of scope of work plus maximum budget.

Major risk factor for the client:

- Incompetent contractor.
- Flawed project administration and follow up.
- Exceeding project budget.

Contract model: unit rate/charter

When to apply?

- When engineering is not yet finished.
- However, the client knows what needs to be done and production volumes are roughly known.

- When activities to be performed are roughly known.
- When activities to be performed are repetitive in character.
- When the scope of work is not yet exactly defined; however, the work needs to be started quickly without delay.
- Often applied as a side arrangement to the main contract to settle for variations.

What information is to be obtained from the client?

- Specifications.
- Conceptual design.
- Bill of quantities.
- Definition of unit of performance.
- Agreement on how quantities are measured.
- Agreement on who measures quantities.
- Agreement on what penalties will apply.
- Technical information, drawings, maps.
- Time schedule and milestone dates.
- General conditions.
- How calculations are made.
- How payments will be made.

Major risk factor for the client:

- Incompetent contractor.
- Flawed project administration and follow up.
- Exceeding project budget.

Contract model: time charter

When to apply?

- Client has undefined scope.
- Client values the contractor's expertise and security of supply.
- It concerns a critical assignment and a small sum compared to the main contract.
- The work needs to be started quickly without delay.
- In case no exact volumes and planning can be provided.
- When the client wants to secure availability of the contractor's expertise and capabilities.
- When the client wants to secure availability of equipment for an unknown period.

What information is to be obtained from client?

- Client needs to be able to describe performance to be obtained from the contractor.
- Client needs to describe when to start with work, i.e. activities.
- Functionality and capacity of equipment to be known.
- General terms and conditions of contract.

Major risk factor for the client:

- Incompetent contractor.
- Flawed project administration and follow up.
- Exceeding project budget.

Contract model: Design and Construct

When to apply?

- When the client does not have sufficient expertise and capability in-house.
- When the client wants to benefit from the contractor's specific expertise.
- When the client wants to transfer part of the design risk to the contractor.
- When the client wants to obtain best value for money from the contractor.
- When the client wants to obtain lowest lifecycle cost.
- When the client has sufficient time for a tender.

What information is to be obtained from the client?

- Clear and transparent scope of work and objectives.
- Well-articulated expectations by the client.
- Complete data set, including all available research reports.
- Clarity about future use and circumstances.
- Legal contract and standard terms and conditions.
- Communication and decision-making structure of client organization.

Major risk factor for client:

- Scope changes.
- Work variations.

Contract model: DBFM

When to apply?

- In case the client wants to realize the project but financial resources for investment are not available upfront.
- The client is primarily interested in the functionality of the solution to be provided.
- In case the client wants to realize lowest operations cost during the lifetime of the project (lowest total cost of ownership (TCO)).
- In case the client wants to transfer risk for budget overruns to the contractor.
- In case the project to be built will generate revenues.

What information is to be obtained from the client?

- Description of functionality of solution to be provided (capacity, future use, number of users, etc., now and in the future).
- Business case, i.e. feasibility study.
- Cash-flow forecasts (max–min scenarios).
- Business model, i.e. how investment will be paid back.
- Bonus/penalties for delivery of project milestones.
- Intended time schedule for project realization.
- Bonus/penalties in case of non-availability of building/road.
- Limiting factors such as:
    - Current infrastructure.
    - Stakeholder requirements.
    - Soil condition.
    - Reimbursement of tender costs.
    - Risk analysis.
    - Financing structure.
- Payment schedule.

Major risk factors for the client:

- Operating model, i.e. business model.
- Internal decision-making structure.
- Internal governance structure.

- Contractor's decision-making structure.
- Contractor's governance structure.

Contract model: DBFMO

When to apply?

- In case the client wants to realize the project but financial resources for investment are not available upfront.
- The client is primarily interested in the functionality of the solution to be provided.
- In case the client wants to realize optimal operations cost during the lifetime of the project (lowest total cost of ownership (TCO)).
- In case the client wants to transfer risk for budget overruns to the contractor.
- In case the project to be built will generate revenues.
- In case the client wants to transfer the risk of operation to the contractor, both technically and financially.
- In case the client wants to increase quality of the permanent works in fulfilling its functional specification.
- In case the client wants to make use of the contractor's knowledge and innovation power.

What information is to be obtained from the client?

- Description of functionality of solution to be provided (capacity, future use, number of users, etc., now and in the future).
- Business case, i.e. feasibility study.
- Cash-flow forecasts (max–min scenarios).
- Business model, i.e. how investment will be paid back.
- Bonus/penalties for delivery of project milestones.
- Intended time schedule for project realization.
- Bonus/penalties in case of non-availability of permanent works.
- Limiting factors such as:
    - Current infrastructure.
    - Stakeholder requirements.
    - Soil condition.
    - Reimbursement of tender costs.

- ○ Risk analysis.
- ○ Financing structure.

Major risks for the client:

- Operating model, i.e. business model.
- Political stakeholders.
- Internal decision-making structure.
- Internal governance structure.
- Contractor's decision-making structure.
- Contractor's governance structure.

This list of contracts shows that contract management is a quite complex issue. Different contracts are used for different situations. In order to give this complex subject, some structure, standard contracts have been developed to help employers and contractors in their contract negotiations and discussions.

8.7. How standard contracts are used

When contracting for complex projects, employers may use standard contracts. However, employers will deal with these templates differently. Some employers may use a certain standard and adapt some contract clauses in their own interest (often without informing the contractor). Next, large investors (such as international oil companies) use their own contract templates. The structure of these contracts resembles that of standard contracts. However, some clauses may be more detailed and less objective than those of general standard contracts.

The different contract models can be applied using different contracting modes. A differentiation is made usually between "contracting as a war game" versus "contracting as a vehicle for collaboration". Depending on the mode that a certain party may want to adopt, a different contract model will be preferred. The attitude towards the other party, the corporate culture, management style, etc., may also determine the choice of or the preference for a certain contract model (see Table 8.4).

As we have argued, employers usually prefer fixed-price contracts, based on a clear allocation of risks between the contract parties involved. As our experience has shown, better contract outcomes are realized when contract parties engage in a collaborative mode, rather than a war game mode. Maintaining a collaborative mode during the lifetime of a contract is extremely difficult. In practice, the personal relationship between parties may be subject to major changes as the project gets to the stage of completion.

Table 8.4. Contracting modes and contract models.

	Contracting as 'wargame'	Contracting as collaboration
Relationship	Adversarial	Collaborative
Contracts	Hard contracts, e.g. • Lump-sum, fixed-price contracts • Penalty-based contracts	Soft contracts, e.g. • Reimbursable, open-cost contracts • Incentive-based contracts
Risk allocation	Risk at contractor	Risk sharing

8.8. Collaborative contract models

Collaboration among partners in the contracting value chain can be fostered in different ways. Supply-chain collaboration may be fostered through "back-to-back" agreements and incentives, i.e. performance contracts with subcontractors and suppliers. More intensive collaboration is realized through joint venture contracts. A joint venture is a business agreement in which parties agree to develop and maintain, for a defined period of time, a new legal entity and new assets which are financed by the parties involved. They exercise control over the legal entity and consequently share revenues, costs and assets. A joint venture takes place when two parties come together to take on one project. In a joint venture, both parties invest in the project in terms of money, time and effort, to build or execute a complex project. Since the cost of executing infrastructural and/or construction projects is generally high, a joint venture allows both parties to share the burden of the project, its risks as well as the resulting profits.

Joint venture agreements (with or without a vertical split of risks and rewards among contract partners) may be arranged among the main contractor and some competitors that are interested in tendering for the same, large project and the main contractor and its key subcontractors.

An alternative is the alliance contract. The difference with the joint venture contract here is that the employer is one of the contract parties and takes an active stake in the project outcome. Alliance contracts by nature are highly complex contracts to manage. However, they enable full alignment of the contractor's and subcontractor's interests with those of the employer. These contracts are used for large infrastructural works, where contract partners need to not only construct the works, but also need to maintain, operate and finance the project during an important part of its lifecycle.

Below, we summarize the major elements of both joint venture and alliance contracts.

Contract model: joint venture

When to apply?

- When the contractor has insufficient capability and capacity.
- If the assignment is too big for one contractor.
- When many specialist disciplines need to be integrated.
- When we want to engage a specialist subcontractor at the tender stage.
- When we want to engage in an exclusive relationship with a strategic subcontractor.

What information is to be obtained from the client?

- Permission from the client to be able to submit a bid using a joint venture.

Major risk for the client:

- Internal decision-making structure.
- Internal governance structure.
- Contractor's decision-making structure.
- Contractor's governance structure.

Contract model: alliance contract

When to apply?

- Project is complex and requires innovative solutions, which need to be developed jointly by contract parties.
- Project risk is too large to be carried by just one party.
- Contract parties have complementary expertise and knowledge.
- Client wants to work in close collaboration with the contractor.
- Typically spans multiple contracts and projects over a long time period.

What information is to be obtained from the client?

- Success criteria. When is the collaboration for both parties successful?
- Commitment and institutional trust among parties involved.
- Business case from the client.

8.9. Summary

This chapter dealt with the different contracting models that project managers can encounter in daily practice. First, we identified three contract-pricing mechanisms, and here the actual context will decide the best pricing mechanism to use. These contextual factors include the employer's ability to specify exactly what he wants, the time and expertise that he has available, and the experience of the employer with a specific contractor. Next, contracts may differ depending on the payment mechanisms, whether they are made upfront, during the execution of the work according to pre-arranged milestones, or after the work has been completed. Is some cases, the contractor is not paid for his construction work at all, since the income needs to be generated by operating the works delivered (in the case of DBFMO contracts). Finally, contracts can differ based upon the allocation of risk between employer and contractor. The more integrated contract models assume the contractor carries most of the risk. Contract models, in practice, reflect a mix of these three elements. Variation is endless, which is why no contract is the same. Important contract models in international contracting are: Construct, Design and Construct, EPC and DBFM(O) contracts. These may be complemented with joint venture and alliance contracts.

Each of the contract models represents different roles and responsibilities, as well as liabilities, for the employer and contractor. Contractors should be aware that when a D&C contract applies, or an EPC contract, they are responsible, under foreign legal systems, for checking all data which has been provided by the employer. This is particularly true for an EPC contract, where the contractor commits himself to Turnkey delivery of the installation or the work, intended by the employer.

Standard contracts can facilitate discussions and contract negotiations significantly. They are the result of the expertise and knowledge of international professional engineering associations and therefore highly recommended.

Besides contextual factors, the choice of a contract model may depend on the contracting mode between parties. Of the two extremes proposed, the collaborative mode should be preferred, given its far better outcomes in practice. However, opportunism and focus on short-term results may get in the way of adapting these modes in practice.

It should be realized that creating one-sided contracts will lead to a conflict system, in which each party will seek its own benefits at the cost of the other party. Therefore, the purpose of a project and contract organization is to create a cooperative system. This is achieved by creating common objectives, the alignment of all key partners involved and properly incentivizing the contractors.

When choosing collaborative contracts, the client must not needlessly interfere in the contractor's work. Every employer gets the contractor that he deserves!

Part III

Project and Risk Management

Chapter 9

Risk Management in Projects

9.1. Case — Contractor withdraws from negotiations due to risk exposure

On February 14, 2012, the oil and gas press announced the following:[1]

> The Australian subsidiary of Belgium's Dredging, Environment & Marine Engineering NV (DEME) has been awarded a €916 million ($1.2 billion) dredging contract on the Chevron-operated Wheatstone liquified natural gas project in Australia. Its subsidiary, Dredging International Australia, will carry out the dredging of the 17-kilometer-long access channel, the maneuvering area, the berths pockets and the tug harbor for the 8.9 million tons per annum LNG project near Onslow, Western Australia.
>
> The contract was awarded by US company Bechtel, who is in charge of the front-end engineering and design work of the project, and DEME stated it would be carried out in close cooperation with US-based Great Lakes Dredge & Dock.
>
> A large seagoing, self-propelled cutter suction dredger, a medium trailing suction hopper dredger and two backshoe dredgers will be used to carry out the contract, while the total dredged volume is expected to be more than 26 million cubic meters.
>
> Work on the contract is scheduled to start at the end of the year with a planned completion date of December 2015.
>
> Work on the foundation phase of the Wheatstone LNG project commenced late 2011 and will include the construction of two LNG trains and a domestic gas plant, with first LNG shipments planned for 2016.
>
> Chevron holds 73.6% operated interest in the Wheatstone LNG project along with joint venture partners Apache with 13%, Kuwait Foreign Petroleum Exploration Company with 7% and Shell with 6.4%.

[1] News at http://fuelfix.com/2012/2/13/deme-wins-1–2bn-wheatstone-contract, January 23, 2013.

On the same day, the Dutch newspaper NRC Handelsblad published the reason why Boskalis, together with its partner Jan de Nul, withdrew from further negotiations on the same project. According to Boskalis, Chevron intended to transfer too many risks to the contractor. Besides its regular staff, the contractor would be obliged to hire local personnel. Due to the tough safety and environmental regulations, it was expected that more personnel would need to be hired and higher wages would have to be paid. All future wage increases were to be carried by the contractor. The dredging companies Boskalis and Jan de Nul presented their reservations, stating that these cost increases should be carried by the employer. A second reservation was a cap on liability, whereas the employer asked for unlimited liability. The client refused to accept these risks and therefore declined Boskalis's offer. As a Boskalis spokesman said: "It was a beautiful project, but we did not want to run the risk."[2]

9.2. The many faces of risk

Transferring risk to a contract partner is one of the many policies used to handle project risks. The case shows the way Chevron and its engineering firm Bechtel intended to transfer certain risks to one of its contractors on the Wheatstone LNG project. Some risks may be transferred to a contractor, others cannot be transferred. It depends on the specific risk involved and the risk appetite of the contractor.

There are other ways for handling risks than just transferring them to contract partners. In this chapter, we will distinguish between various kinds of risk, their origin and source. We will investigate how risks can be reduced and minimized. Some risks cannot be managed and must be accepted as a fact of life; projects without risks do not exist. Risk management is part of project management, and effective project management requires that risks are identified upfront at various stages of the project. Risks differ per type of project. The risks for a 'construction-only' contract are much more the employer's responsibility than the contractor's. Under an EPC/Turnkey project, the contractor is prepared to accept most risks because he is of the opinion that he will be able to handle these more effectively than the employer.

Depending on the project, the qualifications and competencies of project managers will vary. A Construction contract requires a qualified technician, who is able to deliver the required quality within the agreed timeframe and

[2]J. Leyten (2012), Boskalis laat order lopen wegens risico's, *NRC Handelsblad*, February 14, 2012.

within budget. A complex DBFMO contract, however, requires a manager who is prepared to delegate many of his own tasks to assistant managers and specialists. He needs to understand how the project will help the employer to implement his strategic plans. Hence, he needs to be able to cooperate with all stakeholders in the project. That is a different task than completing a project according to technical drawings and specifications.

In this chapter, we will discuss the most common risks in projects and the many possibilities regarding how to handle these. Furthermore, we will discuss some cases where, due to unforeseen risks, projects turned into financial losses. As will become clear, a risk that is overlooked at an earlier stage of the contract life cycle can easily cause losses or damages at a later stage.

Besides project risks, we will discuss some other risks that may be beyond a project manager's competence, but may threaten the entire company. In short, these risks are: asset-impairment risk, competition risk and reputation risk. Concluding this chapter, we will summarize the most important key factors when dealing with project risks.

9.3. Definition of risk

There are many definitions of the word "risk". How a person defines risk is dependent upon his/her position in society, education, profession and personal opinion. A financial manager, who is responsible for managing risks in international transactions, will define risk in a different way than an engineer who is responsible for a design for permanent works that have to be realized in a foreign country. The two persons may have completely different views on the same international contract.[3] Risk is defined as the effect of uncertainty on the realization of certain objectives, whether positive or negative.[4] The Project Management Body of Knowledge states:

> A risk is an uncertain event or condition that, if it occurs, has a positive or negative effect on a project's objectives. Where there is risk inherent with any project, the

[3] For those project managers who want to learn the financial manager's views on risks, we would recommend: M. Crouhy, D. Galai, R. Mark (2006), *The essentials of risk management*. New York: McGraw Hill, pp. 26–36; R. A. Brealey, S. C. Myers, F. Allen (2008), *Principles of Corporate Finance International Edition*. New York: McGraw Hill, pp. 722–754. Furthermore we recommend: A. van de Ven (2001), *Development of risk management and accounting*, in M. van Dealen and C. van der Elst (2001), *Risk management and corporate governance, interconnections in law, accounting and tax*. Cheltenham and Northampton, MA: Edward Elgar Press, pp. 7–55.

[4] ISO 31000, Risk management, principles and guidelines on implementation, International Organization for Standardization, Geneva, 2009, p. v.

> project manager and project team should be constantly aware of any risks that will impact the successful completion of any project. One way to accomplish this is by completing a risk analysis for any identified risk and to review risks periodically with the team.[5]

Consequently, risk management is the identification, assessment and prioritization of risks, followed by coordinated and economical application of resources to minimize, monitor and control the probability and/or impact of unfortunate events.[6] This definition refers to "positive or negative effects". In the construction industry, risk is mostly associated with a negative effect, i.e. a threat. This negative view towards risk is included in the following definition: "Risk is a threat to an organization (or a project) that reduces the likelihood that the organization (or the project manager) will achieve one or more of its objectives."[7] Uncertainties, as soon as they become apparent in projects, are considered to be risky. When a risk is identified, action is required. You do not let the risk exist without taking mitigating measures. Risk is a danger, and the responsibility for handling risk must be allocated.[8] Derived from the definition of enterprise risk, as published in COSO (2011),[9] we prefer the following definition of risk management in projects:

> Risk management is a process, effected by top management, project management and all personnel, fully or partly responsible for (parts of) a project, applied in strategy setting and across the enterprise, designed to identify potential events that may affect the project, and manage risks to be within its risk appetite, to provide reasonable assurance regarding the achievement of the project's objectives.

A more simple definition, which is a little less abstract, is given by Walters (1999): "Risks are possible occurrences, which, in the event they occur, have a negative effect on the achievement of the prior chosen boundary conditions

---

[5] Project Management Institute, PMBOK Guide, 3rd edition, p. 373.

[6] D. Hubbard (2009), *The failure of risk management: Why it is broken and how to fix it.* Hoboken, NJ: John Wiley & Sons, p. 46.

[7] R. Knechel (2001), *Auditing, Assurance and Risk.* Cincinnati, OH: South Western College Publishing, p. 13.

[8] M. Power (2007), *Organized uncertainty — Designing a world of risk management.* Oxford: Oxford University Press, p. 5.

[9] Committee for Sponsoring Organizations of the Treadway Commission (COSO), Enterprise Risk Management — Integrated framework, Executive Summary, New York, AICPA Inc. COSO II report, p. 16.

of the objective of the project."[10] In that context, risk management is defined as follows: "Risk management is the identification, the analysis and quantification, the fixation in a systematic control planning, and following those actions the execution, the control and the correction of risks."[11]

9.4. Risk management and contract type

In general, parties could allocate risks using a few rules of thumb. It would make sense to place project risks with the partner who is best capable of *controlling* the risk in question (rule 1). A risk that could be carried by more partners should be *shared* between such partners (rule 2). Furthermore, a risk should be allocated to the partner who is able to bear such risk at the *lowest possible cost* (rule 3). And finally, a risk that cannot be estimated, or cannot be handled or cannot be borne, should come from the account of the party who initiates such risk (rule 4).[12] A further, generally accepted principle is that all risks incorporate a price that cannot be avoided. Risks come at a price. In the end, in all projects, risks are paid for by the employer, his stakeholders or both.

These rules may be acknowledged when discussing how risks are to be allocated among contract partners. The risk profile of the project at hand and the way parties want to allocate risks among themselves may be key parameters in deciding what contract type to go for. In practice, it is the employer who decides about the contract type in the first place. Usually, the employer initiates the pre-contractual relations by issuing an invitation to tender to prospective contractors. The contract type is mostly chosen at the employer's convenience. Different contract types will result in different pricing mechanisms. Project types may be considered by two criteria: the contract type and the price-setting mechanism.[13]

[10] B. G. Walters, L. J. A. M. van Griensven, M. M. G. van Rosmalen (1999), *Management van Projectmanagement — Het managen van multiprojecten en programma's*, Berenschot Osborne BV, p. 97.

[11] B. G. Walters, L. J. A. M. van Griensven, M. M. G. van Rosmalen (1999), Management van Projectmanagement — Het managen van multiprojecten en programma's, Berenschot Osborne BV, p. 97.

[12] L. de Boer (2006), Turnkey en design & construct: concepten, aansprakelijkheid en risico, in van den Berg & Jansen, *De ontwerpende bouwer*. Tjeenk Willink: Schoordijk Instituut, p. 209.

[13] See also Chapters 4 and 8 for more details.

Contract type

The most classical contract type is the Construction-only contract. The employer orders the design with a separate contract partner, be it an engineering consultant or an architect, or a company who combines both activities. When the design is ready and accepted by the employer, he awards a contract to the contractor. Usually, such a situation results in three contractual relationships (see Figure 9.1).

This contract type has been used for centuries. It represents a pragmatic approach, which is preferred for realizing relatively simple works, where the employer is in a position to choose between several designers and several contractors.

The architect/engineer has to deliver a good design, which enables the contractor to estimate its risks when tendering for the construction contract. The employer will be liable for any design errors. He may request that the architect/engineer correct his design errors. In the event such errors do result in extra costs for the contractor, those costs can be claimed from the employer. The liabilities of the contractor are limited. He has to study the design beforehand and is obliged to warn the employer in case certain design faults have been discovered. If so, he should inform the employer and ask the employer to have them corrected in time.

During the last five or so decades, many other contract types have become popular. In general, employers have shifted more risks to the contractor. Today, contractors are increasingly requested to assume design and engineering responsibility for the project for which they tender. There are many reasons for this common trend. First, there is the increasing complexity of projects. The Design and Construct contract (D&C) is attractive for employers, who are not in a position to design a work or to manage a separate design

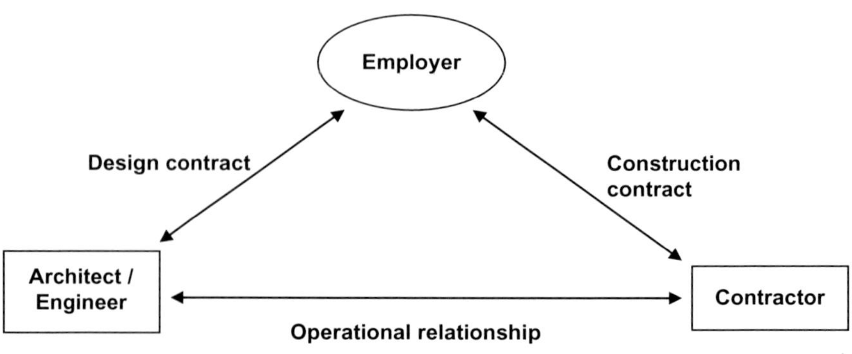

Figure 9.1. Contractual relations in the classical construction-only contract.

contract. Today, this is relevant for many public authorities, who over time outsourced their specialist engineering capabilities. As a result, they became more dependent for design and technological knowledge on their contractors. Adding the maintenance of realized permanent works to the contractor's responsibility was a logical next step. Having the project financed by the contractor was another step. Over time, PFI contracts were issued by public authorities in many EU countries to realize complex infrastructural works.[14] The final step in this development was to have the works actually managed and operated by the contractor. With each step in this development, the contractor assumed more risk, responsibility, and hence, risks and liabilities. Figure 9.2 shows the process.

Construct	Design&Build	Design&Build	EPC-turnkey	DBM	DBFM	DBFMO
Employer's design	Contractor's design	Contractor's design	Contractor's design	Contractor's design and Maintenance	Contractor's design + finance + maintenance	Contractor's design + finance + maintenance+ operations
Re-measurable	Re-measurable	Lump sum	Lump sum	Lump sum	Lump sum	Lump sum / Re-measurable
Descriptive specification	Descriptive specification	Descriptive specification	Functional specification	Functional specification	Functional specification	Functional specification

Figure 9.2. Increasing risk allocation for contractor at increasing complexity of contract type.[15] (Source: Heerema Fabrication Group.)

[14] Private Finance Initiative (PFI) is a way of creating "public–private partnerships" (PPPs) by funding public infrastructure projects with private capital. See: Investopedia, January 2013; Reform of the PFI, www.hm-treasury.gov.uk, December 2011.

[15] FIDIC published a standard contract called Design & Build; in this chapter, both Design & Construct and Design & Build are used interchangeably.

Of course, the reality is more complex than represented by Figure 9.2. To cite an example: in practice, DBFM contracts, which are based partly upon a lump-sum remuneration, are used while the remaining part of the contractor's work is paid through re-measurable installments. In all contract types, mixtures of pricing mechanisms can be applied. This also holds for the payment methods that are used.

Pricing mechanisms and payment methods

The way in which payments are agreed is crucial for the contract parties. Where parties agree upon a lump sum, the contractor is responsible for managing unforeseen hindrances and problems. When parties agree that the contractor will be paid per unit rate, all of the contractor's performances are reimbursable. Here, the contractor has to endeavor to do his best; the contractor has to make the proper arrangements for assuring that his equipment and personnel are qualified, but the contractor is relatively certain to be paid. He is paid per man hour, per cubic meter of sand or slurry, which have been produced, or the tons of concrete that were delivered. Depending on the pricing mechanism, the certainty about the contract sum may differ significantly. This is illustrated in Figure 9.3.

9.5. Risk policy of contractors

A formal, consistent risk policy is a must for each contractor. Such a policy would provide guidelines for management and staff, specifically for those persons who prepare tenders and who execute projects. Also, external stakeholders are expressing increased interest in how a contractor handles project and business risk. Risk policies are part of annual reports. For listed companies, an extensive explanation of their financial accounts is mandatory. A simple risk policy provides clear instructions to all financial managers, tender managers, engineers, project managers, contract managers, procurement managers and legal counsels on how to deal with risks when working with projects. An example of a contractor's risk policy is mentioned in Box 9.1.

The contractor's risk policy contains instructions for various disciplines within the company. The first three items of the list in Box 9.1 represent general statements, related to behavior, which the board is recommending to all persons involved, especially its own staff. The next statements, i.e. items 4 to 7, are promises that the company will respect the financial regulations that apply. In the event that this company is a listed corporation on one of the

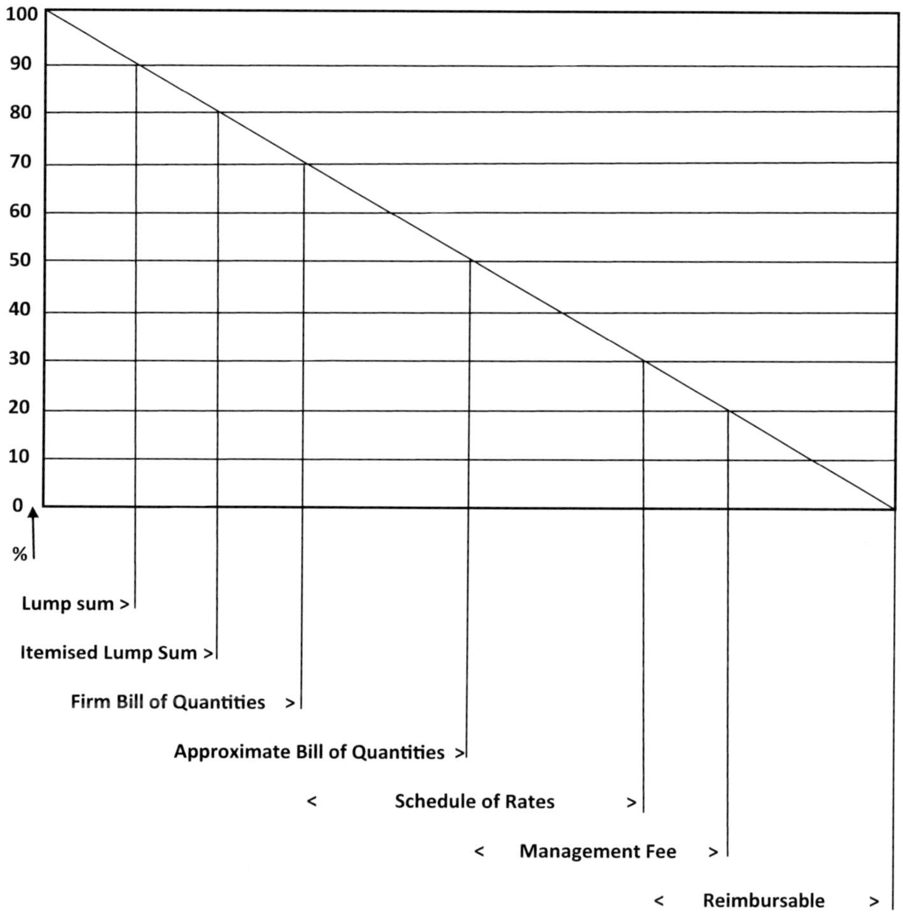

Figure 9.3. Relation between risk and payment method. (Source: Heerema Fabrication Group.)

European stock markets, these items are compulsory. They are mentioned here — and in most annual reports we find the same firm statements — but if they were not mentioned, they would still be applicable. A company cannot and should not escape from compulsory legislation.

Statements 8 to 11 contain useful information for all stakeholders. Here, the financial stakeholders, such as shareholders, bondholders, banks and other financial institutions are informed about the most important financial risks of the international business of a contractor who is operating in foreign countries. Besides the identification of these risks, the board informs how these risks are handled and will be handled.

Box 9.1. Guidelines for risk management.[16]

Board of Management's Business Guidelines

1. We continuously strive to improve all aspects of our operations, including technology, people and operating methods. We look for more effective ways to plan and execute our projects, while maintaining a flexible and creative approach that makes the most of our growth opportunities.
2. We seek to monitor and evaluate all areas of risk on an ongoing basis as part of our commitment to ensuring the sustainability of our business. Our commitment to maintaining the highest standards of corporate governance is the basis of our ability to maintain operational excellence throughout the organization.
3. We consider ourselves responsible for the excellent quality of our work, our engineering standards and our services; we believe that providing such excellent quality is the only reason for our existence in our field of business.
4. The Dutch Corporate Governance Code, Code Tabaksblat, which came into force on January 1, 2004, revised in 2009, which applies to Dutch companies listed on the stock exchange, is respected in full.
5. The consolidated financial statements and the accounting explanatory notes are prepared in accordance with the International Financial Reporting Standards (IFRS), as adopted by the European Union, and with the Dutch legislation at part 9 of Book 2 of the Netherlands Civil Code Book.
6. IAS 11 (International Accounting Standard 11), Construction contracts, 2009, is respected.
7. Work in progress is valued at the cost price of the work done, plus a part of the expected results upon completion of the project in proportion to the progress made and less progress billings, advances and provisions. Provisions are recognized for expected losses on work in progress as soon as they are foreseen, and deducted from the cost price; if necessary, any profits already recognized are reversed.

(*Continued*)

[16] J. van der Puil, A. van de Ven (2009), Going for it… or not?, Module Finance & Risk, Case 1, Part 2, TiasNimbas Business School, Tilburg, September, p. 2–3.

Box 9.1. (*Continued*)

8. The company's main financial risks include disruption by political developments and violence, and the risk of non-payment by clients. These risks are covered by credit-insurance, bank guarantees and advance-payments.
9. Positions in non-euro are fully hedged as soon as they occur.
10. Financial derivatives (such as options, interest swaps and futures) for hedging currency risks, fuel cost risks, risk of cost of materials and/or other risks are only used if there is a physical underlying transaction.
11. The company has large amounts outstanding in the form of bank guarantees or surety bonds (guarantees from insurance companies), usually in favor of customers. The company should maintain adequate credit and bank guarantee facilities at its disposal.
12. The company never accepts, neither directly, nor indirectly, contractual liability for any loss of use of plant or equipment, loss of profit, loss of contracts or such like.
13. We keep our equipment, plant, materials, vessels and vehicles insured for full replacement value and against damages up to €20,000,000 per case, with an excess of €250,000.
14. All projects beyond €1,000,000 should be covered by a CAR insurance, to be arranged by the employer, or by ourselves.
15. We permanently maintain insurance for claims, damages, losses, expenses, arising from injury, sickness, disease or death up to €10,000,000, with an excess of €250,000.
16. We permanently maintain insurance for third party liability for property other than the referred works up to an amount of €50,000,000, with an excess of €250,000.
17. Per contract we do not accept total contractual liabilities higher than 50% of the contract price.
18. In the event we have to accept liability for technical data and information put at our disposal by third parties, such data and information must be checked and verified by a second neutral third party, independent of the employer and ourselves.
19. No tender is accepted without a reliable level of planning, risk analysis and the financial estimate having been carried out first.
20. Increasing shareholder value is of the utmost importance.

Items 12 to 17 mention contractual risks, as well as tortuous risks. Loss of use or profit of business partners is never accepted; consequently such risks are not transferred. These risks are extremely difficult to cover through insurance, and, if so, at very high cost. Items 13 to 16 may concern claims from both contractual parties, as well as third parties. The way such risks are handled is mentioned, including maximum amounts.

In explaining the insurance policy, the statements mention the respective excesses. An excess in an insurance policy is the amount of the damage incurred, which is equivalent to the insured person's/company's own risk. For instance, in the event of an insurance claim amounting to €300,000, while the excess is €250,000, the insurance company will only pay €50,000 to the insured person/company. In case claims come in over the maximum amounts, the company will have to defend itself in court or settle the matter peacefully, the company being liable for the excess.

Items 18 and 19 mention two technical risks. These statements are a bit tricky. They represent simple principles, but in engineering activities, many more risks are present. Item 18 is applicable when tendering for Design & Build and EPC/Turnkey and related orders. It may happen that the employer comes up with a design and wishes to transfer the complete liability for this design to the contractor. The company's risk policy here is that external checks will have to be carried out. For example: we (the first party) receive an order from a project developer (the second party) for the design and construction of a business building with two floors, the suggested location being somewhere in Africa on spot A. The order states: sandy soil (information), foundations 160 deep, 80 wide, brickwork (technical data). The details come from an advisory consultancy X (the third party).

Our policy: we commission an independent party (a second neutral third party) to verify:

- Whether spot A is indeed on sandy soil.
- Whether the aforementioned foundations are indeed suitable for the design for which we will be responsible.

Such technical policy normally follows after dramatic experiences from past projects, where things really went wrong, causing an important financial loss.

Finally, the shareholders will be satisfied with statement 20. That is why they will not sell their shares. Hopefully the company's dividend will be satisfactory.

9.6. Identification of risks

A risk that is not identified cannot be handled. A risk may result in an unpleasant occurrence. As soon as a risk that we feared has actually happened, the risk no longer exists. The uncertainty has become reality. Immediately, the situation has changed. When the risk has turned into effect, all preventive actions have become superfluous. Now the project manager has to deal with the unpleasant situation that resulted from the risk, or — if no better options are available, has to accept the situation.

A risk management policy is aimed at preventing such unpleasant occurrences. Different organizations have different policies. All such policies start with the identification of all project risks. In all norms, articles, scientific publications,[17] management systems[18] and courses,[19] this is the first step to take. It seems so simple. In practice, again and again, this is when the first mistakes are made. No project escapes from a number of overlooked risks. The non-discovered risks are an unknown number. When we begin a project, we do not know that they exist, we do not know how many they are. We have confidence in ourselves; that is a good thing. If the unforeseen happens we will find a solution.

Risk management in practice: observations from the Swania case

The International Contracting Program was developed by the Company Specific Programs Division of TiasNimbas Business School. The contents of the program were defined in close harmony with the three founding international corporations, i.e. large international contractors. The program has been conducted and facilitated many times by the authors. Project directors, project managers, contract managers, tender managers, commercial managers, procurement and financial managers, senior field managers and in-house legal councils participate in the program. Before starting the course, the participants are requested to prepare a tender for a harbor with some office buildings and adjacent roads for a potential employer. All participants receive the same invitation to tender, along with appendices such as drawings,

[17]See, among others, N. Crockford (1986), *An introduction to Risk Management, 2nd edition*. Cambridge: Woodhead Faulkner, p. 18.

[18]For instance, P. M. Hut (2008), Project Management Process, Phase 2 — Planning — Create Risk Management Plan, http://www.pmhut.com/project-management, January 2008.

[19]J. van der Puil (2010), The Swania Project: Are we going to tender? Rev. 1, TiasNimbas Business School, Tilburg, not published.

specifications, attachments and a draft contract.[20] One of the tasks they need to prepare is to: "Make a list of all risks that are to be found in this invitation to tender." On the first day of the course, tender teams are formed, when participants may review their preparations. The groups have to present a tender proposal and elucidate their tender policy. All risks are scored on a tender scorecard. For each identified risk, the group is awarded a number of points. The group with the best score wins a prize; the presentation follows on the second day of the course. At the end of this chapter, a proof of answer is presented in the form of a participants' scorecard (see Box 9.5). The results of the group scores are listed in Box 9.2.

In June 2012, the core module took place 13 times. A total of 58 subgroups, in general consisting of 4 or 5 participants, collaborated on the assignment. In total, 253 participants followed the course.

Here we present our observations with regard to the table presented in Box 9.2, on how participants deal with tendering and risk management.

A few observations about risk identification

A number of evident risks are always mentioned by the participants, such as the required delivery period, the tight planning, missing information about soil conditions, the foreign legal system, quality of local labor (where participation of such is required), unforeseen problems in getting local licenses and permits on time, the unpredictable price variations for fuel and raw materials, back-to-back contracting and dispute resolution. However, participants usually have less awareness of risks on a higher project level, including multiproject risks, political, economical, financial, legal and trade risks.

While the participants carefully scrutinize the presented contract and the scope of work, they can miss the project's non-technical issues, which the employer intends to realize. Most participants fail to analyze the project from the perspective of the employer and its stakeholders. It is just this way of "looking at your project through the employer's eyes" that can make the difference compared to competing contractors. When a tendering contractor makes clear that he is prepared to take care of the employer's major concerns and worries, he will create a preferred position in his negotiations.

[20]The lecturers here apply the Harvard case method. See M. McNair and A. C. Hersum (eds.) (1954), The *case method at Harvard Business School*. New York: McGraw Hill; J. S. Hammond (1976), *Learning by the case method*. Boston, MA: Harvard Business School Publishing Division, Case #376–241; R. Corey (1998), *Case Method Teaching*, Boston, MA: Harvard Business School Publishing Division, Ref. 9–581–058; M. Robinson (2010), *How to write a case study*, William Davidson Institute, Note 1–429–140.

Box 9.2. Tender prices and risk management in the Swania case — risk identification — results per course and per sub-group.

Month	N[21]	Risk score	% of max. score	Av. risk score of group	Av. % of max. risk score	Price in € × 1000	Average pro-posed tender price € × 1000	Remarks
2009/ 2010								
	4	209	45			129.800		
	4	177	38			129.500		
	4	135	30			128.500		
	3	217	47			136.472		
June 2009	(15)			185	40		131.068	
	6	245	53			127.600		
	6	145	31			120.750		
	6	191	41			127.270		
	5	190	41			136.000		
Sept 2009	(23)			193	42		127.900	
	5	246	53			131.140		
	5	135	29			129.000		
	5	129	28			142.162		
	4	115	23			134.800		
Nov 2009	(19)			154	33		134.275	
	4	144	31			130.000		
	4	249	54			122.300		
	4	145	31			142.990		
	3	139	30			119.240		
	3	129	28			139.828		
Feb 2010	(18)			161	35		130.871	

(*Continued*)

[21]N = number of persons in sub-group.

Box 9.2. (*Continued*)

Month	N	Risk score	% of max. score	Av. risk score of group	Av. % of max. risk score	Price in €×1000	Average pro-posed tender price €×1000	Remarks
	4	172	37			133.100		
	4	210	45			121.220		
	4	179	38			128.400		
	4	195	42			129.000		
Mar 2010	5	210	45			144.000		
	(21)			193	41		131.144	
	6	235	51			119.700		
	6	322	69			108.660		
	5	337	72			121.334		
	5	270	58			129.995		
June 2010	(22)			291	63		119.922	
	4	275	59			130.000		
	4	120	26					118.800[22]
	4	252	54			138.000		
	4	204	44			150.000		
Sept 2010	5	589	62			137.000		
	(21)			245	49		134.760	

2011/ 2012	N	Score	%	Av Risk score	Av %	Price	Av price	Remarks
	4	175	34					No price stated

(*Continued*)

[22] Indicative price, exclusive risks.

Box 9.2. (*Continued*)

Month	N	Risk score	% of max. score	Av. risk score of group	Av. % of max. risk score	Price in € × 1000	Average proposed tender price € × 1000	Remarks
	4	185	36			131.670		
	4	325	63			126.900		
	4	310	60			129.998		
Feb 2011	(16)			249	48		129.523	
	5	372	72			144.500		
	5	224	43			137.896		
	5	257	50			139.700		
	5	245	48			122.128		
	4	315	62			136.000		
May 2011	(24)			283	55		136.045	
	4	257	50			129.997		
	4	280	54			124.234		
	4	359	70			128.000		
	4	225	44			137.000		
	4	325	63			126.000		
Sept 2011	(20)			289	56		129.046	
	4	279	54			138.776		
	4	95	18			129.900		
	4	289	56			135.700		
	4	187	36			125.000		
	4	319	62			138.875		
Dec 2011	(20)			233	45		133.650	
	4	364	71			134.300		

(*Continued*)

Box 9.2. (*Continued*)

Month	N	Risk score	% of max. score	Av. risk score of group	Av. % of max. risk score	Price in €×1000	Average proposed tender price €×1000	Remarks
	4	357	69			129.957		
	4	222	43			133.007		
	4	265	51			125.763		
Feb 2012	(20)			302	59		130.757	
	3	265	51			126.170		
	3	275	53			146.312		
	4	322	63			139.110		
	3	227	44			130.165		
May 2012	(13)			272	53		135.439	

Almost all groups attack the case from a dyadic perspective. They think "it is contractor against employer". A small number of groups pay attention to a possible early involvement of a very important subcontractor, which has to cover about 25% of the project value. These groups show their attention to the supply-chain perspective. None of the groups could mention a value-chain perspective; neither could a network perspective be discovered in the participants' presentations.[23]

One of the teachings of the exercise is that it is almost impossible that one tender team is able to recognize all risks in a set of tender documents.

A second teaching is that various teams come to different lists of risks and they price these risks differently. Often risks were priced by intuition. However, a more systematic approach could easily pay off.

To overcome such shortcomings, contractors, ideally, should form cross-functional tender teams for important tenders. The composition of such a team should consist of at least a financial expert, a legal counselor, a specialist

[23]For the various perspectives, see Chapter 4, Section 4.4.

on subcontracting and procurement, a design engineer, a project manager and a contract manager.

For very important tenders, the contractor should preferably create two different tender teams, separately working on the same tender. The teams should consist of at least one senior, experienced engineer together with a younger, talented upcoming technician. The combination of such characters will be beneficial for the results, and significantly improve the contractor's hit rate on tenders.

The spread in the various scores

The maximum score was 72% of the risks to be discovered. The lowest sub-group score amounts to 18%. The average risk score is about 47%. The reasons why some sub-groups have much better results than others are:

- Superior preparation of the tender by individual participants.
- Participants come from different disciplines.
- The knowledge and know-how of the participants are complementary.
- Different team roles are represented by the individual group members.
- Presence of an excellent project secretary.
- Cooperation and respect between team members.

The price differences

The sub-groups presented their lump-sum tender price. The lowest price was €119,700,000, while the highest was €150,000,000, which is 25% higher than the lowest. There are different ways to arrive at a price:

- The team starts a cost estimate: all materials, cost of subcontractors and the most important service providers, the cost of the equipment and the wages are added.
- This bare cost price is increased by costs for general overheads, historical experience for unforeseen disappointments, often called "general risks", and some risks which can be quantified.[24]

[24] Sometimes contractors have different past experiences with different contract forms, causing application of different percentages in excess charges above the bare cost price, for instance, 2.5% for construction contracts, 3.5–5% for D&B, 4.5–6% for ECP, 5.5–7% for DBM, 6–8.5% for DBFM and 7–12% for DBFMO contracts.

- Next, the team starts with an initial tender price, and proceeds by making an inventory of all risks that were detected. Next, each risk that is accepted will increase the fee. As a result the team presents an "all in" tender price to the employer.
- Or, the team starts by stating its reservations, which represent the risks that the contractor, for his own reasons, is not going to accept. These risks are priced, and presented as a separate list next to the (cost-based) tender price. As a result, the team presents a "rock-bottom" price, which is to be increased based upon further negotiations with the employer on the reservations made.
- Finally, the profit target is added.

During the tender process, it is difficult to calculate the price exactly. There are a number of risks that are impossible to quantify. Here, some guessing is necessary. You may call it intuition.

The role of risk appetite

Price differences also originate from the tender teams' risk appetites. The more hungry to score, the lower the tendered price. A remarkable finding during our discussions on the complex Swania case was the unstructured approach through which participants assess risk, which is why we discuss this subject in the next section.

9.7. Categorization of risks

Risks can be categorized as follows:

- Market risk.
- Credit risk.
- Financial risk.
- Operational risk.
- Legal and regulatory risk.
- Business risk.
- Strategic risk.
- Reputation risk.[25]

[25]For further reading, see M. Crouchi, D. Galay, R. Mark (2005), *The Essentials of Risk Management*. New York: McGraw Hill, pp. 26–36.

- Contractual risks.
- Design errors in employer's design.
- Own design failures.
- Executional risks.
- Defaults of contractor's subcontractors, service providers, and suppliers.
- Political risks.
- Risks in local labor.
- Risks concerning HS&E.

If possible, the risks should be quantified in terms of money, although at many tenders this will be impossible.

An alternative way of categorizing risks is to classify these according to the source from which they occurred. Hence, operational risks may be categorized into:

- Interruptions, such as natural events including heavy rain for a day or two, heavy wind, disasters, strikes, holds by suppliers and vendors.
- Bottlenecks in capacity, both in one's own project organization, as well as the subcontractor's.
- Distortions in the supply chain.
- System distortions, such as IT interruption.
- Errors in forecasting, which become evident during execution.
- Missed milestones in planning.
- Infringement of intellectual property, resulting in a hold on use of material or software.
- Bottlenecks in supply, such as an unexpected bankruptcy of a supplier.
- Financial risks at a subcontractor/supplier.

A third way to categorize risks could be the following:

- Employer — main contractor — subcontractors / service providers / suppliers, i.e. categorization based upon the stakeholders related to the supply chain.
- Engineering — procurement — subcontracting — execution — delivery — guarantee period, i.e. sequential perspective.
- Demographic — economic — social — technological — environmental — political.

In practice, it appears that categorizing risks in a systematic way will aid the tender team to observe more risks than without such categorization.

9.8. Managing risks

Risks can be managed in several ways. The best way is to secure a high level of quality assurance and quality control for the design, the operational and work processes and the management of the company. To arrive at that goal, highly qualified staff is a prerequisite. Investing in excellent management and personnel is even more important than investing in up-to-date equipment.

Experienced management and staff are able to estimate risks and to mitigate these.

Avoiding risks is a good practice in contracting. Putting redundant elements in the design, in development, in research, in execution, in documentation, in reports and records and in contract management represents an investment that will pay off later.

A further technique of handling risks is to transfer these to other parties. The contractor may refuse to accept a risk, and transfer it to the employer together with the message to "please find out yourself". When the contractor deliberately accepts a specific risk, he may transfer this to subcontractors, service providers and suppliers. However, in some cases, such actions may be deceptive. Depending on the specific contractual arrangements and the applicable legal system, the contractor may remain responsible and liable for all risks towards its employer, employer's stakeholders, its own stakeholders and third parties. Transferring risks to other parties is basically not the same as mitigation of risks and designing measures to avoid these.

A contractor may seek for insurance to cover certain risks. When insuring risks, a contractor is transferring risks to an insurance company. Or so it seems. In fact, the risk is *not* transferred. The risk remains where it is. The agreement with the insurance company gives the contractor the right to receive a certain financial compensation for the losses incurred, which will be paid to the contractor as an effect of the occurrence represented by the risk. Insurance is certainly not equal to minimizing risk and risk avoidance.

In summarizing, we are convinced that minimizing and avoiding risks are the best ways to overcome project risks. The other, additional measures cannot be neglected and may be used as well.

Risk assessment

Classifying risks into small — average — large risks is normal practice. There is, however, a fourth kind of risk, i.e. unacceptable risk. These are the items for which a reservation has to be made in the tender. The contractor is tendering, subject to the non-acceptance of such risks. This means that the contractor is informing the employer that he has to find other solutions for the risks involved than to transfer them to the contractor.

A project manager cannot manage all project risks at the same time. When executing the project, you have to select the items that deserve your personal attention. In order to select the most important risks, a risk matrix can be helpful. On the y-axis we put the financial impact of each identified risk. The x-axis represents the likelihood with which a risk factor is expected to occur. This is illustrated in Figure 9.4. The project manager has to concentrate on the risks in the outer segments, i.e. the risks marked A. Then, he needs to concentrate on countermeasures, which can be used to minimize the negative effects of the specific risk element.

Designing a risk matrix, as suggested, is far from easy. It requires a thorough understanding of the business and the project at hand, and a lot of practical experience. Assessing the financial impact, as well as the chance of occurrence of a certain risk factor, is a matter of judgment. This would call for a multidisciplinary approach, where different experts are able to expose their views. Having such discussions actually may be more useful than the outcome. It will create a common understanding about the challenges that lie ahead. Quantification of the effects of certain risk factors is, in many cases, an arbitrary matter. However, in the contracting industry, it is possible in some cases to estimate the financial impact of risk factors. For example: when a shipment for critical project goods is late, we may calculate the effect on the time

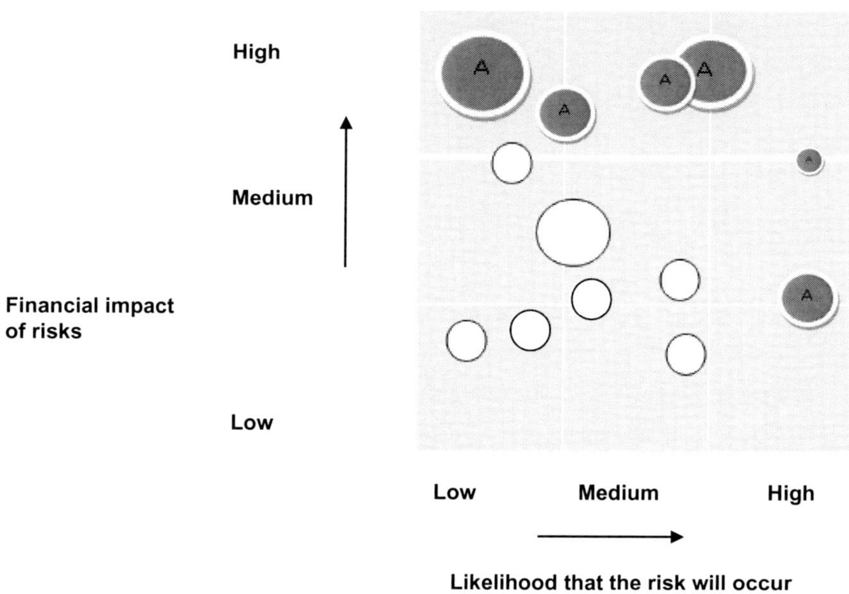

Figure 9.4. Example of a risk matrix.

schedule of the project, to be followed by the calculation of the penalty on the missed milestone. But it is more difficult to estimate the likelihood that the shipment will be late. Problems in estimating risks often lie at the root of discussions between different staff members at the contractor. Different stakeholders within the contractor's organization may convey a different attitude towards risk. Cummins (2011) states the following on the issue:

> When assessing risks most organizations tend to be too optimistic. Certain stakeholders in the organization have an interest in estimating the risk as low as possible. For example, the sales team has an interest in doing business rapidly and will be inclined to assess business risks to be low. Research by the International Centre for Complex Project Management (ICCPM) revealed a similar tendency among business executives — it termed this "the culture of optimism" — and their findings have been cited by a number of leading politicians, including the UK's Minister of Defence. In addition, optimism is fed by, for example, severe competition or social pressure. This means that you should have a clear understanding of all risks involved, qualify those risks and be subsequently able to financially quantify (= cost) those risks.[26]

9.9. Contract cycle and risk management

During the contract cycle risk management has a different role.[27]

When preparing the tender documents, the categorization and the identification of the various risks of the tender at hand are of primary importance. The tender department has to coordinate the different actions of the different departments: engineering, planning, finance, procurement, project department; while the sales department will be involved in permanently contacting the foreign (hopefully future) employer by forwarding questions about doubtful and unclear elements in the presented tender documents to the employer. There is much uncertainty in this phase of the contract cycle. Guessing based on experience will be necessary. Time is always short when preparing for tenders. Specifications for important subcontractors have to be prepared, an action that requires time, while subcontractor's quotations are needed in just a few days or a few weeks. A number of uncertainties usually still exist when the tender date comes near. Finally, the tender manager has to decide either to exclude certain risks at the expense of the employer if the risk occurs, or to add a certain amount of "general costs for unquantified risks" to the bare cost price.

Some risks may be calculated. For instance, a foreign currency may be hedged with the support of a commercial bank. Fuel costs may be hedged if the project's time span is not too uncertain. The same is true for raw

---

[26]T. Cummins, M. David, K. Kawamoto (2011), *Contract and Commercial Management: The Operational Guide*. IACCM. Zaltbommel, NL: Van Haren Publishing, p. 60.

[27]See Chapter 5.

materials, such as steel and cement. These are "clear figures", but a good tender manager is aware of the hidden uncertainties behind the clear figures. Another conflict in the Middle East will influence the market price of crude oil immediately. No one is able to predict whether it will happen or not, which country it might concern and if the oil price will vary slightly or show a steep increase. Still, the tender manager will have to decide upon a price in the tender, which normally will remain firm for some 120 days.

When negotiating the contract, the risks will be discussed with the employer. A keen employer will try to analyze the contractor's various cost elements and calculations. Some risks cannot be mitigated, while neither the employer, nor the contractor, is in a position to influence these. This is the case, for instance, with risks for which there is a hedging market: some raw materials, fuel and currencies. It is either the contractor or the employer who has to take these risks, or parties may share these risks. When discussing the financial part of the tender, the employer will understand that the contractor wants to be compensated, but he does not want to pay more than the "correct price" for the hedge. The employer may be of the opinion that the premium for the hedge is too high. He may state, "my bank will ask a lower price for that". In such an event, the risk should be transferred to the employer. If the employer is seriously convinced that the currency exchange rate will not change in the future, he may take such a currency risk at his own expense. However, when doing so this will increase the project's risk considerably.

Only after execution of the complete project will parties know for sure whether such transfer of risk has been wise or not. Box 9.3 shows an interesting example of differences of opinion between an employer and a contractor. It shows sequential negotiations, where the contractor did not want to accept the currency risk. The contractor's currency is in euros, which is why he needs to be rewarded in euros. The employer has foreign trade relations both in US dollars and in euros, which is why he wants to pay partly in euros and partly in dollars. His national currency is linked to the dollar. The contractor's first tender price was offered in January 2007, when the tender was negotiated for the first time; for the hedge, the contractor included €800,000 in his price, which at that moment came down to $81 million. The second set of negotiations took place in May 2007; again the contractor included €800,000 for the hedge. Meanwhile the currency exchange rate had changed: the euro gained more value to the dollar. That is the reason why the employer, at that moment, had to pay a higher price for the same scope of work, i.e. $87 million. During these negotiations, the employer expected that the currency exchange rate would come back to what he called a "more realistic balance". At that moment, he gambled. When in October 2007 the final negotiations resulted in a firm contract, the currency exchange rate again had moved to the employer's disadvantage. His total price in dollars amounted to $92 million, which represented a price increase of 13%, compared to the initial tender 10 months earlier.

Box 9.3. Transferring currency risk.[28]

1.

Tender
May 2006

First offer
January 2007

Payment in US$	Payment in €	Exchange rate	Cost of hedge	Total cost for employer
$40 m	€33.3 m	1.20	0.8 m	$81 m

2.

Tender
May 2006

2nd negotiations
May 2007

Payment in US$	Payment in €	Exchange rate	Cost of hedge	Total cost for employer
$40 m	€33.3 m	1.38	0.8 m	$87 m

3.

Tender
May 2006

Finalization
October 2007

Payment in US$	Payment in €	Exchange rate	Cost of hedge	Total cost for employer
$40 m	€33.3 m	1.54	0.8 m	$92 m

This case shows the impact of currency exchange rates. A contractor should avoid speculating on price variations of raw materials, fuel or currencies. Contractors should build beautiful works for the world. Gambling with prices is not their core business.

After landing the contract, the project manager is chosen. He is available only when his previous project has finished. Here, a new risk appears. The way

[28]The example is taken from P. van Zwieten (2009), Handling financial risks in project tenders, Presentation Module, *Finance & Risk*, December 9, presented at TiasNimbas Business School, Tilburg, the Netherlands.

the new project manager is informed implies a lot of risks. Normally, the project manager is still working on his previous project when he gets his next assignment. Until then, he has not been involved in the preparations of the project and might not be aware of its history. Immediately after being appointed as project manager he has to study all the important aspects of this brand new order. These imply the scope of work, the contract with its numerous appendices and enclosures, the foregoing correspondence and the drawings. He is informed by the people who did the negotiating. Normally, the new project manager will need from a few days up to a week to get involved with the main lines of the project. He starts the job under time pressure. In practice, it happens that the time schedule as agreed upon with the employer is already jeopardized during the first weeks of the new, freshly signed contract. It may be the tender manager's responsibility to present all details of the foregoing events in a logical order; in reality it is often difficult to get all the relevant pieces together for a perfect start.

Large and experienced employers, having to award very large and complex contracts, increasingly require that the project manager for the future contract will be present during all negotiations. This is common practice when dealing with complex contract forms as EPC/Turnkey, DBM, DBFM and DBFMO. Those negotiations may take a year or longer. Consequently, the prospective project manager will have to prepare all meetings, and becomes in this way acquainted with the ins and outs of the project. He will take notes on the meetings and later, during execution, be aware of the objectives and key issues, which the employer, including its stakeholders, had in mind from the outset. The presence of the future contract manager during negotiations eliminates — or reduces — the risk of misunderstandings during execution, which originated from the tender phase. The cost of such tenders — whether they result in contracts or not — may amount to €100,000–300,000 or more. That seems a lot of money for contract preparation. But such costs should be considered as a small investment in minimizing large contractual risks.

During execution the project manager has to steer his project through rocky waters. If risks are well identified and thoroughly discussed, and countermeasures have been designed and prepared, the project manager will succeed in delivering a profitable project. When time goes by during execution, the risks will disappear slowly, according to the IFSR formula:[29]

$$\text{Profit} = \frac{\text{Total cost incurred to date}}{\text{Total cost estimated to complete}} \times \text{estimated profit.}$$

[29]The International Accounting Standard 11 (2009) of the International Financial Reporting Standards (IFRS) describes in Paragraphs 22–24, 30, 32 and 36 how contract revenues should be estimated.

Each day of execution, the chances for a profitable project increase.

After taking over the works, some repairs may need to be done. For DBM, DBFM and DBFMO contracts, the contractor will be responsible for a number of years. Under such contracts, the employer did not in the first instance contract for the delivery of a works; on the contrary, he contracted for the availability, i.e. usage, of the works by the employer. Hence, payment only commences after delivery of the works.

9.10. Risk appetite — risk pressure — risk exposure

Different companies may show different attitudes towards accepting and taking risks. Some contractors are very conservative and unwilling to enter new markets or take unknown risks. These are stable and reliable contractors, applying their great experience in their fields of expertise. Other contractors like to enter new fields of technology, like to respond to new challenges as presented by employers and do engage in new types of contracts. Those contractors show risk appetite, which is necessary to enter into new markets, to tender to new employers for whom the contractor never worked before, to apply new technologies and to gain experience with more risky contract types.

Top management may press contract directors and project managers to fulfill contractual obligations according to agreed-upon time schedules against the agreed fixed budgets. Exerting pressure on project managers and contract managers may lead to increasing and unacceptable risk exposure.[30]

Figure 9.5 was derived from Robert Simons (1998). We added contract types, employers and subcontractors, since each of them represent different risks. Figure 9.5 identifies six fields of risks, each of which is divided into three sub-fields. Each square represents one kind of risk to be judged using scores ranging from 1 to 5 (low–high). The maximum possible score in each line of risks is 15 points, the maximum possible total score therefore is 90 points. A low risk contractor will score approximately 6 to 30 points; an average risk for a contractor will be approximately between 31 and 60 points, whereas a company which scores over 61 points should be qualified as a great risk-accepting contractor.

A company that has the strategic intent to grow is obliged to take more risks than its competitors. Growth in general is a result of success. At the same

[30] See Chapter 1 for a dramatic example.

Evaluation in figures from 1 to 5 per square						Score
Growth	Press for performance	+	Rate of expansion	+	Inexperienced personnel	....
Market Economies	New demands from employers in existing markets	+	Appetite to enter into unknown markets	+	Accepting strict conditions from new employers	....
Culture	Rewards for challenges and risk-taking	+	Top executives resistance to bad news	+	Level of internal competition	....
Contract Type	Avoidance of construction at reimbursable prices and strict planning	+	Appetite for integrated contracts: EPC-turnkey	+	Appetite for integrated + maintenance + operations: DBM/ DBFMO	....
Employers	Aversion against regular clients at lean profits	+	Accepting changing functional specs during execution	+	Appetite for war-employers at high profit margins	....
Subcontractors	Selecion of subcontractors and service providers at lowest price	+	Detailed instructions +requirements to subcontractors	+	Incidental relationships with subcontractors	....

					Total score	....

Figure 9.5. Risk exposure calculator for international contractors. (Source: Derived from Simons, 1998.)

time, growth incorporates important risks. New personnel are needed; new personnel have no experience, or less than the personnel that have worked for the company for a number of years. New personnel means incorporating increased risks.

The internal culture of the company plays an important role in risk management. If the personnel are rewarded — in whatever form — for results after having fulfilled risky operations, the internal risk appetite will be increased. Another factor is the readiness of top executives to hear bad news. When top executives normally react in a negative or blaming style, project and contract managers will look for their own solutions, while postponing reporting the bad news at a higher level. In doing so, the risk may increase. If one succeeds and achieves a narrow escape, one may feel comfortable, and next time be prepared to act in the same way. The level of internal competition may increase risk exposure when project managers are competing for the most rewarding projects, which are linked to personal bonuses.

As explained before, risks increase for contractors when engaging in more complex contract types. A contractor who is prepared to accept complex contract types is exposed to risks, while a conservative contractor who stays with the well-known level playing field of the construction contracts, with a descriptive scope of work, will not suffer from great risk exposure. On the other hand, such a contractor will not be able to grow and expand his business.

Choosing new markets or new employers represents a separate risk field. There are conservative employers, e.g. conservative public institutions, who prefer well-engineered designs and well-calculated tenders. On the other hand, there are private companies, which, in their own markets, are suffering from strong competition from their rivals and pressure from their shareholders. Their own culture is rather demanding and competitive, a reason why they expect such a mentality from their contractors. This may explain why contracts may be entered into and executed from a "war game" perspective, rather than from a collaborative perspective.

Consequently, a contractor with a great risk appetite is in need of subcontractors, service providers and suppliers with an identical mentality. Subcontractors who want to do work for such contractors have to understand their role. The contractor is willing to accept risks, but he, in his turn, will require the acceptance of risks from his subcontractors for their own part of the work. In such cases, the contractor should be backed by excellent subcontractors. The main contractor certainly will want to engage subcontractors in managing and mitigating his risk exposure.

9.11. Strategic risks[31]

Thinking about risks, we have to widen our view and look beyond the project manager's or project director's horizon. Beyond project risks, the contractor's company is constantly exposed to other risks than represented by projects only. We refer here to risks that result in such dramatic losses that the continuity of the company is jeopardized. In such an event, these risks are strategic. Robert Simons (1998) systematically identified and described such risks.[32]

Operational risks

Normally, in our experience, disasters that might happen to strike projects are never caused by only one single cause. There is always a complex of multiple causes that result in disastrous effects. Operational risks may be reduced by various techniques. The standardization of work methods and control of key processes, total quality management, benchmarking, engineering studies, permanent training of key staff, research and development, evaluation of errors made in regular processes and projects in order to learn from previous failures, and improvement programs are examples of measures that can be taken to mitigate risks.

Asset impairment risks

An asset is a resource owned by the contractor to generate cash flow. Asset impairment risk is the risk that equipment and main operational assets lose their capability to generate sufficient future cash in a limited time span. Asset impairment becomes strategic in the event the company's assets are no longer suitable for the company's long-term survival.

Competitive risks

Competitive risks result from changes in the competitive environment that could affect the contractor's ability to win future projects. Competitors may propose better solutions and superior designs when tendering, or more

---

[31] This paragraph was inspired by Robert Simons, 1998 (see note 32), but adapted to the contractor's business.

[32] R. Simons (1998), *Identifying Strategic Risk*, Harvard Business School, Note No. 199–031; R. Simons, *Identifying Strategic Risks in Performance Measurement & Control Systems for Implementing Strategy, Text & Cases.* Upper Saddle River, NJ: Prentice Hall, pp. 255–274.

sophisticated maintenance plans for the employer's future permanent works, or more intelligent financial arrangements. Another strength of competitors may be in meeting the customer's preferences in the timely foreseeing of their constantly changing needs to realize their strategic goals. Competition is felt where strong rivalry between contractors exists. Demanding employers, for whom in the past many works were successfully achieved, may choose to switch suddenly and award contracts to other contractors. Competitive risk becomes strategic risk when a contractor, after several attempts in different tenders, with the help of its existing technical know-how, its equipment, and with the support of its regular subcontractors and service providers, is no longer able to win projects, not even at cost price.

Reputation risk

Reputation risk occurs when a contractor's problems or the contractor's way of working negatively affect stakeholders' perceptions of the contractor. Key stakeholders are, of course, employers, who are necessary for generating incoming cash flows. But other stakeholders, such as politicians, the press, subcontractors, service providers, suppliers and vendors, trade unions and the like, may affect the contractor's reputation in a negative way, which may result in loss of sympathy from the public. The result may be that the contractor will suffer from stricter regulations by competent authorities; that recruiting young, talented personnel becomes more difficult; that many young engineers do not respond to job vacancies; that subcontractors and service providers, suppliers and vendors do not offer their best prices; that trade unions will interrupt operations. Reputation risk is always translated into financial losses. However, such losses are difficult to quantify.

Strategic risk management — boardroom issue

When a company fails to manage its risks, bankruptcy is not far away. During the last two decades, the general public was taken by surprise in some cases (such as Parmalat, Enron, Fortis, ABN Amro Bank and, more recently, SBM Offshore in 2012). Citizens wonder how fraud and mismanagement, which were conducted by top management, could go on for such a long time. In the case of fraud and mismanagement, the top management of any company may find itself before a criminal court. After a thorough investigation of hundreds of court cases, the most frequent reasons for corporate failure were listed by Daniella Strik (2010). A short overview is summarized in Box 9.4.

Box 9.4. Most frequent reasons for corporate failure.[33]

Most frequent liabilities of board members:

1. Adopting a strategy that entails too much risk.
2. The board takes a decision without investigating the possible risk involved.
3. The company does not have risk management and internal control systems.
4. Possible risks have been investigated, but have not been identified.
5. A choice for an inadequate risk response has been made.
6. No criteria or guidelines have been established for managing identified risks.
7. There is no periodical assessment of the actual exposure of the risks to the established criteria.
8. There is no contingency plan.
9. Further to suspected incidents, no questions have been asked or further inquiries made.
10. No corrective measures have been taken.
11. In cases where established criteria have not been met, they are neglected or amended without inquiry.
12. Failure to inform co-directors.
13. Making misleading public statements on risk management.

The list reveals which mistakes board members were sentenced for by courts in many countries. The list does *not* give us any insight into the many mistakes, misjudgments and failures that were never discovered and remained hidden behind profits on other successful projects.

9.12. Conclusions and recommendations

Risks are possible occurrences, which, in the event they occur, have a negative effect on the success of a project. Risk management is the identification, analysis and quantification of risks, and the translation of these in a systematic risk-mitigation plan, which allows for proper control, reporting and

[33] D. Strik (2010), Grondslagen bestuurdersaansprakelijkheid. Een maatpak voor de Board Room (Basics of governance accountability. Tailor-made for the boardroom.), Erasmus Universiteit Rotterdam. Deventer: Kluwer.

follow-up. A large variety of risks exists. Each project has its own risk profile. Contract type and payment mechanisms of a contract give each project its unique color and flavor.

A written company policy on risks and risk management may serve as a compass when riding the waves of project management. Different tender teams may arrive at different risk assessments, and as a result, may come to different tender prices and proposals. It is nearly impossible to recognize all contract and project risks during the tender phase of a contract.

The best way to minimize risks is to have excellent Quality Assurance (QA) and Quality Control (QC) in place and to recruit excellent project management and staff. Building in redundancies in design, engineering, research and development (R&D), documentation, reports and records, and contract management will also be effective to mitigate the consequences of project risks. Other options are measures aimed at minimizing risks, avoidance of risks, insurance of risks and transfer of risks. Finally, not accepting certain risks can be a wise policy.

Systematic categorization of risks and a systematic approach towards risk management facilitate detection of risks in tender documents at an early stage. Next, it will enable a more complete picture of the risk profile of the project involved.

For important tenders, a contractor should consider working with two competing tender teams, who work separately on the same tender. The teams should consist of both senior, experienced engineers and newly qualified ones with good potential. The combination of such talents will be beneficial for successfully submitting proposals for tender.

In order to select the most important risks, a risk matrix should be used: on the y-axis, the financial impact of each identified risk is presented; on the x-axis, the likelihood of occurrence is stated. The project manager has to concentrate on the risks in the outer segments of the risk matrix. He will primarily concentrate on mitigation and avoidance of these risks.

Risk appetite leads to optimistic estimates when dealing with risks. A careful risk analysis and risk-mitigation plan may keep discussions within the company at a realistic level.

Essentially, the board of directors is responsible for effective risk management. If things go wrong, the board is liable for the financial losses and sometimes even subject to prosecution. It is up to all managers and staff to prevent such events from ever happening.

Appendix 9.1.

Box 9.5. Participants' model score card.

Case 1: Going for it... or not?
Mr. Ing. John van der Puil[34]

1. Evaluation of the performance of the participants (2009)

The most important risks were taken into account
GR = great / important
NA = not acceptable

When participants mention the relevant risks, the following score is booked:

	Kind of risk	GR	NA	Score	Participants' Score
0	**Swania / our counterparty Geenco / tendering**				
0.1	What kind of country is Swania?	X		10	
0.2	Relation to UN, Unesco, World bank, IMF	X		10	
0.3	What kind of a company is Geenco?	X		10	
0.4	Sufficient budget for Variations if any?	X		10	
0.5	Employer = Engineer — one and the same party			10	
0.6	In which way is Geenco going to evaluate the different tenders, ours' as well as our competitors'?			5	
0.7	Should we establish our own company or affiliate in Swania?			5	
0.8	Will Geenco appoint a competent Project Manager?			5	
0.9	Will Geenco in future appoint an Engineer as per FIDIC?			5	

(Continued)

[34]© John van der Puil, Engineers & Lawyers, Rotterdam. The author wishes to express his gratitude to Erik A. Kruizenga, M.Sc. for his initiative, help, suggestions and valuable comments.

Box 9.5. (*Continued*)

	Kind of risk	GR	NA	Score	Participants' Score
0.10	Available health care in Swania?			5	
0.11	Validity of tender 120 days			2	
0.12	Planning data missing in tender documents			5	
1	**Design and Planning**				
1.1	Design, FIDIC 4.10, Design data to be checked by third party	X		10	
1.2	Responsibility, FIDIC 5.1, Contractor responsible for design	X		10	
1.3	Standards, FIDIC 5.4, Country's technical standards?	X		10	
1.4	Planning — impossible to meet required date		X	10	
1.5	Time needed for testing soil and ground levels + sub-soil	X		10	
1.6	19 or more months delivery time for complete works in case of unproblematic soil conditions[35]			10	
	18 months			5	
	17 months			0	
1.7	Error in our own Preliminary Level One Planning			10	
1.8	Interface with other contractors / coordination at site			10	
1.9	Defects notification period			5	
1.10	Import licenses for our own equipment?			5	
1.11	Availability Project Manager			5	
2	**Location**				
2.1	No reliable soil and ground test available at the moment		X	10	
2.2	Ground conditions at bay below water surface		X	10	

(Continued)

[35] Score for item 1.6 is 10 points maximum.

Box 9.5. (*Continued*)

	Kind of risk	GR	NA	Score	Partici-pants' Score
2.2	Heavy rain	X		5	
2.3	Quality of the available sand for concrete			5	
2.4	Site Data FIDIC 4.10			5	
2.5	FIDIC 4.12 — Unforeseeable physical conditions			2	
2.6	FIDIC 4.24 — Fossils, etc.			2	
2.7	Unknown environmental restrictions			2	
2.8	Access routes and harbors			5	
2.9	Availability of gas, water and electricity			5	
2.10	Unexploded objects?			5	
3	**Finance**[36]				
3.1	Currency US $ and Swania $	X		10	
3.2	Non-payment of instalments	X		10	
3.3	Advance payment	X		5	
3.4	Payment bond or bank guarantee	X		5	
3.5	Payment guarantee from World Bank?	X		5	
3.6	Cash flow = timely payment instalments	X		10	
3.7	Maximum liability < 50% of contract price	X		0	
	< or = 30%			10	
	< or = 20%			20	
3.8	Financial losses in the event of *force majeure*	X		10	
3.9	Procurement: cost of raw materials — fixed price to be quoted	X		10	
3.10	Fuel price variation	X		10	
3.11	Import duties on materials or on our own equipment?	X		10	
3.12	Set off not acceptable (looks like hidden consequential loss)	X		10	

(*Continued*)

[36]Deviations from tender documents.

Box 9.5. (*Continued*)

	Kind of risk	GR	NA	Score	Participants' Score
3.13	Taxes to be levied on our own temporary cabins or equipment?			5	
4	**Subcontractors and suppliers**				
4.1	Dredging, price, availability ship, subsurface not yet known		X	20	
4.2	Local subcontractors, staff and labor, permits	X		20	
4.3	Availability of adequate equipment at local subcontractors			10	
4.4	Is Geenco going to nominate certain subcontractors?			10	
4.5	Back-to-back contracting	X		10	
4.6	Fluctuation in steel price	X		10	
4.7	Availability of concrete mill in Swania	X		5	
5	**Own equipment pm**				
5.1	Availability and conditions own equipment			5	
5.2	Import licenses for our own equipment?			5	
	Standard insurance (pm)				
6	**Additional costs**				
	Pm: not yet known				
7	**Variations**				
	Pm: no Variations found in tender specification				
7.1	Not to exceed x % (for instance 15 or 30%) of the contract price			5	
7.2	Not to decrease the scope of work over y% (10 or 20%) of sum			10	
8	**Risks and liabilities**				
	CAR insurance to be taken out by our own company	X		10	
9	**Risk and contractual responsibilities**				

(*Continued*)

Box 9.5. (*Continued*)

	Kind of risk	GR	NA	Score	Partici-pants' Score
9.1	Consequential losses; not applicable, FIDIC 17.6	X		10	
9.2	Maximum liability: to be stated in Letter of Tender: = 50% of contract price or less, FIDIC 17.6 Note Finance, sub 3.7				
9.3	Maximum delay on penalties < 200 days			5	
9.4	FIDIC 17.1 — Tort			5	
10	**Language, Legal and Disputes**				
10.1	Contract law Swania		X	10	
10.2	Changes in Swania law[37], rules and regulations		X	10	
10.3	Dispute resolution, DAB to be appointed	X		10	
	Maximum score			**465**	

2. Price to be quoted

11	**Price in tender**				
	110.,000.000 or less			0	
	119.000.000 = + 8% Overhead			10	
	130.000.000 = + 8% Overhead + 10% design + risk			20	
	135.000.000 = + 8% Overhead + 10% design + risk + profit			30	
	Over 135.000.000			40	
	Reservation if suction dredger needed[38]			10	
	Maximum score			**50**	

(*Continued*)

[37] Changes in law or regulations might be incongruous to foreign companies.

Box 9.5. (*Continued*)

Total maximum score	
1–10	465
11	50
Total	515

3. **Reservations in tender**
   - Investigation for ground and sea levels and sub-soil, state of affairs and planning time
   - Sub-soil and hydrological conditions at the site, FIDIC 4.10

   It is impossible to tender a firm price without having these data investigated by a neutral expert.

   - Required Completion Date
   - Swania law and changes in Swania law, rules and regulations.

4. **Compulsory items in preparing the opinion**
   - Time planning of the project
   - Financial planning
   - List of risks and how to accept them, avoid them or contract out.

Tilburg / Rotterdam, February 2011
JP

[38] Business ethics 11. See Risks, line 4.1.

Chapter 10

Managing Variations in Contracts

10.1. Case 1 — Permission for a technical variation[1]

There was a lump-sum contract to build a series of iron buildings.[2] The contract said that no alterations should be made without a written order from the engineer. During construction, the contractor faced practical problems in getting through-girders. The engineer allowed him to use more expensive girders of a heavier weight. When the work was finished, the engineer issued certificates where, as a deviation from the original specification, the applied girders were mentioned. The contractor claimed extra payment for the extra weight of the material. The court's judgment was clear. There was no written order from the engineer, as required in the contract. Furthermore, engineer's certificates were not written orders. So the claim was excluded by the terms of the contract. It was one of the first cases on the widespread problems and legal cases on variations. The verdict came from an English judge. In other judicial systems, the outcome would not have been different.

10.2. Case 2 — Instructions versus variations[3]

This case played out exactly a hundred years after the first case on changes in a contract versus variations. In the meantime, contractors apparently had not (yet) learned their lessons. The contract stipulated that the engineer could instruct the contractor to carry out "any variation that he thought might be

[1]Tharsis Sulpher and Copper Company vs. McElroy & Sons and Others, 1878.

[2]The verdict mentions "iron buildings". Now we might refer to "steel structures". But note: in England during the 19th century, complete manufacturing halls were constructed out of steel, although "iron" was the word used.

[3]Hersent Offshore S. A. and Amsterdamse Ballast Beton en Waterbouw B.V. vs. Burmah Oil Tankers Ltd, 1978.

necessary for the completion of the works, but no variation was to be undertaken without a Variation Order in writing from the Engineer".

During execution, the engineer changed several technical issues. A year after completion, the contractor asked for extra payment. The employer felt this was a little bit late. Before a court of arbitration, the argument was put forward that the engineer gave instructions to vary the design of the riser support structure. This instruction was not confirmed in writing. The arbitrators discovered another clause in the contract. The notice of intention to claim should have been given as soon as possible after the instruction. So, the employer was not liable to pay for the extra work to the contractor.

Reading the above cases, we discover how judges (and arbitrators) operate. A judge reads the claim. He reads the contract to know what parties agreed amongst themselves. He considers the facts: what happened exactly? He is obliged to do so, because the claim is based on the facts. Then his most important work starts: he compares the claim with the contract, with jurisprudence and with the law. The verdict follows. The key issue when discussing variations is what the parties really did agree upon.

This chapter deals with contract variations, changes and instructions. Sometimes these words are synonymous, and sometimes not. That depends upon the definition chosen, specifically the definition in the applicable contract. The International Accounting Standard 11 gives a definition of a variation as "an instruction of the customer for a change in a scope of work to be performed under the contract". In the two above cases, changes were introduced; in the second case, even on the demand of the engineer, acting on behalf of the employer. In both cases, the judge and the arbitrators did not find reasons for extra payment for the additional work and materials.

Furthermore, we have to pay attention to claims. More than once, it has happened that an employer or an engineer, acting on his behalf, issues an instruction to a contractor, which could be considered as a variation, but is not recognized as such by the employer and the engineer. Thereupon the contractor may issue a claim for extra funds and/or change of the time schedule.

Variation orders result in many problems. Variations may mean the difference between a financially interesting contract or a disastrous contract. The first problem that may arise here is what is the difference between a variation and a change? More important is the second issue — how should the contractor operate in order to get paid for the extra work due to a variation? We will analyze the issues.

In this chapter we will mention some definitions of variations, while noting that there is not one definition, but rather that standard contracts have different ideas on the subject. We will see that variations may concern many aspects of work to be accomplished. Procedures for how to agree on a variation are rather strict. On the other hand, variations may open a possibility to book extra turnover for the contractor. Some cases of successful changes in contracts and in scope of work will be discussed. We will come to the conclusion that, in some types of contracts, variations are good opportunities for the contractor, while in other types, the contractor has to undertake much more risk. Variations are out of the question in most EPC/Turnkey contracts, especially where consequential maintenance by the contractor is involved. We will conclude that variations should fit within the framework of the chosen typology of the contract. For instance: a Construct contract should not be altered into a Design & Construct contract by means of a variation.

10.3. Definitions of variations

Many definitions of the word "variation" exist. As introduced above, the International Federation of Financial Standards issued the International Accounting Standard number 11, which is applicable to construction contracts:

> A variation is an instruction of the customer for a change in the scope of work to be performed under the contract. A variation may lead to an increase or a decrease in contract revenue. Examples of variations are changes in the specification or design of the asset and changes in the duration of the contract.[4]

This definition is sufficient for accounting purposes, but not for managing projects.

Many standard contracts mention more details, in order to prevent confusion.

FIDIC

The FIDIC red book (construction contract) defines a variation as:

> Any change to the works as per sub-clause 13.1, i.e. any change of quantities and quantities of items, changes to levels, positions and/or dimensions of any part of the works, omission of any part of the works, any additional work, plant, or services, including any associated tests on completion, boreholes or any other testing, changes to the sequence of timing.

---

[4] IFRS, International Accounting Standard 11 (IAS 11), Construction contracts, staff consolidated version as of September 16, 2009.

The FIDIC yellow book (D&B contract) defines variation in a different way, i.e. as any change to the *employer's requirements or the works*;[5] it does not mention the list of variations as mentioned in the FIDIC red book. The reason is that, in the red book, the employer is responsible for the design, while in the yellow book, the contractor is responsible for the design.

The FIDIC silver book (EPC/Turnkey contract) uses the same phrasing, i.e. *employer's requirements for the works*.[6] However, here, the contractor's task is wider than in D&B contracts; although the wordings of the clause are almost identical to those of the D&B contract, the context is different. Under an EPC/Turnkey contract, a contractor is unable to ask for variations in case the employer's ideas are unclear, or errors, inaccuracies or omissions have incurred in the contract. The idea is that the contractor, in entering into an EPC/Turnkey contract, is the expert and has much more knowledge of the works that are to be realized than the employer. Variations are restricted to immutable data, definitions of purpose intended by the employer, criteria for testing and performance of the completed works, portions, data and information which cannot be verified by the contractor.

These are general rules. In specific situations, parties may deviate from these principles. However, in deviating, they should take care that the main idea of construction versus D&B, versus EPC/Turnkey, should be maintained.

The FIDIC blue book on dredging and land reclamation defines a variation as a change to the specification and/or drawings (if any).[7]

LOGIC

The most important LOGIC contracts deal with Construction, Marine Construction and Mobile Drilling Rigs. Construction and Marine Construction contracts are near to each other in typology and phrasing.

Both contracts define a variation as an instruction from the employer. A list of possible issues is summed up: additions, omissions, substitutions and changes in quality, form, character, kind, position, dimension, level or line and changes in methods of construction; acceleration of the work;[8] and reprogramming the work.[9] Any instruction will constitute a variation.

---

[5] Emphasis added.

[6] Emphasis added.

[7] FIDIC Form of Contract for dredging and reclamation works, blue book, clause 22.1.1.

[8] Slight difference in wording between LOGIC Construction and Marine Construction, clauses 14.1. iii.

[9] LOGIC Construction and Marine Construction, clause 14.1.

However, instructions to fulfill obligations under the contract are not regarded as variations.[10] The contractor has to start working on the variation, even if the conditions for price and planning are not yet completely settled.[11] Uninterrupted, speedy activities on the work site are more important than the related conditions. The contractor is not in a position to not start the work on the variations, by arguing that the deal should be 100% clear. However, for variations under the Marine Construction contract, within the 500 meters sector from oil and gas production facilities, the contractor shall not be obliged to start work or activities before being sure of the details of the variation, including liabilities of both parties.[12] This last restriction is made because safety around drilling rigs has priority above speedy work.

The LOGIC Mobile Drilling Rig standard contract is extremely short on variations. A definition is lacking. Variations are left to the "mutual agreement of the parties".[13] The reason is clear. This is an EPC/Turnkey standard, where basically the contractor is responsible for the complete design, engineering, procurement, construction and delivery, up to operation and maintenance, as stated under the clause regarding the contractor's general obligations.[14] Entering into such a contract implies that all risks are for the contractor's account.

The standard contracts make clear that variations must contain one or two of three elements, or all three: change in the scope of work, change of the planning schedule and change in price.

10.4. Events resulting in variations

All standards have different definitions for "variation". But under all contracts, variations may be caused by many occurrences. Box 10.1 lists possible reasons why variations should be agreed upon.

A change does not necessarily represent a variation. When the project is under way, many reasons for variations may occur. The typology of the contract plays an important role in determining whether extra payment and extra time are permitted, or if the agreed-upon scope of work should be altered. We have to distinguish between an agreed scope of work and the contractor's own specifications. In a Turnkey contract, the agreed-upon (functional) scope may stay as it is, while the contractor internally decides to change its technical

---

[10] LOGIC Construction and Marine Construction, clause 14.2 (c).

[11] LOGIC Construction and Marine Construction, clause 14.1 (b).

[12] LOGIC Marine Construction, clause 14.1 (c).

[13] LOGIC Mobile Drilling Rig, clause 11.

[14] LOGIC Mobile Drilling Rig, clause 4.1.

Box 10.1. Reasons for issuing a variation order.

- A change in the quantity of an individual item.
- The late issuing of instructions, documents or drawings by the engineer.
- The loss or damage to the contract works arising from excepted risks.
- The location, altering, protecting, offsetting or reinstating of a utility not indicated in the contract documents.
- Protection and complying with the engineer's directions for the treatment of treasures (artifacts and the like) if not otherwise provided for in the contract documents.
- Late provision of documents or materials by the employer.
- Failure by the engineer to properly carry out his or her duties as required by the contract documents.
- Inspection, recording, measuring and testing ordered by the engineer, not provided for in the contract documents, which comply with the requirements of the contract documents.
- Failure by the engineer to carry out inspection at the time when requested, causing delays and extra costs.
- The engineer requesting works to be opened up for inspection, if the works comply with the contract documents.
- Failure by the engineer to issue completion certificates or defects liability certificates on time, causing delays and further costs.
- Works suspended by the engineer, causing delays and further costs.[15]

Further variations may result from:

- The engineer directing or changing the order on which the work carried out is based.
- Unforeseen physical conditions.
- Occupancy of the works by the employer causing delay or cost not otherwise provided for in the contract documents.
- Defects found during the defects liability period, for which the contractor is not liable.
- Cost resulting from royalties, fees or tolls imposed by the government or local authority, which were not foreseen.
- Work directed by the engineer under provisional sums, prime cost sums and contingency sums in the contract documents.[16]

---

[15] This list was derived from the Standard Conditions of Contract, NZS 3910:2003, New Zealand. It helps to consider classification of instructions and requirements in any project situation.

[16] The second list is cited from M. Abernethey (2007), So what constitutes a variation?, *Contractor*, Volume 31, May 4.

specification to arrive at the employer's intended goal. Table 10.1 provides an overview of the possibilities to request variations for different types of contracts. Where "depends" is mentioned in Table 10.1, the referred applicable contract may give a clear answer and indicate the correct solution.

In the list in Table 10.1, we supposed that the reasons for the changes were initiated by or attributable to the employer. Even in those cases, a change does not always result in a variation. There are no clear and unique answers to general questions about whether a certain circumstance will result in a variation; it always has to be considered on a case-by-case basis. Besides the contract documents, the details of the change have to be considered. We recommend, in case of a change, to first check the contract. What has been agreed upon? Who is liable for the costs involved in the change? Is there a reason to apply the *force majeure* clause? Which effects due to the change can be foreseen by the change? Is there any reason for issuing a variation?

Instructions, clarifications, interpretation of drawings, specifications, digital information and notifications are normally not considered to result in a variation. In the event that the employer gives you instructions, check your scope of work: is the work resulting from the instructions part of the scope of work or is it a variation? If so — ask for it in writing.

A brief note on the Dutch UAV 89, the UAV 2012 and the UAVGC 2005 is appropriate. The rules of the latter differ slightly from a regular FIDIC D&B contract. The UAV[17] standards are national standard contracts for the Netherlands. We will shortly discuss some items in the two UAV standard contracts, because there are some remarkable differences compared to the international standards, which are worth mentioning. UAV1989/UAV 2012 mentions the variation in various clauses:

- Art. 13 Changes of dates and completion date.
- Art. 29 Dimensions or state of existing works and site.
- Art. 34 Execution of works and additional payment.
- Art. 35 Additions and omissions.
- Art. 36 Specification.
- Art. 39 Difference in adjustable quantities.
- Art. 40.7 Payment.

The same is true for UAVGC,[18] where the rules for variations are subdivided into different kinds of variations and accessory procedures. UAV is

[17] In Dutch: *Uniforme Administratieve Voorwaarden* (Uniform Administrative Conditions).

[18] In Dutch: *UAV Geintegreerde Contracten* (Integrated Contracts).

Table 10.1. Variations, changes and reasons for variations in various types of contracts.

Causes initiated by employer	Construct	D&B cost-reimbursable	D&B Lump sum	EPC/Turnkey
Postponement of delivery date by employer	Variation	Variation	Variation	Depends
Scope of work changes	Variation	Depends	Variation	No
Change in employer's requirements	Variation	Variation	Variation	Depends
Late provision of drawings by employer	Variation	Variation	Variation	N.A.
Late payment	Variation	Variation	Variation	Depends
Labor disputes	Depends	Depends	Depends	Depends
Poor drawings / specs	Variation	Depends	No	No
Arguments about engineer	Depends	Depends	Depends	N.A.
Behind planning schedule	Variation	Variation	Variation	Depends upon causes
Problems with contractor's subcontractors	No	No	No	No
Additional work	Variation	No	Depends	No
Modified work	Variation	Variation	Variation	No
Re-work	Depends	Depends	Depends	No
Physical objects	Variation	Variation	Depends	No
Time of the year	Variation	No	Variation	No
Location	Variation	Depends	Depends	Depends
Revised drawings	Variation	Depends	Depends	No
Holds on drawings	Variation	No	No	No
Change of employer	No	No	No	No
Change in personnel	Depends	No	No	No
Change law and regulations	Variation	Depends	Depends	Depends
Late issue materials	Depends	Depends	Depends	No
Bankrupt subcontractor	No	No	No	No
Wrong coordination at site by employer	Variation	Variation	Variation	N.A.
Sequence of work initiated by employer	Variation	Variation	Variation	N.A.
Method of construction	Depends	Depends	Depends	No

(*Continued*)

Table 10.1. (*Continued*)

Causes initiated by employer	Construct	D&B cost-reimbursable	D&B Lump sum	EPC/Turnkey
Major design changes	Variation	Variation	Variation	Only in case of functional changes in capacity
Change in functional spec	Variation	Variation	Variation	Variation
Change in test method	Variation	Variation	Depends	Depends
No access to site	Variation	Variation	Variation	Variation
Required acceleration	Variation	Variation	Variation	Variation

the most extensive standard on variations. For specifications, here — like in the other standard contracts — written instructions are required. The clause is comparable to the above-mentioned standards, but differs in the details, whereas maintenance is included as well.[19]

The UAVGC 2005 is a FIDIC D&B contract, somewhat comparable to the FIDIC yellow D&B standard. Here again, variations should be in writing, while a list of examples is suggested: scope of work, choices of execution, documents accepted, accepted agents and subcontractors, accepted work and accepted results.[20] This list has a different character than the above-mentioned lists of FIDIC and LOGIC. It has to do with the Dutch habit of employers who do some design work themselves and present that in their tender documents. The UAV and Dutch law hold the employer responsible for the work done by him and the variations he orders. This responsibility should be verified by the contractor, but basically the employer is responsible. This is an important difference with the FIDIC yellow (D&B) and the LOGIC Mobile Rig 1997 standard where the contractor is liable for the complete design.

10.5. How to handle variations

Variations are a fact of life. Variations are obligatory for contractors. Most standard contracts do not leave much room for contractors to refuse variations.[21] Employers may instruct contractors to accept variations. The

[19] UAV89, clause 36.7.

[20] UAVGC, clause 4.1.

[21] FIDIC Construct, D&B, EPC/Turnkey, subcontract, sub-clause 13.1. FIDIC D&LR, clause 10. CMM, sub-clause 38.1 and 38.9. LOGIC Construct and LOGIC Marine Construction, clause 14.1. LOGIC Drilling Rig: none.

reason behind this is practical. When a future project is envisaged, the employer usually needs a lot of time to come to a final conclusion. Once the decision is taken, often the project is immediately under pressure. Hence, the project looks favorable at this moment under the actual circumstances. But economical, political and financial situations may change. So speed is necessary. An engineering firm is invited to produce its drawings and specifications as soon as possible. Even preliminary specifications are used for tendering; drawings containing encircled notes such as "Hold" or "Preliminary" and "to be decided in concert with contractor" are often seen in tender drawings. A *perfect* finalized set of drawings, issued for construction and ready in the tender phase maybe exist, but not in the construction industry. When the employer is in the process of tendering with a number of contractors, the engineering firm is often still working on many of the details. This is often the situation when the contractor has to tender under construction. This process of ongoing design work may continue during execution of the works. This is why variations are a fact of life in international contracting.

Variations when tendering

"The variations should be recognized during the tender process", some alert project directors used to say. Tendering against cost price and making profit out of the variations is a well-known policy when going for tender. Whether this policy will be successful depends upon the employer, his financial possibilities and reputation, the engineering firm and the hunger for work.

When going for tender, an experienced contractor knows what will happen. After having studied the tender documents, drawings, specification and scope of work, the contractor may discover several flaws in the employer's specifications. What to do? You may put forward questions and ask for clarifications. In a situation of transparent competition, the employer will have to publish your questions and produce his answers in a notice of clarification.[22] In such a case, your competing contractors, who will make an offer in competition, will also be aware of the discovered flaws and the employer's clarification.

Another policy could be to leave the issue, keep silent and not ask for a clarification. If you win the tender, the flaws in the specifications may be a good reason for a variation in case of a construction contract. Note that the

[22] The non-discrimination principle of the EU directives.

contractor's maneuverability is limited due to the following standard contractual arrangements:

- The contractor shall be responsible for the adequacy, stability and safety of all site operations and all methods of construction.[23]
- Before accepting the order, he has to check the tender documents carefully.[24]
- The contractor shall be deemed to have obtained for himself a full understanding and knowledge of the nature of the work, the description of permanent works if applicable, and of the prevailing conditions under which the work must be performed.[25]

For a plant/D&B contract, the contractor's opportunities to request variations are more limited. Here, he is responsible for the design, execution and completion of the works; when completed the works shall be fit for purpose, as defined in the contract.[26] The contractor shall scrutinize the employer's requirements, including design criteria and calculations, if any. It is possible to do this after having received the letter of acceptance. The employer or engineer has to decide whether a request for a variation will be honored or not.[27] Above that, the works shall include any additional work, which is necessary to satisfy the employer's requirements. This means that all works — even if not mentioned in the contract or scope of work — which are necessary for stability or completion, or safe and proper operation, have to be provided for by the contractor.[28]

When tendering for an EPC/Turnkey project, the contractor's room to maneuver is the most limited. The contractor must scrutinize the employer's requirements prior to the base date (the starting date of the project); keep in mind that in this case the employer does not need to hand over a design, given that the design is the contractor's responsibility. The employer is *not* responsible for errors in his own requirements, as originally included in the contract.[29] The clause on variations — although in almost identical wordings as in

[23]FIDIC red book, sub-clause 4.1; UAV, para. 6; LOGIC, clause 6.
[24]FIDIC Construct/FIDIC D&B, par. 6, LOGIC Construct and Marine Construction, para. 6.
[25]CMM, sub-clause 5.1.
[26]FIDIC yellow book, sub-clause 4.1.
[27]FIDIC yellow book, sub-clause 5.1; LOGIC para. 14. 9.
[28]FIDIC yellow book, sub-clause 4.1.
[29]FIDIC silver book (EPC/Turnkey), sub-clause 5.1.

the FIDIC red and yellow books — should be read in a completely different context.

The procedure to agree upon a variation

Standard contracts describe in a high level of detail how to agree on variations. Normally, the procedure has a standard routine for an offer to be prepared by the contractor, which has to be accepted in writing by the employer or the engineer. These procedures are not identical in the different standard contracts. When entering into a contract, project managers and contract managers should study the applicable procedures. It often happens that payment of variations is refused or delayed in the case that the proper procedure was not followed. Problems occur when the contractor's offer is not in accordance with the wishes of the engineer or when its consequences in terms of price and time schedule are not acceptable to the engineer. Mutual consultation is recommended in such situations. The engineer may withdraw his idea for a variation as well.

Mostly, the initiative is with the engineer in charge, who becomes aware of shortcomings of the design in a construction agreement or additional items in a D&B contract. The employer as well is in a position to order variations. We are of the opinion that employers should refrain from initiating variations without consulting or informing the engineer in charge. He should have the overall view of the scope of work without losing sight of any details. The engineer has no authority to change the contract. That is the employer's exclusive right. But in the event a contract is changed, the engineer should be informed by the employer. Handling variations effectively calls for excellent communication between engineer and employer. Unfortunately, this is not always the case.

All standards for construction and D&B have opportunities for contractors to initiate variations. Variations may be caused by an omission or an error in the design (construction contracts) or an occurrence during execution. Variations often are necessary when the employer's engineering department is still in the process of engineering, while the contractor is already in the process of execution.

The contractor may ask for explanations of drawings, specifications and designs, but should keep in mind that explanations in themselves are no reason to ask for a variation.

It is practical to mention not only the main consequences of a variation in its description, but all consequences. At least three elements have to be clearly defined in the variation order: (1) change in the scope of work, (2) price changes, (3) change of the time schedule and its implications on other activities or earlier variations.

All other clauses, terms and conditions of the contract should remain unchanged. The variation should be governed by all existing contract terms. In the event a variation only serves to adapt the planning schedule, the other elements (change in the scope of work and price consequences) are filled out as "nil". We recommend keeping records in a joint (digital) list with access for all parties concerned.

Contractor's request for variations

What happens in the event a contractor is of the opinion that an instruction, a demand, a wish or an explanation of a certain drawing or specification from the engineer or the employer gives rise to extra payment or an adaptation of the time schedule?

Some standard contracts contain clauses where the contractor may ask for a variation, such as the Dutch CMM standard contract,[30] the Norwegian Fabrication Contract,[31] the FIDIC blue book for dredging and land reclamation,[32] the LOGIC Construction and LOGIC Marine Construction[33] and the CRINE standard contract for Mobile Drilling Rigs.[34]

In other standard contracts, the contractor's option to request a variation which will give rise to additional payment or an extension of the time schedule is absent. Such is the case in the FIDIC red book for construction. Here, the only option for the contractor to initiate a variation is in the case that he sees possibilities that are beneficial for the employer.[35] If so, the contractor should submit a written proposal which will, if adopted, accelerate completion, reduce the cost to the employer and improve the efficiency or value to the employer. Here, variations are to the benefit of the employer. In the event the contractor considers himself entitled to any extension of time or any additional payment, the contractor is obliged to issue a claim under the claim

[30] CMM, article 38.2.
[31] NF, article 16.1.
[32] FIDIC blue book, article 10.4 and 10.5.
[33] LOGIC Construction, 2003 and LOGIC Marine Construction, article 14.3.
[34] CRINE Mobile Drilling Rigs, 1997, clause 12.
[35] FIDIC Construction, clause 13.2.

clause of the contract.[36] In FIDIC's standard subcontract the same regulation is applicable. The engineer and the employer may initiate variations, but the subcontractor lacks such possibilities.[37] If the subcontractor considers himself entitled to any extension of time or any additional payment, he has the option to issue a claim to the contractor under the claim clause of the subcontract.[38]

In the FIDIC yellow book there is no option at all for the contractor to claim any variation, which is obviously clear, as he is responsible for the design.

In the FIDIC silver book for Turnkey projects, the same situation exists as per the FIDIC red book: the value engineering clause is applicable, but here there is no option for the contractor to be remunerated.[39] In the FIDIC silver book, as in FIDIC yellow, there is no option for the contractor to ask for a variation. The contractor's demand for extension of time or additional payment should be based on the claim clause.[40]

Under the Dutch UAVCG (integrated contracts) standard, the same regime is applicable as per the FIDIC yellow book.[41] There is no option to request a variation, but there is an opening for issuing a claim.[42]

Handling variations

Project managers and contract managers are wise to develop a certain standard procedure to be followed. In Box 10.2 we give an example of a standard procedure.

For suggestions of standard forms for variation orders, see the enclosure at the end of this chapter.

---

[36] FIDIC Construction, clause 20.1.

[37] FIDIC Subcontract for Construction, review draft, 2008, clause 13.2.

[38] FIDIC Subcontract for Construction, review draft, 2008, clause 20.2.

[39] FIDIC EPC/Turnkey, clauses 13.1 and 13.2.

[40] FIDIC EPC/Turnkey, clause 20.1.

[41] In earlier editions of the FIDIC standard contracts, we found the same system. FIDIC leaves no room for a request for variations by the contractor; if so, the general paragraph for claims should be applied. The Conditions of Contract (International) for Works of Civil Engineering Construction, March 1977 (construction only) contain regulations for "Alterations, Additions and Omissions" (para. 51). Here, there is no possibility for the contractor to ask for a variation. Instead, he should apply the general option for "Settlement of Disputes" (para. 67). An identical set-up is mentioned in the first editions for D&B/Turnkey 1995, where clause 14 refers to Variations, while sub-clause 20.1 mentions the ruling for Claims, Disputes and Arbitration.

[42] UAVGC 2005, articles 14 and 44 sub-clause 1, respectively.

Box 10.2. Example of standard procedure for handling variations.

1. First read the contract (or re-read the applicable parts of it) to clearly understand the obligations of both parties. Which procedure for implementing a variation was agreed upon in the contract? Is there any good reason *not* to follow this procedure and how do I manage a deviation from what has been agreed upon and signed by my board of directors/CEO/CFO/responsible management? Which representative of my counterparty will sign the eventual variation?

   Is there any provision in the contract to settle unclear wordings, if any? Are there any contradictory clauses in different enclosures? If so, is there a hierarchy of documents laid down in the contract? Is the required or supposed change extra work or was it an implied obligation on the contractor's side? If the contract is unclear at that point could we settle it in close harmony with the representative of the other party?
2. In the event the engineer or the employer asks for a variation, investigate the activities the contractor has to perform. Many contractors have standard templates for dealing with variations, which have to be filled out. Check existing and agreed-upon documentation, drawings, specifications, schedules and digital presentations.
3. Note the required materials, equipment and labor.

   Note the other relevant aspects, for instance, the scope of work, the planning schedule, the conditions, the circumstances and the uncertainties. Do not forget the risks incurred.
4. Have the cost calculated.

   Is the value of the change within the financial limits of my authority or financial mandate?

   Is the requested change really a change of the scope of work? Or do we have to consider it as a new assignment? If not, what should be done now?

   A contract may prescribe how the variation shall be evaluated, for example either:
   - An agreed lump sum.
   - Appropriate rates, mentioned in the contract.
   - In the absence of appropriate rates, the rates in the contract that come closest to the referred work on the variation.[43]

(*Continued*)

[43]FIDIC blue book, clause 10.2.

Box 10.2. (Continued)

These elements are mentioned in the FIDIC blue book. Mind that all contracts differ on their valuation of variations. The red book has a different method of valuation.[44] Calculating costs of variations is never a routine job. Don't forget to include costs off site.

5. Issue the required notice to the other party.
   In most contracts, a procedure for handing over notices is laid down.
6. Wait for a reaction. Mind the time limits as agreed upon in the contract.
   In most contracts, a response time is mentioned. If no reaction comes, do not hesitate to send a reminder, preferably by mail or letter with a date.
7. A variation is a deviation from an existing contract. It needs at least two signatures to be of legal value. When the confirmation comes from the other party check the signature.
8. Mobilize the needs for the agreed-upon variation, i.e. personnel, material and equipment. Keep records when you initiate the variation and when you are available to start the execution of the variation.
9. Keep records about the execution of the variation and the impact of the variation on the regular activities.

10.6. Refused variations and disagreements

The contractor is not bound to all variations. The employer has to remain within reasonable limits. Grounds for a contractor to refuse variations are:

- The impossibility of obtaining the necessary goods.[45]
- The variation will affect the safety or suitability of the works.
- The variation will have an adverse impact on the achievement of the guarantees.[46]
- The variation results in work that exceeds what parties could reasonably have expected when the contract was concluded.[47]
- The variation has nothing to do with the work.

[44] FIDIC red book, clause 12.3.
[45] FIDIC Construct, D&B, EPC/Turnkey para. 13.1. UAV: none, LOGIC: none, CMM: none.
[46] FIDIC D&B and FIDIC EPC/Turnkey para. 13.1. UAV: none, LOGIC: none, CMM: none.
[47] Norwegian Fabrication contract, article 12.

Other reasons for a contractor to refuse could be the impossibility of mobilizing sufficient equipment in time or to contract necessary subcontractors or service providers. Another reason for refusing a variation might be the intolerable disruption or disorder of the activities on the site or the non-availability of the required competencies at the contractor.[48] Anyhow, the spirit of all standard contracts is that the contractor should cooperate with the employer in the employer's interest. Even if a specific variation clause is missing in a contract, the contractor can refuse a variation if he can prove to the employer that such a variation would endanger the employer's interests.

A limited number of variations

Some contracts contain rules for the limitation of variations. UAV mentions plus or minus 10–15% for the contract price. LOGIC mentions "reasonable limits". The Norwegian text says "what reasonably was expected". These clauses may help contractors to refuse further variations in the event the total of 15% (UAV) has been reached. In those cases parties need to renegotiate the terms and conditions.

FIDIC does not mention limits. The Dutch CMM contract explicitly mentions that there is no limitation whatsoever on the number, individual value or the aggregate effect of the variations the employer may wish for. However, all variations must have a relation to the work. The contractor has to warrant that it is able, within reasonable limits, to mobilize additional personnel and equipment at short notice to perform a variation.[49] The clause was written to avoid misunderstandings between parties.

Disagreement on terms of the variation

What should be done if the contractor and employer cannot come to terms about a proposed variation? In any case, the work should not be interrupted. The show must go on. The existing time schedule should not be put in danger because of quarrels between the engineer and project/contract manager of the contractor. Different standard contracts show diverse provisions on the subject. In FIDIC standard contracts there are no clauses on disagreements. This means that the general detailed FIDIC ruling about dispute adjudication would be applicable. It depends on the impact of the variation concerned

[48] UAVGC, para. 14.6.

[49] CMM, sub-clause 38.8.

whether parties want to enter into such a procedure for a variation. This should be considered on a case-by-case basis.

LOGIC instructs the contractor to keep reports and records of the disputed variation work. If not, the contractor may forfeit any right to receive any adjustment to the contract price and/or schedule of key dates.[50] LOGIC has no clause to stop or interrupt work. The employer has to take the contractor's objections into account "as it considers fair and reasonable". The contractor at all times will have the option to discuss the matter.

The contractor's alternative attitude could be to give written notice to the employer that disagreement exists, and continue the disputed extra work on a day-by-day basis at rates — if any — that were agreed upon elsewhere in the appendices of the contract. He may invite the engineer to sign the daily reports, records or the notices in the minutes of the meetings. After taking over the work, the contractor may re-open the discussions with the employer based on the earlier disagreement and the records signed by the engineer. The contractor at that stage will not be in a comfortable negotiating position. But it might be better than remaining frustrated while the work still has to be finished.

The CMM standard contract foresees a mini-trial, held by a neutral expert, who is nominated by the parties. If the parties do not agree, a neutral authority will appoint the expert. In the meantime the project must go on.[51] The contractor has to keep reports and records on the disputed variation.

The UAVGC arranges for a mini-trial by experts.[52] This is either a single expert, who has special knowledge of the business, or a committee of three persons. It is different from arbitrage, it being less formal; the experts may hear the parties, take notice of the contract clauses and specifically of the technical, financial and planning details of the issue at hand. Sometimes the experts bring the parties together in a compromise. The clause about the procedure is extensive. It certainly will take some time, at least some weeks. The UAVGC entitles the contractor to compensation of cost or extension of time.

The two systems (LOGIC and CMM on the one hand, and UAV on the other) clearly reflect a cultural difference between operations in the oil and gas business, and works to be constructed on shore in the Netherlands, where the public authorities were partners when negotiating the contents of the UAV, and were bound to general legal rules of good public administration,

---

[50] LOGIC, clause 14.7 (d).

[51] CMM, clause 38.3.

[52] UAVGC, clause 45. Unfortunately some important employers in the Netherlands used to delete this practical option to settle differences of opinion.

which have to be respected by the government. Pressure on the time schedule is acceptable, but the rights of the contractors count as well. UAV had to find a reasonable compromise.

10.7. Variations that usually do not change contracts

The contract should specify which persons are authorized to agree upon variations. Mostly this authorization — which in fact is a power of attorney to act on behalf of the company of the contractor — is transferred to the project manager, a contract manager, a legal counsel or their superiors. The persons who are authorized to act on behalf of the employer must be mentioned as well. Variations concern the scope of work in the broadest sense, prices and time schedules. Basically, these representatives should refrain from altering clauses of the contract itself, including the appendices and enclosures.

The responsibility of other departments in the organization of the contractor may also be a factor. Think about the appointment of personnel for the project (HRM department); supplies and consumables (procurement department); insurances (insurance department); definite take-over procedures; *force majeure*; and changes in law, disputes, responsibilities and liabilities (legal department). The treasury department will be involved when payment conditions have to be changed, and do not forget the engineering department when construction issues are to be discussed, while the survey department may be questioned when quantities and qualities are discussed.

Variations do not change the text of the contract — neither do time sheets. In a case between a dedicated service provider, acting as a subcontractor, and a contractor, the contract between the employer and contractor contained a variation clause, mentioning the rates per hour worked. The contractor and subcontractor agreed upon the clause on a back-to-back basis: rates per hour worked, less 5% general overhead costs for the contractor. After completion, the employer wished to discuss the hours worked by the subcontractor, with the employer stating that too many hours were noted down in the reports.

An agreement on the number of hours was reached between the employer, contractor and subcontractor for the subcontractor's considerable extra work. These revised time sheets were the subject of legal procedures. Before court, the subcontracting service provider stated that his standard general service conditions should be regarded as applicable to the extra work; they were mentioned at the bottom of all time sheets, as the revised time sheets were accepted by both employer and contractor. These time sheets were signed by the employer. The subcontractor had good reasons to see these general conditions applied. They contained important exonerations with regard to liabilities, and gave reasons to invoice interest for late payments. In short, the validity of the time sheets was subject to the court's decision.

Fortunately the (English) court did not agree with this argument. A time sheet is meant for accounting purposes only. These time sheets cannot change the clauses of the applicable contract, as earlier agreed upon.

10.8. Variations that changed contracts

Still, it is possible that, due to a variation, the contract itself has to be adapted. That is the case if, for instance, the financial impact of a variation is such that the contract sum, including accompanying schedules to the contract, is changed. Such schedules may be one or more of the following documents: schedules of payment, parent company guarantee, the performance security, the surety bond, the advance payment guarantee, the retention money guarantee and the payment guarantee by the employer. The contract is changed, as the schedules are part of the contract. But the contract itself remains the same contract, even in the event that some clauses may be adapted.

It may happen that variations are so fundamental that the object of the contract is changed to a different one than initiated originally by the parties. In such a case, it is the actual contract that has changed.

We give some examples from past experience. The first example mentions a variation that was of such essence, that the judge awarded a complete additional order to the contractor.

The first example — as shown in Box 10.3 — mentions a variation.

We will mention a second example of a variation that changed a contract. Here the scope of work was fully underestimated during execution. Box 10.4 describes the situation. The description of the scope of work was clear. Under the same contract, a variation clause was included, mentioning rates per man hour and use of equipment. During execution of the work, these appeared to be much greater than expected. Next, the question came up: who had to bear the risk of the unforeseen extra workload? Both parties relied on contract clauses that worked out to their own advantage. The employer stated that the scope of work was clear, which was true. The contractor referred to the variation clause. How would a judge decide on this matter?

Box 10.3. The birds' island — a variation order that resulted in a second contract.

The contractor booked an order to dredge Larne Lough in Ireland and to deposit the dredged material in areas approved by the public authorities. It was intended that the dredged material would be deposited elsewhere in the lough. However, the local population resisted firmly and this plan had to be changed. An alternative solution was found: to use the material to create a bird island in the lough. The contractor argued that making an island for birds was different work than just depositing the dredged material. This should not be considered as a variation to the existing contract, but as a separate contract, the contractor stated. Taking care of the stability of the soil, the provisions to make stable slopes at the shores of the island, was much more work than the employer was prepared to accept. The judge accepted the contractor's arguments.

The judge considered the construction of the birds' island to be fully and completely outside the scope of the original dredging work and, therefore, constituting a new contract.[53] There was no variation, but a completely new order, resulting in the employer having to re-negotiate an order, which at the moment of negotiation, was already completed.

The provisional sum, in regard to the "defined work", was related to asbestos removal of a kind and quantity that would not interfere with the planning schedule. The volume of asbestos found was far beyond the expectation of the parties and did affect the progression of the work. Accordingly, the additional work should be valued in accordance with the variation clause.[54] Apparently, the judge agreed with this view. He considered that the variation clause should have priority to the agreed scope of work, as described in the contract. What is remarkable is the business common sense that the judge showed in his verdict. It seems reasonable that the extra costs in this case

[53] Blue Circle Industries Plc vs. Holland Dredging Company (UK) Ltd, 1987.
The example was taken from Manches Interface, Newsletter, Summer 2008, p. 4, www.manches.com, January 23, 2013.

[54] This case was taken from Geoff Brewer, Brewer Consulting, London, Newsletter CJ-9929, 2000.

Box 10.4. Appearance of asbestos during demolition of two tower blocks.

A specialized service provider was awarded a contract to demolish two tower blocks. During execution of the work, more asbestos was discovered than was described in the scope of work. The newly discovered asbestos was mainly in the form of additives to paint, while thermoplastic floor tiles contained small quantities of asbestos as well. After discovering this, the employer instructed the contractor to suspend the work. Lengthy discussions with the Health and Safety authorities followed. A revised method of dealing with the asbestos was introduced. The planning schedule had to be changed. The contractor, Demolition Services, claimed an extra £300,000 for the interruption, idle equipment and the extra man hours spent on the varied working method. The employer, Castle Vale, referred to the scope of work and refused any extra payment, as well as a variation. The schedule of works contained provisions that required the removal of "asbestos-based materials". The contractor had to identify and dispose of any asbestos, toxic waste and the like. A provisional sum of £5,000 for additional asbestos removal was included, described as "defined work". The employer stated in court that the literal meaning of the scope of work had to be followed. All asbestos had to be removed as part of the work, against the lump-sum price agreed upon.

The contractor thereupon argued that he would not have entered into the contract at the same price if he had known beforehand that the asbestos was not only in the form of sheets or lagging (it was described in the scope of work as such), but also in other forms.

The judge considered that business common sense should play an important role in interpreting the written contract and the scope of work:

> There must be ascribed to the words a meaning that would make good commercial sense if the Schedule of Works were issued in any of these situations, and not some meaning that imposed upon a contractor a financial liability of unknown extent that no businessman in his [right mind] would be willing to occur [sic]. The fact that a particular construction leads to an unreasonable result must be a relevant consideration. The more unreasonable the result, the more unlikely it is that the parties can have intended it, and if they do intend it, the more necessary it is that they shall make their intention abundantly clear.[55]

[55] Demolition Services Ltd vs. Castle Vane Housing Action Trust, TCC, January 12, 1999.

should come from the employer's account, the employer being the owner of the building to be demolished.

Changing a variation clause by conduct of project managers

A contract to build a pharmaceutical works contained an extensive procedure for variations. Time was of the essence. The employer granted an important incentive to the contractor for early completion. The employer was in urgent need for extra production capacity because demand for its (patented) medicines was high and extremely profitable. The two project managers sat together and decided — without officially informing their top management — to cut corners and to apply a simplified variation procedure. Each Friday afternoon, they would discuss and price the required variations and sign on Saturday mornings. At completion, the employer only paid for 20% of the variations agreed upon in such a way. The contractor required payment of the outstanding 80%. Parties decided on an alternative dispute solution. They invited a retired judge of the local court of appeal for binding advice to decide "as he thinks reasonable". His opinion would have obligatory force. Here again, the decision showed a very good feeling for the reasonable business solution. Remarkable again is the way in which the clauses of the contract were used to come to an honest verdict. After ample hearings and investigation of the relevant details, the binding advisor came to consider the following, as identified in Box 10.5.

The employer had to compensate the contractor for the outstanding amounts.

10.9. Variations that change the typology of the contract

In construction contracts, it may happen that parts of small engineering jobs are left to the contractor. Most standard contracts have a provision for such activities.[56] In practice, one should be aware that variations remain within the typology, the scope and the character of the standard contract that was originally chosen. In the event that variations in a construction contract should oblige the contractor to perform important design work, the discussion may arise as to what extent the contractor's responsibilities for such designs will be expanded. A construction contract was not written for extensive design

[56]FIDIC red, sub-clause 4.1.

Box 10.5. Changing a variation clause by conduct; opinion in binding advice.

Deviating or changing one or more conditions of a contract is outside the project managers' authority. Such authority is only given to the persons who legally and officially represent both companies of employer and contractor, such as CEOs. Project managers have to stay within their limits of respective power of attorney. However, in this special case other considerations have to be kept in mind.

The employer had good business reasons to speed up the time schedule as much as possible. This was explicitly laid down in the contract, mentioning a fixed bonus sum per week of earlier completion. Both parties were aware of the importance of earliest possible completion, which was mentioned in the contract. The binding advisor found out that the good cooperation between the two project managers resulted in two months earlier delivery. This was due to the circumstance that variations, which were of the essence of the critical path in the complicated planning schedule, were not presented to the official "variations committee" which had to decide upon the allocation of budgets. This cutting corners was to the benefit of both parties. The financial advantage for the employer was tremendous, resulting in a turnover of at least $8,000,000, due to earlier supply of medicines. This amount was much higher than the sum of the 80% of the non-paid variations, which were capped at €1,100,000. In paying 20% of the variations, the employer implicitly accepted the project managers' deviated variation method. This acceptance by conduct was conflicting with the clause on openness, fairness and transparency elsewhere in the contract.

responsibilities. The outset was different, and the overall intent of the original standard contract was construction only. In practice, it is quite common that, during construction, calculations and drawings are made up by a contractor, and agreed upon by a written variation. This should not cause any legal problems. But what happens when variations cross the borders of the typology of the chosen model? In such a case, the responsibilities and the liabilities of the contractor will go much further than the text of the contract spells out. That will result in friction between the parties' intention and the wording in the contract. This should be avoided.

Box 10.6 describes the development of good ideas and the history of the negotiations. They were based on excellent relations between the two parties. The dredging work was not the contractor's first job in the country. The

Box 10.6. Design responsibilities in a dredging contract for a foreign employer.

A dredging company was awarded a contract for maintenance dredging in a river, including arranging for some new slopes and finishing touches. The work was simple; it would take some six months. Parties entered into a dredging contract according to the FIDIC blue book.[57] However, the contractor was able to amend a few clauses to his advantage.

There were no particular conditions. All necessary information was provided in an appendix, which went with the contract. It was a relatively straightforward project. Before coming to terms, the parties came together. The contractor assisted the employer in making drawings and specifications before the full scope of works was agreed upon, including some simple design work related to the dredging job to be done by the contractor. This was related to the depths, the shore revetment and the slopes.[58]

A fixed price, lump sum was agreed upon, to be corrected by the bill of quantities. During execution, there was an engineer and a quantity surveyor present, as well as a representative of the employer.

A couple of weeks after the beginning of the execution of the work, the representative of the employer asked the project manager whether he would be interested in doing "some small design work" as an extra on the running contract. It was the design for a piece of quay near the slopes, which the contractor should arrange for. "Can you make that for us?" The project manager wanted to please his customer and answered: "Of course we can." Together the men went ashore, where the representative showed the exact spot where the quay should go. The project manager praised the representative for his good insight and said that this would be an ideal location. A month later, the representative came back, together with his boss, a young woman with a master's degree in civil engineering and a husband in politics. She said that the quay was discussed with "the [top] management", but its length should be a little longer, i.e. 80 meters. After approval of the design, the quay should be built, including the improvement of the adjacent road between the local motorway and the quay.

(*Continued*)

[57] FIDIC form of contract for dredging and reclamation works, 2006.

[58] The FIDIC blue contract has some provisions for design work by the contractor; see clause 5.

Box 10.6. (*Continued*)

The project manager, who was eager to be complimented by his boss in the home office, confirmed the meeting and wrote down in his day report that the order for the quay was booked. Just in case, he asked the representative and the woman to sign his day report; to his astonishment they both signed. "Price to be agreed upon after contractor's definite confirmation of this variation." The project manager informed his head office in his home country and started waiting for his salary increase next December.

A month later, the head office — after the chief engineer and the manager, responsible for the cost calculation, visited the site — wrote to the employer mentioning the budget price. The latter's reaction was positive. In a transparent way, the documents would be published locally; this operation was necessary to meet the national law on the contracting out of public works. But the employer did not expect any suitable tender from any other contractor.

Last but not least, the employer proposed that the contractor would be responsible for the maintenance of the quay and the connecting road for the duration of ten years, while the price of the quay would be paid in twenty, separate installments every six months. It appeared that the employer had more than sufficient budget for maintenance of the complete river, the locks elsewhere in the river, the slopes, etc. for the coming ten years, but lacked any budget for construction of the quay. It could not pay for the quay in only one shot.

The contractor had good reasons to stay within the framework of the existing contract on dredging. That contract was in favor of the dredging company. Limits of contractor's liability, consequential losses, margin in time schedule, risks and insurance — all of these important legal clauses were to the dredging firm's advantage, compared to other contracts at hand. The employer, as well, wished to regard the extra work as an extension of the running contract. The contractor should not include costs for a second mobilization; the employer was familiar with its good engineering and clear methods of communication, while the personal relations and the methods of cooperation were positive. Never change a winning team, the woman said. Concluding that both parties strongly preferred to stay within the existing blue book contract, parties nevertheless had to find their way.

employer was a ministry, where the extensive staff was strong in politics, but weak in technology and engineering. There was a political decision that the river would serve the increasing inland navigation in the coming years. The few technicians were under heavy pressure "to get things done in time". They concentrated on the speedy pace, trusting the well-known contractor to use its know-how. Legal affairs were not taken into account. Discussions concentrated on how to come to business at short notice. The contractor, with his appetite for further orders, saw a good opportunity to make this customer a regular and reliable cash cow. During negotiations, no lawyers were involved.

In the meantime, the nature of the existing contract changed. Now this was no longer "some small design work", belonging to the dredging contract. This was work under a FIDIC D&B standard contract, while the financing aspect turned it into a DBFM contract.

Consequently, it would be favorable to interpret the construction of the quay as an extension of the existing dredging contract. However, some obstacles were to be taken into consideration. First of all, the question should have been raised whether clause 5 of the blue book concerning design by the contractor should be applicable to the original dredging contract. After all, the object of the existing contract was just dredging with some additional work. Was it possible to have the FIDIC yellow book (D&B) apply to just the variation and not to the original contract? Another question: the prevailing clause for variations only authorized the *engineer* to order variations, so could the employer issue such important extensions?[59] The engineer was not present during the negotiations. Besides, the standard dredging contract contains a standard procedure for variations, which requires an offer from the contractor, which should be accepted by the engineer. These obstacles are not that difficult to overcome.

FIDIC's notes for guidance, which go with clause 10, mention the situation where variations may require the mobilization of further major *dredging* equipment provided that the time and cost effect can be agreed in advance. Here, with no extension of the dredging work, but in asking for a quay of 80 meters, completely different equipment will be needed. This should be brought in by the contractor.

The notes on the blue book recommend that in the event of the above situation, the employer and/or the engineer should enter into the earliest discussion with the contractor to agree an amicable way of allowing the contract to proceed. In addition, the engineer may apply this principle to any variation

[59] See FIDIC Dredging and Reclamation standard contract, sub-clause 10.2.

by requiring the contractor to submit quotations with time and cost effects for agreement prior to his issue of the variation. It would be in the interest of both the employer and the contractor if variations could be issued for which both time and cost effects were agreed. The contract allows, however, for the issue of variations in the event that this has not been possible, that the engineer entitles the contractor extension of time[60] and the variation is valued at appropriate new rates, or rates which the engineer considers appropriate.[61]

In general, such comments are useful as long as the variation stays within the context of the typology of the applicable standard contract base, i.e. either Construction, Dredging and Reclamation or D&B. But these comments were not written for variations that go beyond the original contract type.

The existing contract could have been reformed with the help of Particular Conditions. The disadvantage of this option is that the particular conditions have a rather high ranking in the sequence of priority of clauses.[62]

One may conclude that, in this case, a contractor found himself trapped (from a simple construction contract) in a DBFM contract.

In concluding, variations cannot be used for fundamental extensions of work or when important additional work is to be executed under a different contract type. In the case in Box 10.6, where a financing element was introduced into an existing straightforward dredging contract, the conditions of the contract should be re-written for the design, construction, maintenance and financing of the quay. But, in practice, this would mean that two different kinds of contracts would have to be integrated into one document, which for many reasons should be avoided. Our recommendation would be to prepare and arrange for two different contracts.

10.10. Conclusions

Variations are a fact of life. Each standard contract contains its own clauses on variations. One has to understand the typical contract form in order to be successful in managing variations.

- Read the project contract. What exactly is a variation under the contract and how should it be valued?
- Find out the hidden variations in the tender documents and choose your tender policy with regard to variations.

---

[60] FIDIC Dredging and Reclamation, sub-clause 7.3.

[61] FIDIC Dredging and Reclamation, sub-clause 10.2.

[62] See FIDIC Dredging and Reclamation standard appendix.

- Make sure that the people running the job fully understand how the variation clauses fit into the contract. Help from the legal department is very useful. Monitor your staff. Let the project manager and contract manager sit together so that they have an identical understanding of the options the variation clauses may open during execution of the contract.
- Always keep your eye on the instructions and requirements of the employer. An employer or engineer may, in good faith, be of the opinion that he simply gives verbal explanations about documents — this may in fact be a variation, which is reason to ask for an amount on top of the agreed contract sum. If the employer or engineer gives instructions, check your scope of work. Is it included in the scope of work or is it a variation?
- Don't hesitate to ask for variations yourself. Mention the grounds for your request for a variation. Write the letter yourself in your own wording and have it checked beforehand by your lawyer — not the other way round. Make your letter short, clear and fair.
- In the event the contract leaves no room for asking for a variation, do not hesitate to issue a claim for extra payment or a change in the time schedule. Justify your claim.
- You are not always obliged to accept any variation. You should never put your original obligations at risk for a variation.
- All changes are not necessarily variations for which the customer is obliged to pay. Any change implies risks of hindrance to regular work, disruption, disturbance to planning and costs related to idleness.
- Always respond in writing to questions, remarks and to correspondence received from the engineer and the employer.
- Check whether the variation orders are signed by the authorized person. Follow the procedure to agree upon a variation. Confirm oral promises in written and dated statements — e-mail is useful.
- Keep records and reports of your variations and their execution, and give copies to your counterparties. They will appreciate your transparency.
- Keep your files in order — day by day.
- Keep daily diary notes on your project and do not forget to make notes about the outstanding variations that have been offered, but not yet approved, by employer or engineer, which represent obstacles in relation to the next milestone of your planning schedule.
- Do not leave a discussion about a variation unsolved. If you wait too long with your request for extra payment, and it comes to legal procedures, a judge or arbitrator may be of the opinion that you were too late in requesting a variation order.

- Remember that a variation might change your contract type. Don't go ahead without the help of your legal department. It is not that simple.
- When the variation is executed and finished, ask the engineer or your employer to confirm his acceptance and inform your administration immediately.
- Your job is to execute projects against a profit. Whenever you have to go to court to get paid for variations, your best weapons are your excellent files and well-organized paper work. It may represent the difference between a tremendous loss on the project or a successful case.

Variations make the difference. By completing works, variations may represent huge losses or pleasant extra profit. You have to supply two things: good-performing works and your excellent files. The profit is in the paperwork.

Enclosure

Number:
Project:

REQUEST for VARIATION

Initiated by: Employer

Name of representative:

Description of request for Variation:

Reason for request for Variation:

References specification/appendix/deficiency (sheet):

Attached no of pages: ..

Date and signature Employer's representative:

---------------------------- ----------------------------

Date and signature for receipt of request by Contractor:

---------------------------- ----------------------------

This document is valid only if dated and signed by both Employer and Contractor.

Number:
Project:

PROPOSAL for Variation

Based on Request(s) for Variation nr.: ....dated ....

Proposed Variation (incl. Reason for change):

Consequences of change to be investigated? **YES/NO**

Number of manhours involved in change or investigation: ....

Financial consequences for Employer? **YES/NO**

Amount: ....
Increase / Reduction
Valid until (date): ....

Additional materials **YES/NO**

Consequences for payment schedule? **YES/NO**

Consequences for planning? **YES/NO**

Other consequences/remarks or references:

Attached number of pages: ....

Date and signature Contractor: ....

Proposal approved? **YES/NO**

Date and signature Employer: ....

Changes or investigation carried out? **YES/NO**

Changes tested? **YES/NO**

Cleared (date): ....

Implement changes or start investigation only after Employer's approval.

Part IV

Legal Issues in International Contracting

Chapter 11

Letter of Intent and Memorandum of Understanding

11.1. Case — The missing reports and the missing permits

As the project manager of an international dredging company, suppose that you are confronted with the following situation:

In the past, you managed projects for the North Bay Port Authority for more than 10 years. A few weeks ago, the North Bay Port Authority urgently requested that dredging work start on Friday July 6, 2012, for a job that will probably take six weeks. Expansion of port construction activities is dependent on your delivery date — dredging is in the critical path of the North Bay Port Authority's network planning. You contacted your head office, which freed up a dredge urgently. The ship is lying off shore on July 5, 2012. However, the North Bay Port Authority has not provided the required soil surveys, which are part of its verbal invitation to offer. Moreover, it forgot to arrange for the necessary government permits; this will take at least another three weeks. Without reports and permits, the customer cannot issue a purchase order. You are faced with a large loss due to equipment sitting idle, and your boss is not going to be pleased. Your customer feels sorry for the situation, but cannot provide any financial compensation. It goes without saying that you urgently contacted the North Bay Port Authority's responsible account manager. Immediately, he argued that a *force majeure* situation was at hand.

What is the case? The permits have to be issued by the competent authority for this matter, i.e. the Ministry of Environment, Trade & Industry. This is a different institution than the North Bay Port Authority. This hindrance lies outside the Port Authority's control. For the time being, the permits are not going to be issued, because of lack of personnel. And this is due to discussions in Parliament that 9,000 workers at the Ministries are supposed to be made redundant; due to the bad national financial situation, these persons could be dismissed in the near future. A friend of the account manager stated off the record that permits might be ready within three weeks, but he could not take a risk to guarantee this statement.

As far as the soil investigation is concerned, the account manager has to admit that "it is possible" that the handing over of the soil surveys "could be the North Bay Port Authority's responsibility". But he "did not think that [he] made a firm promise on that subject", because he is "dependent upon others in his complex organization". But, finally, all discussions on this item are in vain, given the fact that the missing permits are a complete show stopper.

So here you are: there is no written contract; there is a verbal agreement with the account manager, who in your opinion is a reliable man. Now questions arise: is a verbal agreement as good as a written agreement? Is the account manager authorized to ask for a dredger? Is this "asking for" the same as awarding a contract for dredging for a period of about six weeks? Is the Port Authority liable for your costs for the idle dredger, inclusive of the costs of well-qualified and trained manpower? Should we claim the losses and should we do so on the texts of the previous contracts? If not, which rules are to be applied for claiming our losses? If we have to present our claim at a court, which court and which legal system has to be applied, given that the Port Authority has a different nationality than our company? There are many more questions to be put. These are the issues to agree upon in the event things are not running as they should. A good contract contains agreements on what will happen in the event things occur that are not in line with your agreements.

Landing complex contracts requires that contract parties take time to explore how to cooperate on the intended project. A Letter of Intent is a commonly used vehicle to allow for such exploration. First, the employer wants to find out whether the preferred contractor is able to do the job and wants to explore his workmanship and experience. Next, the contractor wants to have a number of issues clarified by the employer, which at the moment of tender are not clear in the scope of work and tender documents. A Letter of Intent may be used as a preliminary formal written contact between parties to sort things out. Another popular pre-arrangement which is used by parties is the Memorandum of Understanding. The role and importance of both types of documents are the subjects of this chapter.

11.2. Letter of Intent — definition

When engineer Joe Aigboduwa, representing the contractor Westminster Dredging and Marine Ltd, signed a Letter of Intent, received from the intermediary engineering company Lidan Engineering Ltd, representing his employer, he could not know beforehand that at least five extension letters would follow before the actual execution of the intended work could start. The letter was clear and certainly not short (see Box 11.1).

A Letter of Intent or LOI is a document outlining the intention of one party or intentions between two or more parties in order to arrive at a (preliminary) agreement or to finalize terms and conditions of a contract

Box 11.1. Letter of Intent: example.

We, being the employer, refer to your proposal for the project (where the project was described and the proposal was identified), which proposal was revised and clarified by exchanges of correspondence. We call your proposal hereafter the Draft Contract.

It is our intention to award to you, being the Contractor, a contract for the performance of the Work. It is our intention to continue finalization of the Draft Contract with a view to entering into a contract for the Work as soon as practical, but no later than the validity period of this Letter of Intent.

It is agreed that the further terms and conditions applicable to the performance of the Work under this Letter of Intent shall be those contained in our invitation to Bid for the pre-loading and soil monitoring (follows identification of the invitation to bid).

Contractor shall, at the option of the Employer, enter into the Contract on the terms and conditions in the Draft Contract with such amendments as necessary. Employer may terminate this Letter of Intent at any time acting in his sole discretion on prior written notice to Contractor.

This Letter of Intent shall terminate on the earlier date of:

- Execution of the Contract.
- 60 calendar days from the Effective Date of this Letter of Intent.
- Termination of this Letter of Intent by employer.

All work performed under this Letter of Intent by Contractor shall be deemed to have been wholly performed under the Contract. All other conditions shall be as under the Contract.

which is under further negotiation. A LOI expresses the intention to come together, and to arrive at a substantial contract. A LOI may relate to a wide range of contractual situations, such as a follow-up on a proposal that has been submitted to a future employer. It may also relate to a joint venture agreement with another contractor. Thirdly, it may relate to an alliance agreement with a subcontractor or service provider. Normally, the party who sends a LOI will ask the addressee to countersign. When this is done the obligations mentioned in the LOI become mutually binding upon both parties.

Any LOI may be used to clarify the key points of a complex transaction for the convenience of the parties. It may also be used to declare officially that the parties are currently negotiating, as in the preparation of a tender, the preparation of a joint venture, the investigations for financing a project or to arrange for future maintenance of an asset to be constructed. Finally, it may be used to provide safeguards in case a deal collapses during negotiation.

11.3. Is a Letter of Intent legally binding?

A party that sends a LOI to another party commits itself to that which is promised in the letter. So, if the LOI says that the signee will negotiate with the other party to arrive at an agreement, the party is obliged to really negotiate and to come to terms with the addressee of the LOI.

Is a LOI a contract or an agreement? The answer to that question depends upon the contents of the document itself. In the event parties just limit the wording to the promise to meet and to talk, you may say that talking is not identical to a legally binding obligation. But if the document contains promises on how to negotiate and additional issues are accepted, such as exclusivity and confidentiality, these may become legally binding.

In the event an employer sends a LOI for construction of a harbor at a defined place on the map, it is clear that only one harbor will be built. In many LOIs, the term "exclusive" is used. In such a case it commits the employer not to negotiate with different contractors on the same subject.

Very often a LOI contains more obligations than just the promise to negotiate. It often happens that certain facts and figures still have to be verified in order to come to the agreement which parties want to enter into. Further detailing of the design might be required, or further soil and sub-sea conditions have to be assessed in order to come to a complete scope of work. These activities may bring further costs for one or both of the parties. In such a case, the employer may promise to do further research at his cost during negotiations or parties may divide the efforts and costs involved as suitable. In the above case (see Box 11.1), there is work to be performed. The letter mentions pre-loading and soil monitoring: payment for those activities will be as per the contract under negotiation. In the example, those parts of the LOI are indeed legal obligations. Once signed, the contractor cannot refuse to perform them.

LOIs resemble formal contracts, but in their entirety are usually not completely binding for the parties. However, LOIs may contain provisions that are binding, such as non-disclosure agreements, a covenant to negotiate in good faith, or a 'stand-still' or 'no-shop' provision promising exclusive rights to negotiate.

Standard contracts, such as the FIDIC, LOGIC, CMM and BIMCO do not have provisions for a LOI. Most of these models contain procedures for formation of the contract. The normal procedure is that the employer invites the contractor to submit a proposal based upon the tender documents, which the employer had prepared. The contractor's proposal is the binding offer to come to the agreement. Following such a proposal, the employer sends his acceptance. By accepting the proposal the contract is closed. The acceptance in some standard contracts has a defined name, such as the letter of acceptance under FIDIC standards. Mostly a different procedure is applied: both parties sign the Form of Agreement, as is the case under LOGIC and CMM, but FIDIC uses such forms as well. The LOI is not mentioned in these standard contracts.

In conclusion, international contracts in most legal systems are free from conventions. There are some countries that require a written form. Nothing obstructs signing a LOI, whereas in standard contracts the wording "Letter of Intent" is rare.

11.4. Letter of Intent — validity and risk

It is possible to state a certain time span in the LOI during which the intentions of both parties will continue to exist. However, if such a time limit is mentioned, care should be taken that it is stipulated what will happen when the time is up. Are we going to continue our efforts to negotiate, or will the conditions and assumptions be altered, or is it just over and out?

In the above-mentioned case, the day after the expiry of this LOI, parties entered into an Extension Letter for another 60 days. In all aspects, the LOI remained unchanged and in full force and effect. The contractor duly signed the Extension Letter.

In this actual case, there were five extensions before the contract was closed and execution of the work could commence. During this period, parties continued to work on soil monitoring and outlined further details of the draft contract.

In the event parties do not mention a validity period for a Letter of Intent, a 'reasonable' period should be taken into account. Given the fact that different persons always have different opinions about the word "reasonable", and persons always plan to understand this word to the advantage of the company they represent, it is strongly recommended to state its validity in the LOI and what will happen in the event the date passes without the intended result.

Here, some financial aspects of the LOI should be considered. Given that the LOI has been agreed, should the contract sum already be booked as turnover during the actual book year or should the contractor await the arrival of the final letter of acceptance for the final contract? The same question arises in the case in which the contract is (partly) paid in a foreign currency. Should we accept the risk of currency conversion, or should we cover that financial risk by hedging the contract sum on the financial market? Financial governance rules arrange for these matters, as well as the internal financial policy of the contractor. Normally, contractors make profit in building beautiful assets, not in speculating with currencies, which means that they will avoid any currency risk under all circumstances.

11.5. Memorandum of Understanding — definition and objectives

A Memorandum of Understanding (MOU) is a document describing a bilateral or multilateral agreement between parties. It expresses a convergence of will between the parties, which is expressed by an intended common line of action. A MOU is often used in cases where parties either do not imply a legal commitment or in situations where the parties cannot create a legally enforceable agreement. In fact, it may be considered as a more formal alternative to a gentlemen's agreement.

The objectives of a MOU are threefold. First, it is used to clarify the key points of an intended cooperation between parties for their convenience. This may be the case when preparing for a complex project between an employer and a contractor, or when arranging for financial funding for a future project. As such, a MOU may be used when preparing for the organization of a complex project, where responsibilities among parties need to be carefully defined and where contractual conditions for the intended cooperation need to be outlined in a fair level of detail. In all of these cases, parties take note of each other's positions, possibilities, responsibilities and liabilities. Second, a MOU may be used to declare officially that the parties are currently negotiating, as in the preparation of a tender, the preparation of a joint venture, the investigations for financing a project or to arrange for future maintenance of an asset to be constructed. Finally, the MOU may provide safeguards in case a deal collapses during negotiation.

In some cases, depending on the exact wording, MOUs can have the binding power of a contract. Just like in the case of LOIs, it depends what was agreed in the MOU. Contracts do not need to be labeled as such to be legally binding. Whether or not a document constitutes a binding agreement particularly depends on the presence or absence of well-defined legal obligations in the text of the document. This can include specific disclaimers of legal effect, or failure of the MOU to fulfill the elements required for a valid contract. As is the case with LOIs, the same clauses may be used, such as secrecy clauses, promises to negotiate in good faith, and the obligation to refrain from contacts with third parties about identical issues.

11.6. Differences and similarities between LOI and MOU

Indeed, there is a specific difference between a Letter of Intent and a Memorandum of Understanding. A LOI outlines the intent of one party towards another with regard to an agreement, and may only be signed by the party expressing that intent, whereas a MOU must be signed by all parties for it to be valid. Nevertheless, LOIs are often incorrectly referred to as MOUs and vice versa. In the above described case, the LOI was countersigned by the contractor. The difference with a MOU did not exist. In that situation, employer and contractor could have made up a MOU as well.

Depending upon the subject and the object of the MOU, it is possible that the parties are bound to each other for a certain period. It should be mentioned in the MOU what will happen after that period has expired.

The original wordings of the LOI and MOU have their roots in common law countries. When searching the Internet for definitions and clarifications, the reader is confronted with Anglo-Saxon terms and conditions. One should be aware that in case of legal conflicts, the judge will apply his own legal system in most cases. Obligations for negotiations are explained in different ways in one country or another. Therefore, it is recommended to mention what law system will apply to the LOI or MOU.

In practice, different terminology is used. Popular terms are letter of agreement and gentlemen's agreement, the latter of which normally does not stand before court. The concept of a LOI is almost similar to a "heads of agreement", a "term sheet" or "discussion sheet".

11.7. Letter of authorization and other letters

Sometimes the term letter of authorization is applied, for instance when the potential contracting parties want to be informed about data and facts that are not always available to third parties or to the public. Think about other quotations at hand; a dredging company will not want the competition to become aware of the details. Think about available or non-available budgets for a job; a port authority normally is not obliged to publish those figures. By means of a letter of authorization, parties may authorize the other to become aware of such information. Sometimes a letter of authorization foresees the investigation of unknown data. The potential employer may authorize the addressee to spend a certain sum of money for soil and sub-sea investigations. The results of such activities may be important during the coming negotiations.

In business, a letter of authorization is applied for many other objectives. It may be a written confirmation of a person's rank, authority, ability to enter into a legally binding contract, take a specific action, spend a specified sum, or to delegate his or her duties and powers.[1] In the construction industry it is applied to authorize a party to invest or to spend some money.

In common law, it is usual to name certain official statements. Other typical terms are: letter of advice, letter of agreement, letter of acceptance, letter of award, letter of instruction, letter of assignment, letter of refusal, letter of indemnity, letter of attainment, letter of award, letter of comfort, letter of guarantee, letter of commitment, letter of delegation, letter of credit. The meaning of such terms is available on the Internet at www.businessdictionary.com, but note: these terms are applied in various situations. Read the content carefully; it is the content of the signed document that counts, not the definition of a dictionary or an Internet site.

11.8. Conclusions

In international contract law, both the LOI and MOU are very practical vehicles to proceed in cooperation with a foreign partner, where a 100% binding contract would not yet be feasible.

Normally, a LOI is not a contract. However, it happens that parties accept some obligations to fulfill. In such a case, these obligations must be met. A party commits itself to what was agreed upon in the LOI, nothing less and nothing more.

---

[1] http://www.businessdictionary.com/definition/letter-of-authorization.html, January 23, 2013.

If parties do not want third parties to become aware of their negotiations, they have to insert a secrecy clause; if parties do not wish the other party to negotiate with other parties, they have to insert an exclusivity clause.

It is recommended to mention a legal system that is applicable to the LOI. It is also recommended that a term of validity is inserted, and further, what will happen in case the date passes.

A MOU differs from a LOI. It may be used in other commercial relations than just employer and contractor or service provider. It may concern cooperation, a joint venture or the organization in the preparation of a complex project. An MOU should be signed by all parties concerned.

Chapter 12

Signing the Contract — Pitfalls

12.1. Case — Post-tender additional work

Project manager Robert Gootsmark was angry; and not just a little bit. Everything went smoothly, the cooperation with the employer was better than ever. His company had done more than necessary to meet the employer's contractual requirements. He had showed interest in the employer's problems with its financial stakeholders and had helped him to find satisfactory solutions. Robert followed his company's slogan: if you can help the employer where possible, do so. And now, Robert understood that he made a terrible mistake. On his desk was a short letter. The letterhead showed that it came from the employer's legal department at its head office. We refer to Box 12.1.

It was the first time Robert saw the name of Abraham Peerings, LLM, whoever that might be. During negotiations, the legal aspects of the agreement were the responsibility of the employer's contract manager, who knew a lot about engineering and design. Robert never asked whether he was a lawyer or an engineer. Anyhow, he worked closely together with the leading negotiator. The fact that the just-arrived letter was dispatched by the

Box 12.1. A letter from the employer's legal department.

Regarding your invoice on "completed extra work" nr vxx/6789, dated January 30, 2012, we regretfully have to inform you that the described work is part of the agreed Scope of Supply. Following clause 34.8 of your contract xyz, the costs for the referred work are for your account and are included in the total contract price. We have the pleasure to herewith return your above-referred invoice for the amount of US$ 1,200,000.

Should you wish to receive further information on this subject, please do not hesitate to contact Mr. Abraham Peerings, LLM, on his direct number...

employer's legal department indicated that the employer wanted to play it hard. "This business is a war business," Robert said to himself. The employer's negotiator played the good guy. The legal department in reality was the bad guy. Robert now had to deal with the bad guy.

The agreed extra work was specified during further negotiations after the tender was accepted. At that time, the confirmation e-mail, stating that Robert's tender was "fully and completely accepted, subject to some minor discussions on details" had landed in the contractor's contract manager's inbox. But the contract itself was not yet signed by the two parties. Both CEOs would sign within a few days. Shortly after having dispatched the e-mail, the employer's technical department came up with an extra module on the deck of the tendered rig. Thereupon Robert had immediately mobilized the engineering department and the tender manager to come to a moderate price increase of approximately $1 million, which was acceptable to the employer's engineers. This was noted in the minutes of the meeting, signed by Robert himself, but not countersigned by the visiting representatives of the employer. A few days later the contract was signed. The Form of Agreement was not changed, neither was the total fixed price. But Robert had incorporated the extra module on the deck in the specification.

When the module was installed at the site, Robert suggested that the extra invoice should be dispatched to the employer's actual representative. This man was new on the job, after having taken over from the man who did the earlier negotiations. His resistance struck Robert. His response was a little stiff, saying: "You must not be astonished that I am working to strict budgets — that is company policy here; but I'll find out what I can do for you." Robert re-read the awful contract clause. It said:

> 34.8. Entire Agreement
>
> The Contract constitutes the entire agreement between the parties hereto with respect to the Work and supersedes all prior negotiations, representations or agreements related to the Contract, either written or oral. No amendments to the Contract shall be effective unless evidenced in writing and signed by the parties to the Contract.[1]

Robert also checked the complete Scope of Supply — five volumes, each five kilos — and found out that, indeed, the module was included. His own initials were at the bottom of the page. Robert reviewed the minutes of the meeting when the extra order was passed. This document was not countersigned by the employer's representatives.

[1] LOGIC Construction 2003 and LOGIC Marine Construction 2004, clause 34.8.

12.2. Inaccurate technical negotiations and discussions

In the above case, the dispute regarded an extra module at extra cost. Similar cases were about:

- An obligation of a contractor to take over the employer's engineering work which, after verification by the contractor, happened to contain serious miscalculations.
- Extra work outside the scope of work due to more severe regulations of classification societies, insurance companies or competent authorities which, at the moment of signing the contract, were not available.
- Delivery of employer-supplied items, agreed upon during negotiations; however, the contractor understood this would be without cost for the contractor.
- Employer-provided information, promised by the employer's engineer on the project without cost for the contractor.
- Employer-provided engineering, without extra cost for the contractor.
- Advance payment in line with other stipulations of the contract for issues outside the tender documents.

These discussions arise when a contract contains a so-called "four corner clause". Such a clause is also called the "entire agreement clause" or the "integration clause". It defines what is and is not a part of the agreement. It simply provides that the final agreement made by the parties supersedes any terms discussed or proposals exchanged in earlier negotiations. Only what has been written between the "four corners of the sheet of paper" forms the agreement. Under contracts containing a four corner clause a contractor is not entitled to any extra payment in the event that work was done that was not specified in the documents mentioned in the contract. Not everyone is as unlucky as Robert. It happens that exceptions occur, as seen in Box 12.2 and Box 12.3.

Box 12.2. Not entitled to remuneration; nevertheless compensated.

During execution of a complex steel structure, the project manager of the main contractor organized daily "toolbox" meetings. All subcontractors at the site came together. Daily instructions were noted in daily reports, the so called "toolbox minutes", which were drafted by a project buyer. When a subcontractor asked the buyer to

(*Continued*)

Box 12.2. (*Continued*)

take notes in the minutes at the toolbox meeting for extra payment of extra work, the main contractor's project manager intervened, stating that such work at first glance might have been considered outside the subcontractor's scope of work and outside his accepted and agreed upon tender. However, the main contractor stated: "This work had not been executed after issuing a variation order, signed by both parties, while ... as such the referred 'extra' work would not be considered as extra payment, but simply had to be regarded as work performed after 'normal technical' clarification."

Unfortunately for the main contractor, the subcontractor's project manager had kept copies of all previous toolbox meetings. In one of the meetings, it was noted that the main contractor was himself offered extra work that was not mentioned in the scope of work, but was ordered as an extra by the employer during execution at the site. The subcontractor requested an extra work order but the project manager for the main contractor tried to argue that he only got a "technical clarification" of existing drawings and thus none was needed. But the subcontractor's project manager remarked that in one of the earlier meetings it was noted that the employer's main contractor was honored with extra payment for the job. So, the subcontractor's project manager won the argument.

The subcontractor consequently claimed an honorable back-to-back situation in good faith. The main contractor's project manager could not deny that he himself was successful in obtaining extra payment for extra work outside his own four corners contract. So he reluctantly had to agree on a "post-execution variation", all in the presence of the other subcontractors.

Box 12.3. Fair trade and good faith.

Another case is the willingness of a contractor to produce portal legs for an oil rig, based upon the employer's engineering. The referred engineering was submitted to the contractor by the employer and performed by an outside engineering firm, but not verified by the employer. The main contractor, who worked under a D&B contract, afterwards had to re-work the underlying calculations, which resulted in an increase of the steel weight of the permanent works. The extra cost involved amounted to approximately

(*Continued*)

Box 12.3. (*Continued*)

€4.5 million, equal to 2% of the contract price. Based on the LOGIC entire contract clause, the employer refused payment for the extra cost. The contractor had to find a way to escape this loss by suggesting a non-legal, but "business-like" solution. Strictly according to law and order, the contractor had no title to claim for extra payment. But based on "fair trade and good faith", a different solution had to be found. And so it was.

Technicians may question why a four corner clause should be part of a contract. If the work is done, why refuse payment for the extra cost? The answer is simple. One has to bear in mind that all financial documents will be verified by accountants. In the event that, in a four corner contract, work is done and paid for outside the four corners of the contract, the serious suspicion of malversation will arise when such work is not covered by a variation order. The verifying accountant will be obliged to report the deviation under the applicable accounting standards. As such, a credit invoice at an amount of €1 million or €4.5 million is a serious dent in the accountant's report.

12.3. The objective of the four corner contract

There are good reasons for drafting clear and unequivocal project contract documents, and forgetting about all previously discussed alternatives of ideas, designs, draft constructions, preliminary sketches, draft proposals, discussions and exchanges between consultants, architects, designers, engineers, tender teams, development officers, strategic officials, competent authorities, classification societies, pressure groups, politicians, other opinion leaders and board opinions. Certainly, after years of study, aligning conflicting interests, conflicting reports and the struggle for sufficient budget allocation, one has to draw a line somewhere. Now, this is what the project is going to be; forget all troubles from the past. This is certainly true for projects with a long and troublesome history. A simple contract clause will put an end to all previous documents and discussions. LOGIC respects that principle. Those contracts are called "four corner contracts", or "entire agreements". It is called "endorsement of preliminary documents". The CMM standard contract follows the same principle.[2]

---

[2]CMM standard contract for the Oil and Gas industry in the Netherlands, 1992, note 10 to model Form of Agreement.

Under the FIDIC standard contracts, we do not find strict exclusion of previous documents. But FIDIC mentions the documents that together form the agreement. Documents that are not explicitly mentioned in the contract are not part of it. Basically, under FIDIC, as well as under LOGIC, only those documents which are mentioned explicitly in the contract are applicable. By way of exception, FIDIC may facilitate the possibility to add or to change the contractor's original tender. If post-tender negotiations are permitted, and changes in specification or price are agreed, then the original form of contract can still be used after the parties have made and initialed the appropriate changes to their respective documents. The contractor thus makes a revised offer in response to the employer's revised tender documents and the revised offer is accepted by the employer signing and returning the acceptance form. If the changes are extensive, a complete new Form of Agreement should be completed by the parties.[3]

12.4. Priority of documents

A construction contract usually consists of various documents. It is important to note the priority of documents, as they may contain conflicting clauses. Such priority is necessary to arrange for the potential battle of the forms.

Documents forming the Contract, listed in the order of priority, are:

(a) The Agreement
(b) Particular Conditions
(c) General Conditions
(d) The Specification
(e) The Drawings
(f) The Contractor's tendered design
(g) The bill of quantities
(h) . . . .
(i) . . . .[4]

When agreeing on the list of documents, parties may delete or add documents if needed. It is not impossible to have the minutes of the previous meetings added to the contract documents, when negotiating the final version of the contract. If that is done, the minutes should be signed by authorized persons from both parties.

[3]FIDIC note on paragraph concerning Agreement, p. A, blue book, 2006.

[4]This example is taken from FIDIC Dredging and Reclamation, the blue book, Appendix on sub-clause 1.1.1. — 1.3. Other FIDIC standards have comparable listings.

Documents which have only a faint relationship with the agreement are not part of the deal. Authorizations of public authorities are no part of a contract; neither are previous studies of engineering companies and laboratories, or statements from pressure groups. The standard CMM contract has an extensive list, indicating the compulsory priority. It also means that documents that are not listed are not part of the contract. The CMM contract lists the following documents:

- Form of Agreement.
- Standard conditions.
- Pricing schedule.
- Scope of work.
- Time schedule.
- Technical specifications.
- Drawings.
- Administrative procedures.
- Appendices, such as:
  list of company-provided items, list of company-provided services, list of contractor-provided items, list of technical information and services, list of special equipment, list of company-provided technical information, list of company approved subcontractors, list of contractor's representatives and key personnel, list of company's representatives and key personnel, insurance policies, health and safety manuals, environmental measures, QA/QAC manual, bank guarantee, parent company guarantee, reports and records, transport of personnel, equipment, company-provided items, contractor-provided items, penalties, notices, deviations.

12.5. Conclusion — A few days of painstaking work

When everything seems clear to sign the Form of Agreement, it is good to have the contract engineer and the contract lawyer spend two days or more in a room without telephone and e-mail. They should check all documents that together form the contract. These may include several binders of specifications, drawings, calculations, descriptions, memoranda, norms, HS&E regulations and the like. It is better to spend sufficient time on the checks than to find out later that some millions of dollars or euros are at risk or lost. In the event the contract needs to be signed in a hurry, because one of the parties is under pressure for whatever reason, please realize that someone — and mostly that is the contractor — is put at extra risk.

Chapter 13

Liability Versus Responsibility

13.1. Case — A loss-making project and its malfunctioning project manager

"Now, Mr. Dragon, we are here to finally discuss and close the case of your faulty performance in the Elephant's Island Project. You admitted that the company provided you with the necessary means and manpower to start your mobilization in time, but nevertheless you took too many days to set off to the site. Your crew was ready and your assistant warned you to speed up, but you did not. Therefore, you missed the shipping date and had to wait for the next ship. You lost 11 working days. On the site, your communication with the local authorities was so bad that we got a phone call from the town office, asking for an explanation. You again lost some four or five days, before we could settle the case. Consequently, your platform works at the yard started three weeks behind planning schedule. The rainy season started and you were unable to make up your arrears. Your team was not very positive about your leadership and some of the workmen did not consider you as the right man at the right place. Furthermore, we had that incident concerning the local safety regulations, which you were unable to settle yourself. The company could not send its invoice for the fourth installment of €11 million, when the platform was not ready according to schedule. And finally, the client wants to cash the penalty of 0.1% for each week in late delivery in missing that milestone. That is an €11,000 penalty per week. Our lawyers had their hands full due to misery caused by you. It will be impossible for you to repair the bad reputation that the company has to carry from now on, nor can you compensate for the financial losses."

Dragon listened. He thought about his early years at high school, where his notes always were the best in class. He thought about his advanced studies in civil engineering, with his brilliant final thesis on the finite elements method, which could save up to 15–20% steel weight on foundations and pillars. He thought about the personal friendly speech of the dean when he passed with distinction. He was never good in rugby, that is true, but he was the most promising young engineer in the country. And now this.

"Are you with us, Mr. Dragon?"

"Yes sir, I mean, you are completely right, I think so."

The CEO continued while the Chief HRM absently looked out of the window. Both men were well-dressed, in neat gray suits, not the kind of workers' shirts and jeans that project managers wear on duty. Dragon had put on a tie for the occasion.

"I think that you should symbolically contribute to a part of our losses, in accepting that we punish you with 11% of the penalty the company suffered. We will deduct €1,000 from your salary, starting next month. What do you think about that?"

This chapter deals with the difference between personal responsibility, duty and contractual liability, and accountability of a company, a corporation or any other contracting party in commercial deals. When solving legal conflicts, it is important to distinguish between these terms. We will explain using the practical case described above. Next, we will analyze the case.

13.2. The project manager's labor contract

A person is responsible for his actions and behavior. In the above case, the project manager acted in a way that resulted in the wrong decisions. He was late when preparing the mobilization. His behavior was such that he was not accepted as a good leader of a project team. His assistant warned him beforehand, but in one way or the other, all of this did not result in the performance the company promised to its employer. Dragon was responsible for the performance of his task. Such non-performance should have consequences. But should Dragon participate in the losses of the company? We have to consider his legal relationship with the engineering company. This relationship is built upon a labor contract. That is quite different from a contracting or construction agreement between an engineering company and the employer who wants the work to be executed. Figure 13.1 provides an overview of the legal relationships between the parties involved.

The project manager's legal obligation to his employer, i.e. the contractor, is in fulfilling a project management task. Some project managers are able to fulfill their job without any apparent effort. Others, such as the project manager at hand, miss deadlines, are unfortunate in their communication with others and do not get the support of their workers. A task is defined as a set of activities and duties, described in a task description. The execution of tasks

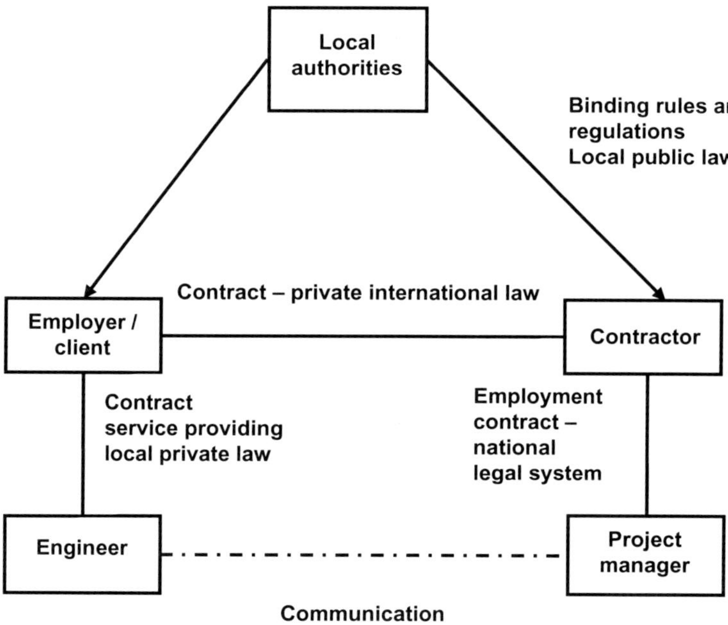

Figure 13.1. The legal relations between owner/client, contractor, local authorities, engineer, and project manager.

and jobs is assessed using a formal evaluation system. A task may be defined in terms of arriving at a certain result, such as the successful execution of a scope of work against a fixed budget in an agreed-upon time schedule. Any project manager is *responsible* for such a task. The good performance of such a task cannot be enforced through intervention of a judge. If the project manager does not succeed, he is not liable for the financial losses of the company. Such liability is part of a completely different contract, i.e. the contract between the contractor and his counterpart, being the contractor's client.

13.3. The contractor's construction contract

A company is liable for meeting its legal obligations. Such obligations may be part of a contract or may emerge from the law in general. A wrongly performed or missed contractual obligation results in a default, which will be settled as written down in the contract documents. In many cases, a penalty or liquidated damages, in case of late completion of a milestone, will have to be paid by the contractor. In the event the contractor does not perform what was agreed upon in the contract, the employer may go to court and ask for a verdict. A contractual obligation, which is expressed in a formal contract, is enforceable by contract parties before court or before arbitration, if such is mentioned in the contract. Since the project manager's company was the party who engaged in the contract, the company is contractually *liable*, and *can be addressed to appear in court*, for the missed milestone or the bad performance. Therefore, in the case of severe failure, the employer will sue the company of the contractor, rather than its personnel who were responsible for the work.

13.4. Legal liabilities after unlawful actions

An individual as well as a legal entity are both responsible in the event they commit an unlawful act.[1] That responsibility is derived from legal regulations, after the non-respecting of, for instance, HS&E rules. Such an unlawful act is called tort.[2] Here, a person as well as a legal entity is liable for damages resulting from tort. In such cases, the verdict is based on tort law and not on the employment law, referred to in Section 13.2.

In contracts, the meaning of the words "responsibility", "liability" and "accountability" are interchangeable. The exact legal meaning has to be found out in the context of the referred clauses.

13.5. Indemnities

Accidents may occur during any project. No one wants them to happen, but they are a fact of life. In construction contracts, parties beforehand stipulate how the liable party should compensate losses of the suffering party.

In general, an indemnity is a sum paid by one party to another party by *way of compensation for a particular loss* suffered by the other party. This may concern a sum paid by a contractor to an employer or vice versa, or by a subcontractor to any other subcontractor, client or contractor, or any third party — even third parties that have nothing to do with the project at hand. Forms of indemnity include cash payments, repairs, replacements and reinstatements.

Losses, which need to be compensated for in a project, may relate to damage to a person, such as death or injury, or loss of/damage to material objects, which are in the person's possession or are in the possession of a legal entity. Damage to companies may be in the form of physical damages, loss of profits, loss of business opportunities or loss for damage to reputation.

---

[1]Synonyms for legal entity are: legal/artificial/juristic/corporate/fictitious person. Also the wording legal body/entity/persona/corporate body and corporation are used. Source: van Dale (1991), *Great Dictionary, 2nd edition*, the Netherlands.

[2]For further explanation of this subject, see Chapter 15.

All international standard contracts have specific clauses on indemnification by the parties concerned. Parties want to agree beforehand and to be sure what will occur in the event something happens that nobody wants to happen. The clauses normally describe how to arrange for compensation, exonerations if any, waivers or limitations of indemnities, the limits of the amounts to be paid by one party to the other, and the formalities on how a claim should be brought to the attention of the other party and the eventual other consequences.

13.6. Non-contractual damages

When, during the execution of a work, a contractor, subcontractor or service provider accidentally causes damage to a third party, and there is no previous contractual relationship between such parties, the civil law of the relevant country will be applied to solve the matter.

An example that may serve here is the case where a truck driver of a sub-supplier of the employer, when fulfilling an activity for the employer's project, gets hurt by an act of a contractor or subcontractor or service provider at the site. Such an accident may result in illness, disability or even death. The general ruling in any legal system is that there should be compensation. But legal systems differ to a great extent. This is true both for the amounts awarded and the procedures to be followed before court. The reason for this is the degree of judgment that is called upon in assessing pain, suffering, lost income, gender, position in society, age of the victim, nature and extent of the injury, family relations of the victim, compensation of social security, if any. Therefore, the outcome of these procedures, in any legal system, is somewhat unpredictable. We will deal with this type of damage in more detail in Chapter 15, when tort is discussed.

In the case described by Box 13.1, the inhabitants did not address their claim to the indemnitor. The inhabitants claimed against the city, which in its turn answered their claims and provided repairs as soon as possible. The cable was part of the electricity network, serving the city. The city summoned the contractor. As the parties were related by a contract, this was a contractual claim. Under a contract, parties may come to other agreements than in civil law. So they did, and then the relevant contract clauses on indemnities were applicable.

The outcome of the claim depends on a few circumstances. Essential here is whether the repair was that urgent that it was not possible to allow the contractor to carry the work out himself. If that was the case, the contractor should compensate the city, although taking into account the agreed-upon maximum

Box 13.1. The damaged power cable and the indemnification.

In a foreign city, a railway tunnel is being constructed. Contract parties are the city and a civil contractor. During the construction works, the contractor damages a power cable belonging to a utility company owned by the city, after which half of the city is without electricity for four hours. The city officers, who are afraid that the city will be sued by inhabitants, feel forced to have the cable repaired at short notice. Hence, the city summons the contractor to repair the cable, starting the same day. The contractor is not able to start this repair work immediately. Thereupon the city orders a third party to repair the cable within one or two days. Next, the city claims a significant amount for repair and damage from the contractor, based upon the appropriate indemnification clause under its construction contract. The contractor refuses to pay for the claim, explaining that he was not given sufficient opportunity to execute the repair work himself, as agreed upon under the contract for the construction of the tunnel.

under the contract. If the repairs could have waited a few days, the contractor is still liable, however to no more costs than he would have spent himself.

13.7. Direct versus indirect or consequential losses[3]

Damages are sometimes divided into direct versus consequential damages. Direct or incidental losses include the costs needed to remedy problems and to put things right. Take, for example, a truck driver whose truck is hit at the site by a heavy crane used by the contractor. Direct damages consist of the mobilization of the damaged truck to the garage for repairs, and the repairs or replacement cost for the truck, during the time it is out of order. In the event the truck driver owned the truck and worked for his own transport company, it is obvious that he suffers from a lack of income (or turnover) as well. The claimant may also be entitled to any consequential losses. These are the lost profits that the claimant could have been expected to make in the period when the truck was under repair.

Recovery of damages is subject to the legal principle that damages must be proximately caused by the wrongful conduct. This is known as the *principle*

[3] In UK common law, the words "indirect losses" and "consequential losses" are synonymous.

of proximate cause. This principle governs the recovery of all compensatory damages, whether the underlying claim is based on contract, tort or both. Damages are likely to be limited to those reasonably foreseeable by the defendant. If a defendant could not reasonably have foreseen that some loss would occur by his actions, there may be no liability for such loss. Suppose, for instance, that the day after the incident the truck driver had a job to go from Amsterdam to Kiev and back at a very profitable rate, including tolls and excellent meals, but — because of the accident — was hindered in his performance. Then, the question arises whether such indirect loss is subject to the liability of the responsible party. In different legal systems, this question is dealt with in different ways.

13.8. Damage to contractual parties

Most standard contracts arrange for a cap[4] on the contractor's liability for a work.[5] In general, it is suggested that the overall cap on the contractor's liability in respect of damage to the works is limited to a percentage of the value of the contract, or the amount stated in the agreement.

Above that, all standard contracts exclude liability for loss of use of the permanent works, loss of business, loss of profits and so on.[6]

Standard contracts have similar clauses on liability and indemnities. Most contracts (Construct/D&C/DBM/DBFM/DBFMO) state that there should be a causal relationship between liability for certain kinds of damage and the amounts that are bearable for the parties, given their financial position. Obviously, parties should work together to mitigate damages to the maximum extent possible.[7] Limitation of liability is, in general, an accepted deviation of the general rules in common law and of many civil-code books used in various legal systems.

It is good practice that liability for indirect (or consequential) damages *vis-à-vis* the contractual party is excluded and/or capped. This is not true for damages done to third parties, as these by definition are not part of contractual arrangements.

---

[4] Cap: a maximum amount to be paid in case of a flawed performance.

[5] Not all contracts include a maximum on the contractor's liability. It is in the contractor's interests to have a maximum agreed upon in all construction contracts.

[6] In practice, some potential clients and investors apply their own templates for draft contracts, where the excluding clauses are not included. Lawyers and tender managers should be aware that such standard arrangements are mentioned as reservations when tendering.

[7] Also M. A. B. Chao-Duivis (ed.) (2011), Dutch construction contracts: views from abroad, *Instituut voor bouwrecht*, p. 84.

13.9. Negligence

In the event of damages, there is often a certain negligence on the part of the participant. However, with regard to negligence, a distinction needs to be made. There is negligence, gross negligence and there is willful misconduct.

When a tort action is committed, there is always negligence in one way or another. When someone acts and causes damages on purpose, or if he nonchalantly does not think about the consequences of his behavior, the law is severe. That is the case in most legal systems. A general rule of thumb in those situations is that there is no maximum in compensation. In most legal systems, this means that even in the case of damages to contractual parties, damage resulting from gross negligence and willful intent can never be capped.

13.10. Insurances

All standard contracts include provisions for insurances. These normally include, firstly, the contractor's professional liability for the design. If the contractor in this respect is negligent, the resulting damages should be covered. In the event of construction contracts or dredging contracts, where no design obligation is incurred, such insurance will be left out.

A second type of insurance is for works, plant, materials, contractor's documents, files and the contractor's equipment. This insurance has to cover loss or damage from any cause, except the professional liability mentioned above. The employer in his tender documents may require the contractor to include this insurance in his proposal. In certain circumstances, the employer may decide not to insist on insurance by the contractor, but to arrange insurance himself in respect of the works and third party liability.[8]

Third, standard contracts mention insurance against any party's liability for any loss, damage, death or bodily injury that may occur to any physical property. The damages from accidental acts are covered under this insurance.

A common fourth type of insurance covers the contractor's liability for claims, damages, losses and expenses arising from injury, sickness, disease or death of any person employed by the contractor, subcontractor, service provider or any other of the contractor's personnel. This insurance should compensate the referred financial losses and is meant to protect all personnel working for the contractor.

---

[8] Many varieties of clauses are at hand, for instance, FIDIC, D&B 1995, pp. 23–25.

There are many more kinds of possible insurances for projects. We just mentioned the most likely types. The applied names of various types differ depending upon the insurance company or country. Some other regular types are contractual liability insurance, workers' compensation insurance, employer's liability insurance, professional errors and omissions insurance, completed operation insurance, car insurance, owner-provided or contractor-provided wrap-up insurance, business interruption insurance, terrorism insurance and hurricane insurance, to name a few.[9]

13.11. Conclusions

Responsibilities that result from an employment contract are of a different nature than liabilities that result from a contract between a client and a contractor. In the event a natural person does not fulfill his task, he in general will not be liable for the financial damages.

A legal entity that is in default after non-fulfillment of its contractual obligations is liable for the resulting damages.

Concluding, we can summarize indemnity clauses as the specific arrangements made by parties to a contract to hold each other harmless in case things go wrong during a project. Parties can agree to maximize the amounts to be paid in case one party incurs damage because of the malfunctioning of the other party. In many legal systems, amounts to be paid cannot be capped in case of gross negligence or willful misconduct.

Insurances serve to cover the financial consequences resulting from damages caused by parties to the project. In general, insurances cover the works and everything that might be damaged or lost, the contractor's professional responsibilities in case of design errors, the liability to third parties and the risks run by the contractor's personnel.

---

[9]For further understanding of some basics of insurances, see Kit Werremeyer (2006), *Understanding & Negotiating Construction Contracts*. Kingston, MA: Reed Construction Data Inc., pp. 93–124.

Chapter 14

Guarantees and Warranties

14.1. Case — Guarantee issues

In a discussion between an employer and a contractor about an oil platform, which was delivered on the basis of an EPC contract, the employer stated that the contractor had not provided for a coating system that was fit for purpose. This was assessed and reported by an independent, specialist consulting firm. Therefore, the employer summoned the contractor to take corrective measures immediately. The damage involved would, according to the contractor's specialists, amount to at least $1.5 million for the contractor. A discussion with a subcontractor on how the cost of the damage could be split was leading nowhere. As many weeks went by, the employer became impatient and ordered another specialist coating firm to do the repair work. Given the speedy work that was requested and the special scaffolding that needed to be contracted, this subcontractor produced a steep bill, charging over $2 million. Since a bank guarantee was originally agreed when signing the EPC contract, the employer decided to call in the bank guarantee for this amount. Obviously, this sum was taken from the contractor's bank account. This action spread rumors at all levels of the contractor's head office. It also created some unrest at the subcontractor's office that provided the coating system and who also had provided a bank guarantee to the contractor, albeit for a much lower amount.[1]

The case perfectly describes the social atmosphere within the company's offices when a bank guarantee is called in by a client. The staff are astonished, furious and irritated. Why is the customer that unreasonable? We did everything as agreed upon. Can't they see that they are completely wrong? They did it without warning us. The bank informed us, but said that nothing could be done and that the bank's reputation would be involved if they did not pay.

[1]A. van Weele, Compliant to customer specifications and still having problems, Case 5, Core Module, International Contracting Program, TiasNimbas Business School, Tilburg, 2009.

The bank guarantee was called in shortly before the end of the guarantee period. This is a period agreed upon between the employer and contractor, during which the contractor was bound to repair shortcomings.

In spoken language, the words "guarantee", "warranty", "defects liability" and "performance guarantee" are often applied in the same sense. In relation to the good performance of the contractor, there are many more terms and expressions, such as "bonds" and "on demand guarantee" versus "conditional guarantee". Also, words like "surety" and "representation" are used. To avoid confusion, Box 14.2, at the end of this chapter, explains the meanings of most current expressions.

In this chapter, we will deal with the meaning of these terms and how they may serve to come to clear agreements with counterparties. In most contracts in international contracting, guarantees are arranged for. As these contracts very often are written in the English language, the wording of guarantee clauses is linked to basic principles of UK contract law. Therefore, we will explain basic principles underlying guarantee clauses according to common law,[2] but do not to forget other legal systems. In doing so, we will provide definitions of guarantee, explain what elements of the contractor's performance may be subject to guarantee and how a guarantee can be called upon. We will discuss the similarity and difference between a guarantee and a warranty.

14.2. A guarantee by a third party

A guarantee implies an agreement by one person or company to another person or company to be liable for a debt, a default or a failure of a third person or company. That is the essence for a third-party guarantee. Cumulatively, the basic requirements are:

- There must be three parties involved: a) the principle creditor or beneficiary (usually the employer); b) the debtor, who is the person in debt or who should do something (usually the contractor); and c) the guarantor, the person or company who promises to be liable in the event the original debtor does not fulfill his obligations (usually the contractor's bank).
- There must be a primary liability between the two other persons or companies other than the guarantor. The guarantor is only liable in the event the original debtor does not pay what he should pay or do what he should do. That is a secondary obligation.

[2] See Chapter 24 for different legal systems.

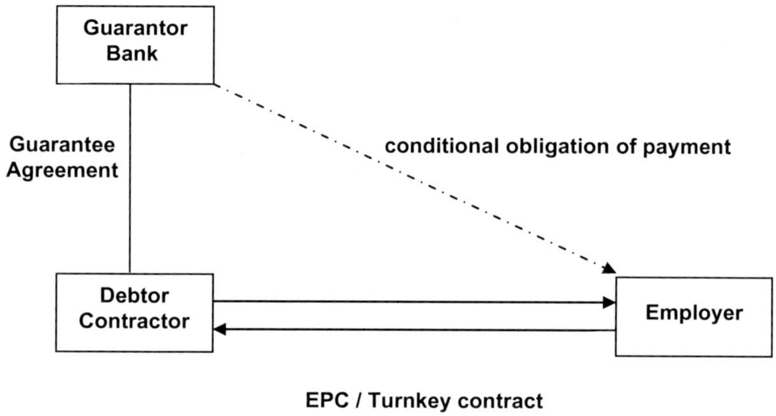

Figure 14.1. Schematic overview of the case study represented above.

- The guarantor has no relationship to the contract between the principal creditor and the principal debtor. He is only — and in no other way — connected by his guarantee.[3]

We analyze the above-mentioned case:

- There were three parties involved: a) the employer, being the beneficiary: b) the contractor; and c) the bank, who promised to pay on the demand of the employer.
- There was a primary contractual relationship between employer and contractor, who had agreed to be liable for fitness for purpose of the platform during a certain period. The secondary legal relationship is the liability in the event the contractor, to the opinion of the beneficiary, did not properly perform his primary obligation under the contract.
- The bank did not have any relationship to the contract between the beneficial employer and the contractor. The bank did not enter into an agreement with the employer.[4] The contracting relations are shown in Figure 14.1.

Conditional guarantee

While the guarantee is a secondary obligation to a contract, the guarantor might not be bound to pay in the event the principle debtor is not liable; then

[3]C. M. Schmitthoff and C. A. G. Sarre (1984), *Charlesworth's Mercantile Law, 14th edition*. London: Steven & Sons Ltd., pp. 481–482.

[4]Instead of by a bank, a guarantee could have been given by a parent company, a surety company, an affiliated company or any other third party.

the guarantor is not liable either. The same idea is that the guarantee will be void in the event the original contract is ended or terminated, unless otherwise agreed in the written guarantee. Here a warning is in place. When, for example, a bank in the Netherlands, located in Amsterdam, issues a security bond in favor of an employer in, for example, the Great Republic of Swania, no one should be surprised that Swanian Law is unclear on this subject. Even in the event in which the contractor has all legal reasons to terminate the contract and leave the site, the bank should not be surprised if the guarantee is called upon by the employer. In such situations, the bank obviously should not pay (due to the termination of the main contract, the guarantee has become void). However, if the bank does pay, the contractor will have great difficulty in getting the amount due repaid by its employer. The main teaching: when terminating a contract with an employer, also inform the bank immediately and — if possible — terminate the guarantee arrangement in writing.

Unconditional and irrevocable guarantee — the on-demand guarantee

In practice, conditional guarantees are becoming rare in international contracting. Most employers insist on unconditional guarantees. In the event they call on the guarantee there is no room for discussions with the bank as to whether a contractor is in default or not. Upon calling in the guarantee, the bank's obligation is not only a surety, but the call makes it a primary obligation. The word "irrevocable" means that the bank may not withdraw from its obligation to pay during the term of validity mentioned in the written guarantee. The normal procedure for calling in such a guarantee is the following:

- The contractor has, in the sole opinion of the employer, not fulfilled his obligations under the contract, either in whole or in part.
- The employer informs the guarantor about the amount, in the opinion of the company, that is or will be due to the employer from the contractor and asks the guarantor to pay.
- The contractor has received written notice that the employer is going to draw funds under the terms of the guarantee.
- The guarantor pays the requested sum.[5]

---

[5]Text derived from Explanatory Notes on Standard Construction/Modification/Maintenance Contract for the Oil and Gas Industry in the Netherlands, September 1993, pp. 73–74.

In UK law, a guarantee must be in writing. There should be a good reason for the guarantor to give the surety. But it is not necessary that its reasons are noted in the written document representing the guarantee. Take, for instance, a guarantee on the good maintenance of permanent works during the 12 months after completion. The contract mentions that the contractor shall present a bank guarantee of 5% of the contract price, as a certainty that it will perform its duties under the contract. The bank will not mention or refer to the terms and conditions of the main contract. The bank will mention its proper conditions and limitations. The employer may draw the guarantee under the bank. However, discussions about defaults of the contractor are none of the bank's business. The employer has to respect the conditions of the guarantee contract itself and nothing more than that.

The employer, when receiving the document, printed on the bank's stationery and signed by an authorized representative of the bank, has no right to be informed about the business relations between the bank and the contractor. That remains the bank's secret.

To prevent discussion, it is wise to mention the legal system under which the guarantee is issued. When the legal system is not mentioned in the guarantee contract, the law of the issuing bank is applicable. However, this general rule is not accepted in every country.

A guarantee may be issued for one contract only. However, it is also possible to draft a guarantee for a continuing series of activities. When contractor A agrees to have a dredger available for any dredging work along the coast of country Z over a number of years, the employer and contractor may agree that one guarantee will be issued during the many years that the dredger will be busy, notwithstanding the fact that the dredger may be laying idle between two jobs.

The basic objective of a guarantee usually is to pay a sum of money. However, a guarantee may also relate to a promise to execute or finalize a scope of work in the event a contractor fails to do so. Such a guarantee may be given by a holding company, which supervises several operating companies. This is called a "parent company guarantee". A guarantee may contain a promise to have a scope of work performed or finalized by a third party to the satisfaction of the employer in the event the original contractor fails to do so. The cost for such an operation will not be borne by the employer. How the contractor and the third party settle the costs is not the employer's business.

Civil law also contains rules for the guarantee when three parties are concerned.[6] Here we may distinguish between different forms of guarantee:

- Bank guarantee "on first demand". The payment by the bank is due after a notice from the employer that a claim to the contractor exists. The bank has to pay because the guarantee is a primary obligation.
- Guarantee against certain documents, written by neutral specialists, giving their legal or technical opinion stating the contractor's default.
- Guarantee against documents, containing a court's verdict or an arbitration verdict or a confession of the contractor to its default.
- Other guarantees against documents. Such documents should be specified in the written guarantee.[7]

The heading of the document — what has been written above the document containing the guarantee — is of no importance. What counts is the exact content of the document. The strict text of the bank guarantee must be followed when the guarantee is called upon by the employer, as well as when the bank needs to decide whether or not to pay.[8]

Indemnity

An indemnity clause differs from a guarantee as follows: 1) there are two parties only, 2) the person or company who gives the indemnity is primarily liable and there is no secondary liability and 3) the person who gives the indemnity has a clear interest in the transaction.[9]

In English law, a contract of guarantee must be in writing, while in the case of an indemnity, this is not required. The major difference is that an indemnity is provided by one of the contract parties itself, whilst a guarantee is always provided by a third party at the request of one of the contract

[6] Dutch civil code book, article 7: 850–870.

[7] J. M. van Dunné (2004), *Verbintenissenrecht — contractenrecht, 5th edition*. Deventer: Kluwer Law and Taxation Publishers, pp. 510–511.

[8] HR June 6, 1995, NJ 639, nt PvS, Gesnoteg — Mees Pierson; HR March 26, 2004, NJ 309, nt PvS, Anthea Yachting Co. — ABN AMRO.

[9] C. M. Schmitthoff and C. A. G Sarre (1984), *Charlesworth's Mercantile Law, 14th edition*. London: Steven & Sons Ltd, London, pp. 482. About the difference between indemnity and guarantee, see also G. H. Treitel (2011), *The Law of Contract, 13th edition*. London: Sweet & Maxwell, pp. 165–170.

parties. In international contracting, indemnity clauses are usually part of the contract; sometimes separate deeds are drawn up.[10]

14.3. Bonds

Bid bond

A bid bond is a written guarantee from a third-party guarantor (usually a bank or an insurance company, a surety company or a parent company) submitted to an employer (a principal, client or customer) by a contractor (bidder) with an offer or a tender, generally called "a bid". The handing over of a bid bond means that the tendering contractor feels himself bound to his offer.

A bid bond ensures that, on acceptance of a bid by the employer, the contractor will proceed with the contract. Normally, the contractor will have to replace the bid bond with a performance bond in the event the contract is awarded. In the event the contractor should not fulfill his obligations under his tender, the guarantor will pay the employer the agreed-upon amount as mentioned in the written bond. The guarantor will pay the employer the difference between the contractor's bid and the next highest bidder. This difference is called liquidated damages, which cannot exceed the amount of the bid bond. Another option is that the guarantor has to pay the full amount as mentioned in the bond, notwithstanding that the price difference was less than the guaranteed sum of money. The payment amount of a bid bond, if cashed by the employer, is recovered by the guarantor from the contractor. Synonyms for bid bond are "bid guarantee" or "bid surety".[11]

Performance bond

A performance bond is a written guarantee from a third-party guarantor (usually a bank or an insurance company, a surety company or a parent company) submitted to an employer (a principal, client or customer) by a contractor on winning the bid. A performance bond ensures payment of a sum (not exceeding a stated maximum) of money in case the contractor fails in the full performance of the contract.

Performance bonds usually cover a certain percentage of the contract price and replace the bid bonds on awarding of the contract. With a performance bond, the payment amount is recovered by the guarantor from the

[10] For indemnities, we refer the reader to Chapter 13, Section 13.5.

[11] www.businessdictionary.com/definition/bid-bond.html, January 23, 2013.

contractor, if cashed by the principal. Such a bond is also called a "standby letter of credit" or a "contract performance bond".[12]

14.4. Guarantee and good workmanship

The term "guarantee" may also relate to the performance of the contract. The contractor has to guarantee its good workmanship and excellent quality.[13] A contract may state, for example, the following:

> The Contractor warrants and guarantees that it has performed and shall perform the Work in accordance with the provisions of the contract, and that the permanent works will be free from defects.[14]

The Dutch UAV 1989/2012 is a construction standard, in which the employer is responsible for the design. Yet, the specification may provide that one or several parts of the works must be guaranteed. That means that the contractor is bound, from his own account, to remedy all defects occurring in those parts of the works during the warranty period.[15]

We can conclude the following with regards to guarantees on performance in international contracting. Firstly, when dealing with guarantees, it is important to analyze what type of contract a guarantee arrangement relates to. A guarantee under a construction contract will be different from a guarantee under a D&B contract, an EPC/Turnkey or a DCFM contract. This is related to the difference in risk allocation between these types of contract. Under a construction contract, the contractor has to perform according to the design of the employer. Under a D&B contract, the contractor is responsible for the design as well, and as such, it must be fit for the agreed-upon purpose. Under an EPC/Turnkey contract, the contractor has to prove that the works are operational. Under a DBFM contract, the contractor is responsible for fitness for purpose during an agreed-upon period, which mostly is longer than a defect liability period after a construction or a D&B contract. Next, think carefully about exactly what performance

---

[12] www.businessdictionary.com/definition/performance-bond.html, January 23, 2013.

[13] In consumer law, a guarantee is primarily a way for a vendor, a supplier or a service provider to fix his legal obligations. People proudly say: "I got 2 years 'guarantee' on my new mattress." In practice, that means that the vendor will supply another item if the delivered one was no good.

[14] LOGIC Construction, 2003, clause 29.1. LOGIC Marine Construction, clause 29.1.

[15] UAV 1989/2012, clause 22, sub-clauses 2 and 3. Clause 22 of the 2012 edition is more in line with the basic risk allocation of this standard contract: employer responsible for design; contractor responsible for the execution.

has to be guaranteed. Also, is a third-party guarantee to be issued by an outsider to the main contract? Or is the guarantee provided by your own company? Be mindful about the authority of the third party to provide the guarantee to you. Also be mindful of circumstances which are outside your control that may influence the drawing of the guarantee by the other party.

14.5. Warranties

In contract law, a warranty relates to a contractor's obligation that goods or the work delivered shall meet specified requirements as to quality or function. In business and legal transactions, it is an assurance by one party to the other party that specific facts or conditions are true or will happen; the other party is permitted to rely on that assurance and allowed to seek some type of remedy if it is not true or followed. The word "warranty" — although not correct — is also applied in the sense of a guarantee, as described above under Section 14.2 and Section 14.3.

Warranties can be explicit or implicit. An implied warranty is one that arises from the nature of the contract, and the inherent understanding by the other party, rather than from explicit formal clauses in writing. In international contracting, the contracts usually vary widely. However, some warranties are so clear that they need not be written down in a contract. In a construction contract, a warranty on delivering good workmanship and good construction works is superfluous. When a contractor accepts a Design and Build contract, it is not necessary to stipulate that the contractor warrants the design to be first class and that it meets the employer's requirements. In a similar way, an EPC contract covers the implicit warranty that the functional specification, submitted by the employer, shall be met when commissioning the work. Yet, many contracts frequently show such clauses.

Contractors need to be careful in accepting warranty clauses that go far beyond what commonly is agreed in standard contracts. This may be demonstrated by the following clause, which was taken from a recent case study. The specific warranty clause stated the following:

> There will be no limitation whatsoever on the number, individual value, cumulative value, the aggregate effect, of the Variations that Owner may request Contractor to implement. However all Variations must have a relation to The Work. Contractor ***warrants*** that it is able to mobilize additional personnel and Equipment at short notice, to perform a Variation.[16]

---

[16]CMM standard contract, 1992, article 38, sub-clause 8.

Such clauses may cause discussions to emerge during the project if the employer commissions a variation order, referring to this specific clause.

The discussion presented in Box 14.1 relates to a situation where project manager George Fisher was summoned to his head office to give a quarterly report on his two-year project in a faraway country. George had to manage an extension of a major tank park near a beautiful bay. The employer issued a contract for a scope of work that would enable vessels to load and unload aggressive chemicals. These vessels were to be connected to the nearby refinery by specific alloy tubing and piping, which were to be

Box 14.1. The employer requests excessive extra work to be done.

"No, Peter, you know what they are doing is most unreasonable and unfair. We are doing our best to please them in every aspect of their complicated project. We are successful in doing so. For a year and a half, we have remained within schedule, we did not miss any milestones, notwithstanding the circumstances. We acted in a transparent way, we performed all the overdone quality testing and got the certificates in place on time... and now they squeeze us by issuing an impossible variation order, which they can handle themselves..."

"Well George, I think you are a victim of your own success."

"How is that?" George asked.

"It is clear. Our client faced a hell of a lot of problems. Last year they were fined by the competent local inspection bodies for violation of environmental regulations. They lost precious time. Now they have run into trouble with their own planning schedule. They know that we keep promises and do good work on time. They cry for help with this action. What would you do in such a situation?"

"No Peter, this is not crying for help. They are just trying to squeeze us and to get us into trouble. I told them four or five times that we have no welders available at short notice. Mind you, this tubing is an alloy steel; it is not just another carbon steel pipe. I cannot put unqualified welders on this extra job and they know it."

"Did you accept this extra order, honestly George, not even verbally?"

"No Peter, I swear. I even had noted in the day reports that such work could be done only after our own obligations, I mean our own scope of supply. That would mean that we could only finish it after nine or ten weeks, but they want to have it done when the jetty will be put in operation. That is expected at the end of next month."

connected to the infrastructure to be built by the contractor. The contract involved was a construction contract.[17] The entire project, commissioned to the contractor, involved civil works, mechanical works, electronics work and installation. Now George's welders were busy welding the alloy tubing and pipe work for the commissioned infrastructure. While the employer wanted to update his facilities for the production of hydrocarbons, the three projects, i.e. the tank park with new vessels (George's scope of work), refinery update and alloy piping of the jetty (the employer's own tasks) had to be finished at the same time; trials were planned for the end of the following month. The employer itself, however, was late in contracting for the supply and installation works for the alloy piping. In order to save its own situation, it commissioned the work at a rather late stage from the contractor through a variation order. This, obviously, put the timely delivery of the main contract in danger.

The acceptance of the specific warranty in the variation clause during the negotiations of the main contract, obviously, lies at the heart of the problems that appeared later during project execution. Issuing the variation order at hand by the employer seems to be in line with the main contract. Obviously, the employer uses this clause to its own benefit in order not to lose face with its own internal stakeholders. What should the contractor do in such a case? Should the contractor permanently have a group of extra personnel available for eventual variation orders of this nature? Should he negotiate a revised time schedule? In this case, the contractor might have been legally bound to accept the variation order. But he could not, and that is why he did not. Notwithstanding, he needed to take all kinds of measures in trying to mobilize personnel, equipment and material to execute the extra work as soon as possible and, at the same time, deliver the main work at the pre-arranged schedule. The project manager found himself in a difficult position.[18]

A warranty for good performance is violated when the promise is not realized, i.e. when materials are not as should be expected, at the time of the testing. The contractor should honor the warranty by making a timely repair or a replacement. The same is valid for bad workmanship. Normally the contract describes what should happen in the event that the quality of materials or workmanship is not what normally can be expected. If that is not described in the contract, how to act is to be found in the civil law of the legal system

[17]The contract referred to was based upon the FIDIC standard Construction contract, but many clauses were re-written by the employer and extra obligations were added.

[18]There is no clear standard legal answer to this. Whether the contractor had to pay for the extra costs involved is doubtful in this case. In practice, these issues are discussed between parties on a case-by-case basis.

applicable to the contract. Although not described as such in most standard contracts, parties may arrange for an "extended warranty". In this case, the contractor provides a guarantee for replacing and/or repairing and/or redoing the deficient performance of the works that have been delivered, if reported within the extended warranty period.

In complex transactions, owners and contractors may make specific representations and warranties to each other. These are statements by which one party gives certain assurances to the other, and on which the other party may rely. In this context, a representation is commonly a declaration of a specific fact that can be verified to be true or not, for instance, "the contractor represents that it is a corporation duly organized and validly existing under the laws of Germany".

Note the warranty clause in the case of Box 14.1. The contractor, when negotiating the contract, did not foresee that the owner could use this clause in the way he did in the final stage of the project. The contractor in good faith believed that the clause did not represent more than a general promise that it could mobilize sufficient personnel in case that would be necessary.

For very risky operations, contractors, owners or insurance companies may appoint a *warranty surveyor*. That is a person or an institution, such as a certifying authority or a classification society, whose task is to inspect and judge certain operations or results. They act as technical advisors for approval and acceptance of any given result or risk concerning the performance of the work and the persons acting as their representatives. Legally, the warranty surveyors have an advisory role. In practice it is not wise to overrule or to deny their opinion. In the event of a warranty surveyor appointed by an insurance company being ignored, it would mean taking over a certain risk without being covered by the insurers. Discussions between a warranty surveyor and a project manager who ignores his advice are risky. The insurance company appointed the expert to be informed about the situation at the work site. In the event of damages at a later stage, the insurers may refuse to pay compensation.

14.6. Decennial liability

In a number of countries, the constructor of a work is liable, not only towards the employer, but also towards the owner of the building or the purchaser, or the person who makes use of the work. This liability concerns damages, even resulting from soil instability, which imperil the strength of the works (for instance, a building) or which, affecting one of its constituent parts, render it unsuitable for its purposes.[19]

[19] Definition derived from Dr. Goetz-Sebastian Hoek, www.dr-hoek.de/en/beitrag, June 1, 2009.

FIDIC standards inform us that "it may be necessary to review the effect of this sub-clause[20] in relation to the period of liability imposed by the applicable law".[21] It is a feeble remark, where some explanation would have been useful. In many countries, mandatory legislation imposes liabilities on contractors for defects in constructions that appear after taking over the works. Those liabilities overrule the liabilities in the standard contracts.

This liability is called decennial because the original legal provision mentioned a period of ten years (a decennium) beginning on the day of delivery of the building. The concept is derived from the French civil code of 1804, one of the three code books that were introduced by Napoleon in France after the revolution.[22] Since then, of course, the issue has been updated; the liability has become more severe.

Decennial liability was introduced in many other countries in a variety of forms. In all of those countries, the legislation is mandatory. It is not possible to contract out of decennial liability with the employer. Even if this is realized, the clause will be invalid in court. The liability concerns the contractor and the "supervising architect" in severe joint liability. Both are responsible. This may mean that an engineer, as defined in the FIDIC Construct standard and D&B standard, will be liable as well in the event of a claim. In certain legislations, the developer or investor in the buildings is also responsible.

Nature of defects

There is strict liability. It concerns any defect in the realized works; defects that were apparent at completion of the work, and those which were hidden and remained hidden until their appearance.[23] Damages resulting from a defect in the soil or sub-soil are included, even in the case that under the construction contract the employer was liable for the accuracy of the data. The principle of decennial liability refers to fundamental defaults; it is not about minor problems, which may be repaired during regular periodical maintenance. The decennial liability refers to essentials of the works wholly

---

[20]The relevant sub-clause in fact is sub-clause 11.10, yellow book, concerning the obligations of parties that remained unperformed after the performance certificate was issued. FIDIC Construction and FIDIC EPC/Turnkey, clause 11.10.

[21]Note on clause 11, Defects Liability, FIDIC yellow book, D&B, p. 12.

[22]French civil code, articles 1792–1793.

[23]In translations of some legislation (Abu Dhabi, Dubai, and UAE Federal civil code book) the wording "latent defect" is applied. A latent defect is a defect that was not discovered or could not be discovered at the time of issuing the certificate of completion. The defect may be of structural or non-structural nature.

or in part, or one of the elements of equipment which render the works or the building unsuitable for its purpose. The latter could refer to elevators in apartment buildings or office buildings, air-conditioning installations or vessel foundations and tubing in chemical plants, fire protection installations in plants, hospitals and hotels. But also simple defects such as loose tiles and leaky roofs may be included in the liability.

The "ten years" period

Most legislations interpret that the liability commences at the date of issuing the completion certificate of the works. In certain situations, the period will be longer than ten years after the taking over of the works. After all, the main contract is fulfilled at the moment at which, after the defects notification period as per FIDIC, the performance certificate is issued. This means that when the defects notification period was two years, while the extension of this period was six months, due to the rework of default, the total decennial liability period will be 12.5 years after taking over the works. Furthermore, some legal systems foresee a claim time barrier, which means that the claimant has a certain period after discovery of the defect to bring forward the claim. Suppose that the damage was discovered on the last day of the extended defects notification period. If that period is three years, the total time during which the contractor is exposed to potential claims will be 12.5 plus three, i.e. 15.5 years after taking over.

Some legal systems have special provisions imposing stricter obligations on contractors. Under French law, for instance, the contractor also has to warrant a two years' *garantie de bon fonctionnement* and a one year's warranty of *achèvement complet.*

Insurances

It is possible to cover the liability under an assurance policy, just like insuring other liability risks at contracting.[24] It is said that such policies are rather expensive, depending upon the country and the amounts to be covered. In some countries, insurance is mandatory, such as in France and in Egypt.[25] However, there are certain exceptions, such as public civil-engineering works

[24] R. Stevenson (2011), *Decennial Liability and Decennial Insurance*, X.L. America Inc, http://resources.xlgroup.com/docs/xldp/decennialliability.pdf, January 23, 2013.

[25] For information about contractors' risks in France, we recommend www.ffsa.fr/sites/jcms/c_51299/how-decennial-liability-insurance-works, July 7, 2012.

and industrial installations for professional activities, such as a factory assembly line, a warehouse, etc., where insurance is not mandatory. In general, the decennial liability is not covered by a Construction All Risks (CAR) insurance policy,[26] neither by Professional Indemnity (PI) insurance.

Impact of decennial liability

The main contractor is obliged to repair, or to rework, or to reinstall or to have the collapse or defect repaired after the claim. There are some exemptions from this obligation such as *force majeure*, which is not often honored, and extraneous events, which are rare.

Various legislations

The French origin inspired many other legislators to copy the concept of strict decennial liability. Other countries or states are: Angola, Belgium, Bolivia, Cameroon, Chile, Egypt, Indonesia, Italy, Kuwait, the state of Louisiana in the USA, Malta, Morocco, Paraguay, Peru, Philippines, Qatar, Romania, Spain, Sweden, Syria, Tunisia and United Arab Emirates,[27] including Abu Dhabi and Dubai.[28]

14.7. Summary and conclusions

There are two kinds of guarantees. There is a guarantee issued by a third person and there is a guarantee for good performance by the contractor. Both guarantees and warranties are valid for a limited period of time, which has to be stated in the written document.

Most employers now insist on guarantees on demand, which are becoming common practice in international contracting.[29] Guarantees issued by a

---

[26] In this respect the wording "All Risks" is misleading, as not all risks are covered by such a policy.

[27] C. Lilley, Contracts of muqalawala and decennial liability: a Middle Eastern perspective, http://construction.practicallaw.com/blog/construction, March 15, 2010.

[28] L. Dale & S. Hunt, Decennial Liability and Latent Defects Contractors' and Developers' Liability in Dubai, www.cmguide.org/archives/2118, January 29, 2010; Al Tamimi & Company, Decennial liability, www.cmguide.org/archives/2118, May 13, 2009.

[29] How to operate demand guarantees in practice is described in the Guide to ICC Uniform Rules for Demand Guarantees, URDG 758 by Dr. Georges Affaki and Sir Roy Goode, ICC Publication No. 702, International Chamber of Commerce, Paris, 2011. This guide is applicable in all sectors and jurisdictions. It came into effect on July 1, 2010 and was officially endorsed by the UN Commission on International Trade Law (UNCITRAL).

third person may be issued by a bank, a surety company or a parent company, or even third companies. They may be conditional or on demand.

A warranty is a statement by a contractor that the work he performs will be free of defects, and if any defects are found, he will repair, replace or re-work the defects. A warranty is also applied in such a way that a party states that certain facts are true. Warranties can be implicit or explicit. In international contracting, warranties are extensively described in contracts, so that from the outset parties may understand what to expect from each other. Insurance companies, employers or certification societies may appoint warranty surveyors to be sure that a certain state of affairs is realized by the contractor. The word "representation" is applied in this way as well.

Bonds are guarantees that are linked to certain phases of the contract cycle. In most cases, this is the tender phase and the phase of completion of the project.

In practice, different terminology is used in international contracting. See Box 14.2, at the end of the chapter, for short descriptions.

Most standard contracts have detailed regulations concerning guarantees;[30] others not at all.[31]

Most standard contracts contain model forms for various guarantees, as noted in Box 14.2. However, when issuing guarantees, international commercial banks have their own templates. After all, it is the content of the statements in the written document that counts.

Decennial liability, which is mandatory in a number of countries, is the strict liability of the contractor and architect of the works. The legislation of the country where the works are situated is in force, notwithstanding that parties may have chosen a different legal system under their contract. In the event parties agreed upon a legal system that prescribes the decennial liability, it will be enforced, even if the works are located elsewhere.

There are some 25 countries or states where the concept of decennial liability was adopted. The concept is the same everywhere; however, details of legislation differ to a great extent. When tendering for projects in a foreign country, one should verify in which way the concept of decennial liability is implemented in the legislation and what risks are to be run outside the clauses of the contract. In the event an assurance is mandatory, it is recommendable to be informed in detail about the cover of the insurance and the cost for a number of years after finally taking over the works. The need for help from local lawyers specializing in construction law and insurance is evident.

---

[30] FIDIC Construction, D&B, EPC/Turnkey, sub-clause 4.2; CMM, 1992, clauses 29 and 30.

[31] LOGIC. This does not mean that under LOGIC no guarantees could be agreed upon between parties.

Box 14.2. Some terms on guarantees, bonds, liabilities, and warranties, applied in international construction contracts.

Term	Short description	Remarks
Advance payment bond	Statement by a contractor that a sum of money received by contractor before starting the works will be used to pay for the contract.	If the contractor misuses the money or in case the contract is void, the amount of money will return to the employer. FIDIC model form in guidance notes on standard contracts.
Bid bond	An assurance provided by a contractor that he will enter into a contract with an employer. Bid bonds may be in the form of a bank guarantee, a parent company guarantee or a surety company guarantee.	In the event the contractor does not enter into the contract or wants to alter the conditions, the employer may call in the bid bond.
Bond	General term for a statement of a contractor, assuring an employer that he will maintain certain promises in relation to a construction contract. Bonds are possible in the form of a demand on a bank, a surety company, an insurance company or a parent company.	If the promises are not kept the employer may call in the bond.
Decennial liability of contractor	Strict liability for the integrity of the works during a period of some 10 years after achievement of the works.	The period is not always 10 years exactly.
Defects liability period	Period between the date on which the work is delivered and taken over by the employer, and the later date as stipulated in the contract.	Also called guarantee period.

(*Continued*)

Box 14.2. (*Continued*)

Term	Short description	Remarks
Express warranty	A warranty in writing.	
Guarantee	General word for an obligation of a third party, where two other parties entered into a primary contract. In most cases, the guarantee is issued by a bank, a surety company, an insurance company, or a parent company or a related third party.	In the event the primary obligation of the committing party is not kept, the beneficiary may call in a sum of money as specified in the written guarantee.
Guarantee against documents	Guarantee which has to be honored by the issuing bank, surety company or parent company at handing over of documents, as described in the written guarantee.	
Implied warranty	A non-written warranty or an obligation of a contractor that can be made up out of the context of a construction contract.	In the event the implied warranty is not respected by the contractor the employer may call him into court.
On-demand bond	The obligation to pay a sum of money, generally to an employer, payable on simple demand of the employer, whereas the employer is not obliged to inform the guarantor of his reasons for his demand.	Most applied form of guarantee in international contracting, much more than guarantee against documents.
Parent-company guarantee	Guarantee issued by a holding company of the contractor.	Model form in FIDIC guidance notes; Idem in CMM 1992 guidance notes.

(*Continued*)

Box 14.2. (*Continued*)

Term	Short description	Remarks
Payment guarantee by an employer	Guarantee, normally by a bank, that in the event the employer fails to pay certain sums of money to a contractor, the bank will pay instead. Often the contractor has to hand over documents as evidence of entitlement to pay.	Model form in FIDIC guidance notes.
Performance bond	General word for an assurance of a contractor that the contractor will deliver the project as agreed upon in the contract.	In the event the contractor does not perform as agreed, the employer may call in the agreed-upon sum of money.
Performance guarantee	See performance bond.	Model form in NF 1992; Idem in CMM 1992 guidance notes.
Performance security	See performance bond.	Model form in FIDIC guidance notes.
Representations	Statements of the parties that certain described facts are true and may be verified.	
Retention money guarantee	A guarantee issued by a bank to an employer to replace the retention money which was paid to the contractor before the end of the defects liability period, to pay a sum of money to the employer as agreed upon in the written retention guarantee.	

(*Continued*)

Box 14.2. *(Continued)*

Term	Short description	Remarks
Surety	A statement in writing that a third person to a construction contract (usually a surety company) will pay a sum of money in the event a contractor does not perform as agreed upon with an employer.	
Surety bond	See performance bond.	Model form in FIDIC guidance notes.
Surety company	A financial institution that specializes in providing guarantees for contractors.	
Tender security	See bid bond.	Model form in FIDIC guidance notes.
Warranty	Statement of a contractor that the work he performed or has to perform is free of defects.	If any defects are found, the contractor is obliged to repair, replace or to re-work.

Chapter 15

Contract Law and Tort Law

15.1. Case — The polluted drinking water

Contractor C has three power generators running at a job site in a foreign country far away. They are fueled with gas oil. The gas oil is supplied once a week by a tractor with a tank trailer. This oil tank has to be filled up five kilometres down the road. A driver of the tractor (part-time employee of a local service provider to the contractor) is on his way to the generators with a full oil tank and wants to take a shortcut. He does not take the paved road, but — totally uncalled for — he takes the dirt road, where there is shingle, sand and rock. The area is full of small hills.

The tractor falls over and gas oil flows away. This is where the reservoir for the local drinking water supply is situated. Two tonnes of gas oil penetrate into the reservoir. The cost of cleaning up is €28,000.[1] The local municipality holds contractor C liable for the damage. The legal relationships are shown in Figure 15.1.

In this chapter, we will explain the difference between the legal consequences from accidents causing damages to contracting parties and accidents to third parties. Third parties have no relation to the contracts.

15.2. Tort, tort law and contractual stipulations

Tort is an unlawful act that causes damage to a person or a legal entity. The primary aim of tort law is to provide relief for the damages incurred.

[1] Paraphrase of HR, March 20, 1970, JN 1970, 251, Doorenbos/Intercommunaal Waterleidingsgebied Leeuwarden.

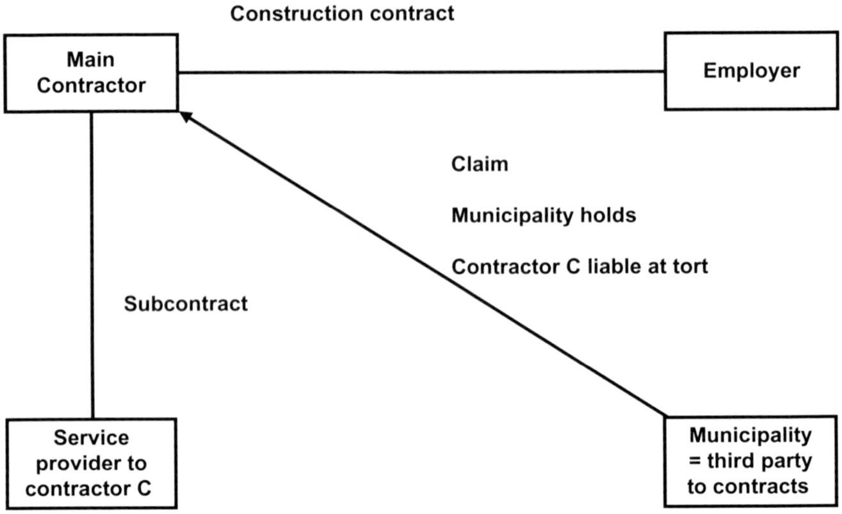

Figure 15.1. Legal relations after tort on pollution of drinking water.

The different kinds of damages resulting from tort are, in more detail:

- Death and injury. Death and injury relate to the (physical) violation of the integrity of a person. In practice, victims, normally being individual persons, are not one of the contracting parties. Contract law in these situations will not, as a rule, be applicable. Instead, tort law will apply. Death and injury cannot be repaired. Here, the suffering by external parties is translated into compensation in the form of a sum of money. The suffering itself, however, cannot be taken away by any arrangement.
- Material damage. Physical damages may concern damages to materials, equipment of a legal entity or to the works, or part of it. They may concern personal belongings of an individual.

In a contract, parties may agree on how they will indemnify each other in the event that one party suffers damages and losses due to the unlawful acts of the other party. The contractor should indemnify the employer on the basis of the applicable contract and vice versa. The contractor has an obligation to be insured thoroughly, which is a basic clause in most standard contracts. In short: parties are prepared in advance in case damage occurs.

With regards to tort to third parties, this is not possible. The legal relationship between the municipality and the contractor in the above case was created by the accident. That means tort law is applicable. The rules of the local legal system are also applicable. The applicable tort law is to be found in the local legal system of the country where the accident occurred.

The local municipality had a choice. It could have addressed the employer, as the transportation of the oil had to serve his project; it could have addressed the service provider, whose driver caused the accident; or it could have addressed the driver himself. It chose the contractor, being the legal entity responsible for the activities at the site and the transportation of the oil.

If the local municipality had addressed the employer, the contractor would have been called upon, based on the contractual agreements laid down in the contract between the main contractor and employer. Instead it addressed the main contractor, who will be in a position to call the service provider in recourse, based on the agreements laid down in the subcontract.

15.3. Tort in general civil law

Tort laws stipulate that the person or company who commits the unlawful act must repair the damage that the other person or company suffers.[2] In general, that is the rule in any legal system. The wording may differ, but the objectives are identical, as in Dutch civil law,[3] which states formally: "The following acts are deemed to be unlawful: the violation of a right, an act or omission violating a statutory duty of unwritten law relating to proper social conduct."[4]

According to civil law, five elements are to be considered for bringing a successful claim on damages that have been incurred by a party:

- An unlawful act or non-action, where action should have been required, resulting in a violation of a legal norm, a regulation or a legal duty or obligation.
- A person's fault or a cause for which he is liable. A person may be a legal entity as well.
- Damage.
- Causality between damage and act.
- The relevant norm should be set in order to protect against the damage caused.

The five elements are cumulative. This legal rule requires some more explanation. The fifth element relates to a situation where norms, which have

[2] Civil code book, article 6: 162.1.

[3] Other continental legal systems contain comparable regulations.

[4] Civil code book, article 6: 162.2.

been set by the legislator or by legislating authorities, are violated. A clear example is that of a dentist who practiced without the proper certification. The other dentists in town wished to hold him responsible and liable for their missed turnover. The violated norm had been installed to protect patients against incompetent persons who are practicing illegally. The norm had not been established to protect against illegal competition between dentists and turnover lost by them.[5]

Another example is the case of the tug-pushed barge Linda, which capsized due to its bad condition, as described in Box 15.1. A convoy of push-barges is shown in Figure 15.2. The High Court agreed that it was true that a safety norm had been violated and that a certificate was issued unduly. But the objective of the norm that had been violated was to provide for the safety of the inland waterways in general. Its objective was not to protect a group of third parties because of the fact that, during inspection, the barge was not proven to be unsafe.[6]

Box 15.1. Barge Linda doing damage to third parties.

A tug-pushed dumb barge, loaded with sand, capsized, causing a near-by dredger to capsize as well, while also damaging two ships at the same time. It happened at night when no one was aboard the dredger and the ships. The cause was the bad condition of the barge's bottom plates, which were so heavily corroded that leakage occurred, allowing water to enter the hold and sand to escape out of it. The barge had been inspected a year earlier and passed inspections. A "certificate of examination" was issued, expiring after seven years. It happened in the south of the Netherlands on the river Maas.

The owners of the damaged ships sued the State of the Netherlands, as well as a number of other authorities, basing their claim on tort at civil law. The State had issued a certificate that was obviously and without any doubt extremely misleading. The owners of the other ships trusted that certified barges would not be in such bad condition that they could cause serious damage to nearby

(*Continued*)

[5] HR January 17, 1958, NJ 1981, 568, Beukers vs. Dorenbos. Nevertheless, the claimants Beukers c.s. were successful because another norm was violated at the same time. After all, the uncertified dentist violated the norm of correct social behavior in relation to the other dentists in town.
[6] HR , May 7, 2004, NJ 2006, 281, LNJ AO6012, nt Hm, Duwbak Linda.

Box 15.1. (*Continued*)

ships. The owners of the damaged ships asked the court to be compensated for their losses by the State. The court rejected and refused to honor the claim, which was confirmed by the court of appeal. The High Court considered that the necessary relationship between the relevance of the violated norm and the damage was absent. It is true that the safety regulations for safe navigation on the inland waterways were violated by the faulty inspection. It is true that this regulation's objective is to safeguard the safety on Dutch waterways in general. However, the High Court argued that the regulation concerned was not enacted to protect the interests of the ship owners who suffered from the wrongly tested push-barge. The claim against the State of the Netherlands could not be honored, according to the High Court. Of course, the owner of the push-barge was and is responsible for its good condition and was to be held liable for the damages that the bad condition of the barge caused to the other ships. However, the State of the Netherlands could not be sued successfully.

Figure 15.2. Multiple barge convoy with four empty barges. Photo taken from the Erasmus Bridge at Rotterdam by Provaart.nl. (Source: www.provaart.nl/images/stories/provaart/ Matricia met 4 lege bakken.jpg.)

15.4. Applicable theory

Reparation can only be claimed for damage which is related to the event giving rise to the liability of the debtor in such a fashion that the damage, also taking into account its nature and that of the liability, can be imputed to the debtor as a result of this event.[7]

In Case 15.1, the standard for charging financially assessable damage is apparent. Note the word "only" in the foregoing legal clause, connecting tort to the obligation to compensate the resulting damages. The word "only" means that other damages are not compensated. The offender is only liable for the event as far as it can be charged to him. That is the law.

Whether an offender can be charged has to be considered on a case-by-case basis. We can use the example in Case 15.1. First, we consider the act, here the deviation in choosing the shortcut. Second, we consider whether such an act was unlawful. That is the case; the unnecessary unsafe deviation during the transport of dangerous, inflammable, polluting matter was not correct. Now the type of liability has to be taken into account. The driver is liable for his act. That is direct liability. There is strict liability, because the truck driver is employed by the subcontractor, which makes the subcontractor liable. The truck is on its way, filled with gas oil for the contractor. This makes the contractor liable as well.[8] Third, we have to regard the type of damage. The fact that the reservoir for the drinking water supply was the scene of the accident is a bit of bad luck; this bad luck is at the risk of the offender. But even if the reservoir had not been there, the cleaning of the polluted soil would have cost a lot of money, too. Fourth, we have to consider the relation between event and damage. These are indisputably present; both in the *conditio sine qua non* theory and in the adequacy theory. In fact, the court applied the theory of the attributable party.[9] And last, we have to verify whether the violated norm was established to protect the damaged interest. That is the case here. The driver was violating an unwritten law relating to social conduct. All required elements are present.

Tort actions are divided into different categories. It is common to differentiate between:

- Negligent torts, which occur when the defendant's actions were unreasonably unsafe.

[7] Dutch civil code book, article 6: 98.

[8] Such liability in civil law could have been exonerated by the service contract between contractor and subcontractor. We leave that option out for the moment in order to better understand how liability works for the contractor.

[9] The theories about causality are explained in Chapter 18.

- Gross negligence torts, which relate to those actions where the liable person or company acted very unreasonably and/or should have been aware that their actions were unreasonably unsafe.
- Intentional torts, which relate to those wrongdoings where the defendant knew that the damage would occur through his actions.

The law is stricter and more severe when the action is done with intent than with normal negligence. Gross negligence represents a situation in between negligence and willful misconduct.

Some legal systems are familiar with extra compensation in the form of a penalty such as "punitive damages" (USA law) or the *peine privée* (French law). In those systems, a victim receives, besides compensation for the damage incurred, an amount of money paid as a penalty by the person liable for tortuous conduct. In other civil legal systems, such actions are not possible. In the event the misconduct contains criminal elements (with gross negligence or willful misconduct), the same unlawful action will be brought to a criminal court, where a fine could follow, or a sentence to prison. The revenues of a fine are for the state and not for the victim. Legislation on this issue differs per country.

Strict liability

Strict liability means that a person or a company is liable, even without fault or negligence. Strictly liable wrongdoings do not depend on the degree of non-carefulness by the defendant, they relate to a situation where a particular action or situation caused damage or danger. An example is a situation where an unsafe chemical product for cleaning purposes was supplied to a construction site by a supplier, where the product put construction workers at immediate risk. Even if the supplier was unaware of the health danger represented by the product, which was supplied to him by a supplier downstream the supply chain, he is nevertheless liable.

15.5. The practical descriptions of standard contracts

Standard construction contracts do not deal with legal topics in a level of detail, such as a court would do. Standard construction contracts, such as LOGIC, BIMCO, FIDIC and the Norwegian standards, describe the limits of liability of the employer and contractor. Standard contracts normally contain a "hold harmless" clause between parties. Standard contracts cannot regulate tort to a third party. Such a party is not yet identified at the moment the contract is signed.

15.6. Conclusions

We might conclude the following:

- In all standard contracts, we find clauses that oblige parties to pay compensation for damages to the other party.[10]
- In all standard contracts, the amounts for compensation of damages can be capped.
- All standard contracts have indemnity clauses.
- Damages to third parties are not related to a certain contract; they are judged by the rules of the applicable legal system where the relevant occurrence took place.
- Standard construction contracts contain regulations for compulsory insurances for tendering contractors and for contracting employers.

Other sections of this book related to tort are: liability versus responsibility, contractual versus non-contractual indemnities, damages, causality and disasters.

[10]In Chapter 19, the knock-for-knock principle, which represents a different setting, is explained.

Chapter 16

Consequential Losses

16.1. Case — The broken mill shaft and the remover[1]

In 1853, a removal company contracted with a mill owner to deliver a broken iron-mill shaft to a manufacturer, which was to make a new shaft using the broken one as a template. The mill owner told the removal company that the delivery was urgent, but not that the resumption of production depended on the delivery being made promptly. The broken shaft was delivered late, and the mill owner sued the removal company for lost profits. The court rejected the claim because, although the removal company knew that the delivery was urgent and that the mill had stopped production, it did not know that the speed of its delivery would affect when the mill could restart production.[2]

This court case, referred to as the Hadley vs. Baxendale case (1854), has become famous in English law. It was the first case on consequential damages. Even now, the English courts refer frequently to this case, the underlying principles of which have held for approximately 150 years.

Under English law — as in the other EU countries and in the USA — a lot of legal cases have been about the damages and consequential losses caused by performance errors. English law has been shaped by the decisions of judges on the basis of disputes taken from practice. Over time, these court cases have resulted in guidelines on how to differentiate between direct and indirect damages. Next, these have gradually substantiated the concept of "consequential losses".

In the above-mentioned case, the removal company was not obliged to compensate the consequential damages of the mill owner. This was based on

---

[1]Hadley vs. Baxendale (1854), 9 Exch. 341; All E. R. Rep. 461.

[2]The description of the case is by Kieron Moore and Barbara Jennings, Consequential losses in offshore contracts, Wikborg Rein Shipping Update, www.ctcplc.com, May 13, 2008.

the finding that he, after entering into the contract, could not have foreseen that the mill would stay idle as long as the new shaft was not at their disposal.[3] The judge's verdict in the Hadley vs. Baxendale case, made a distinction between direct and indirect losses for the first time.

16.2. Liability for consequential losses and contract agreements

Gradually, it has become clear when a party may be liable for losses following a breach of contract. In general, this depends on whether those losses:

- Arise naturally, i.e. according to the normal course of events, from the breach of the contract. These losses, then, are referred to as direct losses.
- Are such as reasonably could have been foreseen by the parties to happen at the time that they drew up the contract as the probable result of the breach of that contract. In such cases, these damages are referred to as indirect or consequential losses.

The word "indirect" in the legal sense is equivalent to "consequential" with regard to damages. In practice, the Hadley vs. Baxendale case implies the following: if, at a later stage, you want to keep open the possibility of claiming consequential losses, you have to inform the counterparty of the risks referred to in the contract. The counterparty is then able to either safeguard itself against the risks, or to increase the price. Of course, for the counterparty, a third option is to turn down the agreement.

Suppose that you, as a contractor, have to perform a modification job on a drilling platform against a functional specification. You finish it on time. However, you find out during a test that there is a technical shortcoming in the new equipment that you installed, which results in a yield of only 97% of the agreed production volume. In this case, you have legally committed a breach of contract. If the turnover loss of 3% is caused by the technical shortcoming of the equipment, this would be considered a "direct loss" according to the Hadley vs. Baxendale case. The productivity loss is directly related to the normal course of events: direct damage. In this case your employer should not present a claim for indirect damage or consequential damage. If no other specific agreements were made in the contract, your counterparty can recoup the production loss from the contractor.

---

[3]For further description of the facts around this case, see G. H. Treitel (2011), *The Law of Contracts, 13th edition*. London: Sweet & Maxwell, pp. 898–899.

16.3. Excluding consequential losses in construction contracts

In the construction industry it is common practice to exclude particular losses. The standard contracts have standard clauses for this. The FIDIC 17.6 silver book concerning Turnkey projects states:

> Neither party shall be liable to the other Party for loss of use of any Works, loss of profit, loss of any contract or for any indirect or consequential loss or damage which may be suffered by the other Party in connection with the Contract, other than...[4]

The LOGIC Marine Construction standard contract starts with its own definition of consequential loss, which reads:

- (i) Consequential or indirect loss under English law; and
- (ii) Loss and/or deferral of production, loss of product, loss of use, loss of revenue, profit or anticipated profit (if any), in each case whether direct or indirect to the extent that these are not included in (i), and whether or not foreseeable at the effective date of commencement of the contract.[5]

Note that loss of production, loss of use, loss of profits, etc. are specifically mentioned. This is done to avoid discussions regarding whether such losses are direct or indirect. Under LOGIC standard contracts, parties are not accountable for the other party's losses of this kind.

How do English judges apply such clauses? Let's have a look at the court case between BHP Petroleum and British Steel (as described in Box 16.1).

Box 16.1. BHP Petroleum Ltd vs. British Steel plc and Dalmine.

The Court of Appeal considered a damage clause in BHP Petroleum Limited vs. British Steel Plc. and Dalmine.[6] The case follows from a contract for the construction of a supply of steel pipes for a gas re-injection pipeline to be installed off shore as part of the Liverpool Bay

(*Continued*)

[4] FIDIC blue, red and yellow books have similar exoneration clauses.

[5] LOGIG Construction, 2003 and Marine Construction, 2004, clause 25.

[6] BHP Petroleum Ltd. vs. British Steel plc and Dalmine (2000); 2 Lloyds Report 277; description of the case is by Kieron Moore and Barbara Jennings, Consequential losses in offshore contracts, Wikborg Rein Shipping Update, www.ctcplc.com, May 13, 2008.

Box 16.1. (*Continued*)

Development. The purpose of the pipeline was to carry the gas by-product of the oil production process to an unmanned platform for re-injection into the reservoir, enabling a more efficient production of oil from the reservoir and postponing the extraction of the gas. No defects appeared in the pipeline until June 1996, when bubbles were seen on the surface, indicating that the pipeline was leaking. BHP Petroleum alleged that cracks in the pipeline were caused by a failure to meet specification limits and claimed against the pipe manufacturer, Dalmine, and the supplier, British Steel, for:

- The cost of inspection and rectification works.
- Installing additional equipment to flare-off the gas while the pipeline was shut down.
- Loss of profits from reduced and deferred production.

The clause in the contract governing liability between the parties excluded:

> ...loss of production, loss of profits, loss of business or any other indirect loss or consequential damages arising during and/or as a result of the performance or non-performance of this Contract regardless of the cause thereof...

The "indirect loss or consequential damages" wording in the contract between BHP and British Steel and Dalmine was considered by the court as the second type of loss covered by Hadley vs. Baxendale, i.e. indirect losses. These can be recovered only if they were considered by the parties involved at the time that the contract was concluded. That loss was excluded by the parties in their contract. Hence, BHP Petroleum was not able to recover the deferred profits, which the court held to be the loss of reduced production: the third type of damage listed above. The contract clause prevented this claim from being approved by the court.

The cost of inspecting the pipeline and remedying the defect — the first kind of damage listed above — was recoverable, because it was neither specifically excluded, nor to be considered as an indirect loss. Inspection costs and rectification are pure direct losses. The first type of damage had to be compensated by British Steel and Dalmine.

Regarding the loss caused by the second type of damage, the court held that it did not have sufficient knowledge of the facts to

(*Continued*)

Box 16.1. (*Continued*)

judge which of the items claimed by BHP Petroleum were covered by the exclusion. Hence, the contractor's decision to install additional equipment could be considered to be a direct damage or an indirect/consequential damage. The court needed more information to be able to come to a decision. Hence, the court appointed a neutral expert in the business to state his opinion whether the installation for flaring-off the rest of the gases should be considered as a direct loss to the pipe leakage or as an indirect one.

16.4. Considerations of direct versus consequential under English law

In the event of contract clauses like "excluded are consequential damages including but not limited to loss of use, loss of profits" etc., there is a problem. This problem relates to how English law interprets the words "consequential damages". According to English law, direct losses are "losses which are natural and usual and can be foreseen without knowledge of special facts" as decided upon in the Hadley vs. Baxendale case described above. Losses that could only be foreseen with specific information are considered to be "consequential".

How are we to make sense of "consequential damages including but not limited to loss of use"? Loss of use is likely to be "direct". In order to explain the differences between direct and consequential damage, let us have a look at another court case, British Sugar vs. NEI (as described in Box 16.2).

Box 16.2. Case — British Sugar vs. NEI.

The draft contract between British Sugar and NEI included a clause that provided that the seller, NEI, "will be liable for any loss, damage, cost or expense incurred by the purchaser arising from the supply by the seller of any such faulty goods or materials not being suitable for the purpose for which they are required".[7]

(*Continued*)

[7]British Sugar Plc vs. NEI Power Projects Ltd, 1997, 87 BLR info TLR 353, 87 LR 42, 1997, EWCA Civ 2438, 1998, ITCLR 128 and 14 Const LJ 365. EWJ No. 1127.

Box 16.2. (*Continued*)

NEI were concerned about this apparent unlimited liability, and commented on the proposed clause by letter, saying that "the company's terms of business trading is that our liability is limited to the value of the contract, and as such we cannot depart from this policy. We regret, therefore, that we cannot accept your proposal for consequential loss".

Thereupon the parties re-negotiated the clause. Parties agreed to the following text:

> The seller will be liable for any loss, damage, cost or expense incurred by the purchaser arising from the supply by the seller of any such faulty goods or materials not being suitable for the purpose for which they are required, save that the seller's liability for consequential loss is limited to the value of the contract.

The contract value was £106,000, but invoking alleged design and installation failures, British Sugar claimed damages in excess of £5 million. Whether they would be entitled to such damages depended on the effect of the limitation introduced by the revised clause, and thus the meaning of the words "consequential loss".

The key question is to what extent is NEI liable? Should the damage be capped at £106,000 or should NEI compensate the excess of £5 million? The position of British Sugar is simple. Referring to the Hadley vs. Baxendale case, the £5 million damages they claimed were to be considered as direct losses. As direct losses were not excluded or limited in the contract, the claim should be legally honored.

Of course, NEI argued differently. NEI argued that the term "consequential loss" had little to do with "foreseeable" (the general concern of Hadley vs. Baxendale) and more to do with the nature of the loss itself. Thus, they argued that consequential loss meant:

> all loss other than the normal loss which might be suffered as a breach of contract, the normal loss being the difference between the value of the goods and services transferred under the contract, and the value of what would have been transferred had the breach not occurred.

The Court of Appeal confirmed the decision of the lower court in rejecting this argument. It argued that, when reading the clause in question accurately, NEI was obliged to pay such damages as followed naturally and directly from any supply of faulty goods or

(*Continued*)

Box 16.2. (*Continued*)

materials. The limitation was to be applied to some other type of loss that did not follow so directly; for example, damage that might follow from special circumstances coming within the second limb (indirect or consequential losses) of Hadley vs. Baxendale. Therefore, £5 million in damages had to be paid by NEI.

Box 16.3 deals with another court case on how to define damages. This case relates to causality where an official was killed due to negligence by one of the subcontractors hired by the contractor.

Box 16.3. Exclusion of liability for indirect or consequential loss.

In the case between the Dutch shipping company Ferryways NV versus the stevedore company Associated British Ports,[8] the judge considered the construction of a clause in a stevedoring contract, which excluded the stevedores' liability for indirect or consequential loss "including without limitation... the liabilities of the Customer to any other party".

The chief officer of the vessel owned by the Dutch shipping company was killed by the negligence of an employee of subcontractors engaged by the stevedores. The chief officer's employer claimed damages from the stevedores. Ferryways NV sought indemnity from the stevedores in respect of sums that it had been obliged to pay to the chief officer's family. The defendant stevedores relied upon the exclusion clause, arguing that the exclusion clause had defined "indirect or consequential" losses as including "the liabilities of the Customer to any other party".

In this case, Ferryways was the employer, being employer in both senses. It is the employer of its employee, the killed chief officer, while at the same time it is the employer in the relationship with its service provider, Associated British Ports. An employee of the service provider's subcontractor committed the tort, resulting in death. This makes the subcontractor liable, due to the rule of strict liability, whereas Associated British Ports became liable for the same reason.

(*Continued*)

[8] Ferryways NV vs. Associated British Ports, [2008] EWHC 225 (Comm).

Box 16.3. (*Continued*)

Now, the agreed-upon clause is applicable to the contract between Ferryways and Associated British Ports.

Keeping in mind the 1854 case of Hadley vs. Baxendale, the court had to consider that the stevedores were responsible for paying damages. Why? It was well-established that the term "indirect and consequential" loss referred to loss which was not the direct and natural result of the breach of contract. Here, the losses suffered were not indirect or consequential. The exclusion clause referred to "indirect and consequential" loss — "very clear words indeed", as the judge remarked. The words "including without limitation" were not sufficiently clear to extend the exclusion of liability to the losses claimed. Rather, those words were intended to identify types of loss that might fall within the scope of the clause, but only if they were also indirect or consequential. So, the stevedores were responsible.

Summarizing the three cases on consequential damage under English law, we have to bear in mind that the English courts rely on the case of Hadley vs. Baxendale, 1854. The House of Lords gave definitions of direct losses and consequential (or indirect) losses. A direct loss is directly related to the breach of contract, or to the tort committed in such a way that it is a normal foreseeable result of the breach or tort. Liability for "consequential" or "indirect" losses results only in the event both parties were aware beforehand of the potential effects of an eventual breach of contract, or tort action.

16.5. Economical losses

An account manager who states that his company's business policy is to accept liability for repairs, re-work of technical defaults and replacement of defective parts up to the value of the contract, but to exclude "all consequential damages", is completely clear when negotiating a tender. Writing this down in the correct wording under a common law system, such as the English system, is another piece of cake. What was really meant was that the account manager's company is not prepared to enter into a contract where it would be obliged to compensate economical losses of its employer. Maybe British Steel–Dalmine and NEI had such intentions when entering into their contracts. Maybe NEI considered that it was unreasonable to be accountable for a loss of £5 million after a contract of only £106,000.

E. Jane Sidnell analyzed over 20 court cases on consequential damages in England and Canada, as well as a number of verdicts by Australian courts. The first limb (direct losses) of the Hadley vs. Baxendale ruling may result in economic losses, which were unforeseen by both parties and extremely high in relation to the contract value. In some cases, courts were reluctant to award extensive losses that could not have been quantified when entering into the contract. Sidnell advocated for a move to revert to the "common understood meaning" of "consequential damages". Such meaning could be "everything beyond the normal measure of damages such as profits lost or expenses incurred to breach".[9] According to Sidnell, "it will be time for the courts to take a more pragmatic approach and give the 'consequential damage' a meaning that accords with the common business meaning as that is the context in which it is used".[10]

However, for the time being: contract lawyers beware. It is still the old rule that is applicable.

16.6. "Consequential" losses under the law of the Netherlands

In commercial discussions, the terms "consequential losses" and "consequential damages" are used as equivalents. Idiomatically such a term is nonsense. A loss is always an effect of some cause. Damage is a result of an occurrence, and therefore all damages and losses are consequential. Yet, in the context of a quick conversation, mostly it is clear what is being said. Consequently, the term "consequential damage" is a pleonasm.

In the Netherlands, the distinction between "direct" and "indirect or consequential" losses is not as relevant as it is under English law. Under Dutch law, one has to find out up to what amount a liable party is accountable for the damages it caused. The logic is the following:

> Repair or compensation can only be claimed for damage which is related to the event giving rise to the liability of the debtor in such a fashion that the damage, also taking into account its nature and that of the liability, can be imputed to the debtor as a result of this event.[11]

---

[9] Clause as agreed upon between two Australian business partners; Environmental Systems Pty Ltd vs. Peerless Holdings Pty Ltd, VSCA 26, 2008, p. 93.

[10] E. Jane Sidnell (2010), Consequential Damages: Are Exclusions of Consequential Damages Inconsequential?, *Journal of the Canadian College of Construction Lawyers*, March, 1, JCCCL 119, pp. 109–129.

[11] Dutch civil code book, article 6: 98.

The courts, on a case-by-case basis, have to consider the relevant circumstances that led to the damage. To be accountable, a *conditio sine qua non* relationship between cause and damage is required.[12] Up to what amount the damage can be ascribed to the debtor in default depends upon a number of facts, such as:

- The type of liability: was there personal responsibility or strict liability? Was it responsibility as prescribed by law, or was it agreed by parties in a contract?
- The type of the damage: was death or injury involved, or was it just a financial or a material loss? Was the damage a very clear loss, or should it be considered as a loss of profit?
- Could the damage be considered a potential foreseeable result?
- The nature of the behavior: was the party in default doing its utmost or not? Was there just bad luck or negligence involved, or gross negligence or even worse — no action at all in a situation where action was required? The heavier the responsibility, the sooner accountability will be assumed.[13]

The court, which has to decide on the liability and accountability of a party in default, has to take into account all relevant facts and circumstances of the case and to assess their interconnectedness. This may explain why the definition of consequential damage in English law is far different from Dutch law. After all, consequential (or indirect) damage in English law is the damage in respect of losses that do not arise naturally according to the normal course of events (these are direct damages), but that, at the moment of concluding the contract, reasonably could have been foreseen to happen by the parties. Here, foreseeability is the crucial element. Under Dutch law, there are four elements that have to be considered on a case-by-case basis. Foreseeability is only one of those elements.

16.7. Legal systems other than English law and the law of the Netherlands

Most international construction contracts are written in the English language. However, the applicable law may differ. It is not always clear beforehand how

[12] For a better understanding of the theoretical issues on causality, we recommend Chapter 18.
[13] Dutch civil code book, article 6: 98.

the wording of "direct", "indirect" and "consequential" are interpreted in foreign legal systems. Therefore, we recommend being precise about what to agree with respect to damages, and how parties will settle the consequences of these. We recommend that parties explicitly put into words what losses will be included and excluded from a party's liability.

Without specific clauses, there is a risk that, for instance, foreign courts will consider loss of profit as a direct loss. If the parties do not want to be liable for loss of profit, this should be specifically mentioned in the contract. In short, undefined terms such as "consequential", "direct", "indirect" and so on leave room for interpretation, debate and conflict at a later stage. It is far better to state explicitly the exact damages that will be excluded.

The drafting of these clauses is a somewhat complex art and should effectively only be done on contracts by lawyers who have an intimate understanding of the applicable legal system and local jurisprudence. We recommend that specific legal advice is obtained to maximize the contractor's position with regard to the concept of losses.

16.8. Drafting clauses on limitation of liability

For contractors and suppliers, we recommend including specific clauses on damages and consequential losses in any contract. These clauses need to exclude, for each category of loss, any risks and damages that they cannot accept. We also recommend that these clauses under common law are drafted as widely as possible to cover against all potential legal causes of action.

Such a clause defining consequential loss could be stated as follows:

> Consequential loss means loss or damage arising from a breach of contract, tort (including negligence), under statute or any other basis in law or equity including, but without limitation, the following:
>
> - Loss of profits.
> - Loss of revenue.
> - Loss of production.
> - Increased production costs.
> - Delay losses.
> - Incremental cost of new equipment.
> - Loss or denial of opportunity.
> - Loss of access to markets.
> - Overhead.
> - Loss of goodwill.

- Loss of business reputation, future reputation or publicity.
- Damage to credit rating.
- Loss of use.
- Indirect, remote, abnormal or unforeseeable loss, or any loss whether or not in the reasonable contemplation of the parties at the time of signing of the contract.

When checking a draft contract, verification of the damage clauses is particularly recommended. In the event the contractor has to accept a foreign legal system, we recommend engaging a specialist local lawyer and having him find out whether compulsory rules exist concerning liability for damages in relation to construction contracts.

In general, standard construction contracts exclude the liability of parties for the other party's loss of use, loss of works, loss of profits, loss of contracts, etc. It is remarkable that even rather experienced contractors make mistakes to their disadvantage when negotiating contract clauses. The perfect example is NEI, which entered into a contract with British Sugar and had to pay £5 million in direct losses on a contract price that was only £160,000.

The term "consequential damage" (or *gevolgschade*) is a non-existent expression under Dutch law. It is often used around the table, but has no legal meaning under the law of the Netherlands.

It is extremely dangerous to agree upon damages in foreign legal systems without the expertise of a local lawyer. Elements like "damages", "consequential damages" and others may have different meanings in different legal systems. If a contractor is forced to accept a foreign legal system, it is necessary to describe extensively what liabilities the contractor may accept and which are excluded from his liability.

16.9. Conclusions

In this chapter, we discussed consequential losses under English law and under other legal systems. We found that there are important differences. We presented a few cases under English law and saw that loss of employer's production may be interpreted as direct loss. Even if contractual clauses to protect contractors were available, English courts nevertheless found contractors liable for those losses. Obviously, the clauses were not sufficiently fine-tuned to exclude such liability. Fortunately, most of the available standard contracts contain clear clauses on losses. However, a warning is in place: where contracts have to be accepted under foreign legal systems, it is advisable to have them checked by local lawyers before signing.

Chapter 17

Intellectual Property

17.1. Case — Inability to perform scope of work due to patent protection

On August 19, 1999 the employer awarded contractor E the reconstruction of a part of the highway Nxxx, according to Specification I&V 23-1999. The contract price amounted to €1,642,000.[1] According to Scope of Work nr. 66420, contractor E was obliged to arrange for thresholds and, near such thresholds, to make layers of asphalt mastic, to be executed in StreetPrint. The employer, a public institution responsible for the maintenance of route Nxxx, intervened and awarded these activities to a third party, named KWS. The contractor E, before the court of arbitration, opposed this action. They did not agree that the employer could deduct the amount that the employer had to pay to KWS from the contractor's invoices.[2]

The employer took its position by stating that it was justified in subcontracting that part of the work to the third party, KWS, and to be compensated for the costs incurred. StreetPrint could be arranged for by a limited number of companies, which had to be license holders of the foreign company that holds the patent; KWS was one of them.

Contractor E defended itself before a court of arbitration. It said that the employer ordered the making of the layers of asphalt mastic, to be executed in StreetPrint at contractor E, and not — as the employer said — to have those activities performed by a licensed subcontractor who has the right to make use of the patent. As stated by contractor E, the employer, after entering the contract, changed the contract by imposing on contractor E that it should pass a subcontract to a qualified license holder. On top of that,

[1] The verdict does not mention the names of the parties, or the location of the road.

[2] Case No. 23.817, Court of Arbitration in the Building Industry in the Netherlands, Aannemingmaatschappij E vs. Provincie X, February 3, 2004.

contractor E had demonstrated to the employer that it was capable of making a comparable product without the need for outsourcing. The employer, however, had passed on this argument, which, in the opinion of contractor E, was not correct. On top of that, contractor E disputed the extra costs involved, which were too high.

The court of arbitration was of the opinion that contractor E, from the outset, should have been aware that StreetPrint may be applied only by an authorized patent holder — read, license holder. However, contractor E announced it would adapt StreetPrint itself. In doing so, contractor E would have infringed the patent right. Contractor E's offer to execute the work itself was in conflict with StreetPrint's patented technical process. The court understood the employer's position in this account. After all, the patent holder could have asked for interruption of the work and the employer could have been accused of cooperating and taking advantage of such infringement. Arbitrators considered that the employer was right in passing the referred part of the work to KWS and were of the opinion that it was reasonable that the cost of that subcontract would be deducted from the contract sum to be paid. Contractor E lost the case and was prevented from infringement of the patent by his employer.

Based upon the arbitrator's verdict, contractor E calculated an amount of €82,270.30. Next, KWS charged the employer €181,064.52 for the StreetPrint activities. So the employer was authorized by the court to charge contractor E for the difference: €98,794.22. This was totally unexpected by contractor E, who had miscalculated the patented work.

17.2. What is a patent?

A patent is an exclusive right to an inventor or his assignee to apply and to make use of its technical invention for a limited period of time. In exchange, the invention has to be described and published.[3] The term "patent" usually refers to the exclusive right granted to anyone who invents any new, useful and non-obvious process, machine, article of manufacture, or composition of matter, compositions of materials, medicines, medical treatment methods or any new and useful improvement thereof. The inventor has to claim that right in a formal patent application.

A patent application must meet the relevant patentability requirements. Novelty and non-obviousness are of the essence. The exclusive right granted

[3] Part of the following text is derived from Wikipedia. Search for "Patent", but note that the author was a US citizen. Patent law differs from country to country.

to a patentee is the right to prevent others from making, using, selling, or distributing the patented invention without permission. It goes without saying that granting permission must be compensated by a fee for the use of the invention.[4] Patent laws should be available in WTO member states[5] for any inventions, in all fields of technology, and the term of protection available should be a minimum of twenty years.[6]

Both natural persons and corporate entities may apply for a patent. The inventors, their successors or their assignees become the proprietors of the patent when and if it is granted. The ability to assign ownership rights increases the liquidity of a patent as property. Inventors can obtain patents and then sell them to third parties. The third parties then own the patents and have the same rights to prevent others from exploiting the inventions. An inventor may also grant a license to make use of the patent; he may license many licensees in various regions. StreetPrint followed that policy. KWS is certainly not the only licensee.

After filing, an application is often referred to as "patent pending". While this term does not offer legal protection, and a patent cannot be enforced until granted, it serves to provide a warning to potential infringers that if the patent is issued, they may be liable for damages.

17.3. Intellectual property and tort

Intellectual property (IP) refers to creations of the mind: inventions, literary and artistic works, symbols, names, images and designs used in commerce.

IP is divided into two categories: Industrial Property, which includes inventions (patents), trademarks, industrial designs and geographic indications of source; and Copyright, which includes literary and artistic works such as novels, poems and plays, films, musical works, artistic works such as drawings, paintings, photographs and sculptures, and architectural designs. Rights related to copyright include those of performing artists in their performances, producers of phonograms in their recordings, and those of broadcasters in their radio and television programs.[7,8]

---

[4] WIPO Patent Law Treaty, Geneva, Switzerland, 2000.

[5] WTO — World Trade Organization.

[6] For basics of copyright, see X. Linant de Bellefond (2002), *Droits d'auteur et droits voisins.* Paris: Dalloz.

[7] The definition is from WIPO, the international organization for intellectual property. WIPO, Intellectual Property Handbook: Policy, Law and Use, Geneva, Switzerland, 2004.

[8] In this book we concentrate on patents and architecture in its phenomenon of art and culture; we leave the other fields out, including science.

The World Intellectual Property Organization (WIPO) is the United Nations agency dedicated to the use of intellectual property (patents, copyright, trademarks, designs, etc.) as a means of stimulating innovation and creativity.

Infringement of intellectual property is related to tort action. Patent law and copyright law are specific parts of tort law. The person or company involved in the infringement is making use of the virtual property of another person. The law protects persons who invested time and money into new technology that is registered as a patent. The law also protects the artistic creativity of new designs of arts and literature. In the construction industry these mainly cover particular aspects such as forms, colors and position of permanent works.

17.4. Patent and patent holder

Case 17.1 describes an infringement of the StreetPrint patent. "StreetPrint" was developed in Canada in 1991 to meet commercial and municipal needs for decorative paving that is durable, economical and maintainable.[9] It is used around the world in about 30 countries. StreetPrint costs just over half as much as bricks or paving stones. It is maintainable, is unaffected by road salt and does not tend to absorb oil. Motor traffic at 50 km/hr produces less noise than on brick or stone road surfaces.[10] Repairs can be made to cracks, tree root problems, settling after soil movements or construction or mechanical damage. Proper installation of this pavement is required. StreetPrint Pavement Texturing© is an innovative technology that produces brick, slate and stone effects using an asphalt base. The process was developed for high traffic areas and is meant to endure unrelenting traffic and weather conditions. StreetPrint also provides cost savings because of its durability, its fast installation process and easy maintenance. The installation process is rather simple. The existing asphalt is heated and the chosen design (brick, cobblestone, etc.) template is placed on the surface. The design is imprinted into the asphalt and the templates are removed. The last step is to apply the high-performance coating that will bond with the asphalt, making it stronger.

---

[9] For information about StreetPrint, see Integrated Paving Concepts Inc., Surrey, Canada; http://www.streetprint.com, January 23, 2013.

[10] The mentioned noise reduction is dependent upon multiple circumstances and method of calculation. We leave those technical details for now.

Work that is executed with a patent or license usually is expensive. The patent holder invested time and money in its invention. Each year, he has to pay for the patent rights in all countries where the patent is registered. He has to contact his licensees on a regular basis, and to cash the license fees. These fees, like the fee KWS has to pay, must be included in the cost to be paid by future employers and contractors, who have no license but still want StreetPrint to be applied.

Contractor E, from the outset, did not realize how the patent system works and why. He thought he was able to perform the work on his own behalf. But as a professional, contractor E should have informed himself about the details of the commercial situation around StreetPrint. Contractor E could not convince the employer of his good intentions. Besides, the employer was worried about being a partner in tort when the contractor intended to infringe StreetPrint's patent rights. The arbitration court agreed with that. Here, a business failure was translated into a legal defeat.

17.5. Architect's copyright

The copyright of the architect is related to the copyright of artists like authors, sculptors, composers and painters. It represents the right to exclusively (re)produce his creation and to show it openly in the public area. Other persons are prohibited to use his design, to copy it partly or wholly. Copyright has two distinct components: the economic rights in the work and the moral rights of the author. The economic rights are a right that is comparable to a right of ownership. They may be transferred by the author to other people in the same way as any other property. They are intended to allow the author or their holder to profit financially from his creation, and include the right to authorize the reproduction of the work in any form.[11] Copyrights are limited in time.[12, 13] Copyright is standardized by several international conventions

[11] Berne Convention for the Protection of Literature and Artistic Works, Bern, Switzerland, 1886, in effect 1887. WIPO, World Intellectual Property Organization, Copyright Treaty, Geneva, Switzerland, 1996, effective 2002. Both treaties are implemented in many countries of the United Nations. Copyright protection differs between the USA and Europe. Software is subject to copyright as well.

[12] European Commission, Duration of Copyright and Rights in the Performances Regulations, No 3297, S.I. No. 158, Brussels, 1995.

[13] Directive 2006/116/EC of the European Parliament and of the Counsel on the term of protection of copyright and certain related rights, December 12, 2006.

outside and inside the European Community. Individual national legal systems differ in details.

The protection of the moral rights of an author is based on the view that a creative work is in some way an expression of the author's personality: the moral rights are therefore personal to the author, and cannot be transferred to another person. Typically it includes the right to be identified as the author of the work and the right to object to any distortion or mutilation of the work which would be prejudicial to his honor or reputation.

Architects accept assignments from employers; those may be people who want to have a new house designed and built, or private companies that want a design for a new office building. Public entities may want designs for public assets, such as a bridge, a raised crosswalk, a parking lot, a multifloor parking garage in town, a theater or a town hall. The employer's description of the asset to be designed and built is mainly (and preferably) functional. When contracting for architectural design, it is common practice that the copyright is transferred to the employer on signing the contract for the design.

Architects are both technicians and creative artists at the same time. They have to make objective technical choices and subjective creative choices.

Objective choices relate to all materials and equipment that the architect applies in his designs. These relate to not only blueprints, technical drawings, detailed specifications, mock ups, descriptions of technical solutions, materials and equipment, but also include existing styles, usual forms and logical concepts which are available on the market. Everything that meets the functional requirements is objective.

Subjective (personal) is everything for which no objective template is available. The architect makes his choices based on his own taste, preference or habit, and his own style. It may be expressed by form or decoration, by color and shape, by surprising and non-conformist conceptions. Those elements of the asset do not follow the historical rules and concepts of common existing construction logic. They are not necessarily as expected. They are not required to meet the functional specification. The choice could have been different. See Figure 17.1 for an example of architectural design.

The distinction between objective and subjective elements in the architect's work is important in finding out whether a creation is subject to copyright or not. Only the subjective elements contribute to the architect's work in his role of creative artist.[14]

---

[14] The description of objective versus subjective is mainly derived from D. F. W. Spoor (2005), *Author's Rights, affiliated rights and the law of data collection, collection rights and practices.* Deventer: Kluwer Law and Taxation Publishers, Deventer, pp. 76–86.

Figure 17.1. The Reina Sofia Museum of Modern Art, Madrid. Advanced technology, from which some components in the upper part of the façade are patented and registered. The form is protected by copyright, which is not registered, but came into existence as soon as the form became available for public view. (Source: John van der Puil.)

17.6. Infringement and enforcement

After infringement of a patent or of an architect's author's rights, the patent owner or the architect may enforce his rights by a civil law suit. Typically, the patent owner will seek monetary compensation for past infringement, and will seek a verdict by the judge prohibiting the defendant from engaging in future acts of infringement. To prove infringement, the patent owner must establish that the accused is making use of his protected inventions. The architect whose work is copied has to prove that the opponent's work is identical to or near to the original architect's design. Normally, the cases are complicated. Technical details are relevant. Often solicitors ask for support from specialists in the business, while courts invite experts to write down their professional legal opinion. The judges may follow these views and opinions, but are not obliged to do so. They have their own authoritative power.

Before tendering, a contractor should be thoroughly informed whether a product or a process required in the employer's specification is protected by patents. Infringement of patents may result in court actions, while the referred project may be interrupted and its time schedule and its budget disturbed.

Patented products, processes, machinery or working methods are more costly than you may expect. However, if they are prescribed by the employer in his project specification, your competitors will be faced with equally high costs; it will not harm your competitive position.

If you are invited to tender based upon an architect's design, note that you are going to be indemnified for your costs in the event someone sues you for infringement of copyright.

If you ever become engaged in a lawsuit on patent rights or copyrights, ask for support and advice from a lawyer who is specialized in this field. The rules differ in all countries, the ways rules are enforced are different and the ways to defend your interests are tricky because of the complexity of the mixture of technology, design and regulations.

17.7. Confidential information and intellectual property in contracting

When employer and contractor are working together, their personnel will be informed about data and information with regard to the project. Sometimes, such information is confidential. That means that one party has to trust the other party not to disclose such information to third parties and vice versa.[15] The knowledge that parties have to exchange in the course of the project may refer to data in writing, in computer programs, in e-mail messages or just verbally during a meeting. It may concern designs, descriptions, calculations, software, tapes, design standards, drawings, technical specifications, instructions, maps, schedules, working documents, procedures, standard forms of letters and subcontracts and the like. Very often such information has commercial interest; it represents a certain value. In such cases, a confidentiality clause in the referred contract is in place. Sometimes the confidentiality is laid down in a separate agreement between parties.

It happens that some information is new in technology, and therefore non-obvious. It may be apt to apply for a patent, but that is not always done. First, it is possible that the information is insufficiently new to be patented, but sufficiently useful to be marked as confidential. Second, it is

[15] CMM standard contract, 1992, clauses 31 and 32. Accompanying notes, 1993, pp. 42–43.

possible that the party concerned started the procedure to apply for a patent, but the patent has not yet been granted. Third, it is possible that the referred party does not wish to go for a patent, but nonetheless is insisting on secrecy.

Some projects need advanced technology, where parties — often it is the contractor — have to be very inventive to arrive at the realization of the functional requirements of the employer. The activities of the contractor in this case partly contain some research and development work. In such an event, the employer and contractor have to agree beforehand about the further rights of the newly developed technical knowledge. There are some basic rules for clauses on proprietary rights, which we recommend considering:

- Contractor's information that existed at the start of the project remains vested in the contractor.[16]
- Employer's information that existed at the start of the project remains vested in the employer.
- Parties indemnify each other for infringement by the other party of intellectual property of any third party.

For newly developed information, a few possibilities are at hand. First, parties may grant each other the use of the newly developed information for the project. Second, parties may agree that the contractor's newly developed information will be disclosed in detail to the employer and that contractor shall assign, grant and convey to the employer all rights, title and interest in and to such inventions. It is then up to the employer to seek patents. In this case, it is reasonable that the employer shall compensate the contractor for the extra work in supporting the employer in such activities.[17] Parties may, at drafting the contract, agree in which party the potential patent or registrable right shall be vested.[18] Parties may agree that such a right may be vested in the parties jointly.[19]

---

[16] The word "information" is to be understood in the widest sense possible.

[17] CRINE General Conditions of Contract Mobile Drilling Rigs, 1997, sub-clause 16.3. CMM standard contract, sub-clause 33.8. Norwegian Fabrication Contract, 1992, clause 33, sub-clause 33.1.

[18] LOGIC Construction, 2003 and LOGIC Marine Construction, 2004, sub-clauses 20.4 and 20.5.

[19] LOGIC Construction, 2003 and LOGIC Marine Construction, 2004, sub-clause 20.6.

FIDIC standards contain clauses for each other's indemnification in case of infringement of a third party's intellectual property rights.[20] FIDIC standards are rather silent about new inventions and potential patent rights or rights that may be registered. The services agreement, which may be applied for engineering services, mentions on the one hand that "anything supplied by or paid for by the Client for the use of the Consultant shall be the property of the Client",[21] while on the other hand, "the consultant retains copyright of all documents prepared by him".[22] But the document does not reveal anything about potential patents resulting from research and development related to the project at hand.

17.8. Conclusions

Infringement of intellectual property rights is a special kind of tort. Patent law and copyright law are specific parts of tort law. A patent is an exclusive right of an inventor or his assignee to apply or to make use of his technical invention. Such invention should be new in technology and it should contain creativity. A patent has to be described and registered. Anyone else may read the description. Everyone will be able to see that the patent exists and how the patent owner can be addressed for permission to make use of his patent or hire the services of a licensee.

A second important intellectual property is copyright. In the construction industry, consulting engineers and architects may be owners of copyrights with relation to their creations. A copyright is not registered. It is a right related to a work of art, of culture or building technology. An architect applies objective elements and subjective elements in the assets to be designed. "Objective" is everything that is necessary to meet the functional requirements of his employer, as well as all available materials and technology. "Subjective" is everything for which no objective norm exists. Here, the architect makes his choices based on his own taste, preferences and style, expressed by form or decoration, by color and shape. Sometimes such creations are surprising and non-conformist. Those elements of the asset do not follow the historical rules and concepts of common logic. They are not required for the functional specification. The distinction between objective and subjective elements in the architect's work is important in order to find out whether a creation is subject to copyright or not. Only

[20] FIDIC Construction, FIDIC Plant and Design & Build, FIDIC EPC/Turnkey, clause 17.5.
[21] FIDIC Client & Consultant Model Services Agreement, 2005, clause 6.
[22] FIDIC Client & Consultant Model Services Agreement, 2005, clause 39.

the subjective elements contribute to the architect's work in his role of creative artist.

When tendering for the execution of an architect's design, a contractor should prevent becoming involved in possible infringements of copyright. In the event the work of the contractor will contain research and development activities, it is necessary to agree beforehand in which party the rights on the newly developed technical information will be vested.

Chapter 18

Damage and Causality

18.1. Case — Malfunctioning struts

In October 2011, an accident took place during construction of a building in the center of Rotterdam. Part of the construction collapsed; as a result, three of the five workers were seriously injured. The newspapers wrote plenty of stories, but were sparse on the causes of the disaster. Later on, it was reported that the struts did not hold. These had been installed to carry just two layers of floors under construction. During the pouring of concrete, the wooden mold with concrete and cement fell down. Were the struts too long for their intended purpose? Were they too thin? Were they not sufficiently strong? What was the real cause of the accident?

The authorities carried out their regular investigations. Having established the real reason for the strut failure, additional questions came up. Authorities started to investigate roles and responsibilities of the parties involved. More particularly, they wanted to know who was responsible and liable for the accident. Who exactly prescribed these struts? What alternative solutions had been considered? Had the workers conducted the work in accordance with adequate instructions? Causes and consequences need to be analyzed first before people, companies and institutions can be held liable.

In this chapter we will deal with causes and consequences related to damages that may arise in projects. We will start our discussion on the kinds of damages that project managers can be confronted with and the way these should be handled. The issue of how to assess causality is discussed.

The international contracting and construction business is not without risk. As constructions and solutions become more complex, business risks, along the contractor's value chain, increase. The contractor must prepare for things that may go wrong during the execution of the project as well as after project delivery. This chapter is about damages that may occur as a result of a contractor's failing performance or accidents. As Figure 18.1 shows, the

Figure 18.1. Collapsed floor as a result of insufficient struts, combined with inadequate verification and coordination, unclear allocation of responsibilities, and lack of overall safety management. (Photo: Royal Dutch Police Service.[1])

damage can be tremendous and may generate a lot of sentiments among the public. The first question that immediately can be and is asked in such a situation is: who is to blame? Another question is: what damage has occurred as a result of the failing construction work?

18.2. Damages under contracts

The word "damage" implies that something is broken. That often goes together with financial losses. "Damages" are a general concept for the different results of wrongdoings, failures, accidents, losses and defaults. Damages may also be the result of inherent causes, such as age or wear and tear.

When losses occur, something is not necessarily broken. For instance, in the event that, after a mobilization, for some or other reason, the project cannot be started until the Portacabins are in place, the contractor is obliged to pay for their rent. That represents a loss, while nothing is broken.

In practice the words "damages" and "losses" are often interchanged.

[1]National Investigation Council, Collapsing of the B-tower Rotterdam, October 21, 2010 report, 112 pages, page 19. www.onderzoeksraad.nl, January 23, 2013. Also B. R. Komat, The collapse of the B-tower Rotterdam, November 21, 2012, 41 pages.

It is important to distinguish between the various kinds of damages, because legal rules for settling the various categories differ. Damages may be incurred by:

- One of the parties to one or more contracts. Here, contract law will apply. However, in some cases, tort law may also apply.
- A party's infringement of legal regulations, such as tax law, HS&E rules and legislation on social security. In such events, tort law or criminal law will be applicable.
- A person or company, who has no contract at all with the contracting parties. We call these non-contractual damages. Tort law will apply here.

Since damage can be caused by different factors, contractual arrangements will differ on how to deal with the consequences. In dealing with this subject, we discuss the factors through which damage and loss can be caused.

18.3. Causes of damages and losses

No completion at all — non-performance

When a contract will not or cannot be completed, it should be formally terminated. In such cases, one of the parties was not able to live up to the agreement. That may be the contractor, who was unsuccessful in delivering the work or a substantial part of it. Usually, such a situation is provided for in the general terms and conditions of the contract. All legal systems have provisions for non-performance; all standard contracts as well. Hereto we use the termination clauses for both the employer and the contractor. Normally, the contractor's non-performance occurs with accumulating delays or with incorrect work that does not meet the required quality standards. The FIDIC standard contracts red, yellow and silver contain extensive termination clauses, which describe in detail when an employer is entitled to terminate a contract.[2] That is the case if the contractor:

a) Fails to supply a performance security or does not follow up on a notice to correct.
b) Abandons the works or demonstrates to stop activities.
c) Fails to comply with the planning schedule, or does not respect a required correction or does not execute corrective work.

---

[2] FIDIC red, yellow and silver books, clause 15. Only the main issues are mentioned here. For details, see FIDIC.

d) Subcontracts whole or part of the work without required approvals.
e) Becomes bankrupt or insolvent, and in the event of liquidation.
f) Is involved in bribery.

The LOGIC standard contracts mention a different arrangement.[3] Three reasons are mentioned for terminating a contract:

a) To suit the convenience of the company (i.e. employer).
b) In the event of any fault on the part of the contractor.
c) The contractor becoming bankrupt or insolvent, and in the event of liquidation.

Materially, the clauses of FIDIC and LOGIC result in the same situation. LOGIC mentions "fault", whereas FIDIC specifies some faults under paragraphs b–d.

The LOGIC Mobile Drilling Rig standard contract differs from the above-mentioned standards; it has ample procedures for termination. Besides the above three reasons, strict clauses apply, such as:

- A *force majeure* condition for an agreed period of time.
- A breakdown of contractor's equipment for a period of 15 consecutive days.
- If the drilling unit is not provided in time, including an agreed-upon time lapse.
- If the drilling unit becomes an actual or constructive total loss.
- If any member of the contractor group fails to comply with business ethics.

Standard contracts differ on this issue. If a contract has to be terminated, it is important to follow exactly the agreed-upon clauses and regulations. Termination has financial consequences for the company. Booked turnover has to be corrected. Registered accountants and tax inspectors will certainly verify whether the termination was executed according to law and order.

Late performance

In international contracting, late performance is translated into cash. Here, we restrict ourselves to the texts of the relevant standard contracts.

---

[3] LOGIC Construction and LOGIC Marine Construction, clause 30.

FIDIC silver translates the delay into damages, which have to be paid by the contractor. Under FIDIC, these delay damages shall be the only damages due by the contractor in the case of such default.[4] LOGIC contains different clauses. Late performance is mentioned under a clause named "liquidated damages", where reference is made to contractually agreed amounts in the event of missed key dates.[5]

These key dates may concern late delivery of goods or services from suppliers or subcontractors, or late (final) completion. Here, contract law also will apply in settling disputes and damages. In the (rare) event a contract does not contain clauses on late performance, the contract law of the legal system underlying the contract will be applicable.

Late performance is a regular issue in international business. The most common solution in contracts is the applicability of penalties or liquidated damages under common law. In practice, important differences exist in handling a claim due to late performance, depending upon the kind of project and interests of the employer. Why would an employer want to be compensated for late delivery? Why would he want a contractor to be liable for that problem? What are his motives?

When a public body — such as a ministry, a city or a department — cannot open a new road with flyovers and access roads at the agreed date, the road users have to drive on the old roads and suffer traffic congestion for a longer time. Civil servants will be working on the project longer, so they cannot work on other useful projects. Indeed, there is some damage to society. The real damage is, however, hard to assess. Contractually, it is translated into penalties or liquidated damages for late delivery.

The real victims are the road users. They are not able to recover their loss of time and extra costs whilst standing still in the notorious traffic jams on the old roads. The risk of such a claim being made against a contractor for this type of loss is extremely small. Car drivers are not parties to the construction contract. Their claim should be based on tort law. As negligence should be proven, road users find it impossible to offer proof of negligence.[6] The contractor will have to pay the contractual liquidated damages or penalties to the public authority that ordered the new road. But the losses of the road users resulting from the delay of large public construction works remain uncompensated.

---

[4] FIDIC red book, clause 8.7, yellow book, clause 8.7, silver book, clause 8.8.

[5] LOGIC Construction and Marine Construction, clause 35.

[6] In continental law systems, five elements have to be proven.

Identical conditions will be applicable for a toll road that was financed with the help of private investors. The investors will miss revenues in the form of toll fees, to be paid by the car drivers who are expected to use the toll road. Here, the investor's direct losses may be claimed from the accountable party. Again, penalties or liquidated damages will be in force.

Incorrect completion under the contract

Incorrect completion means that the work delivered is not complete according to the scope of work, the drawings and specifications, the quality or the HS&E regulations. Examples are: unstable quay walls, quays too short, insufficient depth for mooring ships and less production than agreed upon in specification (gas platforms, pipe lines).

Clauses on incorrect performance are to be found in all standard contracts. The regular consequences of damages, attributable to contractors, are:

- Remedy = repair, redo or replace the defects in work that has been delivered.
- An obligation to make up for the lost time.
- To cover all cost for the extra work and re-work.
- To pay penalties (or liquidated damages) as contractually agreed.
- Suspension of payments.
- Calling in guarantees.
- The termination of the contract if the terms to do so are at hand.

The contractor has to take responsibility for costs. In many cases, the employer probably suffers a much greater loss than the contractor. Sometimes, incorrect performance cannot be undone; or it is too costly or too impractical to repair.

Contracts sometimes contain clauses for missing out on functional specifications in the form of discounts or penalties. These penalties, for instance, are paid for delivering a machine with a lower capacity than was agreed. For example: when building an oil drilling platform, a lower drilling capacity will result in a lower capacity for the exploration of crude oil than agreed upon. This will represent a production loss for the rest of the platform's life span. An employer will, therefore, want guarantees on the good performance of the investment that he is paying for. The contractor, however, would want to limit his liability for the (consequential) losses that such an error in performance could cause. The usual way of implementing that limitation is to agree on a maximum amount (cap) that can be claimed. See Boxes 18.1 and 18.2 for some examples of incorrect performance from practice.

Box 18.1. Examples of incorrect performance with or without a penalty or liquidated losses on functional specification.

- A 445 MW E-turbine, where the specification allowed a margin of plus or minus 1%. At commissioning and testing, the turbine performed at 439.1 MW maximum. Fortunately, the contract contained a liquidated damages clause per MW less capacity. There was a bonus clause for excess capacity, but that clause was not applicable.
- New container ship with specified velocity at 18.2 knots under specified loading conditions and sea conditions. Penalty on less speed 0.05% of the contract sum per 0.1 knot of speed difference. During trials, 18.1 was recorded by the competent authorities. Bonus on faster speed the other way round. But the bonus part of the clause was not applicable.
- Design error in an oil exploration platform. Capacity in all circumstances stays 0.2% under the capacity as agreed upon. Neutral auditors calculated the loss, based on estimated production during estimated lifetime.
- Gas production of platform, which was manufactured under an EPC/Turnkey contract. The measured maximum production capacity accounted for some 1.2% less than agreed upon. Neutral auditors commissioned for a thorough investigation. But their assignment was terminated when it became obvious that the contractor's maximum liability was capped to an amount that was far lower than the actual damage.
- An air pre-heater for a steam boiler, generating steam for electricity generation, did not reach its capacity. Consequently, the steam did not reach the temperature as specified in the contract, but stayed some 12°C lower, which resulted in less MW generation power of the generator. The electricity power-generating company presented its claim based on net present value of its production losses to the boiler manufacturer, who passed it on to its subcontractor. The latter successfully negotiated payment in yearly installments over 11 years. However, due to its lost reputation on the market, the subcontractor lacked further orders after the incident and had to declare bankruptcy after three years.
- Suction-tubing dredger. The tube was too narrow and did not take agreed upon quantities per hour. Re-work was complicated. Although the yard was prepared to do so, the employer needed the ship badly and during negotiations gave in on the subject.

Box 18.2. Some complicated cases to assess and arrange for damage compensation.

- A quay building was put in the wrong position. It was some 22 meters further away from the water than indicated on the drawings. The employer may decide to have the building demolished and to have it reconstructed in the correct position, or to accept the building's position during its lifetime. But if he accepts its actual position it is difficult to find a norm for calculating the loss if he does not demolish and rebuild it.
- Entrance of parking garage with five floors is too low for small buses and vans. It is difficult to arrive at a quantification of the damage. The employer might have so many normal motor cars parked that he may be able to fill up the entire capacity 24 hours per day, 7 days per week. How big is his loss, considering the parking garage was in the center of a big city? Distraught and ashamed over his perceived mistake, the architect committed suicide. In the end, the employer had so many small cars parking permanently that he did not suffer any loss compared to his investment calculations.
- A tugboat was required to sail 11.2 knots in heavy seas. It was designed as a rescue vessel for ships in distress. At trials, it did not go faster than 10.9 knots, while the required power and towing capacity were installed and certified. However, the maximum speed represented a 0.3 knots velocity under specification. What loss will the employer suffer during the lifetime of the vessel? How many times during its lifetime will the rescue boat be in a critical operation where every minute may count? Maybe never. And if that were ever the case, will the employer be the victim? The loss for the 0.3 knots difference therefore can only be assessed in an arbitrary way.

Different legal systems have different rules for the attribution of damages. Outcomes differ per country. Even definitions concerning consequences are not the same everywhere. Therefore, it could happen that a case under the legal system of country A will be viewed differently by a court under the legal system of country B. One universal, unique truth about the how and why of damages and the liability for, or exclusion of, consequential damages does not exist.

Tort

Tort is an unlawful act that causes damage to a person or a legal entity, with whom, as a rule, no contractual relationship exists. The primary aim of tort law is to provide relief for the damages incurred.[7]

When tort applies, identifying the cause and the consequences of the damage incurred is of utmost importance. In capital-intensive projects, usually several stakeholders are involved. In such cases, parties need to establish what cause resulted in what effect. This analysis is necessary in order to determine which party is liable for which part of the damage.

18.4. A theory of causality in business law

Assessing cause and consequence, and the liability for damages of a contractor, a subcontractor or service provider, the employer or a third person is very important. Damages can easily run into six figures. Tort may result in death, injury, physical damage, financial and material losses. Physical damage sometimes can be repaired, but it sometimes happens that parties abstain from repairs.

Where death or serious injury occurs, there is always a strong desire to know what happened. It helps to overcome the sorrow and grief felt by the victim and their family; many times, there is an expressed desire for revenge. When an accident gets lots of publicity in the media, often the general public wishes to "know the truth" so that authorities can be pushed to punish the responsible persons. Next, claims on preventive measures are communicated. How can we prevent similar events from happening in future?

Losses, expressed in financial terms, are caused by undesirable events that either incur costs that could have been avoided, or result in lost income. Damage is always a consequence of some action. Damage always has a cause.

The most commonly applied causality theories when determining damage are: the theory of the *conditio sine qua non*, the theory of the adequate cause and the theory of the attributable cause. The last one is the most practical for lawyers. Each of these theories is briefly explained below.

The theory of conditio sine qua non

When does event A cause consequence B to occur? In other words: when is event B a consequence of event A? The theory of *conditio sine qua non* states that B would not have occurred if A had not happened. This does not imply

[7] For further reading about tort, see Chapter 15.

that A is the only cause for B. In practice, it appears that there were several causes for a certain event. Those causes were all required at the same time in order to make B happen.

When I hoist my sail and there is wind at the same time, my boat will move. If one of the two actions, i.e. events, is absent, the intended effect (moving boat) will not happen. When sailing with strong wind (cause 1), I did not notice a small motor craft because my low sail hindered my observation (cause 2). At the same time, the captain of the approaching motor boat was in the middle of a furious discussion with his fiancée about what restaurant to go to (cause 3), whereas he did not notice (cause 4) that his sailing course was going to cross mine (cause 5), while due to my negligence (cause 6), I did not notice the same. The effect of all causes together is an unintended collision and damage to both boats. All six causes are *sine qua non* causes. If one had not occurred, the damage would not have occurred.

The theory of *conditio sine qua non* is helpful in contract law, but not sufficient to attribute the damage to the party that caused the damage, under the law of tort or under criminal law. To do that, legal experts use an additional theory.

The theory of the adequate cause

There is another theory that for a long time was applied by most courts in Western Europe. This theory looks for the "adequate cause". Only that condition which was — according to generally accepted experience — able or fit to make the consequence happen, is indicated as the adequate cause. The code word here is foreseeability. If sub-supplier X does not supply welding electrodes, subcontractor Y's welder cannot weld. If the steel mill A does not deliver its steel plates in time, subcontractor B cannot bend and roll the plates, while consequently contractor C is unable to deliver its piles for a jetty to be constructed. The damage suffered by subcontractor Y is the consequence of the failure to supply by sub-supplier X. The damage suffered by contractor C is the consequence of the non-delivery by the steel works.

If employer Geenco, being the local harbor authority in a foreign country, who ordered a quay and dredging of the adjoining bay, does not have its quays finished on time, it cannot commence collecting harbor dues. The late completion by the contractor is an adequate cause of the loss suffered by Geenco. That seems reasonable and understandable. The damage was the foreseeable consequence of the concerned cause. These examples are simple because there is only one cause for each effect. However, for legal issues, the theory of the adequate cause is not sufficient. For a better understanding we analyze some legal cases below.

The short circuit

Charles is renting rooms to several people, among who are Adam and Bernard. The rooms are situated over a clothing workshop owned by Charles. All the electrical connections in the building are fed from a single electricity meter board.

The tenancy agreement states that tenants of rooms cannot use electric cookers, kettles or electric plates. Chronologically, the following happens:

1. The sewing machines in the workshop downstairs start running.
2. Adam puts the electric kettle on for tea; this is forbidden by Adam's contract, but Adam has done that before and all went well then.
3. Bernard is going to take a shower; turns on the immersion heater.
4. A fuse blows; the sewing machines downstairs come to a stop.[8]

In physics and in technology, the theory of adequate cause works well. It explains — if the order of events can be reconstructed — which event ultimately, alongside the other circumstances from the *conditio sine qua non* theory, caused the final event (the blowing of a fuse and the standstill of the sewing machines) to occur.

The sewing machines would not have stopped if Adam had not turned on the electric kettle. So Adam's act had an influence on the stopping of the sewing machines. Adam's action was a condition for the final consequence to occur. Event 4 (fuse blowing) would not have happened without 2, putting the electric kettle on (*conditio sine qua non*). Then action 3, the turning on of the immersion heater by Bernard, is the cause of event 4 (*conditio sine qua non*).[9] It was foreseeable that turning on the bathroom heating would cause too heavy a load for the electrical circuit. In the adequate theory, the turning on of the immersion heater by Bernard is the adequate cause of blowing the fuse.

The technical solution for prevention in the future

An electrician, who has to find the cause of the failure, will check why the mains were overloaded. He will conclude that too many amperes were required at the same time. It is not his concern to find the guilty person. He

[8]This example is extracted from J. H. Nieuwenhuis (2003), Hoofdstukken *Vermogensrecht* (*Law of Property*) *7th edition*, Chapter IX, Schadevergoeding (Indemnity). Deventer: Kluwer.
[9]We can take it a step further: the turning on of the electrical sewing machines was also a *conditio sine qua non*. If these had not been turned on, there would not have been any problem.

does not make a distinction between the action of Adam (who was not allowed, according to the tenancy agreement, to use an electric kettle) and that of Bernard (who was not prohibited to shower according to the tenancy agreement). When the landlord asked him to propose a solution to prevent this failure from taking place again, the electrician offered a technical solution, without considering who would do something "wrong". He would check the cabling and verify whether it might stand a heavier electric current. If not, he probably would suggest renewing the cabling and inserting a heavier fuse. Another solution would be to make two separate electric groups for downstairs and upstairs. Those would be the safest and secure solutions in this case. The landlord is given a choice.

A legal solution for prevention in the future

However, if the landlord had asked a lawyer what to do in order to prevent this failure from taking place in the future, the lawyer could come up with a different solution. He could change the tenancy agreement by inserting a clause imposing an extremely heavy penalty (or liquidated damage in the event of a common law system) on infringement of the prohibition clause; furthermore, the landlord should have the option — within the limits of compulsory regulations in the local law — to terminate the tenancy agreement and claim compensation for all costs incurred, ensuring that the landlord would not suffer any damages by reason of the fault committed by the "unacceptable" behavior of the tenant. On top of that, the lawyer could recommend that the landlord paint a clear warning in the tenants' kitchens, stating that the use of electric cookers, electric kettles, electric plates and the like, are strictly forbidden. That written warning could be mentioned in court if it happened again. The lawyer might state before the judge that the tenant acted on purpose or at least with gross negligence.

The theory of the legal attributable cause

The legal expert declares that Adam's course of action was the exclusive cause of the stoppage of the sewing machines. This is related to how the concept of cause is to be handled at law. Turning on the bathroom heating was not prohibited. The legal expert cannot use that action. He can, however, use the condition in the tenancy contract that stipulates that electric kettles are prohibited. The legal expert wants to determine whether the financial damage could be transferred to someone else other than the damaged party. The legal expert is looking for juridical facts. Juridical facts have legal consequences.

A clause in the contract has not been complied with. The lawyer looks for a liable person.

In order to determine whether something is a cause or one of the multiple causes of actual damage, we first have to apply the *conditio sine qua non* theory. Would the damage have occurred if the event, which the legal expert is holding the tenant responsible for, had not happened (*conditio sine qua non*)? If the answer is negative, then there is a legal causal connection. If the answer is positive, we have to investigate the next theory: the adequate cause; and finally, the legal attributable cause.

If, after investigation of the facts given in Box 18.3, it was found that Adam's kettle was on, landlord Charles could blame Adam for breach of contract. Charles could, under the revised contract, try to cash a fine, although Adam's action did not result in the short circuit. Adam, in that case, will have an argument: "Okay, I did put the kettle on and I did put the grid at risk, but it was a calculated risk. I knew very well that the heating in the bathroom was off. So why blame me?"

It is interesting to make a clear distinction between the way technicians and lawyers solve business problems. Technicians will look for technical solutions that will prevent an event from happening again. They are not interested in who is responsible or liable for that specific event. Lawyers are less interested in technical solutions. They will particularly analyze what was contractually arranged by parties. If damage has occurred due to undesirable behavior, they will influence future behavior by stipulating even more precise rights and duties of the parties involved. Apart from that, they will explore who is responsible and, more importantly, liable for the event that caused the damage. When assessing cause and effects among the stakeholders involved,

Box 18.3. Damage due to an unforeseen cause, outside of the tenancy parties.

In the same workshop, some sewing machines are running. An old sewing machine is standing idle, because it is undergoing maintenance; the mechanic has taken the motor out and left the wiring exposed. An absent-minded employee shifts the sewing machine a bit; in doing so she touches the bare wiring, which causes a short circuit and all other machines come to a halt. Adam's electric kettle was also on at that moment. But if it had not been on, the fuse would have blown anyway. The action of Adam is not the legal cause of the event that stopped the sewing machines running, nor is it the physical cause.

lawyers will use different theories. In general, the theory of the most attributable circumstance will be most useful for lawyers.

Calculated risks

In the construction industry, there are numerous "Adams" active during construction and maintenance. They violate contractual and public regulations even though they may have good intentions. The objective of timely completion within tight budget restrictions might lead to actions which do not always comply with standards and regulations. Sometimes such actions may represent a calculated risk; sometimes they may be downright stupid.

18.5. Conclusions

Damages may be distinguished in contractual and non-contractual damages. Damage can be done: (1) to the works, (2) to the employer, his subcontractor and service providers, (3) the contractor, his subcontractors and service providers, (4) other parties related to the project, such as surveyors, supervisors, authorities or (5) to external (i.e. third) parties. Accidents may be caused by the parties 2–5 as mentioned above.

Damages may be at the root of late performance, incorrect performance or non-performance of the contract.

It is possible that several causes combined to bring about an accident. In the event an accident occurs, and, as a result, a multitude of causes and ample discussions about liability take place, we suggest the following procedure:

- List all possible causes, including causes that *prima facie* seem attributable to any other party. This list represents the *sine qua non* causes.
- It is possible that this list includes actions that infringed legal regulations or stipulations under the contract, but did not contribute to the damage. As such, they are not *sine qua non* causes — think about Adam who put his electric kettle on, which was forbidden, but the short cut and the resulting stoppage of the other machines, caused by the exposed wiring of the machine under repair, would have happened anyhow. These "causes" should be deleted from the list.[10]

[10]We do not advocate that these actions should be without repercussions; this chapter concentrates on causality.

- Assess carefully which combination of causes, in your opinion, were the adequate causes to the damage. Mark the party that was at the root of each adequate cause.
- Find out which party is attributable for each of the earmarked adequate causes you found. You may find that information in the contracts and in the legal regulations applicable.
- In the event one or more of the causes are attributable to you, your personnel, your subcontractor or service provider, how to deal with the consequences can be found in the specific clauses of the contract.[11] Do the same for causes attributable to other parties.

In the event one or more adequate causes are not attributable to you or to one of your subcontractors or service providers, you and your lawyer have an argument in the coming discussion with your employer. In the event further consequences of the damage, such as late performance, repair and rework are necessary, their costs should be proportionally allocated to the relevant parties. Sometimes contracts may stipulate consequences of damage where third parties are concerned.

In the event of non-contractual damage — tort and material damage to, or caused by external parties — occurs, the local law will be applicable. However, in the event a hurt person is related to one of the other contracting parties at the site, it is possible that the contract between the hurt person and the other party contains clauses in relation to indemnification.

In the event the damage is personal, i.e. serious injury or death, local law will be applicable and possibly even local public law or criminal law in the case of (gross) negligence.

Always act according to the internal procedures of your company. In all cases, keep extensive reports and records. Take account and archive statements from witnesses. Put them in writing and have them signed by the witnesses. Your in-house legal counsel will assist you.

[11] Most standard contracts have clear and complete stipulations in case of accidents. However, if the contract gives insufficient solutions to settle for the damage, the relevant legislation of the legal system of the contract or the local legislation will apply.

Chapter 19

Knock-for-Knock Arrangements

19.1. Case — The oil platform's broken anchor chain

International Contractors plc was conducting a complicated overhaul/maintenance and modification job at a floating oil production rig for one of the multinational oil and gas companies. The job went smoothly; the weather was acceptable. Materials inflow, up till this point, was according to schedule, due to the wise decision that International Contractors made to outsource the complete downstream supply chain to a specialized service provider. The service provider effectively anticipated the planning schedule, ordered materials in time and provided almost daily shipping services to and from the location near the harbor to the rig. For these shipping services, a special supply boat, including captain and deckhands, was chartered. So all went well.

However, on a dark, rainy and windy night when the captain of the supply boat was working to a 24/7 schedule, his vessel touched one of the heavy anchor chains of the rig. The supply boat was damaged and had to be towed ashore. The insurance company was informed immediately. Repairs were costly. Hiring another vessel at short notice was not cheap. Soon the contractor's project manager, Jim Power, learned that the repairs to the anchor chain would amount to €700,000, while the employer informed him that it preferred to have a brand new anchor chain for the price of €900,000, which was to be put in place by the supplier. Although the liable party, being a sub-subcontractor to International Contractors plc, had no direct contractual relationship with the main contractor, it was clear that — according to normal legislation — International Contractors would be liable for the damage. Jim Power was informed about the way the employer would settle the damage, taking into account that he was not prepared to pay the extra €200,000. However, this was never done. The bill was never presented to International Contractors plc, to the subcontractor, to the owner of the supply boat nor to their insurance companies. This was due to the "knock-for-knock" arrangement, which parties previously agreed upon in the main contract.

This chapter deals with a number of issues related to risk allocation off shore. We will discuss the difference between the liabilities of contractors and employers in normal construction contracts on shore and the liabilities that normally are agreed upon off shore. We will highlight the reasons why the knock-for-knock arrangement is preferable off shore. We will summarize a few historical cases where knock-for-knock arrangements were agreed upon, including their advantages, compared to a situation where these arrangements should not have been agreed. When accidents occur, and liability at tort law is going to play a role in defining the exact liability, there is often a certain degree of negligence. Negligence can be distinguished as regular negligence, gross negligence and willful misconduct. We will discover that it is very difficult to handle these degrees of guilt; hence, the solution is not to distinguish. Insurance companies will cover risks, even if damage is caused by gross negligence or willful misconduct. We will conclude with some recommendations when drafting tenders and contracts.

19.2. Liability for damages in standard contracts

In all legal systems, parties have to indemnify the other party for losses and damages. It is possible as well *not* to do so. In agreeing so with your contract party, you do not indemnify the other party but you "indemnify" yourself. This means you always carry your own losses and damages, caused by accidents, faults or omissions, as does your contract party.

In general, both parties (employer and contractor) to an onshore construction contract are normally liable towards each other for damage from tort. This is one of the basic principles you will find, to a large extent, in all legal systems. The person who does damage has to indemnify the person who suffered the damage. The effect of this general principle varies from country to country, from culture to culture.

In business-to-business relations, it very often happens that this principle is somewhat adapted. In companies' general purchasing conditions, it is often extended in the sense that, if a buyer is legally addressed by a third party and the supplier/service provider of the buyer is involved in the cause of the damage, the involved supplier/service provider must indemnify and hold the buyer harmless for all of the damage, including consequential damage. Indemnifying here means that the supplier/service provider is responsible for the buyer's total damage. On the other hand, sales conditions in general mitigate this principle where possible; for instance, by limiting the seller/

service provider's liability towards the buyer/employer with regard to damages to a fixed maximum amount of financial compensation, or the liability is restricted to replacing the goods that were supplied, at seller's cost.

As the legal arrangements on indemnity from tort vary per country and per legal system, it is customary to arrange for specific and detailed clauses on how to indemnify damages among parties in international contracts. That is why, in all international standard contracts for the construction and offshore industry, extensive arrangements are found concerning liabilities and indemnities. Box 19.1 mentions the regular clauses under FIDIC standard contracts.[1] In order to increase the chance that damages can be claimed and actually paid, these arrangements usually stipulate getting insurance for the related project risks.

In general, the rule behind contract clauses on tort liability is the following: "You are liable for the damage you cause to me and third parties. In case of damage I want to be financially compensated by you."

Box 19.1. Arranging for damage and liability under FIDIC.

FIDIC article 17, red book, yellow book and silver book:

Liability of the Contractor

The Contractor shall indemnify and hold harmless the Employer, the Employer's Personnel, and their respective agents, against and from all claims, damages, losses and expenses (including legal fees and expenses) in respect of:

(a) bodily injury, sickness, disease or death, etc.
(b) damage or loss of any property, real or personal (other than the Works), to the extent...

Liability of the Employer

The Employer shall indemnify and hold harmless the Contractor, the Contractor's Personnel, and their respective agents, against and from all claims, damages, losses and expenses (including legal fees and expenses) in respect of (1) bodily injury, sickness,

(*Continued*)

[1] In the Dutch UAV, UAVTI and UAVGC, you will not find a stipulation about tort. UAV is not an international standard contract. The employer is always Dutch. He will therefore state that Dutch law is applicable to the tender. Hence, the regular rules of the legal system of the Netherlands concerning tort will be applicable.

Box 19.1. (*Continued*)

> disease or death, which is attributable to any negligence, willful act or breach of the Contract by the Employer...[2]

Such liability clauses are common in onshore construction contracts and in dredging contracts.

FIDIC has a standard contract prepared for drawing up contracts with subcontractors[3] in which article 17, "Risk and indemnities", elaborates on the same principle:

Liability of the Contractor

> The Contractor shall indemnify and hold harmless the Subcontractor against and from all claims, damages, losses and expenses (including legal fees and expenses) in respect of ... (c) bodily injury ... etc.

Liability of the Subcontractor

> The Subcontractor shall indemnify and hold harmless the Contractor against and from all claims, damages, losses and expenses (including legal fees and expenses) in respect of those matters ... [there follows references to consequences such as bodily injury, etc.].

19.3. The offshore industry — deviating stipulation

In the offshore industry, it is customary to set the general legal rule aside completely. The rule is adapted as follows:

> When you and I collide with each other (colliding can be taken literally when it concerns parties that both operate their own ship) then we will not hold the other liable for the damage done to each other.

Each party will not hold the other party harmless for damages caused by tort, or any other cause. This so-called knock-for-knock principle means that each party is only responsible for its own losses, regardless of cause. The

[2]The liabilities are not equal back and forth. We will let that difference rest for now. What is important here is the principal rule: one is liable back and forth.

[3]FIDIC Conditions of Subcontract for Construction for Building and Engineering Works designed by the Employer, review draft 2008.

reciprocal indemnities are in effect reciprocal exclusions of liability. The knock-for-knock principle has been broadly adopted in the offshore industry worldwide and has, for instance, been applied in the Norwegian standard contracts 1992 and 2007, where the principle is laid out as follows:

- The Contractor shall be fully responsible for and shall indemnify the Company Group from and against any claim concerning personal injury to, or loss of life of, any employee of the Contractor Group and loss of, or damage to, any property of the Contractor Group arising out of, or in connection with, the contract work.
- The Company shall be fully responsible for and shall indemnify the Contractor Group from and against any claim concerning personal injury to, or loss of life of, any employee of the Company Group and loss of, or damage to, any property of the Company Group arising out of, or in connection with, the contract work.
- This applies regardless of any form of liability, whether strict or by negligence, in whatever form, on the part of the other group.[4]

Each of the parties is liable for its own damage and accidents to its own personnel, equipment and other properties. It is customary to extend this to material and personnel of subcontractors, suppliers, service providers, subsidiaries, affiliated and parent companies. These groups are often referred to in contracts as the Employer Group or the Contractor Group. This is a very simple concept, but in practice, numerous variants and exceptions can be found. The BIMCO Supplytime 2005 incorporates "Owners' Group" and "Charterers' Group" instead of "Owners" and "Charterers" as applied in the BIMCO Supplytime 89. The meaning and interpretation remain unchanged.[5] The groups are very wide indeed. They incorporate "Employers", which include employees, directors, officers, servants, agents or invitees.[6]

Employers in the energy and offshore industry have many valuable and risky installations in use. Consequently, they enter into many construction, modification and maintenance contracts with a multitude of different contractors and

[4] The principle is described here in short. In the standards, the text is more extensive and to-the-point. NTK 07 Norwegian Total Contract for EPC and EPIC projects and NTK 07 MOD Norwegian Total Contract Modification for modification works on existing facilities, both article 30.

[5] BIMCO Supplytime, 2005, sub-clause 14 (a).

[6] Guidance notes: comparison of the differences between Supplytime 89 and Supplytime 2005, commentary on introduction and clause 14.

service providers, who, for their part, have contracts themselves with subcontractors and supporting service providers. The oil and gas drilling entrepreneurs each have their own policy of how to cover their risks. Such a risk policy relates to the type of risks and their size, the typical characteristics of the installations and the organizations concerned. The legal system of their country of location and their own legal system are apparently less important because the knock-for-knock principle is applied worldwide. Such a policy has a large influence on contractual arrangements. In this industry you cannot find two companies using identical contracts; you cannot find two companies that are similar with regard to liabilities/indemnities/insurances. Therefore, deviations from this principle are often made. Where this is the case, contractors should be cautious and consider making qualifications in their bids.

19.4. Example from standard non-construction contract

Here is an example from the BIMCO standard contract for chartering vessels from 1989, article 12. BIMCO, the Baltic and International Maritime Council, is based in Copenhagen.

> No liability of the Charterers:
>
> 12(a) ...the Charterers shall... not be responsible for loss of, or damage to, the property of the Owners or of their contractors and subcontractors, including the Vessel, or for personal injury or death of the employees of the Owners or of their contractors and subcontractors, arising out of, or in any way connected with, the performance of this Charter Party....[7] (See Box 19.3.)
>
> No liability of the Owners:
>
> 12(b) ...the Owners shall not be responsible for loss of, damage to, or any liability arising out of anything towed by the Vessel, any cargo laden upon or carried by the Vessel or her tow, the property of the Charterers or of their contractors and subcontractors, including their offshore units, or for personal injury or death of the employees of the Charterers or of their contractors and subcontractors...[8]

This BIMCO charter contract, which is also used frequently for the chartering of drilling platforms, for example, continues in article 12(b) that

---

[7] Box 19.3.

[8] Box 19.3. The obligations of the two parties mentioned in these clauses are not completely identical. In Box 19.3 at the end of this chapter, the complete clauses are mentioned.

the owner is not even liable when he has been negligent, "even if such loss, damage, liability, injury or death is caused wholly or partially by the act, neglect or default of the Owners". This clause has also been added to the Norwegian standard contracts mentioned above.

This is pushing the limit of liability a bit far. In many legal systems, a party cannot back out of liability when damage is caused by an event where the acting (or failing to act) party has been negligent or has made mistakes. Yet in this Danish model, that is the case.

Robert Gay (2004), states that English law and the English courts have a strong tendency to interpret exclusion and indemnity clauses as not covering the results of negligence. This would mean, for example, that the owners might claim against the charterers if the loss of or damage to the vessel were a result of the charterer's negligence.

However, in this case, the courts should be able to resist their standard tendency. First, the knock-for-knock is mutual: this is not a one-sided exclusion clause. Second, the first part of each limb (the non-responsibility part) is well-fortified by the clauses beginning "even if" and the word "such". Accordingly, these clauses should prevent claims in cases where there has been negligence — even if it can be called "gross negligence".[9]

You could expect those clauses to hold their ground in a court of law under the English legal system. In Dutch law, it is normally not feasible to exclude "willful misconduct" and "gross negligence". This means that, although you can write it down in a contract, if brought before a judge he will not honor the exclusion of liability. The Dutch Supreme Court, being the highest law court, has considered several times that you cannot be exonerated in contracts for damage caused by ethically culpable actions.

Therefore, it is not surprising that in the Dutch CCM standard contract for the Oil and Gas Industry, "gross negligence" and "willful misconduct" are excluded in several places in the article with regard to liability.[10] This is also done at other points in this contract. In short: currently, in Dutch law, when there is misconduct and gross negligence, you will not be indemnified for liability for damages. Please note that the decisions of the Dutch Supreme Court all concerned special situations, in which the exclusion was always unilateral. Where it concerns bilateral exclusions of liability in the offshore industry, the above-mentioned argument of Robert Gay should definitely have a

---

[9]This paragraph is extracted from the comments of R. Gay, Hill Taylor Dickinson, International Law Firm, mentioning problems and pitfalls of the Supplytime 89 Charter, March 17, 2004.
[10]CMM standard contract for the Oil and Gas Industry in the Netherlands, clause 36. 1, 2, 3, 5, and 6.

role to play if the knock-for-knock principle was ever subjected to the judgement of a Dutch judge. A number of Norwegian legal experts also think that willful misconduct and gross negligence should be considered by Norwegian judges.[11]

Claims from third parties

Under the BIMCO Supplytime standards, parties accept a mutual obligation for each party to defend the other if a claim for which the other party is liable is claimed from the non-liable party. This obligation concerns both claims under the knock-for-knock principle and performance claims under the charter party.[12] In practice, this clause will protect financially weaker service providers and sub-subcontractors that might be liable for a default or a claim in tort. An owner — for instance, an oil and gas company — in the event that they are called to court, is held to defend the case at its cost. As there is no recourse possible — that is the core of the knock-for-knock principle — the smaller entity is sheltered.

19.5. Himalaya clause

A Mrs. Adler took suit against Captain Dickson, the master of the P & O passenger ship, the *Himalaya*. Mrs. Adler had been injured when a gangway fell, throwing her about five meters to the quay below. Her passenger ticket contained a non-responsibility clause benefiting the carrier. Suing the shipping company would lead nowhere, and so she took suit in tort against Captain Dickson, the master of the *Himalaya*, as well as against the boatswain, who she held responsible and liable for her injuries. She argued in court that under normal contract law, the defendants (captain and boatswain) could not rely on a term of a contract that they were not party to.

The Court of Appeal declared that in the carriage of passengers, as well as in the carriage of goods, the law permitted a carrier to stipulate not only for him, but for those whom he engaged to carry out the contract. It was also held that the stipulation might be expressed or implied.[13] Since this

[11] C. James-Olsen and J. Heimset (2009), "Knock-for-knock" clauses in offshore contracts; see Wikborg Rein Shipping Update, February 1, 2009.

[12] Supplytime 89, clause 12(b); Supplytime 2005 clause 14(b). The guidance notes mention clause 14(c), which is an error.

[13] Adler vs. Dickson (The Himalaya), 1954, 2 Lloyd's Report 267, 1955, 1 QB 158 [1], http://www.bailii.org/ew/cases/EWCA/Civ/1954/3.html, January 23, 2013. In the case

verdict, all clauses which contain stipulations of exoneration or limitation of liability not only for the contracting party itself, but also for all parties which it intends to engage in fulfilling its obligations, are called "Himalaya clauses". In professional contracting, many Himalaya clauses have been drafted, especially in transport law, benefiting stevedores, service providers, agents, helpers and others. Himalaya clauses are very effective in offshore projects as well.[14]

Definition

A Himalaya clause is a stipulation in a contract in favor of the legal entities and individuals, defined as any and all subcontractors, service providers, vendors, suppliers, employees, servants, agents or other individuals whose services are utilized in the contracting party's performance of its obligations or exercise of its rights under a contract.

A simple example of a Himalaya clause:

> No servant or agent or independent contractor from time to time employed by the carrier shall be liable to the owner of the goods for any loss or damage resulting from any act or negligence on his part while acting in the course of his employment.

This is a very short clause. Wikipedia presents a longer sample clause.[15] BIMCO recommends a much longer and more extensive version, approximately one full page of small print.[16] The clause can be applicable to contracts for work offshore when goods, such as equipment, materials, components and tools are transported to the locations where the work is performed, be it the construction of a pipe line, a wind farm or the maintenance or update of a platform.

Employer group/contractor group

A Himalaya clause is suitable for a main contractor working on board a platform where a great number of subcontractors, service providers and vendors

---

of Captain Dickson, however, the court held that the passenger ticket did not expressly or by implication benefit servants or agents and thus Captain Dickson was held liable in tort.

[14]After this decision, consumer law developed further. An exoneration of liability for a passenger's damage would today no longer hold in court.

[15]http://en.wikipedia.org/wiki/Himalaya_clause, July 19, 2012.

[16]IG/BIMCO, Revised Himalaya Clause, July 2009.

may be active under the main contractor's responsibility. Such gathering of legal entities and individuals is called a "contractor group". This may be the:

> Contractor, contractor's affiliates, participating companies in a joint venture established for the performance of the work, subcontractors, such as but not limited to, its partners, contractors, vendors, service providers and suppliers of any tier and their respective employees, staff, officers and agents.[17]

The contract partner of the contractor is the employer, who has his own affiliations, contractors, subcontractors, service providers and vendors. Together, these are called the "employer group" Box 19.3 at the end of this chapter lists in sub-clause 12 (e), in a rather extensive way, all concerned parties of both charterer and owner. All mentioned parties are indemnifying all parties belonging to the other group.

LOGIC defines the two groups in the same way.[18] The guidance notes of the Marine standard contract stress that the groups imply not only the contractor's subcontractors, but also those subcontractors of any tier who are performing the work offshore at any fabrication yard or construction site.[19]

19.6. The purpose of the knock-for-knock principle

There are several reasons why the knock-for-knock principle makes sense: it makes the risk picture clear and predictable without waiting for disputes over liability to be resolved. After damages on your side, you are not going to dispute the caused losses with your contract party. Whatever the cause may have been, whoever may be the guilty person, you report it to your insurance, or if applicable, you carry the losses yourself.

Accidents at sea and in offshore work are usually not due to one single cause, but to a concurrence of circumstances and unlucky outcomes of actions. These circumstances and human actions can concern various legal parties. It would take a lot of work for the legal experts, insurers, investigators and judges to find out exactly what happened. From those findings, an apportionment of damage has to be set. Experience has taught us that such proceedings can take years.

The knock-for-knock principle reduces insurance costs because each party only needs to insure his own property and personnel. For estimating risks, the

---

[17] CMM standard contract, 1992, pp. 2–3.

[18] LOGIC Marine Construction, 2004 and LOGIC Drilling Rig, 1997, sub clauses 1.1.2 and 1.1.9.

[19] LOGIC Marine Construction, 2004, guidance notes, p. 6.

contractor does not have to take into account the value of the investments of another contractor by order of the employer. The principle is widely accepted by insurance companies and underwriters. It prevents items from being doubly insured. It enables a quick response to disasters that may occur. Box 19.2 gives an example.

It is quite clear that, in the above case, both the hose manufacturer and the contractor felt able to disseminate information about the problem

Box 19.2. The wrongly installed coupling.[20]

A very long, twisting and horizontal oil well, extending around 7,000 metres, was blocked by wax deposits in the production tubing. One way to remove the wax was to circulate hot crude oil to "melt" the wax and enable it to be brought to the surface where it could be removed.

In this case, a coiled tubing unit was used, connected by a hose to a separately fired "hot oil boiler". During the operation, the hose connecting the hot oil boiler to the coiled tubing unit failed, slipping out of its end connection and spraying high-pressure heated crude oil, which subsequently ignited. The oil company had to shut down its oil field, which in turn impacted refinery operations as well. The hose manufacturer/supplier, which had provided the hose under the CRINE Purchase Order Conditions, immediately commenced investigations. The failed unit was returned to Aberdeen where examination showed that a coupling had been put on the wrong way round in the manufacturer's workshop. A product warning was sent out to all purchasers of this equipment by e-mail within one hour of the discovery, containing instructions to check all hoses and couplings. Customers were informed that replacement hoses were being manufactured and would be sent out where needed within a few days. The whole operation was conducted openly and promptly because the manufacturer had immediately admitted that his workers were negligent. Potential damage and injury/fatalities elsewhere were averted thanks to the speedy reaction by the manufacturer. The manufacturer could do this because he did not have to worry that he would be sued for his negligence. Again, because of the CRINE contract and its knock-for-knock terms, the oil company did not claim against the contractor for having to shut down its oil field or the consequential losses.

[20]Case extracted from Alan Thomas, Director of Marine and Energy, CTCS Energy, Aberdeen, UK, www.standard-club.com/docs/mm24.pdf, January 23, 2013.

because they were confident that their contractual provisions would protect them against possible claims. It is not hard to imagine that this matter could have been very different had there been gross negligence or willful misconduct provisions in the contract, forcing the hose manufacturer or the contractor to bear liability for their negligence. They might have been unwilling to give information openly, for fear of inviting claims. At the very least, they might have wished to consult lawyers first, causing delay in the dissemination of vital loss-preventing information. It is our belief that a robust knock-for-knock contracting culture protects the industry from unnecessary insurance and litigation costs. It may also lead to better loss prevention, and a reduction in accidents and their accompanying human and economic cost.

19.7. The unseaworthy tug boat and the gross negligence[21]

A tug owner drew up a contract according to BIMCO's Towhire conditions for a six-month charter in the Kiel Canal. Whilst towing a barge, it came into contact with a dredger owned by a third party and, as a result of this contact, both the dredger and the barge suffered damages which required repairs. The third party (the dredger owner) claimed against the tug owner for his damages and losses, and the owner of the barge also presented a claim against the tug owner for both direct and consequential losses suffered as a result of the damage to their barge.

This particular case focused on one of the knock-for-knock provisions in the Towhire contract form, which provides that:

> loss or damage of whatsoever nature, howsoever caused to or sustained by the Tow [and] loss or damage of whatsoever nature caused to or suffered by third parties or their property by reason of contact with the Tow or obstruction created by the presence of the Tow shall be for the sole account of the Hirer [i.e. the barge owner] without any recourse to the Tug owner...whether or not the same is due to the breach of contract, negligence or any fault on the part of the Tug owner, his servants or agents.

The barge owners argued that the tug owners could not rely on this knock-for-knock allocation of responsibilities because the tug was

[21] Smit International (Deutschland) vs. Joseph Mobeus Bau Gesellschaft GmbH, 2001, CLC 1545. See P. Zeman, Knock-for-knock agreements and seaworthiness obligations, www.danishdefenceclub.com/News/alist.phtml?show=111, June 20, 2003.

unseaworthy (the barge owners alleged that the tug master was in a "constant drunken condition"[22]) and, in other words, the barge owners took the view that the knock-for-knock allocation of liabilities was based on the assumption that the tug was in a seaworthy condition and that the tow was tow-worthy.

The court's decision was based upon what was perceived to be a "businesslike" or "commercial" approach. The court acknowledged that the knock-for-knock arrangement is "a crude but workable allocation of risk and responsibility" (the own risks are borne by the tug and the tow, respectively), "containing a code, apportioning liabilities between parties". The risks are clearly defined, even if the apportionment may sometimes appear to be unfair.

The essence of the verdict lies in the appreciation of the gross negligence aspect. The court consequently went on to say that the introduction of arguments of seaworthiness into this particular knock-for-knock agreement would significantly lessen the effectiveness of the knock-for-knock arrangement of responsibilities. Furthermore, the court also stated that seaworthiness arguments in any event would not play a role in the knock-for-knock agreement due to the express wording of the indemnity clause, which specifically stipulated that the indemnity applied "whether or not the same is due to the breach of contract".

This particular decision confirms that standard form contracts strictly applying the knock-for-knock system can still be relied on to provide certainty with regard to the allocation of risks. This certainty (even if the apportionment sometimes appears unfair) avoids costly and time-consuming litigation.

19.8. The Piper Alpha

The Kieler Canal case was the first case where a UK court recognized the full benefits of the knock-for-knock principle. It was not the first case on the issue. Piper Alpha was a North Sea oil production platform operated by Occidental Petroleum (Caledonia) Ltd. The platform began production in 1976, first as an oil platform and then later converted to gas production. An explosion and resulting fire destroyed it on July 6, 1988, killing 167 men, and leaving only 61 survivors. Total insured loss was about £1.7 billion ($3.4 billion).

[22]The standard form of contract of BIMCO's Towhire was revised in 2008. See https://www.bimco.org/documents/chartering/documents/towage/towhire2008, February 1, 2013.

At the time of the disaster, the platform accounted for approximately 10% of North Sea oil and gas production, and was the worst offshore oil disaster in terms of lives lost and industry impact.

The Piper Alpha claim was finally ruled on in 1994. In this case, the wording of the contract led to a different result.[23] Caledonia, owner of the offshore platform, paid a sum of money to the surviving relatives of an employee of Orbit Valve Co., who died in a fire on board the platform. Caledonia claimed an indemnity in respect of moneys paid; it based its claim on the contract with Orbit Valve, which contained a knock-for-knock clause, which mutually indemnified both parties with respect to their personnel. The clause did not contain anything about parties' negligence.

The Court of Appeal considered that the claim failed, and that the accident, resulting in the employee's death, was caused by Caledonia's own negligence. It was — according to the court — "*prima facie* implausible that the parties would wish to release one another from the consequences of the other's negligence and agree to indemnify the others in respect of such consequences". No recourse was possible. The claim failed.

19.9. Further cases of knock-for-knock

The released and lost tow

Tug owners and rig owners entered into a contract for towing a rig from Brazil to Singapore via Cape Town. In the south Atlantic the tug ran out of fuel. The rig was released from the tug and drifted away. Efforts to salvage the rig failed and subsequently the rig was declared totally lost. The rig owners claimed damages of about $20 million for the loss and the costs of wreck removal. The judges considered that the tug owners "failed to exercise due diligence to tender the tug in a seaworthy condition by commencing the towage with insufficient bunkers". The tug owners could not and did not replenish the bunkers during the towage once it became clear that the tug would run out of fuel. One would conclude that the tug owners would be liable for the damage caused. However, the towing contract was drafted after the knock-for-knock principle, so such loss or damage was at the risk of the rig owners. The tug owners were found not liable. According to the judge, the clause was intended to identify which of the parties was to bear the risk of the

[23] E.E. Caledonia Ltd (formerly Occidental Petroleum (Caledonia) Ltd) vs. Orbit Valve Co. PLC 1994 2 LLR 239, The Piper Alpha.

various types of loss, damage and liabilities. "The allocation of the risks was on a no-fault basis," the judge said.[24]

Far Service

In this case, three parties were operating on an oil rig supply vessel called the Far Service. These parties included Farstad Supply UK.

Farstad Supply entered into a long-term charter contract with Asco for supply work to various oil rigs. When the vessel was in port, Enviroco had to clean up the tanks, while at the same time Asco ordered the captain to move to another berth. An employee of Enviroco opened a valve, causing fuel to leak into the engine room near hot machinery. The vessel caught fire and was badly damaged. Legal relations were as shown in Figure 19.1.

In court Enviroco denied liability. It argued that both Farstad and Asco were negligent themselves. Asco had materially contributed to the accident and should pay at least a great part of the losses.[25] Now the question arose whether Asco could be liable for the damages on the vessel. The text of a part of the knock-for-knock clause was as follows:

> Subject to Clause 33.1, the Owner (Farstad) shall defend, indemnify and hold harmless the Charterer (Asco)... from and against any and all claims, demands, proceedings and causes of action resulting from loss or damage in relation to the vessel (including total loss) or property of the owners, including personal property of owner's personnel or of anyone for whom the owner may be responsible on the vessel, irrespective of the cause of the loss or damage, including where such loss or damage is caused, or contributed to, by the negligence of the charterers...

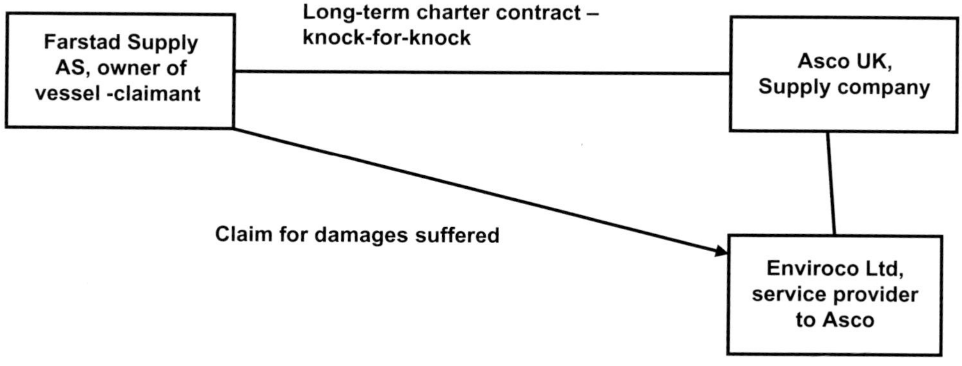

Figure 19.1. Legal relations on the Farstad vs. Enviroco case.

[24] Lloyd's list, http://www.lloydslist.com, February 18, 2009. Also: www.hfw.com/publication/art.

[25] Enviroco based this claim of recourse on a Scottish Act, 1940. We do not discuss that detail here.

In the event Asco would have been sued by Farstad, the latter never would have been liable for the damages. The knock-for-knock clause contained the exclusion of Asco's liability. Enviroco was not entitled to a contribution from Asco and Enviroco was not liable to Farstad Supply. It made no difference whether the contractor Enviroco was involved in the charter contract or not. And it made no difference that the charterer Asco may have been far more or far less to blame for the fire than the contractor Enviroco.[26]

The knock-for-knock principle represents a carefully considered balance between the interests of an owner on the one hand and those of the charterer on the other.

19.10. A bridge too far

The knock-for-knock may lead to what at first instance seems to be an unreasonable solution for damages caused by negligence. But there is a limit, as shown in the Herdentor case. The knock-for-knock principle should be considered in the whole objective of the contract concluded between parties. Where one of the parties is no longer doing anything, the clause will not help him to escape from his responsibilities. The owners of the tug Herdentor were liable for losses of the tow when the tug simply left the tow, and abandoned the towage contract because they booked a much better paid job elsewhere. The court considered this action as a "repudiatory breach of the towage contract". Here the tug owners ceased to do anything at all in the performance of their obligations.[27] But for regular contracts to be performed in good faith the knock-for-knock principle is the most practical. Figure 19.2 shows a tug boat and a barge loaded with materials for a wind farm under construction. Regular risk allocation: parties are responsible for their own risks.

19.11. Negligence, gross negligence and willful misconduct

All aforementioned cases were ruled by common law; verdicts were given by English courts. Common law is case law with great respect for contracts, made up by commercial parties. The development of contract law is driven by the development of the intentions of parties who try to find practical solutions

---

[26] Farstad Supply AS vs. Enviroco Ltd and another (the Far Service), 2010, UKSC 18, Lloyd's List, June 29, 2010. Also P. Dean and J. Koh (2010), Holman Fenwick Willan, http://www.lloydslist.com/art, 29 June 2010; also www.hfw.com/publication/art. See also www.ukscblog/case-comments-farstad-v-enviroco2010-uksc-18.

[27] The Herdentor case, Lessons to be learned from the Herdentor, June 2, 1999, http://lloydslist.com/publications. Also P. Dean and J. Koh, www.hfw.com/publication/art.

for economical challenges. The courts intervene when parties come to dispute each others' opinions when losses occur. The courts look for the law as it was and how it is.

Jennings and Frew (2003) advised against introducing other terms than just "negligence" into contracts.[28] They advocate that the terms "gross negligence" and "misconduct" or "willful misconduct" are left out of the wording of individual contracts. The reason for their opinion is that amendments and exceptions to standard contracts will certainly erode and can affect cover of the insurance companies. In short, this means that when drawing a contract holding a knock-for-knock clause, one should be aware that:

- Contracts must be on standard form, for instance, BIMCO Towcom, Towhire, Heavecom or others.[29]
- Each party should be liable for its own personnel and property.
- Regardless of negligence.
- Each party must indemnify the other.
- The right to limit the cover should not be waived.

The reason is that insurance policies are pooled by various insurance companies. Pools are used for standard covers. "Negligence" is a general standard among insurers. When introducing other gradations of negligence, then the risk can no longer be pooled. This will result in higher premiums for lower covers. And what about non-poolable risks? Furthermore, the differences between "negligence" and "gross negligence"/ "misconduct" are thankfully subjects for solicitors to discuss before courts. Disputes always tie up costly management time, the outcome is uncertain and it has an effect on the company's "insurance record". This means that insurance companies take note on how often a corporation disputes its contracts before courts. Insurers do not like that; they prefer clear cases. There are not many cases on gross negligence or willful misconduct. A definition of gross negligence was given by the High Court in 1997. Here it was established that gross negligence is:

> Something more fundamental than the failure to exercise proper skill and care... [It should be] conduct which a reasonable person would perceive to entail a high

---

[28] B. Jennings and V. Frew, Paper read before the Standard Offshore Forum on November 6, 2003, http://docstoc.com/docs/70763805 and http://llodslist.com/publications/jennings&frew, January 23, 2013.

[29] These are towing contracts. For constructing permanent works, other clauses can be added: the Norwegian Standard Fabrication Contact, clause 30, Liabilities; LOGIC Construction Contract 2003, clause 20, Indemnities; LOGIC Marine Construction, 2004, clause 22, Indemnities.

degree of risk of injury to others, coupled with heedlessness or indifference to or disregard of the consequences...[30]

The one case Jennings and Frew mention defines willful misconduct as: "An action or omission which the doer appreciates is wrongful and yet in which he persists regardless of the consequences and with indifference to the consequence."[31]

The two definitions do not differ a lot. In practice, before court it will be problematic to prove the participant's mindset. Did he have the knowledge; did he have the intention; what was his state of mind when before the act? That is up to courts to finally decide. The author's conclusion is that gradation of negligence will be an obstacle to the smooth insurance of the liabilities of the parties.

However, sometimes you cannot escape from gradations of negligence. The authors recommend that, in the event one cannot escape from wording like gross negligence and (willful) misconduct, one should mention a definition of such words and furthermore limit the exclusions to acts or omissions of the corporate entity, rather than the individuals for which the entity is responsible.

19.12. Negligence in legal systems other than common law

Do other legal systems in various places worldwide respect contracting parties' intentions? Do courts outside the common law countries recognize the legality of the knock-for-knock principle? The Standard (2007) reported that "certain jurisdictions will not uphold a contract which allows a towing vessel to avoid liability for its own negligence and to be indemnified for all losses arising from such negligence".[32] The Standard took a poll on the recognition of knock-for-knock contracts from around the world. That resulted in a number of legal opinions from respectable lawyers. The survey included Argentina, Australia, Brazil, Canada, Chile, China, Denmark, France, Germany, India, Indonesia, Iran, Italy, Malaysia, Mexico, the Netherlands, Nigeria, Norway, Portugal, Qatar, Russia, Singapore, Spain, Sweden, South Africa, Thailand, UAE, USA, Venezuela and Vietnam.

Certain jurisdictions would possibly not enforce the indemnification of liability in case of gross negligence and (willful) misconduct. Among them are Argentina, Australia, China, Italy, Thailand, Venezuela and Vietnam. The

---

[30]The Hellespont Ardent, Red Sea Tankers Ltd. vs. Papachristidis, 1997, 2 LLR 547.

[31]Horabin vs. BOAC, 1952, 2 All ER 1016.

[32]S. Marugason, The Standard, October 29, 2007, p. 1, www.standard-club.com/docs/SB_international_recognition_October2007_disk, pfd, January 23, 2013.

main reason for this is that most of these legal systems contain compulsory legislation that affects the consequences of parties' behavior in the event of gross negligence or (willful) misconduct. When the legal system of such countries is in effect, the contract parties may agree to and incorporate a pure knock-for-knock clause; but in the event parties come to court, the judges will not enforce such an agreement. They will have to rule according to the compulsory rules of the normative legal system.

This means that lawyers and contract managers who have to negotiate draft contracts not only have to consider and appreciate the written texts, but also have to take legal advice from colleagues who are familiar with the legal system mentioned in the draft contract. A question is: in the event of a legal dispute before court, will the court uphold the text as agreed upon by the parties?

In this respect, we consider the market for the construction of wind parks in and around the North Sea. Here we see a number of leading energy power corporations who are active in obtaining concessions and construction and commissioning of installations. This will continue for the coming decades. Important players have different nationalities.[33] Their legal systems are not yet tested on the knock-for-knock principle. Maybe it is wise to negotiate a

Figure 19.2. Sea transport of three wind turbine foundations with sub-piles for wind farm under construction. Best risk allocation is on a knock-for-knock basis. (Photo: SMIT, www.smit.com/tugmagazine/june2011.)

[33] Important market parties are Belgian, Danish, Dutch, English, German, Icelandic, Norwegian, Scottish and Swedish.

different legal system. Just to be sure: agree to UK common law, or, more specifically, English law.

19.13. Preparing a tender with the knock-for-knock principle

When assessing an invitation to tender, the utmost care is advised when assessing risks and liabilities. Based upon the previous text, we suggest considering the following dos and don'ts:

- We recommend the Contractor Group to be as large as possible. The contractor's subcontractors and the contractor's service providers should be included. Even suppliers who deliver their goods at the site and have to install them there should be included. The position of quayside personnel, surveyors and authorities should also be dealt with. Whose responsibility are they, according to the contract? Visitors — think of a group of students who come on a field trip — should be included when covering for liabilities, even when the employer organizes such a visit. There are more people you will not think of straight away. Sit down and think about it when you have the clause of the tender documents in front of you. Situations vary from project to project and from case to case.
- The Employer Group also has to be considered. All other contractors, subcontractors, service providers and officials of the employer should fall under the knock-for-knock principle. If this is not the case, the contractor would need to draw up separate knock-for-knock agreements with the other parties in addition to the main contract, which would generate unnecessarily long bureaucratic processes.
- The tender documents have to be verified as to whether the conceived indemnity is complete. It can happen that — in spite of the application of the knock-for-knock principle — certain risks in the contract are still placed with the contractor. This could represent a certain excess premium for the relevant risk. Be aware of willful misconduct and gross negligence. The best option is to just mention "negligence".
- The amounts to be insured have to be estimated. What risks do we want to cover ourselves for? When we take out insurance, how much of the risk do we cover ourselves? On the list of risks we can then tick off the risks covered under the knock-for-knock principle.
- When dealing with our own insurance companies, it has to be laid down that they forgo their right to recourse. In the event of damage to our

properties, or our people being injured or dying, our insurance should not try to recoup damages from those who have caused the damage. In practice, offshore insurers cooperate with such requests.

- The insurance policy for liability should be in line with the conditions of the contract. It should be ensured that all members of the contractor group, without any exceptions, will be co-insured on the contractor's insurance policy.
- The clause on consequential losses has to be in accordance with the knock-for-knock principle. If we decide to exclude liabilities and indemnities from tort equally, then we should limit consequential losses for damages through shortcomings in the contract.

In short: the knock-for-knock clause in a contract has to be in line with the insurance clauses, as well as with the exoneration clauses on maximum liability of the contractor.

19.14. Conclusions

The knock-for-knock principle is a very practical instrument for settling unexpected and unpleasant damages. This arrangement is well known in the offshore industry. The basic idea is that each party will carry its own losses for damages that unwillfully occurred by actions of one of the contract parties. In most knock-for-knock clauses, gross negligence and even willful misconduct are covered as well. The agreement holds that one party will not knock the other party, and vice versa. It is important that this knock-for-knock arrangement, which needs to be mentioned in the main contract, is transferred and extended to all arrangements with relevant subcontractors and other service providers.

In knock-for-knock, each party is responsible for his own risks regarding sickness, death, and damage. Applying the knock-for-knock principle in contracts results in cost reductions when taking out insurance, especially for parties operating as subcontractors/service providers who cannot afford to run huge risks or pay high insurance premiums.

It avoids duplicating insurance costs by avoiding duplication in the cover needed.

Knock-for-knock arrangements are not only more efficient and less time-consuming, but they also lead to quick responses to compensate technical or human failures.

Box 19.3. Knock-for-knock clause from the "SUPPLYTIME 89" uniform time charter party for offshore service vessels.

12. Liabilities and indemnities

(a) *Owners*. —

Notwithstanding anything else contained in this Charter Party excepting Clauses 5(c)(iii), 7(b), 8(b), 12(g), 15(c) and 21, the Charterers shall not be responsible for loss of or damage to the property of the Owners or of their contractors and subcontractors, including the Vessel, or for personal injury or death of the employees of the Owners or of their contractors and subcontractors, arising out of or in any way connected with the performance of this Charter Party, even if such loss, damage, injury or death is caused wholly or partially by the act, neglect, or default of the Charterers, their employees, contractors or subcontractors, and even if such loss, damage, injury or death is caused wholly or partially by unseaworthiness of any vessel; and the Owners shall indemnify, protect, defend and hold harmless the Charterers from any and against all claims, costs, expenses, actions, proceedings, suits, demands and liabilities whatsoever arising out of or in connection with such loss, damage, personal injury or death.

(b) *Charterers*. —

Notwithstanding anything else contained in this Charter Party excepting Clause 21, the Owners shall not be responsible for loss of, damage to, or any liability arising out of anything towed by the Vessel, any cargo laden upon or carried by the Vessel or her tow, the property of the Charterers or of their contractors and subcontractors, including their offshore units, or for personal injury or death of the employees of the Charterers or of their contractors and subcontractors (other than the Owners and their contractors and subcontractors) or of anyone on board anything towed by the Vessel, arising out of or in any way connected with the performance of this Charter Party, even if such loss, damage, liability, injury or death is caused wholly or partially by the act, neglect or default of the Owners, their employees, contractors or subcontractors, and even if such loss, damage, liability, injury or death is caused wholly or partially by the unseaworthiness of any vessel; and the Charterers

(*Continued*)

Box 19.3. (*Continued*)

shall indemnify, protect, defend and hold harmless the Owners from any and against all claims, costs, expenses, actions, proceedings, suits, demands, and liabilities whatsoever arising out of or in connection with such loss, damage, liability, personal injury or death.

(c) *Consequential Damages*. —

Neither party shall be liable to the other for, and each party hereby agrees to protect, defend and indemnify the other against, any consequential damages whatsoever arising out of or in connection with the performance or non-performance of this Charter Party, including, but not limited to, loss of use, loss of profits, shut-in or loss of production and cost of insurance.

(d) *Limitations*. —

Nothing contained in this Charter Party shall be construed or held to deprive the Owners or the Charterers, as against any person or party, including as against each other, of any right to claim limitation of liability provided by any applicable law, statute or convention, save that nothing in this Charter Party shall create any right to limit liability. Where the Owners or the Charterers may seek an indemnity under the provisions of this Charter Party or against each other in respect of a claim brought by a third party, the Owners or the Charterers shall seek to limit their liability against such third party.

(e) *Himalaya Clause*. —

(i) All exceptions, exemptions, defences, immunities, limitations of liability, indemnities, privileges and conditions granted or provided by this Charter Party or by any applicable statute, rule or regulation for the benefit of the Charterers shall also apply to and be for the benefit of the Charterers' parent, affiliated, related and subsidiary companies; the Charterers' contractors, subcontractors, clients, joint venturers and joint interest owners (always with respect to the job or project on which the Vessel is employed); their respective employees and their respective underwriters.

(*Continued*)

Box 19.3. (*Continued*)

(ii) All exceptions, exemptions, defences, immunities, limitations of liability, indemnities, privileges and conditions granted or provided by this Charter Party or by any applicable statute, rule or regulation for the benefit of the Owners shall also apply to and be for the benefit of the Owners' parent, affiliated, related and subsidiary companies, the Owners' subcontractors, the Vessel, its Master, Officers and Crew, its registered owner, its operator, its demise charterer(s), their respective employees and their respective underwriters.

Chapter 20

Disasters, Damage and Public Investigations

20.1. Case — The collapsed roofs in the Netherlands

In November 2005, several roofs in the eastern region of the Netherlands collapsed due to heavy snowfall. Investigations showed that the heavy snowfall was only a minor cause in most cases. In 15 cases, design errors were the cause of the damage, in four cases construction work had not been executed properly and in five cases the buildings concerned were found to be correct. There was only one building where just the snow load and nothing else had caused the damage. On one other collapsed roof, the snow load was a contributing factor apart from construction errors.[1] The official report mentioned that some hundred buildings were damaged. What is remarkable is the fact that, on some buildings that did not suffer from the abnormal weather situation, the snow loads exceeded the prescribed safety factors, but the roofs were not damaged.[2]

In 2002, heavy rain had the same effect on some hundred roofs with large surfaces. These incidents were investigated systematically by the authorities. Here, the inspections resulted in identical conclusions. The technical guidelines and regulations in general had been followed. However, the design, the execution during construction on site and the maintenance were found to be major causes of the damages.[3]

---

[1] E. J. Kool and T. H. Schmidt, Investigation Report Construction damages due to heavy snow load, www.dakweb.nl/roofs/2006-9/page11.html, January 21, 2013.

[2] VROM inspection — Damages in constructions due to heavy snow load, November 26 and 27, 2005, http://www. Darkweb.nl/roofs/2006-8/RH8-PO8-11.pdf, January 21, 2013.

[3] E. J. Kool and W. P. P. Kloneer, VROM inspection of light flat roofs, VROM distribution number 17056/177, http://www.toitdak.be/instorten/overzicht%20lezingen.htm, January 21, 2013.

In this chapter we will discuss the effects of serious accidents and disasters in the construction industry. We will spend a few paragraphs on the problem of causality.[4] What happened exactly when disaster struck? What was the damage and how was the damage caused? We will discuss different theories regarding causality, both from a technical and legal point of view. Our discussion will make clear that the view of the engineer essentially differs from the view of the lawyer. However, we will argue that society benefits most if both views are combined when analyzing causes and effects of disasters. In some cases, damage from disasters cannot be attributed to one single cause.

20.2. Disasters and public investigations

Disasters are subject to high-interest media coverage. They are often front-page news. The public authorities need to investigate disasters in order to determine the exact causes of the damage, in order to be able to develop preventive measures. Formal investigations also make for hot news. The snowfall, respectively, and the heavy rainfall in the first instance, may lead to conclusions that these are to be considered as acts of God; something that happens according to natural occurrences, where no one can be held responsible, just like the weather, which comes and goes.[5] However, in both cases, that was not the situation. In general, the authorities want to know the exact cause of the damage for three reasons:

- Is someone to blame? Did someone violate applicable rules and regulations during design and construction of the project? Should someone be taken to court, due to the infringement of public law?
- Are the prevailing rules and regulations still adequate for the actual climatic conditions? If not, should they be altered and in what way?
- Is the inspection system that is in place still sufficient for timely detection of faulty construction practices? Does it need improvement or correction in order to better serve the public's interest in the future?

In the event a contractor would have been in default, or in case of infringement of public regulations, such investigations may be used to prove the relevant legal facts.

---

[4]See Chapter 18 for causality theories at law and clauses on *force majeure* in standard contracts.

[5]*Force majeure* is explained in Chapter 21.

20.3. Safety built into construction works — public rules and regulations

In every construction work, a contractor wants to exclude any risk leading to damage. In construction works and when contracting for complex technology, contractors aim to avoid or minimize risks. This starts already when designing technical installations or buildings. We calculate forces on beams and pillars. We specify profiles that are much too strong for their function in the construction, normally four or five times too strong. Classification societies specify minimum dimensions in their construction tables, as do national regulating authorities. Safety systems include redundancies. Implementing two altimeters in airplanes is normal practice; two altimeters are much safer than one. Feeder pumps in chemical plants have bypasses — if one pump is out of order the other will take over. In hospitals, emergency electricity generators are on standby continuously. In order to live up to the public rules and regulations, buffer safety is implemented into the permanent works.

It is not only to the satisfaction of the authorities that we like some extra safety. We calculate beforehand how a certain construction — for instance, a bridge — during the work might incorporate weaker spots and we carefully cover the risks by all kinds of preventive actions and measures. For our computers, we apply power supplies which can overcome the interruption of electricity. We foresee the unforeseen. It is useful. We permanently try to prevent damages. Consequently, many potential risks and damages never occur, because we always have built in sufficient safety measures. That may cost some extra work and money; however, it is certain that in the long run we are happier with this practice.

During execution of a project we take all kinds of safety measures on site. It is compulsory because of the legal requirements, but contractors have their own safety rules above those. In respecting these regulations, the execution of the work will run more smoothly than if we ignore them.

20.4. Learning from damages and disasters

We regularly learn. We learn from incidents, misfortunes and accidents. We investigate after a disaster and we try to avoid such disasters in the future.[6] We study carefully what went wrong. We analyze technical data of collapsed buildings, platforms and bridges; we ask questions, such as "what went

[6] See Chapter 1 for a discussion of the effects of the BP oil spill.

wrong" and "why"? [7] Why do constructions collapse? We find a few reasons, such as aging of materials, natural causes, acts of God, human intervention and mistakes, lack of communication between parties, errors, and flaws in design, execution, operation and during maintenance. Sometimes the regulations were ineffective, which means that these are constantly revised. It is done in good faith. We regularly make progress.

We come together with colleagues and openly admit that we made mistakes of all kinds. These faults are not always restricted to technical omissions. We may have failed to communicate on site with a great number of parties, subcontractors, sub-subcontractors, service providers, suppliers and vendors.

In some parts of the US, landslides may strike the local population, destroying or seriously damaging houses, roads, and infrastructural works, and killing people. The US Department of the Interior and the US Geological Survey systematically study the occurrences and investigate the causes. The object of the studies is to learn from previous disasters in order to better prevent future ones. Emergency alert systems were developed. In practice it appears to be difficult to predict disasters like landslides and earthquakes. Figure 20.1 shows the impact of a landslide close to San Pedro, near Los Angeles, California. Here the question may arise: was this an Act of God or was the damage caused by a design failure or faults during the execution of the contract? We have to assess the relationship between cause and effect in order to find out who is liable for the damage.

In Maastricht, a balcony crashed down from an apartment building. As a consequence two people died. The responsible contractor admitted before a group of construction experts and competent authorities that this could happen in a project where, apart from the Dutch architect, two Spanish architects were involved, while different design engineers worked on the floors, the isocurves and the balconies. The variations that were introduced during the project execution phase were insufficiently communicated to all parties involved. The responsible architect was convicted by a criminal court for death by negligence. The construction company ended up in bankruptcy due to the train of consequences.

After the oil spill disaster in the Gulf of Mexico in April 2011, all events were analyzed and measures were taken to prevent such disasters from ever happening again.[8] When the Twin Towers of the World Trade Center (WTC) in New York collapsed, a specialist in damages on buildings immediately

[7] F. van Herwijnen (2009), *Learning from Disasters*. Zoetermeer: Bouwen met Staal.

[8] See Chapter 1.

Figure 20.1. Landslide near San Pedro, California, on November 21, 2011. Rain exacerbated a slow-moving landslide that left large crevices on a road along the coast. The road broke into pieces that crumbled into gaping holes, while other sections fell into the ocean below. (Photo: USGS: US Geological Survey, www.gallery.usgs.gov/afv2YLk885/large/san_pedro_landslide_knabe.jpg.)

started investigations to find out why both buildings completely collapsed in such a short time after the airplanes crashed into them.

Since the Middle Ages, we have used accidents in order to learn something from them (see Box 20.1).

20.5. Complexity of many simultaneous causes

Damages very seldom arise from one cause only. It is important to distinguish between various kinds of causes. Note that this categorization is different from the one that we presented when discussing causality.[9]

Adequate causes

Adequate causes are those factors that most immediately and proximately caused the damage, that most directly led to the circumstances underlying the damage; or that allowed the occurrence to happen, which caused the damage.

[9]See Chapter 18, Section 18.5.

Box 20.1. Damaged buildings and bridges from a historical perspective.

Cathedral of Beauvais, Beauvais, France, 1284
Dee Bridge, Chester, England, 1847
Tay Bridge, Dundee, Scotland, 1863
Birsbruecke, Munchenstein, Switzerland, 1891
Quebec Bridge, Quebec, Canada, 1907 and 1916
Tacoma Narrows Bridge, Washington, United States, 1940
Second Narrows Bridge, Vancouver, Canada, 1958
Silver Bridge, Point Pleasant, United States, 1967
High-rise flats, Ronan Point, London, England, 1968
Congress Hall, Berlin, Germany, 1970
Hartford Civic Center Arena, Hartford, United States, 1978
Kemper Arena, Kansas City, United States, 1979
Hotel Hyatt Regency, Kansas City, United States, 1981
Schoharie Creek Bridge, Fort Hunter, United States, 1987
Koror–Babelthuap Bridge, Palau, 1996
Millennium Bridge, London, England, 2000
Twin Towers, New York, United States, 2001
Theater Het Park, Hoorn, the Netherlands, 2001
Parking roof, Hotel van der Valk, Tiel, the Netherlands, 2002
Balcony, Living Center Patio Sevilla, Maastricht, the Netherlands, 2003
Terminal 2E, Airport Charles de Gaulle, Roissy-en-France, France, 2004
Gallery Students Apartments, Lent, the Netherlands, 2005
Skating Stadion, Bad Reichenhall, Germany, 2006
Stairs Oudegracht, Utrecht, the Netherlands, 2006
Saint Anthony Falls Bridge, Minneapolis, United States, 2007
Building under construction, Rotterdam Center, the Netherlands, 2010
Town Archives, Koln, Germany, 2011

These factors may be specific events or conditions that existed when executing the construction works. For instance: in a situation where a dimensionally unstable steel support leads to a weak resistance to wind force, the question arises: "who made the error?" Was it the designer in making the drawings and the specifications, or was it the construction company who pre-worked the steel elements? Very often, more than one cause led to the weak resistance of a construction. Anyhow, the unstable steel support was considered to be the adequate cause, besides the extremely strong storm, which the construction should have resisted.[10]

Contributing causes

Contributing causes are those factors that alone would not have led to the damage. However, these causes were significant in contributing to the events or conditions that gave rise to the damage. Such causes need to be proven by presenting compelling evidence, which supports both the existence of the factor and its relationship to the occurrence or severity of the damage.

Possible contributing causes

Possible contributing causes are those factors that are considered to be of minor impact in terms of contributing to the damage; their role in the damage is rather weak or less compelling. However, there is some evidence that they might have contributed to the damage.

Why do we distinguish between these kinds of causes? The answer lies in the question whether a certain person or company involved in a disaster is completely liable for the full damage or only part of it, measured in financial terms. This technique of classifying causes of different character was applied by the Joint Investigation Team, which thoroughly studied the oil spill in the Gulf of Mexico (see Box 20.2). It helps to analyze which party was accountable for a certain cause. In this way it will help judges and solicitors to decide how the damages should be allocated among parties involved.

20.6. The Twin Towers in New York

The investigations into the most dramatic disaster in construction history did not try to find an answer to why the towers caught fire. The most important question was: "Why did the towers, shortly after they had been hit by the planes, collapse so quickly?" The first tower collapsed 50 minutes after being hit by the first airplane, while the second one took more time: one hour and 40 minutes. All experts now believe that it was not the hit by the airplanes, but the fire that destroyed the towers in such a short time. Besides the official reports, there is a supplementary theory, which is not officially confirmed, saying that at the time of the collapse explosions took place in the cellar and the lower floor. But the question remains: "Why did both towers collapse so quickly? What were the real causes?"

---

[10]Proximate cause is synonymous to adequate cause.

Box 20.2. Identifying three kinds of causes.

In Chapter 1, we described how the investigating authorities sharply denounced BP's risk management in relation to the oil rig. All possible causes were listed. In analyzing all causes, they were classified into the categories: a) causes of the failure, b) contributing causes and c) possible contributing causes. As an example, we mention the causes behind the failing cement barrier underneath the seabed.

The Joint Investigation Team (JIT) of the USCG and the BOEMRE classified the various causes that were identified in the investigation of the disaster with the Deepwater Horizon in the Gulf of Mexico in April 2011.[11] Conclusions on Well Design, Cementing, and Flow Path were made:

A. Causes of the Failure of the Cement Barrier

- Combinations of contamination, over displacement, and/or possibly nitrogen breakout of the shoe cement were causes of the blow out.
- Contamination or nitrogen breakout did not affect zonal isolation in the annulus.

B. Contributing Causes of the Cement Barrier Failure

- The decision to set the production casing in a laminated sand-shale zone in the vicinity of a hydrocarbon interval was a contributing cause of the blow out.
- With the known losses experienced in the well, BP's failure to take additional precautions, such as establishing additional barriers during cementing, was a contributing cause of the blow out.
- BP and Halliburton's failure to perform the production casing cement job in accordance with industry-accepted recommendations as defined in API RP 65 was a contributing cause of the blow out.
- BP's decision to set the float collar across the hydrocarbon-bearing zones of interest, instead of at the bottom of the shoe, was a contributing cause of the blow out.
- BP's failure to inform the parties operating on its behalf of all known risks associated with Macondo well operations was a contributing cause of the blow out.
- BP's failure to appropriately analyze and evaluate risks associated with the Macondo well in connection with its decision-making

(*Continued*)

[11] See Chapter 1.

Box 20.2. (*Continued*)

during the days leading up to the blow out was a contributing cause of the blow out.

- BP's failure to place cement on top of the wiper plug was a contributing cause of the blow out.

C. Possible Contributing Causes of the Cement Barrier Failure

- BP's decision to use a float collar that was not sufficiently debris-tolerant was a possible contributing cause of the blow out.
- BP's decision to set casing in the production interval with known drilling margin limits at total depth was a possible contributing cause of the blow out.
- The fact that the Deepwater Horizon crew did not have available to them accurate and reliable flow-line sensors during cementing operations in order to determine whether they were obtaining full returns was a possible contributing cause of the blow out.
- BP's and Halliburton's planning and conducting the Macondo production casing cement job were possible contributing causes of the blow out.
- The failure of BP's well site leaders and the Transocean Deepwater Horizon rig crew to recognize the risks associated with these multiple problems that occurred between April 19 and April 20 was a possible contributing cause of the blow out.[12]

In designing the towers in 1966, the architect and the contractor were faced with the challenge of how to build such a high building with contemporary building technology. The solution they found was to build in steel. Instead of constructing the usual box of bricks, they chose to erect vertical tubing. The core structure of the Twin Towers existed of a closely-boarded fence with about 250 vertical beams, which created the four sides of the towers (see Figure 20.2).

Only small windows were possible between the beams: a good idea for office workers with acrophobia. This framework could withstand wind speeds of 160 km per hour. In the middle of each tower, a column of steel was provided where the elevators and staircases were located. The thick outside steel

[12] Bureau of Ocean Energy Management, Conclusions on Well Design, Cementing, and Flow Path, Regulation and Enforcement, Report regarding the causes of the April 20, 2011 Macondo well blow out, September 14, 2011, pp. 68–74.

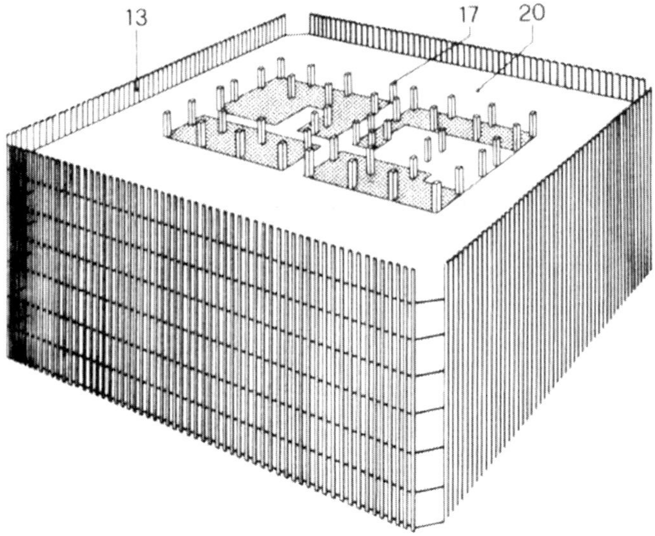

Figure 20.2. Design of the Twin Towers in New York. The outer closely-boarded fence with vertical beams carries half the weight of each floor; the remainder of the weight rests on the central construction. (Photo by US Geological Survey, http://911research.wtc7.net/wtc/evidence/photos/docs/enr.knucles_above_deck_s.jpg.)

walls would carry half of the weight of the 111 concrete floors, the other half resting on the central column.

When the airplanes hit the towers, the outward vertical fences were damaged. Many beams crashed, but the towers stayed in position. The upper floors did not move. Apparently, the safety features that had been built in during the design were holding up. The towers appeared to be capable of withstanding a plane.

However, what was not foreseen is that the wings of the two airplanes, which shortly before the collapse were filled up with 90,000 liters of kerosene each, were pushed into three floors. The kerosene caught fire immediately. A normal office fire will result in an 800 °C heat wave at maximum; here the temperature must have been over 1100 °C (see Figure 20.3). The most probable theory states that the floor beams began to melt, whereupon the concrete fell down in pieces on the underlying floors; after that the central column began to melt, resulting in a situation where the weight of the upper floors was too heavy to be carried any more. Those floors came down. The upper 30 floors came down on the underlying 80 floors. The construction

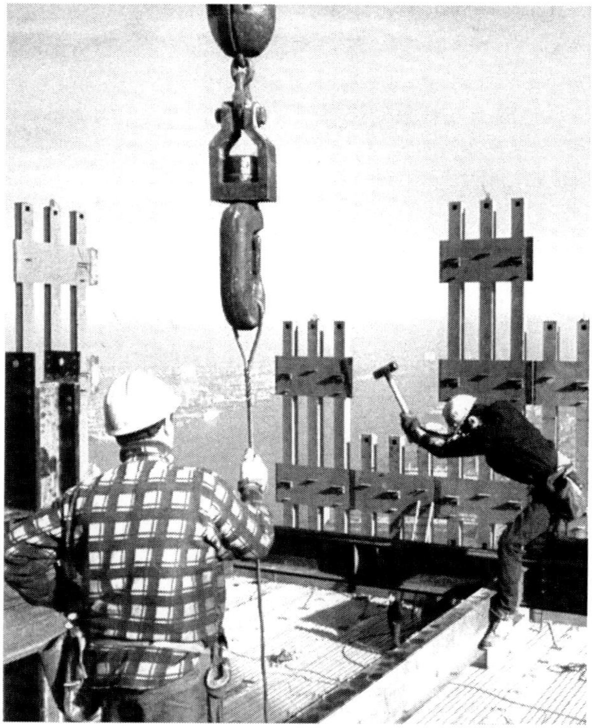

Figure 20.3. Part of the outside wall under construction. (Photo: NIST, National Institute, www.nist.gov/el/disasterstudies/wtc/index/cfm and http://wtcdata.nist.gov/gallery2/d/336400-1/fig-2-7_30.jpg.)

could not withstand this enormous weight. The collapse of these floors in both towers lasted about nine seconds.

Some of the conclusions as officially reported by the US investigation authorities are mentioned in Box 20.3.

Severe disasters may result in new regulations. We mention some of them:

- Fire brigades have to understand that you cannot fight some fires.
- On upper floors more space has to be reserved to allow people to escape. The need for special escape routes has to be foreseen, and they should be protected by extra layers of insulation, which can stand high temperatures for some time.
- More fire-resistant materials have to be developed. Beams have to be thicker and, in combination with other materials, should be able to better withstand earthquakes and fires.

Box 20.3. Causes of the collapse of the Twin Towers (WTC 1 and WTC 2).

Based on its comprehensive investigation, NIST[13] concluded that the WTC towers collapsed due to the impact of the planes on support columns, dislodging the fireproof insulation coating the steel floor trusses and steel columns, and widely dispersing jet fuel over multiple floors, and the subsequent unusually large volume of jet fuel igniting multifloor fires (which reached temperatures as high as 1,100 °C, or 1,800 °F), significantly weakening the floors and columns with dislodged fireproofing to the point where floors sagged and pulled inward on the perimeter columns.

This led to the inward bending of the perimeter columns and failure of the south face of WTC 1 and the east face of WTC 2, initiating the collapse of each of the towers. Both photographic and video evidence — as well as accounts from the New York City Police Department aviation unit during a half-hour period prior to collapse — support this sequence for each tower (see Figure 20.4).[14]

The architect of the Twin Towers, Les Robertson, does not agree that regulations should be made stricter. He states that the best way to avoid this type of disaster is not to fly into skyscrapers with airplanes; that is all.

20.7. The legal importance of distinguishing different causes

The neighbors were enjoying their barbecue. Suddenly they heard a crash. After the cloud of dust had disappeared, they found out that the farmer's barn had collapsed spontaneously. How come? What could have been the cause? Was it a bird that danced too enthusiastically on the roof, or a hungry nest of woodworms whose lunch festivities appeared fatal? We will never know. The only thing we know is that in the last two hundred years, not a single penny was spent on maintenance. Looking for a cause, we probably

[13] NIST was the investigating society for this disaster.

[14] http://www.nist.gov/el/disasterstudi..._wtctowers.cfm, January 21, 2013.

Figure 20.4. The second hit at the Twin Towers. (Photo: US Geological Survey, http://911research.wtc7.net/wtc/evidence/photos/impacts.html.)

would have to choose between old age of the barn and its lack of maintenance.

After investigations by the local police, it was found that the front wall fell down first. That caused the support of the roof at that end of the barn to fall away. The front part of the roof collapsed, taking the complete roof and building with it.

Now suppose that a man put his bicycle against the wall of the barn exactly at the moment the wall fell down. It is obvious that putting a bicycle against the wall could not have caused the wall to collapse. Therefore, no one will argue that the man with the bicycle could be sued for the collapse of the barn.

It may be different in the event a motor car had slightly touched the barn at the moment of collapse. A car is a heavy object; it is not the first time that a house has been damaged by a car. But investigations will show that a motor

Figure 20.5. Suddenly collapsed barn, due to unknown adequate cause. During the past two hundred years, the barn suffered from bad maintenance. (Source: http://www.grenois.com/buurschuur.)

car could not, under normal circumstances, have caused this havoc. The situation becomes different again in the event a truck touched the barn exactly at the moment of collapse. Certainly, in the event the truck was heavily loaded, the police would in the first instance hold the driver — and with the driver the transport company (that is what strict liability means) — accountable for the "accident". The farmer would have an argument to recover the cost of rebuilding the barn, and could see an opportunity to get some money for the necessary reconstruction. It may be non-ethical and conflicting with the rules of good faith in society, but, in practice, it may be that such accidents can be used to obtain compensation of damages, even though they may not be the exact cause.

In court, the farmer would have real and acceptable arguments: "Your honor, my opponent pretends that my barn was in a bad condition due to lack of maintenance. But even if that is true, it stayed upright for 200 years. Now this truck driver came by and touched — I would say he not only 'touched', but firmly hit the front wall — and it suddenly collapsed." So what is the real cause?

The general condition of the barn was so bad that it represented the "real" adequate cause of the collapse. In the event a truck touched the barn at the moment of the collapse, the truck driver could have been held responsible for the accident, where at the same time the maintenance situation of the barn could have been considered as a Possible Contributing Cause or a Contributing Cause. Depending upon the opinion of neutral experts, the farmer could have a real chance getting some money out of the situation.

20.8. Holding the offender accountable in civil law and public law

In practice, there are always several causes when damages occur. In the construction industry it appears to be difficult to determine the amount of the damage that has to be attributed to each party involved. In civil law, we have to translate errors of various parties into amounts of money. The party that suffers the damage can claim financial compensation from the party that caused it. The latter is liable. More often than not, the claiming party has a hand in one of the various causes himself. Things become complicated at that moment. How parties have to deal with such situations depends on the specifics of the case itself. It depends, amongst others, upon:

- The type of contract involved.
- The text of the contract itself.
- Whether the damage is done to a contract party or to a third party with whom no contractual relationship exists.
- The public regulations applicable to the specific case.
- The legal system underlying the contract.
- The legal system related to the place where the damages occurred.
- Other circumstances.

Under public law, a competent authority may start an investigation into a disaster. The aim of the public investigation is to determine whether a person or company is guilty of a violation of the law or any construction regulation. In the event of death and severe injuries, even criminal prosecution is possible. Also, in this context, it is important to know exactly which theories will be applicable to the case and how various kinds of causes may differ in terms of severity. In international construction there is never only one cause of a disastrous event. The victim himself may have contributed to one or more causes, the regulations may have been outdated; there are a great number of possibilities. There is no standard rule for the many, many different situations that may occur.

20.9. Conclusions

In this chapter, we learned that public investigations should serve the public interest. The authorities investigate whether the regulations were respected, whether these are still up-to-date or whether they need to be reviewed and whether the inspections were carried out properly during actual construction.

Regulations relate to issues like health, safety and environment. Usually, redundancy is built into the design construction, operation and maintenance of assets.

Extra safety in design, construction and during execution, even if this is not required by regulations, may cost a little more, but eliminates big troubles later on. With the help of public investigations in analyzing disasters, the construction industry continuously gains experience and knowledge.

In the construction industry, damage is never due to only one cause. Causes may be classified based upon their character, i.e. be categorized into adequate causes to disasters, contributing causes and possible contributing causes. This categorization is useful to get an idea of how an offender should be judged.

Where several causes occur there is always a human temptation to have the full burden of consequences to be loaded on one person or company only. That is not always fair and ethical, but it happens. Good insight in causes and theory about causality is useful in practice.

Chapter 21

Force Majeure

21.1. Case — The loose pontoons

The contractor worked on a project for the maintenance, raising and lengthening of a great number of fascine dams at the salt meadows on the coast of the Netherlands for a period of 36 months. The total contract price amounted to €2,247,000, excluding VAT. The work started on April 1, 2003 and was planned to be completed on March 31, 2006. The employer wished to have the inner dykes storm-safe before the storm season started, that is, November 1, 2003. In the scope of work, it was mentioned that this date was of the essence in the time schedule. The contractor was behind schedule and had to speed up work by putting more manpower and equipment into the works. Unfortunately, during stormy weather, two of the contractor's pontoons came loose from their anchors and ended up in a vulnerable salt marsh area. The fact that the pontoons got loose was considered a default by the employer. Damages were claimed and the contract was dissolved unilaterally by the employer. Before the court of arbitration the contractor claimed *force majeure*, because of the unexpected storm.

The arbitrators investigated in more detail how this could happen. It appeared that these pontoons were fastened by one anchor only, one steel cable or anchor chain and an extendable cable. This happened to be insufficient for safeguarding the pontoons. The arbitrators were of the opinion that the contractor neither claimed, nor proved that the storm was of such unexpected heavy force that the contractor reasonably could not have taken sufficient measures against it. The claim for *force majeure* was not honored.[1]

---

[1] Court of Arbitration for the Building Industry, January 8, 2004, No. 26.187, Firma K. vof — State of the Netherlands.

Hundreds of reasons for force majeure

When reading decisions of the Dutch arbitration court for the construction industry, one can easily get the impression that claims for *force majeure* in arbitration cases are as normal as a glass of beer in a bar in town. Contractors claim *force majeure* for many reasons. Here are some of the arguments given:

- Custom authorities needed too much time when importing building materials.
- National strike in building industry, while contractor fell behind schedule.
- The contractor was awaiting the employer's data. Data was not issued in time and the contractor was not in a position to speed up.
- The contractor was dependent upon the help of third parties, which did not come in time.
- The contractor claimed two weeks late completion because of *force majeure* due to two weeks longer sailing time of the ship carrying building materials from the Chinese supplier; the ship had to deviate from its course due to the Iraq war, and go around South Africa's Cape.
- Inclement weather according to the contractor's general conditions, applicable to the contract.
- Incoming rains in building, which was not yet completely covered; damage due to excessive rainfall.
- The contractor's only construction engineer was ill for seven working days.
- Too many variation orders.
- Very bad communication with the surveying engineer appointed by the employer.
- The employer provided items too late at the building site.
- No connection to the public electricity grid, which hindered completion.
- Leakage after completion not repaired in time due to dependency upon foreign supplier of coating materials.
- One lost day due to testing of building crane.
- Bankruptcy of regular supplier and missing isolating windows — needed extra procurement period for replacing supplier.
- Execution of brick work impossible due to lack of brick workers in extremely tight labor market.
- Tender arriving too late at the employer's premises due to fault at post office.
- Heavy rain during roof construction.
- Heavy pressure of ground water, leading to leakages in cellar.

- Broken fresh water supply system, not in control of the contractor.
- Damage in sewage system.

Contractors are inventive in finding reasons for *force majeure*. It must be said that Dutch arbitrators, in general, are not very willing to honor the wide variety of excuses in their arbitration decisions. Only in very few cases is an appeal on *force majeure* successful in the Dutch arbitration court for the building industry. The court is very reserved on this matter. Where claims were approved in a few cases, the motivation was always extensive, as if the case was very specific and particular.

21.2. What is *force majeure* in international contracting?

Force majeure in international contracting is a delay in fulfilling a contractual obligation of one of the parties to a construction contract, which was:

- Reasonably unforeseeable at the moment of concluding the contract.
- Outside the control of the party invoking *force majeure*.
- Not at the risk of the party invoking it.
- Not to be overcome by the party who invokes the *force majeure*.[2]

The effect of this definition is that only a few items of the above-mentioned list are considered as *force majeure* in the international construction business. The arguments listed in Box 21.1 will usually not count.

Box 21.1. Occurrences that generally will not be considered as *force majeure*.

Customs authorities needed too much time when importing building materials.	Contractor's materials are not outside contractor's control.
Contractor was awaiting employer's data — an investment firm did not issue them in time, contractor not in a position to speed up.	Not outside control of party invoked.

(*Continued*)

[2]Compare Unidroit Principles of International Commercial Contracts, article 7.1.7; Principles of European Contract Law (PECL), article 3.108; the Convention on the International Sale of Goods, article 79.1; the Vienna Treaty, Vienna, 1970.

Box 21.1. (*Continued*)

Contractor dependent upon the help of third parties, which did not come in time.	Helping parties are under contractor's control.
Contractor claims two weeks late completion because of *force majeure* due to two weeks longer sailing time of ship carrying building materials from Chinese supplier; the ship had to deviate from its course due to the Iraq war and sail round South Africa's Cape.	Contractor's materials are under contractor's control.[3]
Inclement weather according to contractor's general conditions, applicable to the contract.	This may be or may not be *force majeure*.
Incoming rains in building, which was not yet completely covered; damage due to excessive rainfall.	Protection against rain is under contractor's control.[4]
Contractor's only construction engineer was ill for seven working days.	Contractor's personnel are under contractor's control.
Too many variation orders.	Not outside control of parties.
Very bad communication with surveying engineer appointed by employer.	Not outside control of parties.
Employer provided items too late at building site.	Under employer's control.
No connection to the public electricity grid, which hindered completion.	Contractor responsible for timely request.
Leakage after completion not repaired in time due to dependency upon foreign supplier of coating materials.	Care for suppliers is under contractor's control.
One lost day due to testing of building crane.	Testing not outside control of contractor
Bankruptcy of regular supplier and missing isolating windows — needed extra procurement period for replacing supplier.	Suppliers under contractor's control.

(*Continued*)

[3] In some contracts provisions for consequences of war between countries are foreseen. Often this is earmarked as *force majeure*.

[4] Some contracts leave room for *force majeure* in case the rain was outside all historical statistical data.

Box 21.1. (*Continued*)

Execution of brick work impossible due to lack of brick workers in extremely tight labor market.	Tight labor market foreseeable at time of conclusion of the contract.
Tender arriving too late at employer's premises due to fault at post office.	Dispatch of tender is at contractor's risk.
Heavy rain during roof construction.	May be or may not be *force majeure*.
Heavy pressure of ground water, leading to leakages in cellar.	Under contractor's control.
Broken fresh water supply system, not under control of contractor.	Possibly *force majeure* depending upon details of breakage.
Damage in sewage system.	If sewage system is part of scope of work then no *force majeure*.

21.3. Some definitions from standard contracts

FIDIC blue book on dredging and land reclamation

> "Force Majeure" means an exceptional event or circumstance which is beyond a Party's control; which such Party could not reasonably have provided against before entering into the Contract; which, having arisen, such Party could not reasonably have avoided or overcome; and, which is not substantially attributable to the other Party.[5]

The four elements of our first definition are materially present in this definition. Under the FIDIC blue book, *force majeure* is one of the defined risks.[6] These risks have particular consequences, as described in this standard contract. The notes for guidance mention a few examples of events that could be considered as *force majeure*. Note that such events will not be considered *force majeure* in all cases. The original requirements from the definition have to be fulfilled.

[5]FIDIC blue book, definition 1.1.16.

[6]FIDIC blue book, clause 6.

"Force Majeure" may include, but is not limited to, exceptional events or circumstances of the kind listed below so long as all of the four conditions stated in the definition have been satisfied:

a) War, hostilities (whether war be declared or not), invasion, act of foreign enemies,
b) Rebellion, terrorism, revolution, insurrection, military or usurped power, or civil war,
c) Riot, commotion, disorder, strike or lockout by persons other than the Contractor's and his subcontractors' personnel,
d) Munitions of war, explosive materials, ionizing radiation or contamination by radioactivity, except as may be attributable to the Contractor's use of such munitions, explosives, radiation or radioactivity, and
e) Natural catastrophes such as earthquake, hurricane, typhoon or volcanic activity.[7]

The FIDIC red, yellow and silver books contain exactly the same wording. Here, the above-mentioned words in the notes for guidance of the blue book are part of the contract text.[8] The FIDIC subcontract does not mention the list; it simply states that provisions of the main contract shall apply to the subcontract.[9]

LOGIC standard contracts

The LOGIC Construction and Marine Construction standards define *force majeure* as well. Elements of the definition are:

- Beyond control.
- Without fault or negligence.
- Unable to provide against the hindrance.[10]
- Above these, the party that is or may be delayed shall use all reasonable endeavors to remedy the situation.[11]

LOGIC standard contracts relate to lateness. They mention a list of events that constitute *force majeure*. This list is exclusive. *Only* the following

[7] FIDIC blue book, definition 1.1.16.
[8] FIDIC red, yellow, silver books, article 19.1.
[9] FIDIC subcontract for construction, clause 18.
[10] LOGIC Construction and Marine Construction, clause 15.1.
[11] LOGIC Construction and Marine Construction, clause 5.3.

occurrences shall be *force majeure.*[12] The list includes similar events as mentioned by FIDIC. However, there are differences. LOGIC occurrences include:

- War, riots, invasion, act of foreign enemies, hostilities, civil war, etc.
- Ionizing radiations, contaminations, etc.
- Earthquakes, flood, fire, explosions, i.e. natural disasters, etc.
- Strikes at national or regional level, etc.
- Maritime or aviation disasters.
- Changes in law, etc.

Under LOGIC, an occurrence may be considered as *force majeure* where exactly the same occurrence under FIDIC would possibly not lead to *force majeure.* LOGIC Construction and Marine Construction do not mention the unforeseeability of the occurrence. In the event the law or the regulations are changed, consequently the contractor may wait for the change before notifying the employer of the *force majeure* situation. LOGIC in general does not stipulate anticipating activities. FIDIC does.

LOGIC Mobile Drilling Rig standard — the former CRINE contract

Elements of the FIDIC norm are part of the *force majeure* clause: beyond control of the parties, without fault or negligence and unable to provide against. Above that, the same limitation of concurrencies is listed.[13]

CMM contract for the Oil and Gas Industry 1992

The definition for *force majeure* under the CMM contract is stated in a different way than under FIDIC and LOGIC; however, the same four elements of the international doctrine are present here. Under this contract we do not find a list of examples as under FIDIC, neither a list such as that under LOGIC contracts.

The CMM definition is a little bit stricter. This is the standard that lists occurrences that *under no circumstances* will be judged as *force majeure.* These are (a) breakdown of any item, equipment, engine, plant, machinery;

---

[12] LOGIC Construction, 2003, clause 15.2 and LOGIC Marine Construction, 2004, clause 15.2.

[13] LOGIC Mobile Drilling Rig, former CRINE standard, 1997, clauses 12.1 and 12.2.

(b) commitments that limit the ability of a party to perform its obligations;
(c) inclement weather.[14]

This standard contract was written for the benefit of employers, contractors and subcontractors, who, in general, were operating on the Dutch part of the continental shelf. It is understandable that bad weather will not qualify as *force majeure*. On the North Sea, inclement weather is normal from October to March each and every year. Why should bad weather be considered unforeseeable? Next, a party is never excused from timely or good execution of its work due to a heavy workload, which it accepted itself. A good portfolio management of orders at hand is compulsory, is it not?

Comparing the three above standards, a *force majeure* occurrence is an exception.

Norwegian fabrication contract

The Norwegians do not define *force majeure* under their standard. The contract says what should happen and under which procedures the notifications should follow: each party shall carry its own costs. When the employer invokes *force majeure*, it will be considered as suspension of the contract and a price revision must follow. The contract schedule must be adapted. After a certain defined time lapse, there is an option to abandon the contract.[15] But what *force majeure* exactly represents is not described. That is not necessary either. Norwegian law is the standard system. In Scandinavian civil law, the *force majeure* subject is sufficiently clear.

Dutch UAV 1989/2012

Under UAV 1989 and UAV 2012, *force majeure* refers to completion. The two clauses on *force majeure* at completion refer to later completion[16] and discounts (read penalties) on late completion.[17] One may get the impression that under UAV 1989/2012 *force majeure* only has to do with completion. However, this is not the case. The standard legal system is the law of the Netherlands, which has ample rules and jurisprudence on risk allocation.

[14] CMM standard contract, clause 44.1 and 44.2.
[15] Norwegian Fabrication Contract, 1992, clause 28.
[16] UAV 1989, clause 8.4; UAV 2012 clause 8.5.
[17] UAV 1989 and UAV 2012, clause 42.3.

21.4. *Force majeure* in the Netherlands' law

Since 1992, the Dutch Civil Code Book has not contained clauses about *force majeure*. Now Dutch law considers whether a person or company is to blame or not to blame when they did not comply with a legal duty or a commitment under a contract. One is in default, but one has an excuse. The law says it in three steps. First, after a failure in the performance of an obligation one must repair the damage. Second, if the default cannot be repaired the damage must be compensated. Third, one cannot be held accountable in case one was legally or physically not in the position to perform.

> Every failure in the performance of an obligation obliges the debtor to repair the damage which the creditor suffers there from, unless the failure cannot be imputed to the debtor.[18] To the extent that performance is not already permanently impossible, paragraph 1 only applies subject to the provision of paragraph 2 respecting the default of the debtor.[19] A failure in the performance cannot be imputed to the debtor if it does not result from his fault, and if he cannot be held accountable for it by law, juridical act or common opinion either.[20]

In what cases the debtor cannot be held accountable are not defined by the legislator. It is all up to how the courts feel that a party should be held accountable, or not, for not fulfilling a legal (contractual) duty. In general, it is hard to get *force majeure* acknowledged before Dutch courts. The key word is not guilt, not negligence, but accountability. Mind that the word "hindrance" or "impediment" is missing.[21] In surrounding countries — with the exception of the UK, which is a case in itself — the word hindrance is always the key word.

In 1968 the hoisting of an airplane wing resulted in damage due to a broken bolt on the crane that was used. The damage was considered not attributable to the crane owner. Here, the High Court of the Netherlands also introduced the possibility of insuring the operation as a possible indication regarding which party had to carry the risk of the damage. Box 21.2 describes the situation as it happened, without mentioning the overall general norms. Compare the figures. If you hire a crane for Fl 17.50 per hour, could you expect that the risk of the damage, over Fl 100,000, should be the crane owner's responsibility?

---

[18] Civil code book, article 6: 74.1.

[19] Civil code book, article 6: 74.2; Paragraph 2 refers to the procedure by which the debtor has to be put into default by his counterparty.

[20] Civil code book, article 6: 75.

[21] For reasons why, see J. J. Nieuwenhuis *et al* (1994). *Text and Comments Civil Code Book.* Deventer: Kluwer Law and Taxation Publishers, article 74.2.

Comparing the two cases on hoisting cranes

In the event of *force majeure*, the losses that result from the damage will have to be covered by the party suffering the damage. Consequently, the damage has to be carried by the party suffering the damage. *Force majeure* allocates risks between parties. It is interesting to compare the two cases mentioned in Box 21.2 and Box 21.3 and list their similarities and their differences. Why, in the first case of the airplane wing, was the damage not attributed to the service provider, while in the second case, the service provider, who had to mount the crane, had to carry the losses?

Box 21.2. The service provider hoisting the airplane wing.

In the early 1960s, aircraft manufacturer Fokker contracted a crane owner to lift a ready-made wing, produced by a subcontractor for a Fokker airplane, from a pontoon, and to put it on a special truck. The truck would further transport the wing to the works. During hoisting, a crucial bolt on the crane broke; the wing fell down and was seriously damaged. The rate for hiring the crane was Fl 17.50 per hour. The cost of the wing amounted to approximately Fl 117,000. The crane owner rendered a service, which should have resulted in bringing the wing safely on the truck. The reason why the bolt broke exactly at the moment that a precious wing was hanging in the cables was never found out. There was no negligence in the procurement of the crane. There was no backlog in maintenance. The inspection certificates were correct. The crane's condition had been verified before hoisting. This really looked like an act of God. No one could foresee the event — no one could have helped. The High Court considered that in such a situation it could happen that the service provider is not accountable for the damage, particularly where the failure of the crane resulted in damage of such a high sum of money that — compared with the cost of hiring — it would be unreasonable to have the risk of the damage borne by the crane owner. Furthermore, the possibility that such a risk could have been covered by insurance, could be an indication that such risk according to general public opinion should not be attributed to the service provider's account.[22]

[22]Free to HR January 5, 1968, NJ 1968, 102, nt GJS, AA p. 441, nt Koster, Fokker vliegtuigvleugel. Related article, Civil code book, 6: 77.

Box 21.3. The broken crane cable.

Van Dijk purchased a second-hand Liebherr crane from Van der Spek. After delivery, Van der Spek was responsible for the maintenance of the crane. Two years later, Van Dijk asked Van der Spek to dismantle the crane, to re-allocate it and to re-build it on an industrial park in the village of Bruinisse. During that operation the hoisting and lowering cable of the crane broke. Thereupon the crane fell down, resulting in material damage of Fl 48,000. The real cause was never found. Van Dijk's insurance company, who had to hold harmless its client Van Dijk, sued Van der Spek for that sum. Van der Spek defended itself as unaccountable because of *force majeure*. The considerations of the High Court were as follows:

> The agreement about dismantling and remounting of the crane was an agreement that should result in a certain effect. That circumstance is not sufficient to hold Van der Spek accountable for the damage in the event the occurrence should have been considered as *force majeure*.

However, according to the High Court, it was Van der Spek who had to state and to prove that a certain cause should not be his responsibility or that the circumstances of the case were such that they had excluded his accountability. Van der Spek just stated in court that he really had used his "best endeavors" and had done everything possible to bring the job to a good end. However, this should not preclude Van der Spek from being responsible for the breakage of the cable of a crane, as the maintenance of that crane was his duty for years. There was no *force majeure* for Van der Spek, who had to compensate Fl 48,000 to Van Dijk.[23]

Similarities are striking. Both cases are about hoisting cranes. In both cases a technical fault was at the root of the incident. In both cases the real cause was never found or explained — one could say that both damages were caused by an act of God. In both cases no one was to blame. Both cases were decided in the same winter of 1968.[23]

The differences are striking as well. When hoisting the airplane wing, the remuneration was low and the risk relatively high compared to the

[23] HR February 23, 1968, NJ 1968,103, nt GJS, van Dijk vs. van der Spek.

remuneration. The service provider did not arrange for insurance, but we know that Fokker had the operation insured, as this was mentioned in the verdict. That means that Fokker took the risk of damage into account. In the other case, while mounting the hoisting crane in Bruinisse, a regular maintenance contract between the owner of the crane and the service provider existed. This maintenance contract had already lasted for two years. You may assume that a firm that contracted the maintenance of the crane is a specialist on cranes and has more technical knowledge about cranes than the contractor, who is the user only. The service provider, who was responsible for the maintenance, could have covered these risks by arranging for an insurance policy and incorporating the premium into the maintenance price. It is reasonable that the risk in such a case should be the service provider's responsibility. The occurrence was outside his control, but the risk was not.

The case was discussed and disputed by legal experts, who were not all in agreement on the outcome. The lesson for contractors is that court decisions will always be disappointing for one of the parties. Either one party or the other will be held accountable for the risk. It is better to have the risks insured effectively, where maximum amounts are fixed in the policies. Such amounts are to be stated in the contracts with employers, with subcontractors, service providers, suppliers and vendors. It is more work to prepare a contract, but it is worthwhile.

21.5. *Force majeure* in English common law

English common law lacks a clear definition of *force majeure*. In common law contracts one often finds a list of possible occurrences that represent *force majeure*. This is identical to the LOGIC standard contracts. English legal textbooks are very brief on the subject, whereas in Belgium, France, Germany and the Netherlands, *force majeure* is an extensive subject in the legal profession.

The first case about *force majeure* dates from 1647. To fight invaders and to fight the resulting civil war, Prince Rupert and his troops occupied a building. For a number of years, the building was not accessible to the regular tenant, who thereupon refused to pay the rent to the owner. When sued before the court, the tenant defended himself by claiming *force majeure*, which was refused by the court. According to the court, *force majeure* may hinder the fulfilling of a legal obligation but not when it is a contractual obligation.[24] Implicitly, the court stated that parties have to agree upon *force majeure* themselves when drawing up contracts. This is exactly what national English, as well as international, standard construction contracts do.

The English Standard Building Contract JCT contains clear *force majeure* clauses. The term *force majeure* has not been defined in this standard as was done in the FIDIC standards. According to Adam Williamson, this must be put down to the circumstance that references to the term are without qualification to interpret the clause.[25] JCT reverts to extension of time for completion of the contract in the case where a "Relevant Event" occurs.[26]

Under FIDIC contracts, a general norm is created by defining the term *force majeure*. The English JCT contract does not follow this construction. It lists a number of possible events. If these occur their consequences might be an extension of time or termination of the contract.

The NEC3 standard contract starts in a different way. There is a clause headed "Prevention".[27] The clause mentions a list of events that prevent the contractor from proceeding with the work, i.e. causing complete stoppage or making it impossible to meet the time schedule. At first glance, this clause gives the impression of being a *force majeure* clause; it is rather close to the FIDIC definition. However, it lacks the element of unforeseeability at the moment of entering into the contract. Instead, NEC3 relates to an event "that it would have been unreasonable for an experienced contractor to have allowed for [... and] that neither party could prevent".[28] This includes the employer. For the contractor, NEC3 is less strict than JCT.

English law has looked with little sympathy upon the contractor. The approach has been that he undertakes an absolute obligation to complete. If the works prove very difficult, or even impossible, to complete then that is the risk he has taken.[29]

---

[24] Paradyne vs. Jane, King's Bench (1647), Aleyn 26, 82, E. R. 897.

[25] A. Williamson, *Force Majeure* and Construction Contracts, Society of Construction Law, meeting, London, February 2012, www.scl.org.uk, January 23 2013.

[26] JCT Standard Building Contract, 2011, clauses 2.29.14 and 8.01.

[27] NEC3 Engineering and Construction Contract, clause 19.

[28] NEC3 Engineering and Construction Contract, clause 60.

[29] A. Williamson, *Force Majeure* and Construction Contracts, Society of Construction Law, meeting, London, February 2012, www.scl.org.uk, January 23 2013.

There are a few cases on the subject, but they are not clear. In one case on the sale of goods, the judge found that *force majeure* was an implied term.[30] In other cases, the terms were too vague, according to the judges' opinion.[31]

Here, a warning is in place when drafting a construction contract. The doctrine of *force majeure* is not clear in England. Common law is very flexible as far as the drafting of contracts is concerned. It is possible to draft a definition of *force majeure*, like the FIDIC models do, and to agree with your employer what will happen in the event of *force majeure*. If this wording is clear and complete, you do not need to go to court ever. In case of problems, you settle with your counterparty as agreed in your well-drafted contract.

Frustration

What happens in the event that parties in their contract do not mention anything about *force majeure*, and the contractor during execution is hindered in fulfilling one or more contractual obligations, which under FIDIC, would be qualified as *force majeure*? English law has developed a rather extensive doctrine about frustration. When the common object of the contract can no longer be achieved because, in light of the circumstances, a situation fundamentally different from that contemplated when the parties entered into the contract has unexpectedly emerged, the contract is at an end, for otherwise the parties would be bound to perform a contract which they did not make. A contract to perform something that is obviously impossible, e.g. to build a castle in the air, is void.[32] This may be said in other ways. Under the doctrine of frustration, a contract may be discharged if, after its formation, events occur making its performance impossible or illegal, and in certain analogous situations.[33] As long as it is possible to fulfill contractual obligations there is no frustration. Box 21.4 gives an example.

Where the continental doctrine of *force majeure* allocates risks under certain circumstances or to the employer or to the contractor, frustration under common law has the same effect. For the contractor it remains hard to have the risks concerned transferred to the employer and to have the extra costs reimbursed.[34]

---

[30] G. H. Treitel (1999), *The Law of Contract, 10th edition*. London: Sweet & Maxwell, pp. 297–298.

[31] G. H. Treitel (1999), *The Law of Contract, 10th edition*. London: Sweet & Maxwell, p. 47.

[32] C. M. Schmitthoff and D. G. Sarre (1984), *Mercantile Law, 14th edition*. London: Stevens & Sons, pp. 155–156.

[33] G. H. Treitel (1999), *The Law of Contract, 10th edition*. London: Sweet & Maxwell, p. 805.

[34] Davis Contractors Ltd vs. Fareham U.D.C., 1856, A. C. 696.

Box 21.4. No labor force available.

The contractors agreed to build 78 houses for a local authority in eight months for £84,000. Because of labor shortages, the work took 22 months and cost the contractors £115,000. They claimed that the contract had been frustrated and that they therefore were entitled to extra remuneration. The House of Lords rejected the claim, as the events that caused the delays were within the ordinary range of circumstances.

> It is not hardship or inconvenience or material loss itself which calls the principle of frustration into play. There must be as well such a change in the signification of the obligation that the thing undertaken would, if performed, be a different thing from that contracted for.[34]

21.6. Consequences of *force majeure*

All standard construction contracts have clauses about the consequences of a *force majeure* occurrence. They may deal with the accountability of one of the parties; they also may arrange that the time schedule will be extended. It is also possible to terminate the contract in the event the *force majeure* situation cannot be resolved within a reasonable period of time. In order to prevent any disputes, it is recommended that parties in concert with each other discuss the consequences of the possible damages, losses and lost proceeds due to eventual *force majeure*. A separate protocol may be drafted, which can be tailor-made and dedicated to the foreseen risk. In the Caribbean a hurricane is not an exception. In Haiti an earthquake may occur. The contractor must bring as much redundancy into his works that he will overcome natural disasters. However, during construction, it may happen that at certain stages of the project a natural disaster will occur. Here a Disaster Protocol may be very useful.

In practice, it is very hard to be compensated for extra costs if *force majeure* occurs. When tendering, contractors should identify all potential risks related to the tender documents. The potential *force majeure* situations especially should be noted. Those risks may be discussed and negotiated before coming to final terms. It might be helpful to exchange views with the potential employer on the issue.

21.7. The Hurricane Protocol

Pictures of beautiful blue seas in tropical areas may suggest romantic holidays. The contractor who builds constructions in areas where hurricanes are common is not in a position to claim *force majeure* when a hurricane destroys part of the work or the complete works. A hurricane is not an unforeseen disaster. After tendering and when negotiating with the employer, it is wise to foresee what could happen in case such a disaster strikes.

Defense against hurricanes is not simple. Wind forces of up to 200 km per hour are possible. In a few minutes complete buildings can be destroyed. Figures 21.1 and 21.2 show damage after the violence of Hurricane Katrina in 2005. The house was destroyed completely; the trees in the background were uprooted. It is possible to build in a hurricane-resistant way. Figure 21.3 shows a hurricane-proof quay with two jetties. The most dangerous hurricane risk lies in the period during execution of the contract on site. It is impossible to overcome or to prevent all damages. But risks can be reduced.

A protocol may be drafted in order to reach a useful disaster schedule, so that parties know what each party should do and not do in such a situation. The foreseen activities can be much wider than the clauses in the standard construction contracts. In fact, such contracts give definitions of *force majeure* and regulate the legal results of the *force majeure* event. Protective initiatives and protective measures are not mentioned.

It is a good thing to be prepared together with the employer. After all, a hurricane brings damages to both parties. You cannot prevent the wind

Figure 21.1. New Orleans, September 20, 2005. Sections of the eastern span of a causeway slid off their moorings and into the lake due to the winds and waters of Hurricane Katrina. (Photo: Win Henderson, Federal Emergency Management Agency (FEMA).)

Figure 21.2. Empire, LA, October 25, 2005. The bridge was closed for almost 60 days after Hurricane Katrina came through the area. Damage to the causeway shown in Figure 21.1 could not be prevented or overcome. (Photo: Robert Kaufmann, Federal Emergency Management Agency (FEMA).)

Figure 21.3. Hurricane-proof and *force-majeure* proof quays and jetties in the Caribbean. (Photo: Ballast Nedam, Nieuwegein, the Netherlands.)

from blowing, but you can defend your employer and yourself as much as possible. What could be planned beforehand is suggested in Box 21.5.

The activities in Box 21.5 are suggestions only. The list should be tailored to the project in question. Note that deviations from the standard construction contracts for the consequences of *force majeure* are possible.

Box 21.5. Possible preventive actions in case of operations in hurricane areas.

- The planning schedule should be fixed in such a way that the most vulnerable activities of the execution will not take place in the hurricane season. Certain activities will not be started in the hurricane season.
- Agree beforehand that normal storms with wind velocity less severe than hurricanes are at the contractor's risk.
- During execution, parties have the obligation to listen to the daily weather forecasts of the local radio and television stations and those of the local Coast Guard.
- Install a disaster team, with leading members of both parties and, if possible, a representative of local competent authorities. Such a team could, for instance, consist of: a representative of the employer and his deputy, the engineer and his deputy, the project manager of the contractor and his deputy, the safety officer, if available, police and/or fire brigade and first aid service. The team may be installed when signing the contract. Around that time, members should come together and exchange data.
- Follow the international color codes for hurricane categories as broadcasted daily:
    - Green: no threat.
    - Yellow: hurricane active, estimate direction and schedule on approximately five days or more away from the works.
    - Orange: hurricane forecast to arrive in the area (define area in numbers of kilometers around the works) between three and five days.
    - Red: hurricane expected in less than two to three days and forecast to pass area
    - Pink: hurricane follows track within the area.

(*Continued*)

Box 21.5. (*Continued*)

- Define activities during various phases:
    - Yellow: all construction activities suspended; disaster team will meet at least on a daily basis.
    - Orange: identify rescue activities that should take place.
    - Red: demobilize and secure equipment, tools and materials.
    - Pink: secure all staff.
- Define damages:
    - Demobilize and secure equipment, tools and materials on the site.
    - Remove and replace non-connected or insufficiently connected materials and components of permanent works from the site.
    - Working time lost by staff unable to get to work during the hurricane.
    - Damage to non-completed parts of the works due to wind, rain and water masses.
    - Damage to completed parts of the works.
    - Cost of delays caused by hurricane, and accelerations to make up for defense against hurricane.
    - Costs of remobilization and cost increases for speeding up time schedule.
- Agreement on costs:
    - Specification of costs to be borne by the employer.
    - Specification of costs to be borne by the contractor.
    - Agree that damages and re-work at contractor's side will be compensated by a variation order.
- Agree on the regular insurance policies and which party has to take out such insurances, and which party has to submit the relevant claims:
    - Verify whether the regular CAR insurance will cover hurricane damages and up to what amount — verify the same for the offices, workshops and equipment.
    - If necessary — according to employer and contractor — take out on-top insurance for the works.
- Agree that a revised planning schedule will be made up after the hurricane.

Figure 21.4. Earthquake-damaged building in Calexico, California, on June 18, 2010, after a 7.2 magnitude earthquake. (Photo: Adam DuBrowa, FEMA Photo Library.)

It is not always possible to prevent all effects of natural disasters in the construction industry. In 2010 a heavy earthquake shook the rigidly well-constructed building of the United States Port Authority in Calexico, California. Notwithstanding the rigid construction, some setting of a part of the outer wall occurred as shown in Figure 21.4. In such an event it is doubtful whether the architect, the design engineer, or the contractor could have prevented the damage. After investigation by the authorities and careful reading of their reports, in most cases some room for arbitrary judgment will remain.

21.8. Conclusions

Contractors often use the term *force majeure* when they run late, where according to laws and contracts this is not justified.

The effect of *force majeure* is that damage is not attributable to a party that was claimed to be liable. *Force majeure* is a legal construction to allocate a certain risk to a certain party. Which party is best situated to reasonably carry the risk involved is the key question when considering future *force majeure* situations.

In general, it is very difficult to be compensated for extra costs when *force majeure* occurs. Clear and extensive contract clauses on *force majeure* are indispensable in any international construction contract. If you have to perform a project in an area that is subject to natural disasters, it is recommended to negotiate and to explicitly state the potential risks and damages and to agree how these will be allocated among all project partners.

Inclement weather in general is no reason to claim *force majeure*. The only way to minimize the risk involved is to build some slack into the planning schedule or to contractually transfer such risk to another party.

In certain areas of the world, tsunamis, earthquakes and hurricanes are foreseeable — in such events, contractors in concert with their employers should take defensive measures to overcome the effects of such natural phenomenon. Actions may be prepared to prevent damage as much as possible. As far as prevention is not possible, the relevant risk may be insured.

Chapter 22

Bribery

22.1. Case — The happy man

Today is Friday. Today, Nicassio is a happy man. This is his first success in getting some more money. He started last Monday as "general facility assistant" at Swania Harbor Facilities for Construction Works Ltd. This is a new company. He finally had a boss again, after all those years of finding food on a day-by-day basis. When he started work, he had received a reasonable advance payment. That had been used to pay part of the outstanding hospital bill, which was urgent, because if the family did not pay that bill, the hospital would definitely refuse any further treatment for his mother.

Mother was the big problem for months. She could not look after the children. She was in bed most of the day, complaining about pain, sickness and nausea. She took expensive medicines, which consumed a great deal of what there was of the budget. Nicassio had pressed his brother and his two sisters for help, without great success. After that he had addressed his uncle Serge; Nicassio's mother was his sister, wasn't she? So the uncle was responsible, that was clear. He should support the whole family, bearing in mind that he had a brilliant position at the Ministry, a sunny house and even a car. The meeting with his uncle was disappointing, but promising at the same time. Uncle Serge argued that he had completely financed the hospital, the long-lasting illness and the funeral of his own mother, Nicassio's grandmother. So now Nicassio should take responsibility for his mother. Uncle Serge gave him the name of a white man, working near the bay in a temporary office with electricity and air conditioning. That man needed a facility assistant. Uncle Serge prepared a work license with official stamps of the Ministry and a written recommendation.

"You go there, you say that you come on behalf of me. If they accept you as an assistant, you accept any salary they propose. The white man will be your boss. There is a chance that this will go on for 21 or 23 months, as long as the construction of the new port facilities will take, maybe longer. But do not disappoint your family. You do everything they ask you to do, you will do the shopping, you have to take messages to other offices, you have to clean cars, you do it, even if they order you to do women's work like hoovering, making coffee and cleaning the pantry. And don't cheat them, do not steal money, they will fire you, blaming me. Good luck."

The white man had smiled, looked at him and accepted. That was last Friday. Monday was Nicassio's first working day. Very soon the first opportunity came. Nicassio had to go to the customs clearance with three bills of Swania $100[1] and an envelope containing papers, like a Bill of Lading and a request for a certificate of import. It was for two containers, arriving from abroad for International Flexible Contractors, a foreign company, which was going to make a new harbor in the bay. The custom officer had recognized Nicassio. They attended the same school in their youth; they played soccer together. They were acquainted. That made things easier. The customs officer had explained that there were extra costs for urgent handling. So the import license would be Swania $150. Nicassio handed over $200. The officer had no change.

"We will leave it like that," he said.

Nicassio asked: "OK, can I have a receipt?"

The officer answered: "Of course you can; here it is," and handed over a receipt on which was written $67.50 for customs clearance.

When Nicassio went back to the office, the white man asked: "How much was that?"

"Three hundred," Nicassio answered.

"Sounds reasonable," the white man said. "You have to sign the cash transaction here."

Nicassio signed. He did not hand over the official receipt of $67.50.

Today is Friday. Today Nicassio is a happy man. This is his first success in getting some more money. Soon his mother would be better again. She could look after the children again. The future was bright and promising.

22.2. Bribery and corruption

Bribery has a long history. There is also corruption, which is operationally defined as the misuse of entrusted power for private gain. According to the World Bank, corruption sabotages policies and programs that aim to reduce poverty. So attacking corruption is critical to poverty reduction. Corruption

[1] Swania $5 equals approximately US $1.

occurs when organizations or individuals, in their activities, profit improperly through their position and thereby cause damage or loss. Most often, public officers are involved. The community trusts public officers to perform their duties with honesty and in the best interest of the public. Corruption involves breaching public trust.

Corruption is very costly for business. It is estimated that the extra financial costs of doing business is about 10% in many parts of the world. The World Bank stated that bribery has become a $1 trillion industry. Note the word "industry". It implies that there are professional underground organizations that make a living from the proceeds of bribery as a business.

Corruption is found in all countries. It is particularly widespread where the legal system is weak, and where the public administration is not (yet?) well developed. Corruption blossoms where temptation co-exists with permissiveness; where institutional checks and balances on power are missing; where decision-making remains obscure; where great inequalities in the distribution of wealth condemn people to live in poverty; where integrity of public procurement is ignored.[2]

Greed, self-interest, the wish to be rich without doing anything, the ambition of less-qualified persons, and avarice are the main causes. Persons in power who are responsible for good governance and keeping the organs of state and the society free from corruption are themselves mostly greedy, selfish, corrupt and incompetent. This is why it is really difficult to combat or eliminate corruption.[3]

Fraud concerns all dishonest actions, also those that are away from public power. In Case 22.1, the "white man" misuses his power in closing his eyes to the bribery committed by Nicassio. He is not entrusted with public power, but with private power, entrusted by the (top) management of International Flexible Contractors, his employer.

Bribery and fraud are committed "to get things done" in a way they should not be done, but where they may be realized "in another way". They serve the contractor to develop smooth operations and relationships, to serve (in)flexible time schedules, to circumvent the possible long-lasting effort and time-consuming methods required to follow the law as it is described. They are means to speed up operations for "a few dollars more", for which one receives immaterial benefit in return.

---

[2]Cited from the Guidelines of the Anti-Corruption Commission of Bangladesh, Dhaka, 2003, www.acc.org.bd, January 21, 2013.

[3]M. Shamsul Hague, Advocate, Supreme Court, Bangladesh. Anti-corruption mechanisms in Bangladesh, 2004, http://www.humanrights.asia/resources, January 21, 2013.

Bribery and fraud are committed by persons with private authority. The white man, being the representative of the contractor, bribed for the benefit of his company. Nicassio bribed for the benefit of his mother. Civil servants are being bribed. They may welcome the opportunity to have an extra income for their services. Especially in countries where the salaries of the civil servants are not always regularly paid, bribery may become normal practice. In such a situation it is a source of income for certain civil servants.

Bribery and fraud are even more serious acts when they are committed with only criminal intentions. All of these bribery actions result in inequalities in the distribution of wealth to the disadvantage of the persons who did not commit such criminal acts.

22.3. Analyzing the small bribe

We may guess why Nicassio comes to his actions. He is rather poor; his children need care. The hospital has to be paid for. Obviously, there is no public health service available unless he is able to pay for the hospital costs himself. Nicassio has no means to do so. We may guess that in Swania there is inequality in the distribution of national income, which goes together with poverty of the lower classes. Giving gifts and perks is part of family duties in Swania. That is what Nicassio asks for from his brother and sisters and from his Uncle Serge. It is not completely Nicassio's fault. In a way, he is a victim of the social reality.

We may feel a lot of sympathy for the poor Nicassio, who cares for his ill mother. But is he honest? We do not think so. He lied to the white man, his hierarchical chief. We may wonder how Nicassio considers the relation with the white man. Are there "chiefs" in Swania in the way we in the West see "chiefs"?

The customs clearance for two containers for International Flexible Contractors comprised four persons, who together were friends in crime. First of all is the customs officer, who keeps the $150 in return for a receipt of $67.50. The surplus is for him. Then Nicassio, who keeps $100 for himself for the benefit of his ill mother. Uncle Serge is a partner as well. Uncle Serge sees a welcome opportunity to escape from bribery himself. He feels obliged to help a sick member of the family — his sister — given the fact that in Swania family matters are important ethical, maybe even legal, obligations, while the burden of the hospital costs should be carried by the whole family. Uncle Serge sends his nephew to the white man. The application for the job is not transparent. There is not a clear procedure where the best candidate can be selected by the boss who needs the assistant. The white man and Uncle Serge are already familiar to each other, most probably for business reasons. If the case ever came before court, it would be very difficult to prove that Uncle Serge willfully recommended to Nicassio that he commit fraud. Still, Uncle Serge is corrupt: corruption involves the dishonest or preferential use of power resulting in one person or organization getting advantages over another.[4] Finally, we consider the white man's position. He did not commit the crime. But he is involved. He did not ask for a receipt. He asked for Nicassio's signature for the cash book. But, being his employer — or his boss — he should have been aware that bribery was in the air. Anyhow, all four are liable for fraud, the one a little bit more than the others.

22.4. The worldwide war against corruption

Legislation, accounting regulations, public information, anti-corruption policy by official authorities, influencing public opinions and stimulation of local economy are the instruments in the worldwide war against bribery. We will discuss some of them.

Treaties and legislation

First there are legal arrangements. Top-down there is a chain of legal conventions, treaties, laws, rules, regulations and recommendations with excellent intentions. The largest institution that has formulated conventions is the United Nations. In 2005, the UN entered into the globally-agreed United Nations Convention Against Corruption (UNCAC). A second instrument is the OECD[5] Convention on Combating Bribery of Foreign Public Officials in International Business Transactions, which was issued earlier, in 1997. Some 40 states signed the 1997 convention. They agreed to adopt legislation to criminalize bribery of foreign public officials as well as assist in prosecuting foreign bribery, providing for corporate liability and imposing proportionate and effective sanctions.

The International Accounting Standards (IAS) are applied all over the world. Listed companies, including banks and insurance companies, are obliged to prepare their consolidated accounts and annual reports in accordance with these standards. This implies that financial reports of each individual

---

[4]Definition of corruption by CPIB, Singapore, 2004. Other legislations have similar definitions.

[5]OECD: Organization for Economic Co-operation and Development.

contract and each individual project have to be in line with those standards. The standards contain ethical rules on integrity and corporate responsibility. In practice, this means that in case a project manager or contract manager acts in conflict with these standards, the board of management, specifically the CEO and the CFO, are held responsible and accountable for the fraud. To prevent such situations, most listed companies have systems to internally check and verify financial reports and records of projects. Consequently, in the event a project manager commits bribery or if he is connected with it, the top management of the company is not in a position to look the other way. Instead, it has the obligation to take corrective action, whatever that may be.

European level of actions against bribery and corruption

In Europe there are actually two conventions in force: the Criminal Law Convention on Corruption of the Council of Europe and the Civil Law Convention on Corruption of the Council of Europe.

In 2003, the European Commission addressed the Council, the European Parliament and the European Economic and Social Committee on a comprehensive EU policy against corruption.[6] The Commission installed the European Anti-Fraud Office (OLAF) and created the Investigation and Discipline Office (IDOC). Criminal laws in the member states should be aligned, as far as the opinion of the Commission is concerned. The Council of Europe created the Group of European States against Corruption (GRECO), which is responsible for evaluation of the impact of corruption in various states and member states of Europe. The European Commission sharpened its specific financing agreements and tender documents with a view to inserting anti-corruption clauses. The European Directives on Public Procurement contain many clauses, which were drafted to prevent bribery and corruption.

National level of crime fighting

We find considerable legislation against bribery in many countries in the world. More often than not, such legislation in foreign countries was issued

[6]European Commission, COM (2003) 317 final, not published in the Official Journal.

after pressure from the United Nations, but also after pressure from the World Bank when awarding a loan to a less-developed or a third-world country. The oldest legislation is found in England: its Statute of Frauds dates from 1677. Actually, on the topic of fraud and bribery, the world's legal systems are far away from each other. The laws are complex and diverse. The descriptions of the acts of offenders are different; the objectives of the respective legislators are also different. Corporate liability is not always considered to include acts of individuals; sanctions are sometimes limited to administrative measures; the offender has to pay a fine and that is it. Sometimes bribery acts are seen as criminal. The sentences vary — in China, individuals may be sentenced to death. In other countries, a symbolic fine is the most severe penalty.

Legislations may describe who can be prosecuted (companies and individuals), if offences committed abroad are inclusive or not; sometimes the role of foreign subsidiaries is targeted. A specific issue can be a bribe in the home country and not in a foreign country.

Much legislation is available in the state's own language; there are many English translations. For a good understanding, the help of a specialized lawyer, who is familiar with the international conventions as well as the criminal law of the respective country, is of the essence. Generally, diverse legislations are changing regularly and are becoming more stringent than ever before. When tendering for work in a foreign country it is useful to be aware of the bribery risks.

The USA

In the United States, a database is published of "big corruption deals". Extracts are published openly.[7] In the US, apart from the local prosecuters, there are two federal institutions active in the war against bribery: the US Department of Justice (DOJ), with whom, after having committed a bribe, a deal can be settled to prevent further prosecution by paying an enormous fine; and the Securities and Exchange Commission (SEC), with whom one may come to terms by paying a sum to escape from a civil complaint. To get an idea of the amounts involved, we are talking about sums between $5,000 and $200 million. If such fines are not accepted — that is a matter of the offender taking his chances — the case is brought before court.

[7]For instance, by the Saunders anticorruption blog: http://www.anticorruptionblog.com/, January 21, 2013.

There is a clear risk that the court will demand a much higher amount, plus a prison sentence. The cases are about funneling sums to government officials in order to receive benefits or to make life impossible for competitors, bribes to retain business in foreign countries, and facilitation payments to a foreign official, to a political party or to a party official with the intention to secure the performance of a governmental action. It is remarkable that various kinds of industries and important service providers, such as telephone companies and insurers, are involved.

The US Foreign Corrupt Practices Act (US FCPA, 1977) was the first statute that explicitly imposed liability on companies and executives who committed bribes in other countries. Top executives in the US were frightened to see themselves prosecuted for foreign operations of faraway subsidiaries or agencies, while they had not been aware of any misconduct of the referred persons. The act leads to improvement of control and accounting in all corners of the world. The act in the past has been enforced very aggressively by the extremely efficient American authorities, who have executive power which crosses borders where no one would expect.

22.5. The UK Bribery Act 2010

Since the 1970s, many initiatives have been developed in the UK, but the UK Bribery Act only came into force on July 1, 2011. This is the world's most stringent anti-bribery act ever; it is even stricter than the USA FCPA 1977 act.

There are persons who commit bribery;[8] there are persons who are bribed.[9] Both commit a crime, according to the new UK law. Bribery could potentially encompass issues such as contracts, non-monetary gifts and offers of employment. Being bribed is possible in:

> any function of a public nature; any activity connected with a business, trade or profession; any activity performed in the course of a person's employment; or any activity performed by or on behalf of a body of persons whether corporate or unincorporated.[10]

This applies to both private and public industry, and encompasses activities performed outside the UK, even activities with no link to the UK.

---

[8] Section 1 of the Act.
[9] Section 2 of the Act.
[10] Section 3 of the Act.

Bribery of foreign public officials is a distinct crime in line with the OECD Anti-Bribery Convention.[11] A person will be guilty of this offence if he promises, offers or gives a financial or other advantage to a foreign public official, either directly or through a third party, where such an advantage is not legitimately due. The inclusion of "through a third party" is intended to prevent the use of employees, agents or intermediaries to avoid direct involvement.

The new act applies to all commercial organizations — including the construction industry and the offshore business — which do business in the UK. This does not only apply to the organization itself; individuals and employees may also be guilty. The offence is one of strict liability.[12] This means that an organization cannot excuse itself by proving that there was no intention or even knowledge that someone was committing bribery in any way. The person in charge and the organization are guilty in any case.

The crime could have been committed anywhere. For a prosecution, the person must have a "close connection" to the UK, which includes being a British citizen, resident or protected person, or a company incorporated in the UK. As stated before, an organization is guilty of the offence if the bribery is carried out by an employee, an agent, a subsidiary or another third party. The location of the offender is irrelevant to the prosecution.[13]

Guidance notes were published by the Secretary of State of the UK. The guidance sets out six principles to be followed in doing business. They cover such topics as Proportionate Procedures, Top-level Commitment, Risk Assessment, Due Diligence, Communication (including training) and Monitoring & Review.[14] The one firm conclusion to be drawn from the guidance is that every commercial organization that might be subject to prosecution needs to have a code of conduct in place that appropriately reflects the guidance. This should ensure that all members of its personnel are fully aware of the risks and are adequately trained. If the company is then charged with the offence of failing to prevent bribery, it would be able to show evidence of the "adequate procedures", which it will need in order to defend itself. Hopefully! Penalties under the new UK law are not light. If an individual is found guilty of a bribery offence, he may be imprisoned for up to

---

[11] Section 6 of the Act.

[12] Section 14 of the Act.

[13] Following the analysis of D. Aaronberg and N. Higgins, who found that: "Therefore, a German business with retail outlets in the UK which pays a bribe in Spain could, in theory at least, face prosecution in the UK." *Archbold Review*, April 2011.

[14] Ministry of Justice, the Bribery Act, Guidance, March 2011.

12 months and fined up to £5,000 or — in some more specific and severe circumstances — face up to 10 years' imprisonment and an unlimited fine. The crime of a commercial organization of failing to prevent bribery is punishable by an unlimited fine. In addition, a convicted individual or organization may be subject to a confiscation order, while a company director who is convicted may be disqualified. Senior officers in a company that commits a general bribery offence will also be liable under the Act.[15]

22.6. Anti-corruption legislation in the Netherlands compared with the UK

In the Netherlands the legislation is clear and strict as well. Active bribery and passive bribery are criminal offences. Bribery outside the country is forbidden.[16] Directors and senior officers (read: the management, specifically the CEO and CFO of an affiliated company, a subsidiary or working group of the organization, including the project managers and the persons who assist them) are subject to prosecution in the Netherlands according to today's legislation. The punishment is heavier in the UK than in the Netherlands: prison terms are longer in England; amounts of fines in England are unlimited in a few cases. There are three remarkable differences, which make the UK law stricter.

First, the law's aggressive character and its far reach abroad. In the event a person commits bribery — it does not matter where in the world — in favor of the organization, the organization is liable. It is then possible that a (Dutch) company will be prosecuted in England in the event the organization has part of its activities carried out in the UK by a subsidiary. The claim will be "failure to prevent bribery", section 7 of the Bribery Act. Here, a stunning example is found: for instance, a company vested in the Netherlands, having activities in England and a subsidiary in a Baltic state, while an employee of that subsidiary on a business trip to Japan, offers a Belgian business partner the opportunity to generate business in Japan, using bribes for private benefits. The company in the Netherlands is liable under UK law.[17] In Dutch law, this is not the case.

Second, there is the explicit article on facilitation payments. These are small sums of money which may be spent abroad to smooth or to speed up

[15]The Bribery Act, section 14.4 (a).

[16]Dutch criminal code book, article 177–178; article 328–362.

[17]M. Vermey and E. Perez (2011), British Bribery Act: The end of the "facilitation payments"?, *Nederlands' Lawyers' Magazine*, February 11, 6, p. 366.

normal activities of public servants, which are common practice or normally tolerated in the foreign country. Formally, these payments are not excluded from liability by Dutch legislation; however, in practice, the prosecution policy is such that these are — within reasonable limits — permitted.[18]

Third, there is the heavy burden of proof that is put on the shoulders of all organizations with operations in the UK. The company should actively have introduced and maintained an anti-bribery policy. Top management should be involved in the introduction of such a policy, and there should be a clear code of conduct, available to all members of the personnel, but also to all intermediates, agents, helping hands, subcontractors, service providers, vendors and suppliers. Contracts should contain anti-bribery clauses. Regular, serious, training sessions should be organized, where the project managers and all persons active in commercial relations around projects and procurement should be trained. The burden of proof is on the prosecuted company. It should formally demonstrate that its anti-bribery system is excellent. The prosecution has nothing to prove in court about this issue. It can judge whether it thinks the policy of the defending organization is sufficient or not to prevent punishment. Under Dutch law, the necessity to provide the proof resides still with the prosecution. The UK legislation will result in a lot of work for company lawyers and the nominated compliance officers.

22.7. Diverse legislation and anti-corruption committees

In most countries anti-corruption legislation is part of criminal law. Even countries that are far down on the international bribery index have good legislation on the topic. In general, the legislation in itself is not bad at all. Often English translations are available. Mostly the laws are set up in a systematic way; for instance, they include definitions of acts and persons, the description of offences, punishments, criminal misconduct, investigations by public authorities, competent courts and so on. More often than not a special committee is formed, whose duty it is to investigate and to bring to court suspects of bribery. Those committees are called "anti-corruption commissions" or "anti-bribery committees", "anti-corruption agencies" or "anti-corruption bureaus". We found these commissions in the legislation in Andhra Pradesh, Canada, Hong Kong, India, Kenya, Malaysia, Mauritius,

[18]Directive on prosecution of corruption of public authorities abroad, Aanwijzing opsporing en vervolging ambtelijke corruptie in het buitenland, Ned. Stcrt, July 2, 2007, 24, p. 14.

Namibia, New South Wales, Sierra Leone, South Africa and many others. In South Africa there is a special court dedicated to bribery.

Beside such good legislation and paper work, in many countries information is available on how to fight against bribery and corruption. Such information may be a pamphlet or a booklet in simple and easy wording, which can be understood by the "man in the street" who is not acquainted with difficult legal language. Such booklets contain definitions of corruption and fraud, their dimensions, abuse of power, conflict of interests, abuse of privileged information, indications of suspected actions, information on how and where to "blow the whistle" (inform the public authorities) and the protection of whistleblowers. For organizations, a fraud prevention plan is explained.[19]

22.8. Business reality

On the one hand, we see extremely strict legislation, with the USA and recently the UK on top. In England, significant concerns have been raised, mainly that the new UK legislation may harm British industry's competitiveness in the global market. Some issues of the Act in the UK are ethically problematic but seen as legally permissible. It is problematic that a bribe by a person somewhere low in the organization of a faraway affiliate will have its repercussions in the board of directors, who are not aware of the offences. Other critics complain about the facilitation payments, which are no longer permitted. These are commonplace in many international jurisdictions. The neutral complaint about this legislation may be the question of whether English departments[20] and parliament really believe that this act will reduce bribery in the world.

Many people have serious doubts on the effectiveness of the various official Anti-Corruption Commissions, which are found throughout the world. It is clear that most of them are not as effective as intended on paper. More often than not, these commissions are found in poor countries, which are rather low on the bribery ladder. The reason might be that policy makers do not really wish to change the reality of regular bribery. Around a president and his political friends and families, a clan of important persons is formed in the center of the state's government. Politicians, public institutions, generals and private companies are linked tightly by relatives and family ties. A concentration of power is in operation. This clan is in a position to profit in a

---

[19]For instance, the South African booklet, Blow the whistle on fraud and corruption, 2002, 12 pages.

[20]For instance, the Department of Justice and the Foreign Office.

more favorable way from the national product than would be possible in a modern, open economy. It is in the interest of the clan to remain in power and to only admit persons with identical ideas on key positions to private companies, ministries and public services.

The diplomatic representatives of such countries are not in a position to refuse and not sign the international treaties on corruption. In the assemblies of the United Nations, no one is in a position to state that corruption is not evil. Consequently, such regimes issue legislation in order to show the world that they behave correctly. But it is window dressing to satisfy donors who finance infrastructure, and international banks who give loans.

For reforms, a law is a beginning only. To be effective the law needs a well-equipped ministry of justice with competent prosecution officers and personnel, while the (criminal) police services should be of A-one standard. Those institutions may be officially present, but if no budget for their services is available, or if the people in key positions are part of the clan, no result in reducing bribes will be realized.

Reducing bribery is not always in the interest of the majority of the state's own public servants. A good working anti-bribery system may hinder its own operations. Anti-bribery commissions are often used to eliminate political opposition and critical individuals who openly question members of the central government. In a country where bribery is an essential element of the reigning powers, it is possible to use the anti-bribery legislation if a member of the clan is too ambitious for his own career, or if he is quarreling with people in high ranks. He is accused of bribery — which is always correct, because everyone in the clan uses the same techniques for their own benefit and the members know that about each other — and condemned to a long prison sentence, where in the newspapers the hot news is spelled out for the public. The World Bank studies the issue regularly and knows better.[21] The reform process is slow. It is difficult to fight bribery.

Individual tender documents

Now, contracts presented by employers with their invitation to tender very often contain anti-corruption clauses. A more formal and strict way of dealing with this is the signing of an anti-corruption acknowledgment statement. This is a model paper, drafted by the (future) employer, which has to be signed by the contractor before entering negotiations. Box 22.1 gives an example.

[21] J. R. Heilbrunn (2007), Anti-Corruption commissions, Panacea or Real Medicine to Fight Corruption?, World Bank Institute.

Box 22.1. Anti-corruption acknowledgment.

The Contractor hereby warrants, undertakes and represents that it has not paid, agreed to pay, promised to pay, authorized the payment of or caused to be paid directly or indirectly in any form whatsoever any commission, percentage, contingent fee, brokerage, gift, of the Employer's affiliate or person, any entity in the State of Qatar or elsewhere, in order to cause the Employer to select the Contractor for the provision of Work or to influence the negotiation of the Agreement between the Contractor and the Employer or to ensure better terms for the benefit of the Contractor.

22.9. How to operate in a faraway country

For the international construction industry the issue remains dangerous. It is impossible to deny all reality and behave 100% correctly in all corners of the world. In traffic, the maximum speed is respected. Yet, going a few kilometers faster than permitted is not always noticed by the police. Besides, there is a small official margin before being penalized. You have to be informed. You have to know the "rules" as they are in practice. That differs from country to country. The investigation to get hold of the relevant information should start even before tendering. It is important to find out how "things are settled" in the referred country. One of the first orientations is the bribery ladder, to be found on the Internet. www.cyborlinks.com gives information about many countries and regions, including the Geert Hofstede Information Website. www.international-business-conter.com mentions behavior and etiquette in many countries, including the Hofstede Analyses. www.transparency.org furnishes information mainly on bribery in various countries, and countries that pay bribes to get a hold on international business. Information available at a national ministry of Trade and Industry is helpful.[22] Plus there are private institutions.[23] Commercial banks have local sources of financial details.

22.10. Conclusions

All project managers abroad know about bribery. All project managers have to deal with it. There is an international war against bribery and corruption

[22] In the Netherlands, the EVD (*Economische Voorlichting Dienst*), department of the Ministry of Economic Affairs, keeps records of foreign countries.

[23] Tropeninstituut Amsterdam.

going on. The laws are becoming stricter. Everyone should be alert when working in a foreign country. All European legal systems include anti-corruption regulations. The strictest legislations are those of the USA and the UK.

In the event a corporation has business relations in the UK, while bribery is committed anywhere else in the world, the corporation is at risk of being sued under the new UK law. It is now necessary to be informed about a corporation's bribery policy. Facility payments are not (yet) prosecuted in many countries. However, it is possible that top managers may adapt the corporation's policy, and the personnel working on a project in a faraway country should be informed.

Chapter 23

Dispute Resolution Mechanisms

23.1. Case — A different time schedule

The plaintiffs, building contractors, submitted to the Leicestershire County Council a tender for the construction of a school, in which they offered to complete the work in 18 months. The council replied "accepting" the tender and forwarded the contract documents. In these documents they specified, for their own benefit and not that of the contractor, the completion period at 30 months, instead of the 18 months referred to in the tender. The contractor executed the contract without noticing this change in the contract period. The officers of the county council realized that the contractor was mistaken about the contract period. There is a direct relationship between the price and the contract period, and if the contractor had made its tender on the basis of a 30-month period, the price would have been higher.[1]

Reading the case, we may understand that the contractor could have two different arguments to ask for extra payments. Firstly, the contractor could have insisted on payment after the completion of the work at 18 months. This most probably was refused by the employer, who was only prepared to pay after 30 months, some 12 months later. Neither was the employer prepared to pay interest for late payment, as we would suppose. We have to bear in mind that interest rates in the early 1960s amounted to 7–9% per annum.

The judge argued that the parties did not have a common intent with regard to the completion time of the project. The judge said that the correct contract period was 30 months (first principle). Secondly, the judge stated that a party (the contractor) was entitled to rectification of this period (30 months to 18 months, second principle). The contractor, in order to be entitled to this

[1] Roberts & Co. Ltd (contractor) vs. Leicestershire County Council, 1961, Ch. 555; [1961] 2 W.L.R. 1000; [1961] 2 All E.R. 545.

change, should demonstrate (read: should prove before court) that the reason why this did not happen — or could not happen — was due to the dishonest conduct of the county council, being the employer.

In fact, the contractor's argument was insufficient to convince the judge that the contract was an 18-month contract. The judge added:

> If, on the other hand, the principle is rested on fraud, obviously dishonesty must be established. It is well established that a party claiming rectification must prove his facts beyond reasonable doubt, and I think this high standard of proof must equally apply where the claim is based on the (second, JP) principle indicated above.

To summarize: in the event the contractor could have proven that the changed contract period was based on fraud, he would have won the case.

The case illustrates the mentality of the judge. The judge adds that honesty is a thing of ethical value, which must be protected by the law. This case is remarkable for a few reasons. It is strange that after a tender the employer (here, the county council) issued contract documents. What kind of documents were those? Could a contractor prepare for a tender without knowing what contract will be applied? Apparently, the contractor's tender documents were not complete. Why did the contractor not notice the change of the completion time? Was the contract actually read and scrutinized by the contractor? Contracts are established between parties through offer and acceptance. When the county council replied, in fact, it made a new offer that needed to be accepted by the contractor. The judge said nothing about that. The judge seemed to argue that it would have been the contractor's duty to amend the contract of 30 months back into a contract at 18 months. It remains unclear at what moment the contractor discovered that the completion time was changed into a 30-month period. Did the contractor do so after 18 months? The verdict does not include details about payment installments, nor about planning details, such as any room for maneuver in the time schedule.

It is questionable whether the same case before a different judge in a different legal system would result in the same verdict. We have our doubts. Sometimes the outcome of a court's decision is difficult to understand. In this chapter we discover why cases in legal systems that are not familiar to us at first glance may seem strange, compared to our way of reasoning.

Therefore we will discuss dispute resolution in its various forms in this chapter. Parties may go to court or appeal on arbitration. However, there are many other ways to deal with disputes.

23.2. What to do when you are summoned to court

You go to court because you are summoned by someone else. That may be a party with whom you have or had a contract. However, it may also be a third party who suffered from an unlawful action from your side. It may be a public prosecutor, who was informed by an official authority, responsible for following up rules and regulations, that you violated the law.

There is another reason why you may go to court, and that is if you want to sue someone else. You do so if discussions to solve a dispute have been in vain. It is far better to avoid courts whenever you can. Or still better, to prevent situations that may expose you to a court case.

Box 23.1 describes how an official letter was delivered at a contractor's head office, after which the project manager had to give details about a previous project.

Being summoned to court is inconvenient. A court case is complicated, time consuming and takes a lot of effort that is not in line with our regular activities. Each case is different from all previous cases, so we never gain a certain routine in court matters. That is different for the professionals, such as judges and prosecutors, solicitors, lawyers and bailiffs for whom court cases are their way of life.

Joe thought about the case with the unwilling Building Technology plc. The project concerned a complex of architect-designed modern buildings. The facades had complicated forms, were prestigious and had different coatings such as handmade brickwork in different colors and special stone plates, which were attached mainly by bolts and nuts, but at some places by means of a chemical adhesive. Building Technology presented a very competitive quote, the reason why this firm got the order for this extensive subcontract. But on site, the workers showed little interest in the architect's creative ideas and did not come up with questions when his drawings were unclear. They just did what they thought they were supposed to do in order not to increase the complexity of operations even further. They did what they thought was best to finish the job as quickly as possible and go home early. Several meetings with the employer and the architect followed. But the subcontractor's main attitude was that the architect's idea of decorating the building was nonsense. The employer did not accept this mentality and Joe had to terminate the subcontract. Discussions about the costs of intensive re-work followed. Finally, Building Technology presented a stiff invoice, which was returned with a firm letter from Joe's contract engineer, stating that the invoice was not justified and that the case was closed.

Box 23.1. A bailiff at the main office.

"Hello Joe, could you please come by one day? My boss would like to meet you. He needs some further information about your earlier project. I am sorry to disturb you. You must be busy."

It was Barbara of the Legal Department at Head Office. She worked for the CEO and the few senior lawyers of the group. All complicated files would pass her desk. She was charming. You would never hear anything about whatever cumbersome case the company was involved in.

"Oh dear, what is going on?"

"We are summoned to appear in court. This morning a bailiff delivered the writ. It is quite a file, some 250 pages, I assume. We have to respond in 12 weeks. But our CEO prefers to take it on immediately; he does not like to be under pressure if further research would be needed."

"Who is making trouble?"

"It is on behalf of Building Technology plc."

When he heard the name, Joe shivered.

"But, that affair was three and a half, maybe four years ago. They were subcontractors on my previous project. The case was settled and completely forgotten."

"The normal limitation on legal actions is five years. We had similar cases that were presented only a week before the deadline. Can we fix a date? The first meeting will probably take a few hours of your time. You are requested to bring the files with you, including all reports and records if available."

"Sure, how about next week? I'll be in the office on Wednesday."

"Fine Joe, would two o'clock be convenient?"

"I am sorry to bother you."

"Don't mention it; it is part of our work."

Reading the summons with the attachments, Joe was surprised about the issues that were presented, which had nothing to do with the bad work of the subcontractor. Building Technology's solicitor listed statements that for a great part were made up and were a far cry from the true state of affairs.

Joe read about himself, his company and his project: breach of contract, tort committed by International Flexible Contractors (Joe's company), misrepresentation by the main contractor (Joe's company again), fraud, deceit and misleading behavior whilst negotiating the subcontract, such that if a subcontractor had known this in advance it never would have entered into the subcontract. Further issues were "the continuous errors in level one planning" and subsequently "in the detailed planning schedules of all subcontractors concerned"; "letters and e-mails that remained unanswered"; a project manager (that was Joe) who "without exception was absent from the site, due to advanced management courses at universities and international business schools"; "surveying engineers effectively incompetent to the interpretation of tests results, which on other building projects would have been approved"; "test procedures inadequate"; "competent authorities issuing unreasonable new rules and regulations when work was going on"; and last, but not least, the "main contractor forcing the subcontractor to dump chemical toxic waste in illegal ways". On top of that, the "main contractor was working with illegal Eastern European workers, which made it impossible to communicate with their foremen".

And that was not all.

Here the solicitor of the subcontractor was starting a "war game", while Joe was not suitable for this struggle. Now IFC, being the main contractor, would have to deny all and play the game according to the rule of law.

After the meeting with the director of legal affairs, Joe realized that the case was not easy at all. The offending solicitor of Building Technology had attached copies of the referred subcontract, together with copies of minutes of project meetings where unsolved problems were identified. Statements of witnesses were enclosed, among them, four with Polish names. They were certainly not illegal — their temporary employment contracts should be somewhere at head office, maybe at HRM or at Procurement — who knew? Anyhow, these four men were in the other camp already and may have been instructed about what to declare and what not to declare. Joe's best counterwitness would have been Peter Jung, his deputy on that project, but unfortunately this man had died in a car accident the previous year. Joe was beginning to realize that statements that are not "completely true", but in the context of the case are not improbable, could play a role in the court's decisions. True facts, which cannot be legally proven, are useless in court.

Joe now realized that the main reason to terminate the referred subcontract was the subcontractor's undisguised contempt for the architect, the employer and one of his stakeholders. Whether that reason would be an acceptable argument for contract termination when cited in court was an open question. If Joe was unable to prove bad workmanship, the court might confirm the breach of contract from IFC's side.

It would have been far better to discuss a reasonable amount to terminate the subcontract three and a half years ago with the disappointing subcontractor, instead of now beginning a legal war that would take at least three to four years. Even if IFC was going to win the case in court, an important sum of money would have to be paid to its own solicitor for the defense.

23.3. Going to court yourself

A contractor may go to court itself, suing employers. The main reason is usually "I want my money!" Such actions should always be well prepared and only take place if ample attempts to settle the case harmoniously failed.

Before calling your solicitor, please sit down, cool down and ask yourself some questions:

- Think why you need a solicitor. Is it for legal advice or are you angry about your business partner, who left you with a burden of troubles, which you had to resolve?
- Does your problem necessarily call for a legal resolution, or can it be handled in another way?
- If you want to sue a (former) business partner, is there a reasonable chance of success?
- If your business partner is going to be sued, is there an affordable and honorable way to settle the case and come to a solution "somewhere in the middle"?
- If you are being sued, is there a way to persuade your business partner to drop the action?
- When one has the choice of initiating a legal action, would this be better — think about time, money, anger, anxiety and the ruined relationship — than doing nothing at all?
- Is the principle that important for you that you can't afford not to sue?[2]

The international contractor's business is to get things done, while satisfying the client, the ultimate client and his stakeholders, and making a profit in doing so. A lawyer's business is to make money at high hourly rates. A lawyer who is good in court will certainly not recommend not suing. He is looking forward to a game, which is attractive for him. In the hands of such a lawyer, the contractor and the lawyer have no common interest. Some excellent lawyers are against mediation. It is much cheaper and much quicker than dispute resolution before court. In John Grisham's novel *The Firm*, it is described

---

[2]M. H. McCormack (1985), *What they don't teach you at Harvard Business School.* London: Collins; M. H. McCormack (1987), *The terrible truth about lawyers.* London: Collins.

how partners of an international law firm in the United States cheated their customers by billing for more hours on a case than they spent. Boxes 23.2 and 23.3 give some paragraphs from this novel.

Suppose that you are 101% right in disputing with your subcontractor, who really was in default?

First of all we recommend contacting your in-house legal counsel. Maybe he suggests re-negotiating the case with your counterparty, but now in his presence. This may help. Your opponent will have to reconsider his position. But if he does not move — not even an inch — you may feel forced to ask your legal counsel to bring the case to court. But look before you leap. Do so in concert with your legal specialists.

What will you win if you win the case? What will be your advantage in business after the subcontractor has lost the case in court? What do you lose after your subcontractor loses the case? After two or three or four years — how much turnover will have been charged by the two lawyers (yours and the subcontractor's)?

Sometimes technical specifications are not 100% perfect — that happens, more often than we wish. Sometimes technical specifications are not feasible

Box 23.2. Padding.

Billing is vital. There is always the pressure to bill more. All we have to sell is our time. Once you pass the bar your billing hours will be mentioned weekly... Before they consider you for partner, you've got to hit sixty hours a week constantly over a period of many years.

Most good lawyers can work eight hours a day and bill twelve. It's called padding. It's not exactly fair to the client, but it's something everybody does. The great law firms have been built by padding files. It's the name of the game.[3]

Box 23.3. Billing time running at lunch.

Mitch had discovered a deli three blocks away from the Bendini Building between Front Street and Riverside Drive, near the river... He liked it because he could sneak away and proofread a document while he ate. Now that he was a full-blown associate, he could eat a hot dog for lunch and bill a hundred and fifty an hour.[4]

---

[3] J. Grisham (1991), *The Firm*. London: Arrow Books, p. 57.

[4] J. Grisham (1991), *The Firm*. London: Arrow Books, pp. 102–103.

in practice. When the problem is technical, do not go to a lawyer for help! He has no knowledge of technology. It will take time and effort to inform him about the technical details. And even if he understands, it is not sure whether the judges will understand, when the lawyer explains such technical details before court.

If you go to court instruct your witnesses together with your lawyer. They have to tell the truth, but it is no good if they talk about issues that are not related to the dispute. If you ever, after many considerations, go to court, go to the best lawyer in town, or one of the best lawyers in the country. That will cost you a good sum of money, but it is better than becoming a victim of legal errors which could have been prevented. Consequently, your opponent will be obliged to consult a lawyer of the same level. Both parties have to spend money on their interests. There will be bills to be paid.

In the event your lawyer leaves his firm, the file is handed over to a colleague. So, now you have another lawyer. He will have to read the file from the beginning. And you will have to explain the whole case — including all details — again. Be aware that these hours are not considered to be billing hours for him — handing over a file to another lawyer should be at the risk of the lawyer's firm. However, better to check your invoices! The client should be in the driver's seat:

- Ask your solicitor beforehand to give an indication of billing hours.
- When receiving an invoice, ask for a minutely detailed time registration and the timesheets: what was the phone call about? Why 30 minutes, where six would be sufficient?
- You have to know how to prevent a lawyer from meddling in situations where "the legal approach" is no good.
- It is your responsibility to stop your lawyer in a timely fashion.
- Your lawyer is a special service provider. In concert with him, you have to agree on the specification of his work.

23.4. Some dispute resolution clauses in standard contracts

LOGIC

LOGIC's main aim is to discuss and to settle disagreements, differences of opinion and disputes between parties themselves before going to court. When such clauses are part of a written contract, a judge may ask parties what they have done to solve the matter together and why they have not been successful. Both parties must have acceptable answers to such questions. The following is how LOGIC arranges for conflict resolution.

LOGIC's sequence:

1. Discussion between representatives, i.e. project managers.
2. Discussion between authorized representatives, i.e. the persons who signed the form of agreement, or the nominees for the resolution of disputes as mentioned in the appendix to the form of agreement.
3. Discussions between the managing directors of the parties.[5]
4. A form of alternative dispute resolution; the specific form is left open to the parties.
5. In the event all previous steps failed, one of the parties may take appropriate action and bring the case to court, after having used its best endeavors to follow the complete steps 1–3.

The work on the project is not to be interrupted.[6] Third parties may have rights, which have to be respected.[7] Arbitration is another possibility, in particular if the international marine element forms the greater part of the work.[8]

FIDIC

The FIDIC standards all refer to a dispute adjudication board (DAB), consisting of one or three members, agreed upon by the parties. FIDIC's cycle is slightly different from LOGIC's.

1. Settle amicably. FIDIC has no escalation levels such as LOGIC.
2. DAB, where FIDIC has extensive rules for adjudication; DAB members to be appointed from the outset, which means when signing the contract.
3. Referral to international arbitration of the International Chamber of Commerce in Paris.

During arbitration, no changes in the obligations of parties are provided. There are many procedural rules under FIDIC, which have to be respected.[9]

[5]LOGIC Mobile Drilling Rig standard, clause 27.1, which does not mention the alternative dispute resolution option.

[6]LOGIC Construction and Marine Construction, clause 37.

[7]LOGIC Construction and Marine Construction, clause 38.

[8]LOGIC Drilling Rig standard, guidance notes, clause 37.

[9]FIDIC blue book, clause 15; FIDIC red, yellow and silver books, clause 20.

The FIDIC white book (client & consultant model services agreement) has a deviating procedure:

1. Resolve problem between project managers.
2. Discuss between the representatives who signed the contract.
3. Mediation, while the mediator — if asked to do so by one of the parties — may give his opinion on the conflict.
4. Arbitration.[10]

CMM standard contract

This standard, like the Norwegian standard and the LOGIC contracts, refers to the national legal system. In line with this, the arbitration of the Dutch Institute of Arbitration is applied. Parties have to try to settle first. If this fails arbitration is compulsory.[11] The arbitrators have to apply the law, which means that they have to judge as judges in court would. They must consider the referred case, consider the facts and, further, should not interpret them as "faithful men under reasonable considerations". The CMM standard has a special clause on fast settlement of disputes on variations by one neutral expert at short notice. No interruption of the time schedule of the work is permitted.

International arbitration

Besides the agreement to go to arbitration, parties also have to agree on the procedure of arbitration. The formal rules of different institutes are different. Various rules exist, such as the rules of the ICC (International Chamber of Commerce) in Paris; other arbitration rules are those of the UNCITRAL (United Nations Commission on International Trade Law) or conciliation under the UNCITRAL Conciliation rules, or the rules of the International Centre for Settlement of Investment Disputes (ICSID) or of the Additional Facility administered by ICSID. It is also possible to choose the national arbitration rules of the country of the employer, although most contractors are a bit afraid of unexpected surprises in foreign rules and regulations. It all depends upon the country in question and its legal professionals. The International Convention on the Settlement of Investment Disputes between

---

[10] FIDIC Client & Consultant model services agreement, FIDIC white book, clauses 43 and 44.
[11] Standard Construction/Modification/Maintenance Contract for the Oil and Gas Industry, 1992, clause 47.

States and Nationals of Other States (the ICSID convention) on arbitration may be referred to, which leads to the application of the ICSID rules. Your lawyer will find the details.

23.5. Alternative Dispute Resolution (ADR)

There are many other ways of settling disputes in order to stay away from courts or arbitration institutes. Together with your opponent you may choose the form which suits the case best.

Negotiation

Parties directly or indirectly communicate about the disputed points. The purpose is to arrive at a deal and enter into an agreement to settle. It is done when parties have an interest in maintaining good relations. It is not wise to apply this form if one of the parties has much power or control over the other.

Mediation

Parties are supported by an independent and neutral third person to facilitate their communication and negotiations. This form can be chosen if parties want to keep or to repair good relations or reputations or if they want to end their disputes without fighting. When one of the parties has too much power over the other, this method is not recommended.

Settlement conference

A neutral third person evaluates the case and gives his opinion according to legal considerations or business positions of the parties; that person may suggest a settlement agreement. The method is to be applied where parties are not prepared to change their positions, but are prepared to listen to each other's arguments. The third person may give his legal opinion and parties may re-evaluate their earlier convictions.

Early neutral evaluation

A neutral third person identifies all disputed subjects between parties and helps parties to come to a schedule of activities to manage the conflict. The neutral person must have knowledge of the business of both parties. His role is to give parties insight into each other's position and interests. This method is preferable where the dispute cannot (yet) be solved by simple judgment of the facts, but where further investigation or testing is required. For complex disputes this is a suitable procedure.

Mini trial

A neutral third person makes use of elements of negotiation and mediation to come to an agreement on the disputed subjects. Parties must have given authorization to the third person to decide on a number of items. The third person judges the quality of proof that parties may bring in. The third person may be invited to give his opinion on the strong or weak points of parties. The method is suitable in situations where parties have reached a deadlock in their communications, but still have an interest in settling the dispute discreetly. The method may secure good business relations.

Summary jury trial

A jury hears short pleas on behalf of both parties and comes to a non-binding legal opinion. The method is appropriate where legal or complex disputes arise and where the public opinion or the opinion of certain business circles is important to parties. The opinion of the jury will assist parties to move closer to each other.

Mediation/arbitration

A neutral third person helps parties in negotiating the disputed subjects. However, in the event parties do not come to a solution, the third person is authorized to decide on the case partly or completely. He may write a verdict that has to be accepted by both parties. This method is a combination of mediation and arbitration. The method is ideal in situations where parties need to maintain good business relations, especially where a solution is needed on short notice. The risk that goes with this method is that in the beginning, parties are reluctant to inform the third person when he is still playing the role of the mediator; a party may be worried that openness will be to its disadvantage when the mediator changes his role into that of the arbitrator.

The self-chosen judge[12]

Parties together appoint a third person to decide their dispute. The third person must have sufficient legal knowledge. Expert knowledge of the

[12] In the Dutch language, *bindend advies*.

parties' business is of great help. Both parties present their arguments to the self-chosen judge, who writes a verdict that is binding for the parties.

In all the above alternatives, the third person may operate in his own style. It is possible to apply shuttle diplomacy between parties, when direct discussions due to personal feelings are less favorable. It is possible to arrange for a common hearing, where parties may comment on each other's arguments. All the aforementioned methods are businesslike methods of dispute resolution. They are all less time consuming, less costly and less stressful than court cases or arbitration. Furthermore, the dispute remains confidential to a great extent.

The next, more drastic steps, are arbitration and legal procedures in court.

There are many forms of alternative dispute resolution; you may, together with your opponent, choose the form that suits the case best. Even if the contract provides for a certain way of dispute resolution, it is always possible to agree with your counterparty that the most suitable way of coming to terms will be applied. If one or another form of mediation does not lead to success, the parties may fall back on court proceedings or arbitration.

23.6. Conclusions

In this chapter we have seen that disputes may be settled in various ways. Besides the normal legal ways to courts and arbitration, there are a number of different techniques of alternative dispute resolution. Even in the case that court procedures or arbitration had been agreed upon in a written contract, it is always possible to agree with your counterparty on another way. Settling conflicts in good harmony is the best option. It is not always possible to come to terms with the way of dealing with differences of opinion, but it is always worth trying. Costs of going to court, as well as costs of arbitration, are high. The leadtime is long. The lawyers are expensive. Trials take their toll on project and contract managers, from staff lawyers to further staff members. That represents energy that could have been spent in a more fruitful way, for instance, building beautiful technical constructions whilst making profit for your company at the same time.

The outcome of cases before courts and arbitration are always unpredictable. You may have "a fair chance", but one is never sure when starting a lawsuit. Estimate the costs and the probable result that you may gain. It is better to settle in a way that is not completely satisfactory than fighting a war for a few years and — even when you win — end in a disappointed mood. Standard contracts discourage the referral to the court by clauses that oblige parties to try to settle before initiating legal proceedings.

Keep files, reports and records of all projects — even keep your personal notes, if any for use in court. A case before a court is complicated, time consuming, costly, and it requires a lot of effort, which is not in line with our regular activities. Statements that are not true or "not completely true", but not improbable in the context of the case, could play a negative or positive role in the court's decisions; it depends which side you are on. Arguments that cannot be legally proven don't favor your position at court.

If we are 101% right and we consider suing our subcontractor, who was really at fault? What will we win if we win the case? What will be our advantage in business after the subcontractor has lost the case in court? It is far better to discuss with a disappointing subcontractor a reasonable amount to terminate the subcontract instead of starting a legal war, which would take three or four years. Think hard before approaching your lawyer. The contractor's business model is to make a profit in getting things done, while satisfying the client, the ultimate client and his stakeholders; the lawyer's business model is to make hours and a turnover at a high rate. A lawyer is a service provider; the client should be in the driver's seat.

Chapter 24

Different Legal Systems

24.1. Case — Exact to specification, but not fit for purpose[1]

Mr. Lynch purchased from Thorne, a builder, a plot of land with a partly erected house on it. Thorne, the contractor, agreed to complete the house in accordance with the plan and specification produced by the contractor and attached to the agreement. The specification provided that the walls were to be nine-inch brick walls. The house was built precisely in accordance with the specification, with sound material and good workmanship, but turned out to be unfit for human habitation because rain penetrated the walls. Three architect experts gave their opinion. Only the wording of the respective opinions was different. But finally, all three were unsurprised that rain could penetrate a nine-inch brick wall. A country court judge found that the contract contained an implied warranty that the house, when completed, would be reasonably fit for human habitation. So damages had to be paid by the contractor. The contractor appealed and won before the court of appeal; no damages. We cite from the extensive judgment:

> For the unfortunate Mr. Lynch obviously one cannot help feeling a great deal of sympathy; but a grown adult man is presumably capable of taking competent skilled advice if he wants to; and if he elects not to do so but to make a bargain in precise terms with someone else, then, though no doubt he does rely upon the skill of the other party in a sense, he assumes that the other party, as was the fact in this case, will do the job he has promised to do competently and, at best, that he believed that the house he is going to build will be a habitable house... But that is far short of importing into the transaction any such overruling condition or warranty ... it would appear almost to involve the result that because the employer elected not to take advice himself, therefore there was some duty of care thrust upon the contractor which should more properly have been borne by somebody engaged by the employer... I can find no room for an implied warranty..."[2]

[1] Lynch vs. Thorne.

[2] Court of Appeal, 1956, 1 W.L.R. 303: 100 S.J. 225; [1956] 1 All E.R. 744.

Appeal allowed. No damages to be paid by the contractor. No re-work to be performed by the contractor.

The key legal issue is that a judge only implies terms in a contract in case the contract does not include clauses about the issue. Here, the house was built exactly to specification. For making the house fit for purpose, a variation would have been required. In earlier cases on implied terms, it was found that such terms may be implied when stipulations about the issue are missing in the contract. Implied terms are not meant to overrule terms that were agreed upon by the parties. Here, the specification was agreed upon.

The case illustrates that the outcome is debatable. Yet, under common law, the result was correct. Why? In earlier verdicts on cases about the issue of implied terms, the courts decided that a judge could add terms to an incomplete contract in order to come to a decision. The legal debate in the case was not on implied terms. The contract was clear, although not fair. For continental lawyers the result might be disappointing. A continental lawyer may ask why the employer should not have the right to get from the contractor a house that is fit for purpose. Moreover, the contractor is a specialist in the business of building houses. You may trust that his specifications are such that the object of a house is that you can live in it happily. Other arguments are the relationship between consumer and professional, which lay more responsibility, or even liability, on the shoulders of the contractor. You may doubt if the same case in 2012 would have the same outcome after compulsory directives of the European Union. The case is a good example of the meaning of implied terms under the English legal system.

24.2. English terminology and international construction contracts

English has become the international language of trade and industry. English, simple in grammar — which makes it easier for a foreigner to learn than any other language — is practical as an instrument to communicate. The English language is very rich in idiom, and therefore is a suitable vehicle of international business relations.

And so, business letters and business contracts are written in the English language. Consequently, English legal wording is applied. And here is the pitfall. Contracts are written in legal English. But legal English in fact is a different language than the everyday English that is spoken in the streets. Legal English is a professional language. It has a special vocabulary. We use that vocabulary — often without being aware that some words have special meanings, which are different from meanings they have in day-to-day life. Further, the words may be explained as if English law was applicable to the contract in question, even if the relevant legal system of a construction contract is a different one. This is the reason why contractors should have some knowledge of English law, its history and its logic. It is interesting to note that a case in English law could have a completely different outcome than if the same case were dealt with under a continental legal system.

In England there are significant cases concerning the interpretation of legal terms. Before court, and especially before the House of Lords, cases were decided by explaining and defining words. We refer to the introduction of this paragraph. Many, many words in construction contracts have a special legal meaning. We recognize the words, we look in a dictionary and we find a meaning. But it is not certain that such a translation is correct in the context of the relevant contract. You may not be aware that there was a case behind the concept of the legal meaning of the word you are looking for. As an example, the word "consideration" has a different meaning in legal English than in everyday English. "Consideration" means that in a contract where one party accepts an obligation to do something, there should be an obligation on the other party's side to compensate for this obligation. If not, there is no contract. So if a contractor is prepared to do something special for you, but before or when making the promise there is no "consideration", no contract exists, and so no compensation is required. When reading an English text, we may not be aware of the danger when we think that we understand everything in the way it is described. Special dictionaries may help.[3] There are many words with special meanings in English contract law and tort law. We mention some of them in Box 24.1.[4] To summarize: the English language is an excellent instrument to write international construction contracts, once you are aware of its pitfalls.

---

[3] P. H. Collin (2007), *Dictionary of Law*. London: Peter Collin Publishing. See www.petercollin.com, January 21, 2013.

[4] For further readings on English legal vocabulary, see: H. Gubby (2011), *English legal terminology, legal concepts in language, 3rd edition*. The Hague: Eleven International Publishing; H. Gubby (2006), *Practical legal English: legal terminology*. The Hague: Boom Juridische Uitgevers.

Box 24.1. Some words in the English language with special legal meanings.

Contract law vocabulary	Tort law vocabulary
Acceptance	Action
Adequate	Aggravated damages
Affirm	Award
Agreements to agree	Balance of probabilities
Anticipatory breach	Breach of duty of care
Battle of forms	Break the chain of causation
Best endeavors	Capacity
Breach of contract	Comparative negligence
Capacity	Contributory negligence
Collateral contract	Conversion
Condition	Damages
Consequential losses	Defamation
Consideration	Discrimination torts
Construction	Duty of care
Contra proferentem rule	Duty to mitigate
Damages	Economic torts
Discharge by frustration	Fraudulent misrepresentation
Divisible contract	Harassment
Entire contract	Immediate aftermath
Equity	Injunction
Estoppel	Joint and several liability
Exclude	Negligence
Express terms	Neighbor principle
Force majeure	Non-pecuniary loss
Four corners rule	Nuisance
Fundamental	Pecuniary loss
Honor clauses	Physical damage
Implied terms	Proximity
Incorporation	Quasi-contractual
Induce	Reckless
Injunction	Remoteness
Innominate term	Slander

(*Continued*)

Box 24.1. (*Continued*)

Contract law vocabulary	Tort law vocabulary
Lapse	Statutory nuisances
Last shot	Strict liability
Letter of intent	Structural settlement
Liquidated damages	Tangible/intangible property
Misrepresentation	Tortfeasor
Of the essence	
Parole evidence rule	
Past consideration	
Presumption	
Proximate damages	
Reliance loss damages	
Remoteness of damage	
Representation	
Rescission	
Sit on the breach	
Specific performance	
Substantial performance	
Unliquidated damages	
Waiver	
Warranty	

24.3. The human need for rules

There are rules in every society. There are rules within countries, within cities, within different kinds of industries, within companies, within families, in sports, in leisure and in training programs (where you have to read the cases beforehand and prepare yourself). There are rules for service providers and subcontractors; there are rules for suppliers and vendors. Some rules are so obvious that we scarcely recognize them as "rules", and yet they are. The project manager of a subcontractor who is invited to perform a difficult welding job is dressed in a different way than the legal counsel who is present when negotiating the subcontract. We need rules: the way we dress up is a rule in society; we like to know how to behave; we like to be part of a group. Books were written about informal rules; there are books on the etiquette of forms of engagement, marriage, birth, dinner and correspondence. Rules are an important part of society.

Rules have two dominant elements. First, they change constantly, and second, they differ from country to country, from city to city, from company to company, from industry to industry. Everywhere in the world the rules can differ from the rules we are aware of in our company, our business, our profession, our country and all the various places we have been.

There are two important groups of rules, which we want to distinguish between. These are the informal rules of etiquette and ethical behavior on the one hand, and the legal rules on the other hand. The main difference is that legal rules can be enforced. This means that somewhere there is a public authority that is capable of maintaining those rules in the event someone does not behave and act according to the legal rules. We concentrate in this chapter on the legal rules only.

In all societies at certain moments, the need will arise to write down legal rules. It was done on stones in ancient Egypt, on clay by the ancient Greeks, in writing in the Middle Ages, in code books in the 18th–21st century in Western Europe, and on the Internet in the 20th–21st century. The first "complete" code book was that of the Roman emperor Justinian (482–565), who codified the Roman civil law in one code book. This good idea was followed by Emperor Napoleon of France in 1804–1806, who edited the French civil code, Code of Commerce and the Criminal Code Book, after the new French Constitution was conceived in 1795. These three books were translated into other languages. After the French initiative, various European constitutions were formed in a democratic way. The idea behind those constitutions was that the total power of a king or an emperor should be divided into three different powers: the legislative power, the judiciary power and the administration of the state, the executional power. The concept is called the "trias politica". The object of the constitutions is that the three powers cannot overrule each other. There is a system of checks and balances. Each power has its own field of action and should act in a pre-described way. In Western society we are of the opinion that this arrangement of power is correct. We feel the need to put that on paper.

24.4. Families of legal systems

This system of dividing the total power of the monarch into three different powers is certainly not the same in all parts of the world. International companies that work in countries of the Middle East, in Africa or Asia know better. In these areas, full power, which is concentrated in one person only, still exists. Not long ago we discussed pricing systems in the construction industry during a course on international contracting. We refer to the short story of the project manager who told us about the local sheik who, on a sunny Sunday, took a trip on his yacht around his newly-built island, which shortly before was created by land reclamation and constructed by the project manager. The sheik was so satisfied with the beautiful new premises, that the project manager was invited to come to the palace the following Monday. Here, a drawing made up by the sheik himself was shown, while the great secretary of the sheik asked for a price per piece — per piece meant simply: a price per island. The offer should be made within one week. In Western Europe, in Australia and in the United States, such a decision — by one man to order an island for himself — is non-existent these days.

In the world, several families of legal systems exist:

- The Roman legal system, which describes open norms in codified rules; codification here is the description of general legal rules. The Roman legal system concerned civil law only; that is the reason why this way of noting rules in codes is called the "civil law system".
- Related to Roman law are the German civil law system and the Scandinavian civil law system.
- Common law systems, which originated from England and Wales, but spread out over large parts of the world during centuries.
- Religious legal systems, based on behavior and religion, which comprise Islamic law, Buddhist, Hindu, Confucianist, Bhutanese and Taoist influences.[5]
- Custom-based legal systems, which are based on local habits and customs.
- Asiatic — the Chinese/Japanese legal systems, which originally were based upon the authority of the emperor.
- EU law, which is valid for economic, monetary and social issues, but only in the member states of the European Union.[6]

---

[5]E. J. Jurji (ed.) (1946), *The Great Religions of the Modern World.* Princeton, NJ: Princeton University Press; H. Smith (1957), *The Religions of Man.* New York: Mentor Book, The New American Library; L. Woodhead (ed.) (2003–2007), *Religions in the Modern World.* London: Routledge.

[6]For different sources on the issue, see: CIA field listing, 2012; List of country legal systems, http://eu.wikipedia.org, January 21, 2013; Snapshot on Different Legal Traditions, Université d' Ottawa; R. David and J. E. C. Brierly (1985), *Major Legal Systems in the World Today, 3rd edition.* London: Stevens & Sons.

A legal system consists of a very large set of rules.[7] Differences in legal systems have their origin in factors like climate, history of the population, economy, religion and authority of great leaders. In many countries, the law is a model for how society and visitors, including foreign contractors, should function. In some countries the law is a vehicle to suppress individuals who do not behave as the legislator prescribes. But, in general, legal entities and individuals are protected by the system as long as their behavior is in line with the relevant rules, whatever they are. Many legal systems have the objective to influence human behavior in their daily activities.

A legal system is not the only way to influence human behavior and to contribute to the wellbeing of citizens. Religion is another important vehicle to achieve that goal; prayer and meditation may help people as well. In many cultures it is important to live in harmony with your neighbors, while the law is not a vehicle to enforce such goals. "I'll sue you and I see you in court" is an expression that will not be understood in a legal system based on Taoism. Under such a system, the obligation to come to terms is more important than a dispute about a sum of money. The project manager should be aware of such differences. It may happen that a representative of an employer is not happy with the behavior of the contractor and its personnel. He may prefer to discuss these issues before discussing details related to the scope of work and the time schedule.[8]

24.5. The Roman civil law system

Emperor Justinian's mission was to restore the power of the Roman Empire, which at the beginning of his reign was relatively divided. At that time the Roman Empire consisted of two large parts: a western part and an eastern part. Justinian wanted to bring these two together again and run the Empire as one entity. An important vehicle for this was to build one single legal system, which should be applied everywhere in his empire. Open norms were described in general concepts. When a case was presented to him, the judge (i.e. the praetor on the local market place) could analyze the case and compare it with the rule to be applied. In the code book, the judge could find the "solution" for the relevant case (see Box 24.2).

The Roman law system lies at the root of the French law system. The French codification in the 19th century had different objectives than the

[7] For a more extensive definition of the word *recht* we refer to J. van den Berg, Nederlands Juristenblad, NJB March 1992, No. 13.

[8] For further reading, see Chapter 25.

Box 24.2. The hired slaves and the discovered treasure.

Publius lent two strong, white Nordic slaves to his friend Geraldus. Geraldus said to Publius that he needed the slaves for land cultivation aside his existing garden. The slaves had to turn the rough soil at least two spits deep, as Geraldus's wife had the idea of planting beautiful flowers in the new area. All weeds had to be put aside carefully. The parties agreed on a price per day, good food included, and a completion time. One day, when the sun was setting in the west, his slaves came home and reported to Publius that they found about a hundred golden coins of foreign currency while digging deep. They collected the coins, carefully washed them in the brook, put them in a vase and handed them over to Publius. Geraldus, who was informed by his own slaves, and hearing the news the next day, immediately reclaimed the coins from Publius, arguing that the coins were found on his premises and consequently — according to the code book of Justinian — he had complete legal title to them. Publius, however, stated that he did not lend out gold-diggers, but just slaves for land reclamation. As the object of the contract was land improvement and nothing else, Geraldus had no right to claim the coins, as nothing was agreed upon that issue in the contract.

The next day, the friends went together to the praetor on the market place. The praetor listened carefully to their different arguments and tried to find the norm in the code book. It was his job to compare the case to the norm and to come to a reasonable verdict. In the presence of witnesses the praetor gave his binding opinion.

For curiosity's sake: the outcome of the verdict in classical Roman law was 50/50 for the two parties. The case is still current. It is far better to foresee such a situation and settle the case beforehand when negotiating the contract. We find a clause for identical cases in FIDIC standard contracts.[9]

Roman codification. The republicans of the revolution wanted a clear set of rules, which should be comprehensive for every citizen. That was the reaction against the arbitrary regulations, together with the local taxes levied by the noblemen, who at the same time had the power to punish the farmers and workers at will. Transparency was an ideal of the revolution, as was the role of the judge. The judges of the nation were considered to be the mouth of

[9]FIDIC Construction (red book), Design & Build (yellow book), and EPC/Turnkey (silver book), clause 4.24.

the legislator, who speaks the words of the law.[10] It was a political statement that was realized after the revolution. In the event of tort committed to a third party when a construction — for example, a bridge — collapsed during the course of being built, the three main powers of the nation each played their own role. The legislator had set the rules on what tort is and how should it be handled in court; the administration consisted of the police and the prosecutor who reported what had happened on the building site; while finally the judge would pronounce the verdict according to the rules of law.

24.6. Codification of laws on the continent — law review in selected countries

The purpose of codification as it was realized in France was followed in Belgium, Italy, Luxembourg, the Netherlands, Portugal, Romania and in parts of Switzerland and some other countries. The idea was to arrive at uniform rules throughout the nation. The legislator is responsible for good legislation, while the judges have to follow the laws of the legislator. They apply the laws. If an employer refuses to pay the invoices of the contractor who performed according to the agreed-upon scope of work, the contractor may ask the court to issue a judgment, which will oblige the employer to pay. The judges will study the relevant contract and the relevant details as presented by the parties, find the relevant norms in the legislation and come to a verdict accordingly. If the government, or a public body, refused to issue a license to a contractor, the judges will need — according to the existing rules — to ascertain whether there were legal arguments for the refusal. Crucial in these legal systems is the weighing of arguments on the facts of the case and placing them in the context of the law.[11]

> In other words, a judge reads the law, considers whether the alleged and existing facts fall within the relevant legal provision and, if this is the case, applies the legal rule. The law says that if A occurs then rule B should be applied; in a specific case when A occurs the judge then would apply rule B.[12]

---

[10] Les juges de la nation ne sont que les bouches qui prononcent les paroles de la loi.

[11] This is a simplified description of the judge's working method. In reality, the judge will consider previous jurisprudence concerning the issue; in concluding a verdict, judges will consider generally accepted principles of law, actual juridical views and the particular societal interests involved. It is not the authors' intention to explore these elements within the context of this book.

[12] G. Corstens in response to B. Schink (2011), in *Objective Law and Subjective Judges*. Amsterdam: Editor Cossee, p. 79.

Court cases are dealt with differently throughout continental Europe. In Germany, the Federal Constitutional Court has the power to review legislation and to judge it against the constitution. In practice, this means that this court has the possibility to judge, for instance, the Equal Opportunities Act, or the Technical Education Act or the Act on Public Procurement against the constitution of Federal Germany. In the event such an act should be in conflict with the constitution, the act, or a certain paragraph of it, would be invalid. In Germany — and in some other countries on the continent — the doctrine of judicial review was established. This places much more authority in judges, even political authority, than in judges operating in a system where no judicial review exists.[13] This difference inhibits a much more aggressive attitude among judges in German judicial circles. They may be critical of the law, and at the same time, they are critical of written contracts that are presented to them.

Where the appointment of judges is influenced by political power, the law becomes a weapon in political arenas. In Spain, judges are appointed on the recommendation of political parties in the parliament. In such a system, it is almost impossible to investigate suspicions of corruption by political authorities. The Spanish judge Baltasar Garzón was accused of misuse of power after giving orders to tap telephones of accused persons belonging to another political party than his.[14]

One may ask what use such knowledge brings to project managers in the construction industry. It may illustrate that legal systems are extremely different, that courts in various countries may have different roles. Consequently, judges are formed and shaped in different templates.

24.7. Common law — the English legal system

Common law cannot be understood without being aware of its history. The need for codification of civil rules was never an issue in England as it was in the old Roman Empire and in France after the revolution. England had a different history. In 1066, William the Conqueror from Normandy in France crossed the Channel and won the Battle of Hastings against the King. This William was not English, he grew up in France, and as a bastard he came to England to claim his "rights on the throne". Not only was he a good general of his troops, but as a ruler he also wanted to establish a new society in

[13]The difference in attitude is clearly explained in B. Schink (2011), *Objective Law and Subjective Judges*. Editor Cossee, Amsterdam, pp. 63–77 and pp. 88–90.
[14]M. de Waal, NRC Handelsblad, Friday January 20, 2012, p. 11.

England and Wales. The land was completely claimed by William and divided amongst his friends and subordinates who served him faithfully in various battles. In order to settle disputes, he changed the existing unclear and mixed-up legal regulations of that period. At that time, legal regulations were a mixture of canon law, i.e. church law, Anglo-Saxon customs and Danish customs, the last being a remainder of the Normans who had earlier invaded England. These three systems were inconsistent with each other. There were local interpretations and irregular outcomes of disputes. William introduced the term common law, which meant that this law was common to all men in England and Wales. It was derived from customs and legal precedents. There were no statutes; the system was not codified. Its sources were earlier cases, customs and some textbooks. Later on these sources became insufficient when the civilization developed further. From 1166, statutes were used to govern society. In the 19th century, many statutes were published, which went on into the 20th century and this will certainly not stop in the 21st century. Nevertheless, English law basically is case law. The cases were judged by the courts; hence, the basic principles of private laws were left to be laid down by the courts in light of common sense and experience under the prevailing feudal conditions.[15]

Some aspects of commercial law are codified by statutes, as they were worked out based upon a very long experience (see Box 24.3). There is also legislation about important subjects, which are not covered by cases, since in a case law system the society has to wait until the suitable case is brought before court. An example is the Unfair Contract Terms Act 1977. Here, the legislator took the initiative. The United Kingdom, being a member of the European Union, is obliged to incorporate European legislation into its legal system. As a consequence, this is realized by means of legislation, in practice by new statutes, which sometimes have to overrule the existing case law.

Disputes under common law — as under any continental law — are settled as follows. First you have to try to settle the dispute yourself. If you are not successful you go to court. The loser may address a court of appeal. In the event the loser is not yet satisfied, he may go to the Supreme Court; for ages this final appeal was up to the House of Lords. The consideration in 1066 was that the King would appoint some wise men around him, men who were to be trusted. These men became the House of Lords. They had to take a final decision, which was published. A similar case should be judged in the

[15]See A. K. R. Kiralfy (1990), *The English Legal System, 8th edition*. London: Sweet and Maxwell, p. 1.

Box 24.3. Some important statutes in common law in England and Wales.

Year	Act	Domain
1215	Magna Carta	Relation King/noblemen
1278	Statute of Gloucester	Public administration
1284	Statute of Wales	Public administration
1285	Statute of Westminster	Public administration
1344	Justices of the Peace Act	Public administration
1677	Statute of Frauds	White collar criminal law
1689	Bill of Rights	Human rights
1722	Criminal Law Act	Criminality
1835	Highway Act	Private transport
1861	Malicious Damage Act	Tort law
1872	Licensing Act	Civil commercial law
1893	Sale of Goods Act	Civil commercial law
1894	Merchant Shipping Act	Civil commercial law
1968	Trade Descriptions Act	Civil commercial law
1972	European Communities Act	European membership
1977	Patents Act	Civil commercial law
1981	Supreme Court Act	Administration public justice

same way by lower judges. This gave stability to the system. It is called the doctrine of the binding precedent.

Consequently, the judges play a different role in a common law system than in a continental law system. As there is no legislation from the outset, a new case provides the option for the judge to discover the rule. The rules, "discovered" by the courts of appeal and the House of Lords, are developed on a case-by-case basis. Originally, English contract law and tort law were, as we have stated before, case law.

On October 1, 2009, the task of the House of Lords as the highest appeal court disappeared. It was replaced by the newly installed Supreme Court, existing of twelve member judges, appointed by The Crown. This was in line with the democratic principle of the separation of powers. After all, the House of Lords is a part of the Parliament, which is responsible for legislation; judgments should not be made by the legislator itself. As we might conclude here, although it took them a few centuries, England also adopted the old concept of the *trias politica*.

24.8. A short comparison between common law and continental law

Strong points of the common law system

A revolution, like in France, is not necessary to create a good legal system. No legislation is required to start the system. It started from scratch. The doctrine of the precedence gives stability to the system. Once a case has been decided, you may rely on the judge to decide in the same way as was done in an earlier, identical case. Cases were categorized per subject by academics and professors in universities. Hence, it is possible to search for a certain legal subject and to find the most relevant cases.

A further strong point of common law is the judge's respect for the agreement between parties. Where a contract is clear, a judge under common law will not be prepared to change, adapt or interpret its clauses. Judges under common law in general have a good feeling for business. A judge — if the law permits — will do his best to find a verdict that suits a business attitude.

Weak points of the common law system

There are an enormous amount of cases. The cases opened the opportunity to the courts and the House of Lords to find out what the law was and is. A decision of a court works retrospectively, explaining how the law has been, rather than how the law in a changing society should be in future. A case, however, does not necessarily cover the complete contents of a legal subject, such as tort or breach of contract. When England in the 19th century went through the industrial revolution, new types of business and new types of employers and contractors developed. The changing society required new legislation, where the case method was no longer able to help. Hence, supplementary legislation was necessary.

Some subjects are under-developed under common law. *Force majeure* is one of them. Consequential damages are another. For the construction industry, all common law cases together are not sufficient to draft proper contracts. It is therefore most fortunate that institutions like LOGIC drafted complete sets of standard contracts, which added definitions of important legal issues, as well as the structure of a contract, its formation, the period, contractor- versus employer-provided items, title of materials, assignment and subcontracting, variations, *force majeure*, indemnities, obligations in respect of insurance, consequential loss, termination, drawings and documents, permits and licenses and resolution of disputes. The LOGIC (former CRINE) standards are — to the benefit of the construction industry — better than the civil law part of the common law.

Finally, we have to make clear that the common law system as it was developed in England and Wales was exported to several parts of the world in the 17th–19th centuries. Australia, Canada and the United States have a common law system. However, as time moved on, these legal systems began to show significant differences with the original English creation. Those countries are autonomous and developed their own regulations, statutes and legal provisions. Being a specialist in common law in the UK does not automatically imply being an expert in another common law country. In parts of the former colonies of the British Empire, like India, Hong Kong, Pakistan and Singapore, roots of common law are still to be found, although these basic rules were amalgamated with local customs and religious verdicts and legal systems.[16]

24.9. Various other families of legal systems

There are many more legal systems. We will mention a few only.

Religious legal systems

Religious legal systems are mostly based on words or documents with historic background, and linked to prophets or famous personalities who lived in the past. There are always religious traditions and professions (priests, imams, monks) involved. The systems are, from the outset, conservative; the will of God cannot be changed by legislators, governments or the interpretation of judges. However, as all societies change, some flexibility is observed, but that differs from place to place. Sometimes locally a certain "freedom" or "flexibility" is present, whereas in other cases the original strict rules and regulations are maintained strongly.

These religious legal systems regulate the internal order of a church as an organization. They rule the complete life of the persons who live in these systems, and include ethical rules and regulations for ceremonies to celebrate birth, baptisms, marriage, raising children, death and heritage. The main types are the sharia in Islamic countries, halakha in Judaism and canon law in the Roman Catholic Church, the Eastern Orthodox Church and the Anglican Church. In only a few countries, the religious legal system is the only one.

---

[16] K. von Benda-Beckman (1998), English Law and the Former British Colonies, pp. 24 – 31; AA47 (1998), 5, 376–383.

That is the case in Bahrain, Brunei, Iran, Kuwait, Maldives, Mauritania, Oman, Qatar, Saudi Arabia, Sudan, United Arab Emirates and Yemen. In practically all other countries, the religious legal system exists besides a national system of law, resulting in a mixed system together with civil law and/or common law. Egypt, Indonesia, Jordan, Malaysia, Morocco and Syria are examples of countries with mixed legal systems.

Contracts in English are applied normally, agreed upon and executed. The international models of standard contracts are used regularly. In many cases, the national law of the contractor has to be accepted as the legal system ruling the contract. That is the case in the Middle East oil and gas countries. Yet, it is not common practice to confront the European contractors with rules and regulations of the referred religious legal systems.

Customary legal systems

The earliest legal systems in human society were customary, based on the customs of a group, a society or a civilization. The rules concern the social relations, as agreed upon by the population; often the rules were not written down. Although there are always sanctions for not respecting the rules, resolution tends to be reconciliatory rather than punitive. There are many African states keeping these traditional legal systems alive, often mixed with the legal system that was brought by colonization. Countries with important parts of customary legislation are found in Africa, the Pacific Islands and in the east.

Asiatic legal systems

The most well known are the Chinese and the Japanese legal systems, both originally based on the authority of the emperor. As the emperor in Japan has lost influence and respect, the original authority is fading. The Chinese emperors disappeared. Both civilizations need much economical and business law for ruling their complex societies, resulting in extensive legal regulations that follow the Western example.

In October 2011, the Chinese government issued a white paper on the Socialist System of Laws, which is edited in Chinese characters.[17] The regime stated that the system includes some 240 effective laws on various subjects, some 700 administrative regulations and over 8,600 local regulations. Governing China by law is a "fundamental principle for the Communist

---

[17]Socialist System of Laws with Chinese Characters, Beijing, Xinhia, October 27, 2011.

Party", the authorities said. The system relates to issues such as civil and commercial laws, administrative laws, economic laws, social laws, criminal laws, litigation and non-litigation procedures, including human rights, environmental protection and the protection of intellectual property rights. The white paper said that China is keeping pace with its development as a socialist country.

US law

The US is a federation and, at the same time, a republic. The federation is formed by 50 self-governing states, each with their own legal system. On many legal issues, there are two layers of legislation, which go together or are separated.[18] The US is to be mentioned here because of its dominant economical position and the characteristics of its civil law system. There is much economical activity within the territory of the US. There is much federal legislation, but in important details, the civil law systems of various states differ. American enterprises do business in many states. In the case of litigation, a contractor who works in a different state than his home state is not always informed about the civil law in the state where the work has to be undertaken. The solution to escape from uncertainties is to draft extremely detailed contracts. American construction contracts include many legal details, more than anywhere else in the world. American engineering firms do likewise. American contracts are extensive and clear. Drafting contracts is an esteemed legal specialism in the US. There are many different types of standard contracts and standard model forms available in the USA,[19] as well as contracts that were agreed upon between public employers and contractors in the past.[20]

The US has a very strong international economic policy. This goes together with rather aggressive laws that sometimes reach far beyond its own territory. The US contains the most lawyers per inhabitant. Its legal universities are famous throughout the world. For political careers or careers in business, a law degree from such a university is a good recommendation.

---

[18]There are other federations of states with several internal legal systems and the two layers of legislation like the USA. We mention some of them: Brazil (26 states), Germany (16 states), India (28 states and seven territories), Mexico (31 states), Nigeria (36 states and one territory) and Venezuela (23 states and one district).

[19]Onecle, Findlaw, Techagreements, Finer Edge, ZIP form, Business Integrety. All institutes have Internet sites.

[20]CORI mentions some 116,000 contracts.

In the US, the Supreme Court is in a position to review legislation issued by Congress. This rule was introduced in 1803. It means that an appointment to the US Supreme Court is highly political. Its members are appointed by the President of the United States; he will certainly consider the political views of a candidate before appointment. It also means that a law that passed Congress is not yet definite. President Obama passed his health reform project in the Congress; that was one of his most important issues in his election campaign. It was his biggest reform project, even bigger than the reduction of the military budget in the US. This reform project could have been frustrated by the Supreme Court. This did not happen. The verdict was not the result of legal issues or conflict with the constitution, but simply a result of a political interpretation. It resulted in some discussions within the deeply divided population, a population with extremely different opinions on poverty, tax levies and the role of the state in society. When the review rule was issued in 1803, the President of the US at that time, Thomas Jefferson, lamented that this doctrine made the constitution "a mere thing of wax in the hands of the judiciary, which they may twist and shape into any form they please".[21] Two centuries later we are reminded of his words.

Socialist legal systems

Socialist legal systems were developed between 1917, the year of the socialist revolution in Russia, and approximately 1980, when the communist regime in Europe was losing economical power. The system blossomed in Central and Eastern Europe, Russia, in socialist nations in Africa and Asia, and in Cuba. The system is based on the Marxist-Leninist concept of the state, the economy and the law. There is a nationalistic republic, practically no (or very little) private ownership, state interference in private-life relations, a strong state control of economy, finance, budgeting, import and export of goods.

China, Cuba, North Korea and Vietnam still have this socialist legal system. Its core function is not to protect human beings against interference of the state;[22] the purpose of the law is simply to strengthen the socialist

[21] Wikipedia entry on the life of Chief Justice of the Supreme Court, John Marshall, 1755–1835, http://en.wikipedia.org/wiki/John_Marshall, January 23, 2013.

[22] Compare, for example, the US Bill of Rights and the Convention on Human Rights and the Court of Human Rights in Strasbourg. The objective of those treaties is the protection of the individual person. This is not in line with socialist legal systems.

orientation of society. Consequently, the individual rights of human beings are of less importance.[23]

Since 1990, the systems have been transformed in all former Soviet republics in Central and Eastern Europe, where the former civil law systems are partly repaired, however adapted to the new economic and social reality.[24]

EU law

For contractors, EU law is embodied in the European Directives on Public Procurement.[25] This procurement law is inflexible, forces public bodies to apply strict procedures and offers many opportunities for suppliers to go to court, in case public bodies have made procedural mistakes in evaluating tenders and selecting the winners. EU law — we should say European Community Law — however, is more than that. It is composed of a system of treaties, which are named after important cities (Rome, Nice, Maastricht, Amsterdam and Lisbon) where important decisions were taken by the governments of the united European nations. Secondary sources of European law are the regulations and the directives (there are over 1,000 directives). The third source is the jurisprudence of the European Court in Luxembourg, where the law is interpreted in the spirit of the economic cooperation between states. In the more than 50 years of economic and technical harmonization, the EU has grown to a system of international law, containing general principles of European law. The start was the internal market with its four freedoms: free movement of goods, capital, services and persons. Afterwards, in 1997, a social chapter was added. This contains items such as health and safety, fair remuneration of employment, rights of workers, vocational training, living conditions, industry relations, equal opportunity and the rule that state enterprises must adhere to the same competition principles as companies. For the contracting industry, EU law means a lot more than just the European Directives on Public Procurement.

---

[23]For further reading, see R. J. Hunter and R. E. Shapiro (2008), A Primer on Important Legal Aspects of the International Business Environment, *Journal of Money, Investment and Banking*, 2, www.eurojournals.com/finance.htm, January 23, 2013.

[24]Alan Uzelac describes the lead that is taken by the legal professionals in the reform process of the legal systems in former Soviet countries: A. Uzelac (2010), Survival of the Third Legal Tradition? *Supreme Court Law Review*, 49 SCLR(2d), pp. 377–396.

[25]See also Chapter 6 of this book.

24.10. Conclusions

Legal English is a professional language, having a special vocabulary. Some words have special meanings, which are different from the meanings they have in day-to-day life. The words may be explained as if English law was applicable to the contract in question, even if the relevant legal system of a construction contract is a different one. One should be aware of using English wording in contracts without being aware of the exact meaning.

Rules differ from country to country, from city to city, from company to company, from industry to industry. Everywhere in the world rules are different from the rules we are aware of in our company, our home business, our profession, our own country. The way of doing business differs all over the world.

Legal rules are brought together in legal systems. Legal systems differ enormously throughout the world. Legal systems have different functions and serve different objectives, depending upon the cultural, political and religious background of nations. Each system has its own characteristics. Interpretation of contract clauses may differ, depending upon the relevant legal system of the interpreter.

Chapter 25

Cultural Differences and Contract Management

25.1. Case — Two cultures meet

Tinus Greenway, the technical director at International Flexible Contractors, a European engineering contractor, suffered from bad sleep. The company's pipeline of new projects was short.

There were not many tenders outstanding at the moment because the global economy was suffering from a recession, which, according to some experts, was going to last for a considerable time. During the past weeks, only one invitation to tender was received, from a foreign company in a foreign country, for which International Flexible Contractors had never worked before. The project comprised the design and construction of extensive port facilities for Geenco, a company that was subject to the law of the Great Republic of Swania. Tinus badly needed this order, an interesting job. But the client was completely new to his company. Tinus wanted to know beforehand with whom he was dealing. So Tinus decided to go and pay a visit to Swania.

At the reception desk of the Swania International Hotel in the capital was a message. It said: "Mr. Peter Abdullah Oshinac will be waiting for Mr. Tinus Greenway at the hotel lobby at 20:00 hours for dinner."

In the car, Mr. Oshinac explained that the restaurant they would go to was owned by his nephew, who started it with the support of family capital, the reason why the best tables in the restaurant were always reserved for Mr. Oshinac. And indeed, in the far corner with a view of the romantic bay of Swania, a table was labeled "Reserved". Two beautiful ladies were smiling at Oshinac.

"Please Mr. Greenway, may I introduce you to my wife Fanny [Tinus shakes hands and smiles] and my daughter Amelia..."

"Just call me Tinus," he said.

During dinner, Tinus talked about the successful history of his company, the projects which it had successfully accomplished worldwide, its excellent staff, its know-how in relation to advanced construction technology, and its perfect relationships with the universities and research institutes. Tinus even made a drawing on the tablecloth to show how the project in the Swania bay should be arranged and what innovative ideas would be proposed by International Flexible Constructors. Oshinac and his ladies listened politely.

Mr. Oshinac informed Tinus about the national economy of Swania, the enormous economic development of Swania, the loan it was going to receive from the World Bank, the Democrats' Party and the elections that would come. Oshinac did not hesitate to confide some family matters related to the Oshinacs. Two of his sons were abroad, one was studying at the Carnegie Institute of Technology, University of Pittsburgh and the other was at Harvard, but recently continued his studies in International Relations at Oxford. Another daughter studied Cultural History in Aix-en-Provence in France.

As for the project, it was important to know that the Minister of Economic Affairs was a brother of his wife Fanny, while the Minister of Internal Affairs was married to a niece of Oshinac's mother. This possibly could soften the relations in passing the order to Greenway's company, Oshinac stated. It became clear that Oshinac did not only represent his own family, but stressed that his family was linked to another important family by marriage. The ladies confirmed what their husband and father was telling Tinus; they kept smiling. The atmosphere was warm and cozy. The music was soft and perfect. The lights on the Swania bay flickered full of romance.

25.2. Introduction

In this chapter we will discuss different cultural aspects around projects. In international project business, national customs, ethical conventions and day-to-day etiquette influence business relations, communications and even the way in which contracts should be read and explained.

We will pay attention to different values in different societies. Our discussion will reveal that people may represent different values and may have different merits, depending upon the society and culture in which they were raised and educated. When dealing with parties in different countries, differences between our culture and that of the contract party become visible. This immediately happens when we cross the border when visiting a neighboring country. Its culture differs from ours.

We will discuss the characteristics of different cultures. We will do so through presenting a few case studies, which are taken from actual experiences of business practitioners. We will show how sometimes communication between a project manager and a deputy engineer (appointed by the employer) may completely get stuck due to our Western way of communicating.

We will briefly discuss the cultural roots of the most important families of legal systems. We will explain why bribery is judged in very different ways across the world. We will finish this chapter with some suggestions on how to deal with different cultures when dealing with complex projects and contracts.

25.3. Cultural differences are all around us

The introductory case shows the differences in customs and behavior between the employer's CEO and the technical director of the contractor. Greenway immediately starts to tell that the company, which he represents, is a perfect match for the works to be realized. Greenway informs his counterparts about the company's technology and experience, assuming that this is important for developing the future relationship. Greenway illustrated his understanding of the scope of work by making a drawing on the tablecloth. That should not be done in a romantic restaurant. The other people listened politely, but it is not clear if this dinner is of any interest to Oshinac and his ladies. Greenway was not very diplomatic when saying, "Call me Tinus", to the daughter of his counterpart — a young lady of about the same age as his own daughter — when she was introduced to him. Maybe such a remark is also "not done" in this country.

Oshinac stressed his excellent family relations. In a country where family relationships matter, this is important. In France, people value a lady by saying "*Elle sort d'une tres bonne famille*", which means that she belongs to the upper tier — the upper-upper class — of the nation. Here, Oshinac gets the best places in the restaurant because of his investments in the place. He mentions what his children are doing, through which he intends to say that he has sufficient funds to finance such expensive stays abroad. Last, but not least, he wants to introduce his ladies to Greenway, confirming his position as a husband and father. In his youth, he was able to marry one of the most important young women available. It goes without saying that she belonged to "the right family". It is not clear whether Oshinac's message was received by Greenway in the way Oshinac intended.

Maybe Oshinac and Greenway started from different objectives. Maybe Greenway wanted to "score" as early as possible in convincing his future client (hopefully) that the potential contract would be in good hands. Whereas Oshinac, during this dinner meeting, wanted nothing more than to explore whether it would be possible to build a constructive, trustful relationship with the director of the European company. Why else, then, would he bring his wife and daughter to the dinner?

25.4. Defining culture

Culture is a term that has many meanings. In 1952, Alfred Kroeber and Clyde Kluckhohn compiled a list of 164 definitions of "culture".[1] However, the word "culture" is most commonly used in three ways:

- Excellence of taste in the fine arts and humanities, also known as high culture.
- An integrated pattern of human knowledge, belief, and behavior that depends upon the capacity for symbolic thought and social learning.
- The set of shared attitudes, values, goals and practices that characterizes an institution, organization, group or a nation.

Out of the many definitions available for this chapter we choose:

> Culture consists of patterns, explicit and implicit, of and for behavior acquired and transmitted by symbols, constituting the distinctive achievements of human groups, including their embodiments in artifacts. The essential core of culture consists of traditional (i.e. historically derived and selected) ideas and especially their attached values. Culture systems may, on the one hand, be considered as products of action, and on the other as conditioning elements of further action.[2]

---

[1] A. L. Kroeber and C. Kluckhohn (1952), Culture, a critical review of concept and definitions, *Harvard University Peabody Museum of American Archeology and Ethnology*, Papers 47.

[2] A. L. Kroeber, and C. Kluckhohn (1952), Culture: A critical review of concepts and definitions. *Harvard University Peabody Museum of American Archeology and Ethnology*, Papers 47.

A more simple definition is the following:

> Culture is the shared knowledge and schemes created by a set of people for perceiving, interpreting, expressing and responding to the social realities around them.[3]

In the remainder of this chapter we will refer to the last definition in most cases. We will find out that culture has a great impact on how to deal with legal issues. We will try to find out how differences in cultural behavior can be explained. Where do these differences come from? Why do other people think differently than we do? We will discuss the work of some important researchers, such as Edgar Schein (Section 25.6), Edward Hall (Section 25.7) and Geert Hofstede (Section 25.8).

25.5. Differences of all kinds

Cultural differences exist among continents, countries, nationalities, regions, population groups, public institutions, such as community councils, regional councils, local committees, associations, foundations, but also among companies and individuals all over the world.

Already within one nation, important differences between groups and regions may exist. In Spain, the Basques consider their culture as a different one to the Spanish; they have their own language, customs and ceremonies. The same is true for Normandy and Corsica in France, for Friesland in the Netherlands and for Bavaria in Germany. In nationalistic China, different populations exist who speak different languages. Although such sub-groups are part of one country and one nation, some differences are so important that the group openly wants to differentiate itself from the overall nation. National differences may give rise to political controversies within the nation. Examples here are the political disputes between the Flemish and the Walloons in Belgium, and the Hutus and Tutsies in West Africa. An extreme example of cultural differences is the apartheid in South Africa, which for decades kept its society apart. Malaysia is a country with a mixed population: over 50% are Muslim Malays, 25% are Chinese and the remainder is a mixture of Indians and smaller ethnic groups. The lobby of the Aboriginals in Australia is strong. Operating in foreign countries implies the risk that one

---

[3] J. P. Lederach (1995), *Preparing for peace: Conflict transformation across cultures.* Syracuse, NY: Syracuse University Press, p. 9.

could easily be involved in incidents among different ethnic and cultural groups. It is better not to become involved in quarrels between these groups.

Even within one nation differences among contractor's clients can be large: ministries, provinces, towns, harbors, airports and hospitals show great differences in terms of policies, decision-making, values and behavior. Each of these institutions has its own specific culture. These clients may operate as a pure public institution, as a private company, a combination of the two, such as a public–private partnership, even with the help of a special purpose vehicle, such as an alliance or joint venture.[4]

The same is true for subcontractors, service providers, suppliers, consultants, engineering firms, architects and individual experts — all of them show different interests and different customs, not to mention the authorities, trade unions, pressure groups, the press and the television. Surveying bodies during execution of the work, such as engineers appointed by the employer, but also labor inspectors, quantity surveyors, tax inspectors, warranty surveyors and customs clearing authorities, all have their own interests and auditing practices, checklists, behavior and "culture".

Also, professionals, such as lawyers, accountants, engineers, doctors and so on, have their own specific culture. They have a certain style of doing things. Their habits, preferences and behaviors have been shaped by similar education, training and interests. They follow professional standards, requirements and commitments. Project managers in construction industries have a culture of their own, which is evident when they are together.

All organizations have their own characteristics, their own culture, influenced and shaped by their environmental context, their history, their purpose and strategy, their interests and the personal views and interpretations of top management. Large organizations have a unique culture; they even embody a large number of professional, i.e. functional, sub-cultures. Mostly there are vision documents, strategy documents and codes of conduct to align the behaviors of all those who belong to and represent the company. Shell may serve as an example here: it has a strict policy in dealing with contractors, subcontractors, suppliers, service providers and vendors. You may rely on it and be confident that Shell's managers and employees will act according to the code. Box 25.1 shows the extensive Shell Code of Conduct (2011). Nowadays, you will find these codes of conduct represented in annual reports and websites of listed companies. Through codes of conduct, companies try to manage, control and influence employee behavior and hence the corporate culture.

---

[4] See Chapter 3.

Box 25.1. The Shell code of conduct.

Shell's Code of Conduct provides practical advice for its entire personnel on how to comply with laws and regulations and how to relate to customers, communities and colleagues.[5] The text is published in Arabic, Chinese, Dutch, English, French, German, Italian, Norwegian, Polish, Portuguese, Spanish, Thai, Turkish and Vietnamese on Shell's website.

The Code of Conduct opens with a letter from the CEO. It says a few interesting things:

> The principles of ethical business behavior are laid down in the Shell General Business Principles (SGBP) and the Code of Conduct. The SGBP govern how Shell companies conduct their affairs. This Code of Conduct describes the behavior that Shell expects of you and what you can expect of Shell. The language is not legal and the Code is more than a set of rules. It should be viewed as an essential guide. The values underlying the SGBP and the Code of Conduct are obvious and universal — honesty, integrity and respect for people. Your conduct will be judged by how you live by those values, and how you have met the intention and spirit of the principles in the Code.
>
> As we strive to improve our performance in a fast-changing, competitive world, we should always remain true to our core values and the SGBP. They are the bedrock of our success, through tough times and good times.
>
> Many of us face legal and ethical dilemmas in our work and must find an appropriate solution or decide how to act. Simply put, in such situations you must follow applicable laws, follow Shell's rules and apply basic common sense and high ethical standards. By doing so you will help ensure that together we do the right thing and that you are never embarrassed to tell your family, colleagues, the media and the public what we have done.

Besides the Code of Conduct, which is applicable to all Shell personnel, the company issued a Code of Ethics for Executive Directors and Senior Financial Officers.[6] This Code of Ethics should be read in conjunction with the Statement of General Business Principles (SGBP) of Royal Dutch Shell

[5] http://www.shell.com/home/content/aboutshell/who_we_are/our_values/code_of_conduct/, January 23, 2013.

[6] http://www.shell.com/home/content/aboutshell/who_we_are/our_values/code_of_ethics/, January 23, 2013.

plc, which governs how each of the Shell companies which make up the group conducts its affairs.

The SGBP has been adopted by all Shell companies and, amongst other things, provides that all persons must avoid conflicts of interest between their private financial activities and their part in the conduct of company business.

This Code is specifically intended to meet the requirements of Section 406 of the Sarbanes–Oxley Act of the US and the listing requirements of the New York Stock Exchange, by providing for a number of implementing requirements in the area of disclosure controls and the avoidance of conflicts of interest. It is addressed to directors and top financial executives.

25.6. Culture — What is behind attitude and behavior?

A popular concept of culture was described by Schein, who found that culture had three different layers.[7]

A first layer relates to the observation that a group of people has assumptions and beliefs. These are fundamental and are "taken for granted". Basic values, when they are sufficiently important, are laid down in laws and treaties. The rule that all people are equal and no discrimination is tolerated is an issue of human rights and is the first clause in the relevant treaty. We all know that it is not literally true. But the rule has an impact on all organizations in countries that signed the treaty on human rights. Nevertheless, the rule is interpreted in different ways in different countries and in different organizations.

The second layer is related to the values that an organization or a nation deems important. Typical values in a business context are: "A promise made is a promise kept"; "All meetings should start on time"; "When there is a problem we will find a solution". When staff members propose different solutions, the boss should make the decision — afterwards, there should be no further comments. These may be examples of a contractor's pragmatic values. Other groups have different values.

The third layer relates to how culture becomes apparent, i.e. visible. Values and culture are reflected in day-to-day life as well as in policy, in architecture, in building design, in technology, in music, in religion, in products.

---

[7] E. H. Schein (1984), Coming to a new awareness of organizational culture, *Sloan Management Review*, 25(1), pp. 3–16. The same model is described by F. Trompenaars (1993), *Riding the Waves of Culture: Understanding Cultural Diversity in Bbusiness*. London: The Economist Books, pp. 22–24.

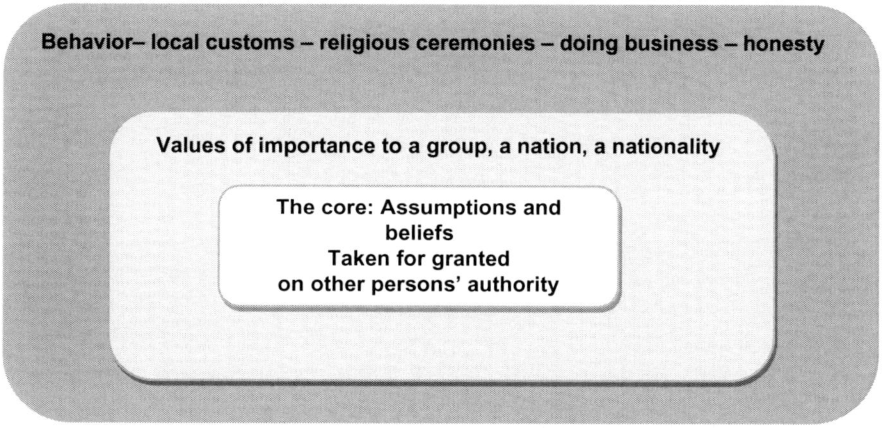

Figure 25.1. The three levels of culture according to Schein (1984).

See Figure 25.1 for a graphical illustration of the three layers of culture, as originally presented by Schein.

A project manager who works in a foreign country does not see the assumptions and beliefs that are at the basis of the cultural values of the people he has to deal with. He just sees and is confronted by the actual behavior, i.e. the outer manifestations of the inner culture. Only the inner culture of people represents the feeling of what is right and what is wrong. These basic beliefs may conflict with basic values of the contractor's civilization. The following may serve as an example here.

In the EU, some basic values were the starting points for the founding of the European Coal and Steel Community (ECSC) in 1952. In 1957, the European Economic Community (EEC) was founded through the Treaty of Rome. In that year the six founding countries started their journey towards economic collaboration. The basic principles for economic collaboration were:

- Freedom of transport of goods.
- Freedom of transport of capital.
- Freedom of transport of persons.
- Free competition is good for the economy and hence for the wellbeing of the people of the EEC. No protectionism whatsoever.

These principles were at the heart of the EEC. Countries that joined the EEC at a later date had to accept these.

However, these principles are not always recognized in other countries outside the EC. In other countries they may even be considered as "strange".

Box 25.2 describes a situation where the principle of free competition is at risk. The case shows that the procedure for arriving at a fair winner based upon open and transparent competition was not realized.

Box 25.2. The preferred subcontractor.

A Western European contractor was awarded with a FIDIC Design and Construct contract for a toll highway in a country somewhere in the south of Asia. In the scope of work, a certain preferred subcontractor was listed, who would construct the 10 toll offices and the adjacent routes around the offices, including some parking lots. During negotiations, the contractor changed the description by adding "or equal".[8] Our contractor did not want to be forced to subcontract part of the work at unreasonable prices and conditions to a local subcontractor. It could happen that the compulsory described subcontractor was linked to the employer — you never know. Free and open competition is a trusted value in Western Europe, is it not?

When awarding the subcontract, it was found that sufficient competition was present. In the local market, several other subcontractors were available, which should be able to do the same job. The contractor dispatched three identical invitations to offer to three different local subcontractors. He received three proposals. It was not surprising that the "preferred supplier", who earlier was mentioned in the first draft of the scope of work, came out best. Its technical solution was exactly as required and, above that, its price was 8% lower than the next best quotation. Our Western European contractor awarded the subcontract to the best bid — the original listed subcontractor.

The project was a few months underway when the project manager of our contractor, by coincidence, discovered that the owner of the preferred (and awarded) subcontractor was the elder brother of the engineer who was appointed by the employer to supervise the contractor's work. The project manager immediately protested, stating that matters of friends and family were given more importance than "a fair and competitive price". In the event variations in relation to the preferred subcontractor should be discussed, the engineer might be in a referee position between the employer and the contrac-

[8]The term "or equal" behind a manufacturer or a trade mark in a scope of work means that the contractor is free to select another supplier or another item when the quality of such is equal to the specified manufacturer or item.

Box 25.2. (*Continued*)

tor. "Such a situation may represent a conflict of interest," our project manager stated.

An official meeting was arranged in the presence of the employer, the engineer, the subcontractor and the project manager. Here, the employer stated that all Asian persons involved were well aware of the business ethics of the contractor. "We know," said the representative of the employer, "that your business ethics dictate that all potential subcontractors available should be given a fair chance to win this subcontract of yours. We know that you will not only consider a good price but that all other elements of the deal will be taken into account in order to arrive at the best Total Cost of Ownership. Well sir, this is exactly what you got." The project manager persisted. It could happen that a variation, which could result in a change in the subcontractor´s scope of work, planning schedule or price, could be influenced by the non-neutral engineer. At that point, the representative of the employer cut the discussion short. In such a case the employer would intervene: the engineer should be passed over and the employer would take a decision directly.

Two years later, the list of all 112 variations was discussed just a couple of days before the final completion date. Not a single variation was found to be related to the doubtful preferred subcontractor (presumably because these had already been settled in one way or another). During execution, some technical discussions took place, which, without any doubt, could have given reasons for the subcontractor to ask for extra payment, which did not happen. The project manager never learned how the employer, the engineer and the subcontractor arranged things, neither did the project manager ask for an explanation. It was the employer´s way of settling things, according to its culture and its values of doing business.

In the example in Box 25.2, the employer was able to circumvent the dilemma of the non-matching principles of the contract partners. It may happen that the way in which local subcontractors are selected interferes with the formal rules of one of the two countries involved. It is not always easy to find a good solution. Sometimes parties may act in what Western companies would consider an unethical way. Box 25.3 gives an example, while Box 25.4 gives a true and historical example, which would be unacceptable in European legislation.

Box 25.3. A borrowed quantity of sand.

A Western minister of Foreign Affairs granted a sum of €8 million to a land reclamation project somewhere in Southeast Asia. Development aid was a heavy political issue in the granting country. "We only subsidize projects, which — without our help — would never have been realized" was the outcome of a political discussion in its parliament. The contractor tendered a fixed price under the condition that the work should be completed before a strict deadline. Next, the contractor waited in vain for the Letter of Acceptance, which did not come. The local authorities would not dispatch the Letter of Acceptance before the official confirmation letter from the Minister of Foreign Affairs of the donor country was in their possession. In the meantime, the contractor's project manager and the representative of the employer were in the process of preparing and harmonizing planning schedules. But they could not start the work before the official confirmation was handed over by the donor's ambassador. They had to be patient as well. Inside information led to the conclusion that the actual donation of €8 million would take "more time", maybe some months. The beneficiary and the contractor were not amused by this news, both for their own reasons. Both wanted to start as soon as possible.

One of the first activities to be executed after mobilization was the raising of a construction area with sand and water slurry. This was planned to be done with the help of a dredger, which was owned by the contractor, and which was lying half a mile away from the coast. The suction dredger would take sand from the sea bed and pump it to the shore via floating tubing. However, if the contractor were to start its dredging activities, the employer would forgo its €8 million donation; this because the donor country would then think that the project could be realized without its donation. Obviously, the €8 million donation would then be put at risk.

A creative solution was found. The dredger stayed far beyond the horizon. The employer's project manager delivered a different quantity of sand at the disposal of the contractor's project manager. "We don't need that heap of sand immediately," he said. It could be transported by lorries at the employer's cost. When the subsidy of the European ministry came off, the dredger could come and replace this "borrowed" sand with the dredged sand and slurry. In this way the work could be started "on time"; at the same time the donation was safe. No official ever found out how things were arranged by the two project managers.

In this practical solution, described in Box 25.3, nothing was stolen, there was no bribery, no party suffered any disadvantage. On the project management level, two planning schedules were aligned. Nevertheless, in the event the operation had been discovered by politicians in the donor country, it could have raised an argument in parliament. Both the employer's and the contractor's project manager took a personal risk. This was done to serve common interests. However, how far should you go as a project manager? Box 25.4 describes a completely different situation. This is a situation that, according to the ethical and legal rules of the one country, is not acceptable, while in the other country no one ever would have made any objections.

Box 25.4. The nuclear power station and the Irish chief safety inspector.

The Indian government wanted independent advice about certain proposals made by American, Russian and French companies to build a number of nuclear power plants. An Irish engineer and scientist, who held a PhD on nuclear safety control, got the job. Beforehand, he had been employed by the British navy as an inspector during the construction of two submarines; at that time he was responsible for the development of the safety procedures on board these vessels.

He did not bring his family to India, but instead could visit home every four months. When the order for the construction of the complete power station was awarded, the Indian employer invited the Irish engineer to stay on board his team during execution of the project. In India the new nuclear-power generating station was to be built upstream on one of the big rivers in the north. From the outset, our Irish scientist was appointed as Inspector during construction, later on as Chief Safety Inspector. The appointment was arranged for by a son of the Rashtrapayee family. A number of subcontracts had to be awarded, which involved our Irish inspector.

In Ireland his wife owned a horse farm. But he was not interested in being a farmer; he liked this challenging job on the power station. A modification and update of the farm could be financed with his Indian salary.

The job was demanding. There were more problems than expected; there were problems that could not have been foreseen. After hours, he had to go to his flat near the construction site in India, which he shared with one of the Rashtrapayee family

Box 25.4. (*Continued*)

members in India, a young mechanical engineer. They both shared a secretary to assist them. She did the cooking as well. She was the cousin of the minister's older brother, an intelligent young woman. She became responsible for smoothing out difficulties when drafting subcontracts. These subcontracts had to be signed by the Chief Safety Inspector, who never asked after the selection process for subcontractors and service providers. In fact, all of them were linked by family relations. Our Irish specialist just meticulously checked regulations and safety procedures and instructed the responsible managers clearly. Because of his expertise he earned great respect for his detailed knowledge and tactful leadership. Later on, the lady stated: "In India we look at family connections and common interest."

Home in Ireland, the upgrading of the farm required much more funding than estimated. This provoked worries and insomnia in India, which were discovered by the secretary. Sometimes female intuition is very useful. At that point, it became in the family interest that the excellent Chief Safety Inspector — who in reality operated as the overall project representative of the employer — should not worry about €100,000. So supplementary funding was arranged for. That was only a very small amount compared to the contract price of the nuclear power station. This charming young lady, a member of the family, had a son, who was three-years-old when the Irish scientist died in Ireland. She was at the funeral in Ireland, but immediately traveled back to India. When the boy was 13-years–old, he was sent to Trinity College, a boarding school, and played cricket in Dublin. After that he went to Dublin University. Why Dublin? To honor his father and because of his Irish blood.[9]

Box 25.4 shows us a conflicting situation between two different cultures. This is an example of infringement of Western criminal legislation as well as infringement of ethical Western principles. The Irish engineer gave his secretary a free hand in selecting the subcontractors and service providers. Formerly — according to European legislation — she was the Irish engineer's responsibility. Here, he misused his position in awarding contracts to relatives, which is forbidden under European legislation. He signed the subcontract documents. Next, he accepted gifts from his employer for his wife's

[9] G. van der Puil (2012), *The Other Ireland*. London: Olympia Publishers. The book is classified as literature and fiction. But fiction is often derived from real life.

horse farm, which — according to the international definition of bribery — must be identified as a criminal act. He had a sexual relationship with a secretary. In Western Europe, this should be a reason to inform the employer, while to prevent further inconvenience at the work site, the secretary certainly would have been replaced by a different person. And last but not least, there is a child. In Catholic Ireland an illegitimate child, hidden away in India during his early years, not born from an honest marriage, was a serious dent in the engineer's family's reputation. In India such a child was a full member of the family. In India, business and family matters are much more interrelated. It is all a matter of different cultures.

25.7. Characteristics of cultures and nations

In doing business, cultural differences may represent obstacles in coming to terms. Marie-Joëlle Browaeys and Fons Trompenaars (2000) analyzed some cases and developed hints for a better understanding of foreign peoples' behavior in conflicting situations.[10]

In his amazing report on international incidents, Paul Verluyten (2007) collected almost 100 remarkable and stunning situations of intercultural clashes in day-to-day life.[11] These concerned local customs, behavior, ceremonial expression of feelings and misunderstandings between business partners. Box 25.5 shows one of his examples.

Box 25.5. Leaving and returning to a meeting when in Brazil.[12]

"I used to work for a company that made parts for big earth-moving machines. One time I was traveling in Brazil trying to persuade a company to sign a frame contract for regular supply of parts to serve their customers, the big contractors in the country.

My partner and I had prepared a PowerPoint presentation for the eight top executives of the company. The meeting had been going on

[10] M. J. Browaeys and F. Trompenaars (2000), *Case Studies on Cultural Dilemmas: How to Use Transcultural Competence for Reconciling Cultural Dilemmas*. Nyenrode: Nyenrode University Press, 11 cases.

[11] P. Verluyten (2007), *Cultures: From Observation to Understanding: A Workbook*. Voorburg: Acco, pp. 91–142.

[12] P. Verluyten, (2007), *Cultures: From Observation to Understanding: A Workbook*. Voorburg: Acco, p. 125.

Box 25.5. (*Continued*)

for an hour, when some people started to get up and leave. They were gone for an hour and then came back in, acting as if they had been gone for only a few minutes. My partner and I were shocked by this behavior. I had no idea why they got up and left for such a long period of time. In fact, I never found out about this strange behavior during the presentation. But I did land the account." (Brooke H., USA).

Which cultural concept might help explain the behavior of the Brazilians in this story? Why did their behavior upset the Americans?

Edward Hall (1976) created some useful frameworks for studying cultural differences.[13] He differentiates among three aspects of intercultural communication that may cause problems or may result in some kind of uncomfortable feeling.

An interesting first difference between cultures is between high-context and low-context cultures. People communicate in different ways. In some cultures, the context of communication is as important as the content. In Asian and Arab cultures, which are seen as high-context cultures, non-verbal communication is important. Silences are normal. What is not said is as important as the concrete context.[14] In the first meetings, one may build a relationship rather than reach a specific conclusion. In business, trust is more important than a written contract. However, at the end of the series of meetings, a contract about quality, quantity, date of delivery, shipping times, custom clearance and Incoterms will be signed. In high-context cultures it is not always wise to say everything. Respect may be so important that you will keep silent on issues that cannot be realized. Discussion is superfluous in delicate situations. Box 25.6 gives an example.

The second dimension, identified by Hall, is presence, i.e. distance between the negotiating persons. For instance, in the UK, Germany, Nordic countries and the Netherlands, people like a certain distance between each other. The handshake is the touch and that is sufficient. In Northern Africa, Egypt for instance, it may happen that someone will speak close to your face. There will be more touching. This may happen at social events, linked with business, for example, a reception.

---

[13] E. T. Hall (1976), *Beyond Culture*. New York: Doubleday.

[14] See Box 25.6.

Box 25.6. About things which could not be said.

An American procurement manager negotiated with a Japanese account manager of a manufacturer of steel tubes. The procurement manager wanted to know why the Japanese firm did not sell a certain type of high-alloy tubing, which, in his opinion, should be within the mill's technical possibilities. The Japanese account manager did not give a concrete answer, but repeatedly stressed the good quality and interesting possibilities of his other products. When the procurement manager insisted on a satisfactory answer, the (Japanese) interpreter intervened: "You have your answer, sir; Mr. Sanowowaya is not able to tell you that his top management decided to restrict the mill's product program to a number of selected qualities, not including the alloy you actually need. Mr. Sanowowaya regrets this very much." In this instance the interpreter was a bridge between cultures.

The third phenomenon, mentioned by Hall, is time. In the US, UK, Germany, Scandinavia and other Western European countries, time is something to be planned and to be foreseen. The meeting should start at 14:00 hours and everybody should be present. If an important person is not present, no important conclusions can be reached, so the meeting has to be postponed to another date, because meetings are there to produce results. Everybody looks for his (electronic) agenda to arrange the next meeting.

Other cultures regard meetings more as a social exchange of ideas, to build relationships or find common ground for further exploration. High-context cultures are not disturbed when the meeting starts an hour later than agreed, or if the appointment is completely missed. In such cases, the meaning of the message is that the time is not yet ripe.[15] "Time is money" is a phrase that sounds very strange here. The absence of an important person does not hinder the meeting from being successful. The other members of the team will inform him anyhow. It even happens that the deciding person is not present during meetings at all. Final decisions can be taken outside of meetings.

Time can play another role. Contractors operate to strict planning schedules in order to keep fixed costs under control. Other cultures may value the moment of the right decision first. Box 25.6 refers to such a situation.

[15] See Box 25.7.

Box 25.7. About sequential time and time as a healing factor.

A Western European project manager offered in writing three important variations to an employer in a country where time schedules are less important than in Europe. The project manager asked often for a decision, given the fact that the planning schedule would be jeopardized, with or without the requested variations. That could result in unpleasant penalties and discussions. The representative of the employer simply answered: "Sir, we understand your position; time will come — time will always come; we have plenty of time; do not feel squeezed in your planning schedules. I feel that you are not happy. So I am sad. I apologize. But the right time will come, I assure you."

25.8. Evaluating cultural aspects according to Hofstede

Hofstede (1980) is seen as the first important researcher of cross-cultural issues in business. Hofstede ranked 50 countries; he questioned 116,000 employees in those countries. He worked for IBM, which enabled him to use questionnaires and feed his findings into a data bank. The results are still useful, although the latest work dates from some 20 years ago. Based upon his extensive research, he developed different cultural indices. Four of these indices relate to: power distance, individualism versus collectivism, uncertainty avoidance, and masculinity versus femininity (see Box 25.8).[16]

[16] G. Hofstede (1980), *Cultural Consequences, International Differences in Work-Related Values.* Beverly Hills, CA: Sage; G. Hofstede (1984), *Cultural Consequences, International Differences in Work-Related Values: Abridged Edition.* Beverly Hills, CA: Sage. Box 25.8 shows material from the 1984 edition.
G. Hofstede (1991), *Cultures and Organizations:, Software of the Mind.* Maidenhead: Mc Graw Hill; G. Hofstede and G. J. Hofstede (2005), *Cultures and Organizations:, Software of the Mind, 2nd edition.* New York: McGraw Hill.

Box 25.8. Cultural criteria according to Hofstede, 1980–1984, 2001.

500 CULTURE'S CONSEQUENCES

Exhibit A5.1 Index Scores and Ranks for Countries and Regions From the IBM Set

	Power Distance		Uncertainty Avoidance		Individualism/ Collectivism		Masculinity/ Femininity		Long-/Short-Term Orientation	
Country	Index	Rank	Index	Rank	Index	Rank	Index	Rank	Index	Rank
Argentina	49	35-36	86	10-15	46	22-23	56	20-21		
Australia	36	41	51	37	90	2	61	16	31	22-24
Austria	11	53	70	24-25	55	18	79	2	31[a]	22-24
Belgium	65	20	94	5-6	75	8	54	22	38[a]	18
Brazil	69	14	76	21-22	38	26-27	49	27	65	6
Canada	39	39	48	41-42	80	4-5	52	24	23	30
Chile	63	24-25	86	10-15	23	38	28	46		
Colombia	67	17	80	20	13	49	64	11-12		
Costa Rica	35	42-44	86	10-15	15	46	21	48-49		
Denmark	18	51	23	51	74	9	16	50	46[a]	10
Ecuador	78	8-9	67	28	8	52	63	13-14		
Finland	33	46	59	31-32	63	17	26	47	41[a]	14
France	68	15-16	86	10-15	71	10-11	43	35-36	39[a]	17
Germany	35	42-44	65	29	67	15	66	9-10	31	22-24
Great Britain	35	42-44	35	47-48	89	3	66	9-10	25	28-29
Greece	60	27-28	112	1	35	30	57	18-19		
Guatemala	95	2-3	101	3	6	53	37	43		
Hong Kong	68	15-16	29	49-50	25	37	57	18-19	96	2
Indonesia	78	8-9	48	41-42	14	47-48	46	30-31		
India	77	10-11	40	45	48	21	56	20-21	61	7
Iran	58	29-30	59	31-32	41	24	43	35-36		
Ireland	28	49	35	47-48	70	12	68	7-8	43[a]	13
Israel	13	52	81	19	54	19	47	29		
Italy	50	34	75	23	76	7	70	4-5	34[a]	19
Jamaica	45	37	13	52	39	25	68	7-8		
Japan	54	33	92	7	46	22-23	95	1	80	4
Korea (South)	60	27-28	85	16-17	18	43	39	41	75	5
Malaysia	104	1	36	46	26	36	50	25-26		
Mexico	81	5-6	82	18	30	32	69	6		
Netherlands	38	40	53	35	80	4-5	14	51	44	11-12
Norway	31	47-48	50	38	69	13	8	52	44[a]	11-12
New Zealand	22	50	49	39-40	79	6	58	17	30	25-26
Pakistan	55	32	70	24-25	14	47-48	50	25-26	0	34
Panama	95	2-3	86	10-15	11	51	44	34		
Peru	64	21-23	87	9	16	45	42	37-38		
Philippines	94	4	44	44	32	31	64	11-12	19	31-32
Portugal	63	24-25	104	2	27	33-35	31	45	30[a]	25-26
South Africa	49	35-36	49	39-40	65	16	63	13-14		
Salvador	66	18-19	94	5-6	19	42	40	40		
Singapore	74	13	8	53	20	39-41	48	28	48	9
Spain	57	31	86	10-15	51	20	42	37-38	19[a]	31-32
Sweden	31	47-48	29	49-50	71	10-11	5	53	33	20
Switzerland	34	45	58	33	68	14	70	4-5	40[a]	15-16
Taiwan	58	29-30	69	26	17	44	45	32-33	87	3
Thailand	64	21-23	64	30	20	39-41	34	44	56	8
Turkey	66	18-19	85	16-17	37	28	45	32-33		
Uruguay	61	26	100	4	36	29	38	42		
United States	40	38	46	43	91	1	62	15	29	27
Venezuela	81	5-6	76	21-22	12	50	73	3		
Yugoslavia	76	12	88	8	27	33-35	21	48-49		
Regions:										
Arab countries	80	7	68	27	38	26-27	53	23		
East Africa	64	21-23	52	36	27	33-35	41	39	25	28-29
West Africa	77	10-11	54	34	20	39-41	46	30-31	16	33

NOTE: 1 = highest rank. LTO ranks: 1 = China; 15-16 = Bangladesh; 21 = Poland; 34 = lowest.
a. Based on EMS consumer survey (see Exhibit 7.3).

Power distance

Power distance represents the social distance between people in terms of hierarchical position. People in certain countries in East Asia with a high power distance would not be able to put questions to superiors. They just wait for orders from above. Accordingly, employees will accept an unequal distribution of power and autocratic leadership. The Chinese author Jung Chang, in her novel *Wild Swans*, reports: "I grew up with the idea that hierarchy and privileges were the most normal issue in the world."[17] Lower and higher ranks are normal and fully accepted. It is as it is.The man in the street is dependent upon the man above him. It happens that a deputy engineer does not feel comfortable when he has to replace his boss if the power distance between engineer and deputy is too large to be bridged (see Box 25.9). Although many standard contracts contain regulations for delegation by the engineer, instructions of the engineer or replacement of the engineer,[18] such legal clauses do not help to change a deputy's normal feelings about his position in a society. You cannot change a strong ethical rule by laying down a different ruling in a contract.

Box 25.9. The deputy engineer, educated in a strict hierarchical society.

A UK-born project manager had to realize a D&B project in the Middle East There were regular contacts with the engineer, appointed by the employer. When the engineer fell ill, the Scottish project manager addressed himself to the deputy engineer and invited this man to his Portacabin to discuss the daily events. This man, however, did not want to sit down in the project manager's office, but preferred to stand upright. He spoke only when he was spoken to. Discussing the coming variations, the deputy always answered in a very polite way, but never answered in an affirmative way. He refused to sign the weekly meeting minutes, nor the notes that were earlier issued with the variations. Investigations later on showed that the deputy only accepted orders from his boss, i.e. the engineer. But given the fact that the boss was ill, he felt very uncomfortable being invited to sit down in the office of a person who, in his eyes, was higher in rank.

[17] J. Chang (1991), *Wild Swans – Three Daughters of China*. New York: Simon & Schuster.
[18] FIDIC Construction and FIDIC D&B, sub-clauses 3.2.–3.4.

In low power distance countries, there is less distance between a manager and his employees. There is less dependence between lower and higher ranked persons. A leader may have formal leadership by appointment of the top management; he will first have to gain respect and prestige before being accepted by the workers as a real leader. The leader may even be questioned by the workers about decisions taken and decisions to be taken.

In Hofstede's ranking, the higher the index numbers for power distance, the greater the gap between management and workers. In Guatemala, Mexico, Panama, Venezuela and Arab countries the power distance is large. In Austria, Denmark, Ireland, Israel and New Zealand, distance between management and lower employees is rather small.

Individualism

Individualism reflects the extent to which an individual relies on a group. In many countries decisions in business are not taken by an individual person, but by a group of people. Belonging to a certain group is important in Asian cultures, be it as a member of a family or as a partner in trade and industry. Much time is spent on maintaining the group's structure. Being a member of a network means obligations, but you may rely on your network for support if necessary.

In other countries individual decisions are appreciated. Managers, as well as individuals, make decisions themselves. Their function is described in general terms and, within their responsibility, they act as they think is good for the result of the department, the firm, the consortium or the alliance. In these countries the limits of power are described in order to protect the (top) managers from decisions that may put the enterprise at risk. But that may go wrong. In Box 25.10 a misuse of a mandate is described. An area manager

Box 25.10. Best intentions and misuse of mandate.

A young promising account manager of a European enterprise was appointed "Area Director" for East Asia. His mission was business development. Top management considered him a reliable person and, without any hesitation, he was formerly authorized to enter into contracts up to €250,000 on behalf of the company. All went smoothly. After three years the turnover in his territory had increased to €8.4 million per annum.

(*Continued*)

Box 25.10. (*Continued*)

In order to save transportation costs, a project was planned to build a small, local factory where part of the assembly of the product could take place in future. Our area director suggested that his deputy, a Chinese engineer, sign the construction contract with the local contractor, saying: "Please Cheng, could you sign this contract yourself; you know more about buildings than I do."

Cheng asked: "Of course sir, can I have a written authorization from you?"

"Of course you can," answered our area director, took a piece of paper and both men signed the authorization.

The fixed contract price was €2,600,000. Unfortunately, the construction project turned into a nightmare and our area director was called to headquarters in order to explain about the misuse of his mandate. He argued that the geographical sector of the contract to be signed was within his responsibilities; hence, without any hesitation he drafted and signed the paper.

passed his own authorization to a deputy manager and authorized the latter to enter into a contract for a much higher value than his own authorization. This was incorrect. But in cultures where individualism is highly appreciated these situations may occur.

The higher the index number for individualism in Hofstede's ranking, the more people may rely on themselves. In terms of individualism, we find countries like the US, Australia, the UK, New Zealand, the Netherlands and Canada on top. These countries rank even higher than Sweden, Belgium, Denmark and Italy.

Other countries like Columbia, Ecuador, Guatemala, Panama and Venezuela show important cohesion between individuals. The group is of primary importance here. Individual decisions are rare. In countries like Korea, for example, people would not be happy if requested to do something a foreign project manager had asked them to do. Hence, the action should first be discussed in the group the subordinate belongs to. Social action in Korea and other Southeast Asian civilizations is carried out with the intent of not allowing individuals to lose face, as this is of importance in this area. A Western project director should be aware of these values.

In societies where individual decisions are important, the question may arise how to keep managers under control. Company bylaws mention which obligations chief executive managers are not permitted to enter into without the written consent of the supervisory board. Obligations for credit loans, mortgages and entering into legal procedures need the consent of the supervisory board. Directors are authorized to sign up to a maximum amount. A procurement manager is given authority to place orders with suppliers and vendors to a certain maximum amount. An internal administrator may execute payments to creditors up to a maximum amount. More often than not, these limits of power are overruled by the management itself and, accordingly, afterwards accepted by the organization. This is inherent to the culture of individualism; in other cultures this behavior would not be accepted.

Uncertainty avoidance

There are people who do not like to live with uncertainties. Everything should be settled and regulated, which provokes feelings of calm and happiness. Those people avoid uncertainty. Uncertainty avoidance reflects people's ambiguity in a group or in a nation. In certain cultures people want a lot of direction from leaders; they are less comfortable with change. Change should be explained extensively to them. If not, they may develop anxiety and stress and their work will be less effective and efficient.

On the other hand, there are nations that are not afraid of change. In these countries initiative and creativity are admired and stimulated. New technologies are developed one after another. People have self-confidence in such cultures.

Belgium, El Salvador, Greece, Guatemala, Japan, Portugal and Uruguay are countries with high uncertainty avoidance. Tomorrow should be like yesterday. Tradition is a must. Parents and grandparents have high status.

On the other hand, Singapore (top), Sweden, Denmark, Hong Kong, Ireland and the UK are countries with low uncertainty avoidance. Here risk means taking chances; risk management is a dominating issue in entering new fields of technology and business. The implications for project managers are obvious. A new project in a country with high uncertainty avoidance may bring stress in local relationships, which may have repercussions when hiring local labor which is needed for the project.

Suppose that a Swedish contractor starts a project in a country like Guatemala or Portugal; one knows even before mobilization what kinds of problems will occur. There will be strong local resistance against the project and against the Swedish managers, whose main issue is to start as soon as

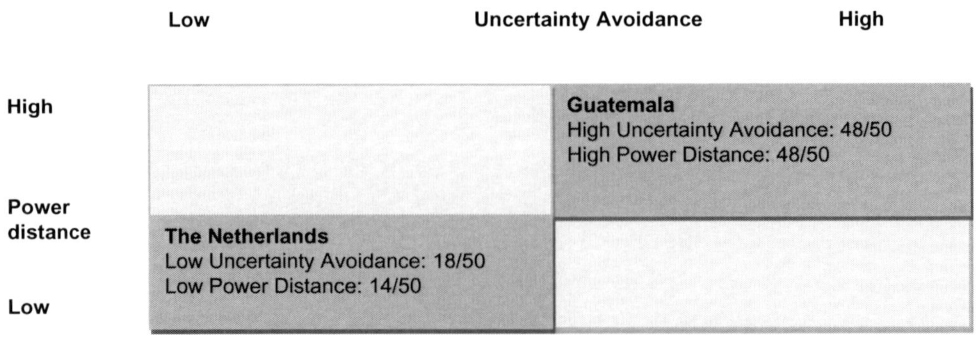

Figure 25.2. Comparison of national characteristics of a contractor from the Netherlands and a subcontractor in Guatemala. The countries show completely opposite cultural elements.

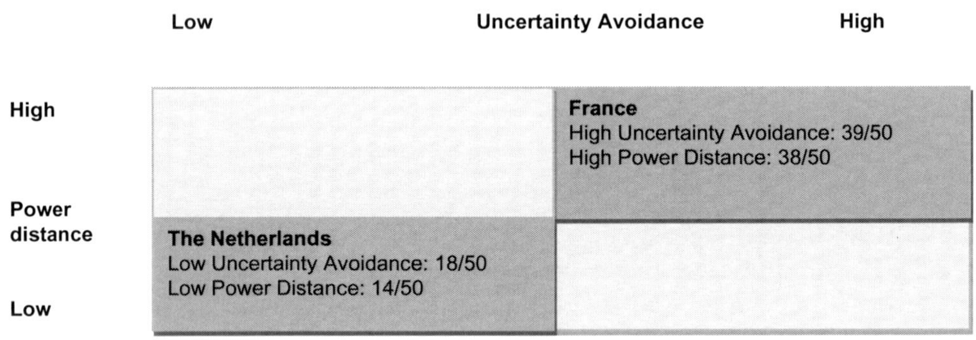

Figure 25.3. Comparison of national characteristics of a legal entity from the Netherlands and a subcontractor in France. The countries show completely opposite cultural elements.

possible and not to pay too much attention to other people. Engineers and technicians, who operate on their manager's positions, used to be especially blind to these kinds of problems. These are not technical, financial or logistical problems; these touch the inner feelings, assumptions and beliefs of human beings. They are much more difficult to identify and to handle than technical issues. Intelligence is not in your favor here. In Figure 25.2 and Figure 25.3 we give some combinations of different cultures where cooperation will be very difficult. The reason is that there are both great distances in uncertainty avoidance as well as in power distance between hierarchical levels of the personnel. Figure 25.4 shows some groups of cultures that are not far from each other.

Low Uncertainty Avoidance Low Personal Distance Between managers and workers			**High Uncertainty Avoidance Great Personal Distance between managers and workers**		
	UA	**PD**		**UA**	**PD**
Denmark	**23**	**18**	**Italy**	**75**	**50**
Sweden	**29**	**31**	**France**	**86**	**68**
UK	**35**	**35**	**Greece**	**112**	**60**
USA	**46**	**40**	**Japan**	**92**	**54**
Netherlands	**53**	**38**	**Spain**	**86**	**57**

Figure 25.4. Differences of national cultures in different countries. Some countries are near to others, while great distances exist between others. Those separations have to be bridged in one way or another when operating in a foreign country. The figures refer to scores in Hofstede's research.

Masculinity/femininity

This is the fourth element introduced by Hofstede. It concerns values that traditionally are considered to be more masculine. Here, we speak about firmness, assertiveness, competition, result orientation and a problem-solving attitude. Women are not primarily involved with "solutions" for problems. Women primarily want to talk about problems and exchange feelings, more than talking about a solution. A solution in itself would not particularly offset the uncomfortable and unhappy feelings.[19]

Japan is at the top of masculinity, together with Austria, Italy, the UK, Ireland and Jamaica, while Sweden, Norway, the Netherlands, Denmark, Finland and Costa Rica are found in the lowest ranks. The latter countries show much more "female" characteristics than the former ones. There is considerable variance between European countries, which means that it is difficult to talk about a "European culture".

The reason why more developed countries show much more feminine characteristics is, in most cases, explained by the economical development of the Western society. After agriculture and industrialization, a third main

[19] J. Gray (1992), *Men are from Mars, Women are from Venus.* London: Harper Collins.

activity was developed in countries with high income per individual: the service industry. The French writer and philosopher Alain Soral explained:

> Consequently, the economic-social feminization does not only mean that the man is slowly losing his muscles in the automation and office work, but, specifically, because he does not need to understand his social role to achieve his tasks, he is not even aware of the fact that the roles are changing that rapidly.[20]

Compared to earlier agricultural and industrial societies, the Western countries show more dominant roles for women in politics, parliament, ministries, art, history, psychology, education, law and business. This means that in decision-making today, more feminine aspects are taken into account than in earlier civilizations.

In the construction industry, as in a few other fields of technology, the conservative bulwark of male decision-makers still hold key positions. Board members, directors, project and contract managers are men. Women work as secretaries, staff members in Human Resource Management or in the laboratories. In the event a woman is appointed as a production manager on a drilling rig, it makes charming news for a magazine. But nevertheless, even in the construction industry, decision-making is slowly changing. More and more feminine aspects are taken into account in construction nowadays.

While respecting Hofstede's four dimensions of culture, the American researcher and consultant Gannon made a number of so-called metaphorical journeys through 28 nations. When executing projects in such countries, project managers are recommended to read about those countries before going to work over there.[21]

25.9. The practical use of cultural elements

For contractors who operate in many foreign countries, Hofstede's study is practical for a first understanding of intercultural behavior. Local subcontractors have different behavior than subcontractors in our home countries. Their experience differs, as well as their know-how; the language barrier may hinder effective communication. But there are other problems which are not

[20] A. Soral (1991), *Vers la féminisation, Démonté d'un complot antidémocratique*. Paris: Editions Blanches/Mango Litérature, p. 111.

[21] M.G. Gannon (2004), *Understanding Global Cultures: Metaphorical Journeys Through 28 Nations, 3rd edition*. London: Sage.

easy to explain and not easy to solve. Maybe their origins come from the country's inner culture. In such situations, the account managers and the project managers, with the help of Hofstede's ranking, may find out what lies behind the observed "strange" behavior. A better understanding of hidden obstacles may help. You may understand why a management style, which you developed in your own culture, does not work in a different culture.

Compare, for instance, your own country's Uncertainty Avoidance ranking with the one of the foreign country that you are going to visit; next, compare your Power Distance with the one of the foreign country. Have a look at the results when a contractor from the Netherlands has to work with a subcontractor in, for instance, Guatemala. Making use of Hofstede's rankings, we find the following figures for the Netherlands and for Guatemala:

Contractor in the Netherlands:	UA 18/50	PD 14/50
Subcontractor in Guatemala:	UA 48/50	PD 48/50.

In Guatemala Uncertainty Avoidance is very important. The country is listed 48 out of 50 countries, while Power Distance is very high as well: 48 out of 50 countries. The Netherlands scores much lower in those two elements. In this country Uncertainty Avoidance is rather low: 18 out of 50, while Power Distance is low as well: 14 out of 50.

After having done this exercise, you may add the other two elements of Hofstede's research. The Netherlands is a country of strong individualism; it is ranked 46 out of 50. Guatemala, on the contrary, is at the bottom of individualism; there are no individual considerations or personal decisions; fulfilling a task on its own will be impossible. Never give a job to one person alone; always ask several men to join you before discussing even the simplest task. Do not be surprised when you ask a question to one person and get a reply that he is going to discuss a possible answer with his colleagues before answering you.

The last element that we compared is the masculinity of the two countries. The Netherlands scores low. It is listed number three from the bottom up. Guatemala is rather low as well, at number 11 from the bottom up. In interpreting the figure of the Netherlands, a small correction should be applied. The figure indicates the complete population, whereas the construction sector in itself is dominated by males. The female elements of the complete society are less prominent in the contractor's company. In this way, Guatemala and the Netherlands may be about equal.

25.10. Changing patterns

The idea that culture could be analyzed was further developed by Trompenaars (1992, 2003 and 2005), who distinguished more aspects on culture than Hofstede. But for a quick scan of a foreign culture where a project has to be realized, the Hofstede index is a good start.[22]

Cultures change as the climate changes. In the last four or five decades, due to the fast development of electronic data interchange, cultures have changed very fast. It is not clear if Hofstede's findings are still valid everywhere.

Yet, the idea behind the analyses is still useful. It may help international contractors to better understand difficulties in work relations when tendering for projects and when execution of the works is at hand. Trompenaars refreshed and renewed Hofstede's ideas and concepts.[23] Further elements were studied by Florence Kluckhohn, Fred Strodtbeck, André Laurent, and Stephen Gatley.[24, 25, 26] The interested reader is referred to these authors.

25.11. Legal reflections on cultural beliefs and assumptions

The above-mentioned studies are related to long-term cooperation, to mergers of companies or to the problem of managing foreign subsidiaries or business units of worldwide enterprises.[27] But the findings are also very useful when working abroad for a limited time span.

---

[22] F. Trompenaars and P. Woolliams (2003), *Business Across Cultures*. London: Capstone Publishing, Chapters 2 and 3; Dutch translation (2005): *Business en cultuur*. Amsterdam: Business Contact. In an earlier publication, Trompenaars summed up seven dimensions as well, but with slightly different terminology and in a different sequence: F. Trompenaars (1992), *Riding the Waves of Culture: Understanding Cultural Diversity in Business*. London: The Economist Books, pp. 29–136.

[23] F. Trompenaars (2007), *Riding the Whirlwind: Connecting People and Organizations in a Culture of Innovation*. Oxford: The Infinite Ideas Company Ltd.

[24] F. Kluckhohn and F. Strodtbeck (1961), *Variations in the Value Orientation*. New York: Peterson.

[25] A. Laurent (1983), The cultural diversity of Western conceptions of management, *International Studies of Management and Organization*, No. 13, pp. 75–96.

[26] S. Gatley, R. Lessem, Y. Altman (1986), *Comparative Management: A Transcultural Odyssey*. Maidenhead: McGraw Hill.

[27] M.J. Gannon (2007), *Paradoxes of Culture and Globalization*. London: Sage Publications.

Inner assumptions and beliefs often originated through historical events and are taken for granted and accepted. Hence, these co-create the core of a nation's values and behaviors. Some of these values are to be found in constitutions and national laws. They often concern religion and family regulations. They may concern business relationships as well. The Mexican constitution has an article on national resources, which may benefit only Mexican people. The clause is a reaction to Mexico's history when foreigners came to Mexico to exploit its silver mines and exported this precious metal, leaving the local population in poverty. Local constitutions and local legislation may contain compulsory clauses that may hinder the contractor's freedom to perform contractual obligations. It is difficult to find out what is hidden behind such regulations. It is best to hire a reliable local lawyer who is aware of such rulings.

It is impossible to be aware of all impacts of all foreign cultures and foreign legislation. That is the reason why all standard contracts describe in detail the important issues of a construction contract. In this way pitfalls are circumvented. Rights and obligations are described in relation to formation of the contract, variations, scope of work, payment, guarantees and bonds, etc.

Contractors should do their utmost to escape from foreign legal systems which are unfamiliar to them. Belgian and French law, as well as some Middle East legislation, have unpleasant compulsory rulings with regard to the contractor's liability.[28] Any foreign legal system may contain inappropriate compulsory regulations and rules that reflect values which are important for the referred country. A neutral legal system, which is acceptable for both contractor and employer, is preferred. Neutral legal systems that are often chosen are Swiss law — which has three languages at its disposal; English law — easy to read and to understand; and private law of the Scandinavian nations. The legal system of the Netherlands is relatively modern — the Civil Code Book was updated in 1992; the legal system is flexible and it contains few compulsory clauses; English texts exist; Dutch judges are strong in foreign languages.

Yet it is impossible to completely escape from the local law of the country where the permanent works are constructed. There is more than just a contract between owner and contractor. Employment legal issues are ruled by the local country. Property law is always local, as is tax law, including custom regulations. The same is true for HS&E rules, which mostly are local.

---

[28] See Chapter 15, Section 15.5.

25.12. Coming to terms with different cultural values

How should you deal with issues arising out of cultural or legal differences? When an issue arises where different solutions could be chosen, depending upon cultural or legal differences, remember that people in different cultures have different ways of thinking due to their cultural roots. A certain preferred solution has its roots in the basic assumptions of the other party's culture. It is of no use to bluntly refuse to discuss a possible way of handling the issue. The following options offer a better way:

- Be aware that the issue has its origin in the cultural or legal roots of your partner.
- Respect the other person's identity, cultural background, and arguments.
- Try to discuss the issue by first listening to the other's arguments.
- State your own position and mention why some "solutions" will not be accepted by your company and yourself.
- Mention various options for how the issue could be handled.
- Try to compromise as much as possible when handling the issue, resulting in a solution which is acceptable for both parties.

The issue of the preferred subcontractor

As an example, we turn to the problem of the preferred subcontractor as described above in Box 25.2. The employer prescribed a certain subcontractor, while the contractor did not want to be bound to only one subcontractor without having a choice. The contractor wanted to subcontract the relevant part of the scope of work in a transparent and competitive way. The contractor foremost wanted to ensure the good quality needed for the job, and a timely completion, fitting into his own planning. These requirements conflicted with the employer's interests, which mainly consisted of transferring the job to a family member. The employer may even argue that it is his money, so he has the right to decide which subcontractor will be selected. To a certain extent this sounds reasonable.

Respect the owner's arguments

Do not deny the validity of the employer's preference and opinion. Ask why he insists on choosing this subcontractor and no other. In the event he, in your opinion, has illogical arguments, do not be surprised — the basics come from differences in cultures between him and you. Different languages are difficult to handle, different cultures even more so.

Make your own point

Try to explain your position and the aspects that really matter to you: best quality. Keep in mind the typology of the referred contract, which means that your company will always be responsible for the outcome of the subcontractor's work, timely completion and best price, which should be transparent. Mention different options for how the issue could be handled.

In this case, those options might be:

- Issuing a variation order, in which the part of the scope of work to be subcontracted will be deleted from your scope of work — a price reduction that will have to be negotiated. The employer in that case will be responsible for the subcontract itself. Coordination should be settled.
- Competitive bidding by different competing subcontractors. This was the way in which the issue was "solved" in Box 25.2 above.
- Issuing the subcontract to the preferred subcontractor, while checking its price, quality and planning discipline as far as possible.
- Execution of the subcontract by the contractor himself.

When listing the different options, describe each option in a dichotomy as per Figure 25.5. Note the valuation of the contractor on the x-axis and the valuation of the owner on the y-axis. The ideal solution is the one that gets 10 for the contractor and 10 for the employer; if it is available, it is noted in the upper-right segment.

This method looks like a recipe, medicine, which "always works". That is not true. This method is only effective if the negotiators are aware of the underlying conditions. First, it is a rational way of handling the negotiations; not all men are rationalists. And second, the negotiators should have the strong desire to reach an agreement. Negotiating skills are necessary. The solution which is the closest to what both parties want, or the best of the worst solutions, should not cause trouble for either negotiator. This chapter does not deal with negotiating although it might be useful to get some practical tips from good books on the subject. We mention Jimmy Carter and Roger Fisher but there are many others.[29, 30, 31, 32]

---

[29] J. E. Carter (1984, 2003), *Negotiation: The Alternative to Hostility.* Atlanta, GA: Emery University Press.

[30] R. Fisher, W. Ury, B. Patton, Getting to Yes, The Harvard Negotiation Project, 1981, 1999; R. Fisher, E. Kopelman, A. K. Schneider (1994), *Beyond Machiavelli: Tools for Coping with Conflict.* Cambridge, MA: Harvard University Press.

[31] H. Cohen (1980), *You Can Negotiate Anything.* New York: Lyle Stuart.

[32] *Negotiation* magazine, Bohn – Stafleu — Van Loghum, Capelle aan den Yssel.

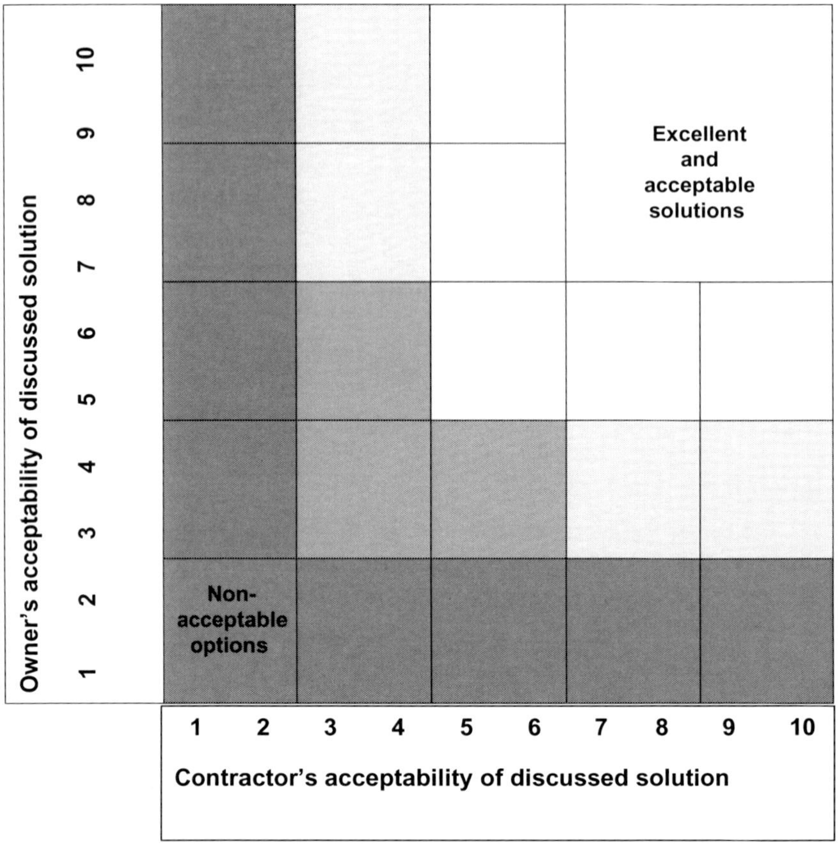

Figure 25.5. Dichotomy noting the employer's and contractor's interests when evaluating options for different practical solutions. 1 means solution not acceptable at all; 10 means completely satisfactory. When a solution is not acceptable to the contractor, value it by noting it from 1 to 4; if it is fully satisfactory value it at 10. Do the same for the employer's position. The ideal solution is the solution that is marked 10 by 10. Parties should strive to find solutions in the upper-right segment: 7–10 for both owner and contractor.[33]

In the case described in Box 25.2, we are aware of the contractor's arguments for refusing to be forced to employ a certain subcontractor without having any other option. We also understand the employer's point of view. The solution of Box 25.2 was satisfactory to the employer; he got his most

[33]The figure is derived from F. Trompenaars, who applied the idea of putting two solutions on two axes for different dilemmas, such as investments against savings, differentiation against integration in corporations. See also M. Hampden and F. Trompenaars (2000), *Building Cross Cultural Competence: How to Create Wealth from Conflict Values.* New Haven, CT: Yale University Press, Appendix 3, pp. 353–358.

important interest by passing the subcontract to a related family or clan member. It was acceptable to the contractor because it was the outcome of a fair bidding process. This solution was not a 10–10 solution. When variations came up, the owner had to circumvent discussions with the contractor. Box 25.2 does not describe how the employer handled that aspect of the issue.

25.13. Summary, recommendations and gentle suggestions

Organizations that operate in a multicultural environment should be aware of the large cultural differences that exist between their own culture and that of the foreign country where their projects are realized. It is very likely that problems will be encountered which were unpredictable and not foreseen when entering into a contract.

Attention has to be paid to those differences that we encounter when operating in a foreign country, where a foreign language is spoken in a climate that is not familiar to us. Better understanding of the backgrounds of human behavior in foreign countries may help us to deal with habits that are unfamiliar to us, and hopefully to come to agreements with people with and for whom we work.

Be aware of your own culture. Before comparing other cultures to your own, you have to understand your own inner presumptions and axioms, which have been taken for granted, and the inner values, which derived from those starting points of inner belief.

Notice that you are part of a nation that has national characteristics. Some ground rules were noted in a constitution, in national laws or in EU rulings, but it is not necessarily true that such ground rules are valid in the country where your project has to be realized.

Respect the foreign culture in your host land. Be aware that sub-cultures exist. Refrain from giving your own opinion about stresses and quarrels between sub-cultures in the country, as you may hurt feelings without knowing it, and it is possible that no one will be willing to explain to you what you did wrong. But not every civilization is happy with the unexpected. Be aware of non-verbal communication, which may differ from the communication you are used to.

Outside of Europe, the European rules and directives for tendering for projects are not applicable. This does not mean that there are no rules at all. An organization that dispatches invitations to tender may be subject to national compulsory rules, which can be applicable to the tender your company is going to send in.

Employers operate from many different legal entities. They may appear as private companies, but — dependent upon national codes — may be controlled by governments, by regions, by powerful families or by autocratic leaders. Your company has to deal with various forms of companies, which from a strict legal point of view, appear to be simple companies with limited responsibility, as we know in Europe. But sometimes there is more behind such a façade.

Know your own code of conduct. Listed companies always have these codes, but non-listed companies have them as well. It may happen that rules in the foreign country of operation conflict with rules from your own code of conduct. It is not always easy to circumvent such situations. Creativity is a must, but you should never put your company in danger.

Note that there is no standard formula for bridging cultural differences. Every case should be judged on its own merits. A mixture of common sense, intuition, experience, respect and interest in the other culture will be a good starting point when differences occur.

When differences hinder execution of the project, try to understand the other party's concerns, which originated from deeper values. Try to exchange views. Try to make your own point, be it of technical origin, a logistical problem, the availability of local labor, the hindrance of local regulations and so on. But also discuss your own interest and the reasons behind your own behavior.

Explain to your counterpart that you are in this country to build a project to the correct quality, with the agreed upon quantities, respecting the local health, safety and environmental regulations, with the local permits, in the right (agreed) time frame and against the agreed price and payment conditions. Try to reach an agreement with your counterpart.

Realize that language may be a hindrance to understanding your foreign partner. When you don't feel absolutely at home in another language, it may be difficult to express your feelings.

Realize that you may ask something that your counterparty cannot accept for reasons which do not seem very logical from your point of view. Respect such impossibilities. Hopefully, that will result in comprehension and sympathy so that a future dispute may be decided in favor of your point of view.

Prevent business problems that arise out of different cultures from becoming dilemmas. Try to list various solutions and value them if they are satisfactory to yourself and your counterparty. Be aware of the differences, respect the differences and come to an agreement. Awareness of cultural differences will give your organization an advantage over your competitors.[34]

---

[34] www.cultureforbusiness.com; http://geerthofstede.com, January 23, 2013.

It is obvious that the last chapter of this book concerns cultural differences. In international contracting the project manager and his team are operating in different cultures to those of their home surroundings. Therefore, the reader of this book has to bear in mind that all chapters are informed by cultural differences. Contracting in a national context is not easy; international contracting is demanding. Apart from technical knowledge, it requires non-technical knowledge, feeling, intuition and, above that, an awareness of the differences between your home country and that of the people you are working with. Principles of behavior are different all over the world; legal explanations of wording may result in different outcomes and solutions, depending upon the legal system where the contractor is executing his scope of work.

Yet, in the interest of his client, the contractor should be aware of differences when performing his task, at the same time minimizing his own risks and those of the other stakeholders involved in the project. This is only possible if all parties in the supply chain work in a cooperative way and in good harmony. For that purpose they need to be able to understand each other.

Index